Errata Sheet

Richard L. Phillips and Contributors
Harvey H. Potthoff: A Life in Process, First Edition (2013).

Pg 83, paragraph 4. Quotation marks should offset quoted material beginning "Dealing with…" and ending "… realizations."

Pg 293, paragraph 2. Should read: "For Potthoff's retirement..."

Pg 401, photograph. The caption incorrectly identifies Patsy Moore with Harvey Potthoff. Caption should read: "Professor Lois Coleman and Harvey at NWU in front of tree planted in his honor." Photograph credit should read: "HHP photograph in Iliff Archives."

Pg. 597: "Metzger, Ellen" should read "Metzger, Eileen."

Harvey H. Potthoff

A Life in Process

Harvey H. Potthoff

A Life in Process

Richard L. Phillips, author and editor
with guest chapters

Cosponsored by The Iliff School of Theology
and Nebraska Wesleyan University

Published by Filter Press, LLC
Palmer Lake, Colorado

Library of Congress Cataloging-in-Publication Data

Phillips, Richard L. (Richard Lee), 1934-
Harvey H. Potthoff : a life in process / Richard L. Phillips, author, editor with guest chapters.
pages cm
"Cosponsored by The Iliff School of Theology and Nebraska Wesleyan University."
Includes bibliographical references and index.
Summary: "Describes the life, ministry, and theology of Harvey Henry Potthoff (1911-2002), United Methodist pastor and professor of Christian Theology at Illif School of Theology and Nebraska Wesleyan University"--Provided by publisher.
ISBN 978-0-86541-151-7 (pbk. : alk. paper)
1. Potthoff, Harvey H., 1911-2002. 2. United Methodist Church (U.S.)--Clergy--Biography. 3. Methodist Church (U.S.)--Clergy--Biography. 4. United Methodist Church (U.S.)--Study and teaching--Biography. I. Title.
BX8495.P68P45 2013
287.092--dc23
[B]

2013010079

Produced with the support of The Iliff School of Theology and Nebraska Wesleyan University. Views, conclusions, or recommendations found in this book do not necessarily represent those of either institution.

Cover photo used courtesy of The Iliff School of Theology. The stained-glass window created by Rev. David Woodyard and presented to Dr. Potthoff, January 25, 1981, now hangs in the Potthoff Seminar Room in The Iliff School of Theology.

Filter Press, LLC, Palmer Lake, Colorado
info@FilterPressBooks.com / 888.570.2663

Printed in the United States of America

Dedication

This book is dedicated to the life, the scholarship, the wisdom, the ministry, the sharing, and the memory of Harvey Henry Potthoff: churchman, scholar, teacher, mentor, humorist, family man, colleague, and friend.

Contents

Acknowledgments

As author and editor of this volume, I am very pleased that The Iliff School of Theology and Nebraska Wesleyan University have co-sponsored this biography. In each case, the eagerness to enter into this project is a tribute to Harvey Potthoff and was essential to the start of the necessary research and writing. The two academic institutions have shared the contractual costs making publication possible.

Former President David Trickett and the officers and staff of Iliff have been wonderful partners in this endeavor. Dr. Trickett was instrumental in committing the money to contract with Filter Press for publication of this book. He also facilitated Iliff providing me with an office with a full computer hookup, printer, and copy privileges in which to do the research and writing. David's tenure at Iliff came to a close before the finish, but I owe him a very grateful thank you for all of his interest and help. Donna Sovern, on the staff of the Office of the President, was a help in many, many ways and was not only very talented but always a delightful person with whom to work.

Dr. Albert Hernandez, Vice President and Academic Dean, and now Acting President, along with Leslie Inman and Alisha Eno of his staff, have been most helpful. Special thanks to Laura Harris of the library staff for facilitating moving the Potthoff-related archives to my office so the research and writing could be joined in the same work area. Laura has also been helpful in document location and preparing photographs for publication. The whole library staff has been helpful at every turn. Mary Sue Alexander, Director of Marketing Communication at Iliff, has been very supportive and helpful with photographic needs. Iliff has been my home away from home (a 30-minute drive to Lakewood) for over a year. Many faculty and retired faculty and staff members at Iliff have been significant helpers in many aspects of my work here. I am most grateful!

To Nebraska Wesleyan University and President Fred Ohles, heartfelt thanks for wonderful cooperation and support with the funds necessary for publication, and for endorsing faculty member Dr. David Peabody as author of the chapter on the eleven years that his colleague Harvey Potthoff taught and was part of the school and community. As cosponsors of this biographical effort, NWU has played a critical role, and in so doing has endorsed me but especially honored the memory of Harvey Potthoff.

Patsy Moore, part-time faculty and former colleague of Dr. Potthoff's, has provided written input and was interviewed by me as was Dr. Peabody and President Ohles. Many others at NWU and in the Lincoln, Nebraska, area have been helpful to Dr. Peabody; thanks to them all. My visits there have been rewarding and facilitated important aspects of this biography. Especially meaningful was the opportunity to visit with former NWU President John White, who was so central in Potthoff's years at that great school. Dr. White, who died shortly after the start of this book, became a close friend of

Dr. Potthoff's. Harvey was very proud of and impressed with NWU and treasured his time there very much. It added greatly to his most productive career. My conversations with Harvey during the last decade of his life often centered on his NWU years. It was a splendid and meaningful chapter in his career.

Even though I have been moderately computer literate for a number of years, the help of the IT department at Iliff was oft used and very helpful for the several months of this project. Without Systems Administrator Will Wedow and Help Desk Technician R. J. Hernández-Días of the Iliff IT Department, there would have been mega delays in getting the text organized and ready for publication. Thanking them here is a mild way of expressing my appreciation.

To David Conner, Tom Wood, David Peabody, Rich Peck, Howard Bailey, Paul Kottke, Amy Phillips, Rick Chappell, Richard Vickery, Gregg Anderson, Alton Templin, Don Messer, and others who contributed to this biography, including submitting reflections: my thanks unending for being guest writers and adding in such splendid ways to my knowledge and to the readers' awareness of the breadth of the life and work of Harvey Potthoff. All of the writers' efforts provided for me and for this book rewards only available and forthcoming from a labor of love. David Conner has also been one of the best consulting friends anyone could ask for in any such undertaking.

Eminent scholar Peter Gay's tribute to Harvey at his memorial service in 2002 is contained in Chapter 15, on Harvey's last decade of life. Gay is an emeritus member of the Yale faculty but could not be reached for added input. Charles Milligan (a very close friend and colleague of Harvey's) was to have been author of a major chapter, but his death came soon after he had begun to assemble materials for writing. Those materials were donated to the project and the archives by his widow, Nancy. Tributes from Charles's writings and his remarks at the Potthoff memorial service are included in this biography; it is a lesser document due to Milligan's untimely death. Even so, his brilliant mind and his penetrating insights have added much to this work.

My wife, Ethel Phillips, has been a diligent volunteer, helping in research, keyboarding, and office tasks including proofreading and textual suggestions. Without her and my cousin Amy Phillips doing the same tasks as a part-time worker and lending her excellent computer skills, the project would have lasted for years and maybe years more! Amy also authored and edited the first part of Chapter 1.

Former faculty colleagues, friends, and former students of Harvey's have responded with reflections of him as teacher, friend, theologian, scholar, mentor, and their inspiration. The pages of this book containing their input have their own special way of revealing Harvey to the readers. Their writings and my personal visits with many fellow Iliffians have enriched both this book and my own knowledge of the man and his work. The input of many individuals who were not students or faculty at Iliff, but who became Harvey's friends or colleagues in other contexts, added greatly, and I am most appreciative of them and to all who added to and supported this project in so many ways. Several persons also made donations to Iliff so that this project could have a modest budget for general expenses and for Amy's hourly part-time work. Even so, most of her effort was a labor of love. Her skills and help were limited, and sometimes interrupted, by fifteen months of dialysis and a kidney transplant, all of which went very well.

For the frequent times Dr. Potthoff and I were able to spend together during the last ten years of his life, especially the last half dozen years, I am so very grateful. I was able to relish the conversations, the shared theological concerns, the love of Iliff, and the stories of NWU (and of Wili Otey) that have characterized more than fifty-five years of knowing one another. Now, just over ten years after his death, I know him even better! This has all informed and enriched my own career and life just as Harvey often did by accepting my invitations to speak in many different places—Baker University, The American Youth Foundation and Syracuse to mention only three.

Late in the research and writing, I was able to be in touch with members of the Potthoff family. I had not had any previous information about many of them, including any way of contacting them. They found me, and then I found more of them. Thus more family information and more of Harvey's history became available to me, including many photographs. Discovery, in so many cases like this, is a source of joy and has been very confirming of so much about Harvey as well as his extended family. Very sincere thanks to all of Harvey's family members for bringing information, pictures, and indeed joy to our work. See Chapter 1 for specific family information.

Central to this work has been the wonderful help and cooperation of Filter Press publishers Doris and Tom Baker. They have been more than willing to respond with suggestions and advice regarding each aspect of the project. Our meetings with them have been a very important ingredient in our work. Our special thanks for all their help and now friendship.

It has been a special joy for me to interrupt "retirement" to fully engage this project. Being back at Iliff and seeing the current faculty and students in today's version of Iliff is proof to me that one can go home in some significant ways. I have appreciated the opportunity and I hope you, the reader, will appreciate the results.

– Dick Phillips, March 2013

Contributors

Following are identifying sketches of those who have written chapters or portions of chapters for this book.

Gregg Anderson: BA, St. Olaf College, 1970; MDiv, Iliff, 1983; DMin, McCormick School of Theology, 1996; United Methodist clergy, chaplain, and senior minister of Aspen Chapel, Aspen, Colorado; from a 1972 start as youth minister, developed the Aspen Chapel from an empty building to a church now forty years old; host of the Iliff-at-Aspen summer school program; hobbies are tennis, skiing, hiking, and biking; member of many boards and agencies in Aspen over the years.

Howard Bailey: BA in Psychology, Hendricks College, 1957; ThM (1960) and ThD (1963), both at Iliff; postdoctoral study University of Minnesota, University of Iowa, George Williams College, Vanderbilt University, Harris Institute, Iliff, St. Paul School of Theology, Lancaster Seminary, University of Nebraska.

Award/Honors: 1957, National Methodist Scholarship and Travel Seminar for seminary students, UMC; 1962, participant, Sixth Biennial Conference on teaching religion to undergraduates, National Council on Religion in Higher Education, Danforth Foundation; 1968, Hill Foundation Fellowship–Urban Sociology Research in Chicago; 1981, Distinguished Service Award, First UMC, Omaha; 1999, Charles L. Calkins Award for Outstanding Leadership in Pension and Benefits Administration, General Board of Pension and Health Benefits, UMC; several publications and research papers including 1963 and 1968 *Iliff Review* articles; served churches in Arkansas, Colorado, and Nebraska; was Campus Minister and Associate Professor of Philosophy and Religion at Dakota Wesleyan University; Dean of Students, Academic Dean, and Acting President of John J. Pershing College; and director of Ministries, NE Annual Conference. Retired in 1998.

Charles R. "Rick" Chappell: graduated magna cum laude in physics, Vanderbilt University; PhD in space science, Rice University; joined NASA in 1974 and was a mission scientist and trained as an alternate crew member for a shuttle mission; 1987–1997, Associate Director for science at NASA's Marshall Space Flight Center, Huntsville, Alabama; 1989, co-founded the Aspen Global Change Institute with John Denver's Windstar Foundation; May 1994–May 1995 worked with Vice President Al Gore to create an innovative K–12 science/education program involving students around the world; September 1966, joined the First Amendment Center at Vanderbilt to conduct a joint project with former NBC *Today Show* host Jim Hartz to examine the media's portrayal and coverage of news related to science and technology (the resulting book was released March 1998); 2002–2009, Director of the Vanderbilt Dyer Observatory. As a scientist and spokesman for the space program, he has been interviewed on NBC's *Today Show*, ABC's *Nightline*, and the BBC; provided color commentary on CNN for space shuttle missions; has testified before Congress on the importance of communicating science to the public; and twice received the NASA Medal for Exceptional Scientific Achievement (1981–1984). Presently he is a Research Professor of Physics in the College of Arts and Science at Vanderbilt. He continues to be involved in teaching and research, is active in science communication, outreach, and education in the community and throughout the nation; and was a guest lecturer in Potthoff's courses in both the Iliff-at-Aspen program and at NWU.

David Emory Conner: BS, chemistry, Millsaps College, 1972; MDiv with distinction 1975 and ThD 1981, both at Iliff; awarded the Elizabeth Iliff Warren Fellowship in 1975–1976 for further graduate study at the Claremont Graduate School, where he studied with John Cobb and simultaneously held a Claremont Graduate School Fellowship. He has been an adjunct faculty member at Iliff and is the author of several published articles, including articles on Whitehead and on Potthoff, and of chapters in books. He has served UM churches in Mississippi and Colorado; is currently pastor of Wheat Ridge UCC in Wheat Ridge; is sporadically a member of the American Academy of Religion; and is a current member of the Institute for American Religious and Philosophical Thought (formerly Highlands Institute). Enjoys tennis, cooking, and playing the piano and has hiked sixteen Colorado fourteeners.

Peter Gay: Born in Berlin, Germany, on June 20, 1923; along with his parents, he escaped Nazi Germany in 1939 and made it to the United States in 1941. The first stop was Cuba, where his parents were delayed; Peter came to Denver and enrolled in Denver University. With a fellow student, he started attending a discussion group led by Harvey Potthoff, and from there he and Potthoff became lifelong friends (see Chapter 8). His last name had been Frohlick ("happy" in German), and he changed it to Gay after his arrival here. He became a US citizen in 1946. He graduated DU with a BA in 1946 and then received the MA and PhD from Columbia University in 1947 and 1951. Gay has received a number of honorary doctorates. Recognized worldwide for his scholarship, writing, and teaching, Gay is an emeritus member of the Yale University faculty where he taught for many years. For his book *The Enlightenment: An Interpretation*, he received the National Book Award, and many other honors have come his way. His biography *Freud: A Life for Our Time* (1988) has been translated into many languages. He has been a scholar of remarkable range, authoring more than thirty books. [This biographical information was collected from several sources including Wikipedia, Denver University, Yale University, and from Gay himself.]

Paul J. Kottke: BA in philosophy and English, University of New Mexico; 1981 Iliff grad; founding Executive Director for Denver Urban Ministries, 1981–1985; Director of Development, Iliff 1985–1988; Pastor Warren UMC,

1988–1994; Senior Pastor of University Park UMC, 1995 to present; Board of Ordained Ministry, 1992–2004; Chair of Religious Advisory Committee for Bridges to the Future, University of Denver, 2002 to present; Registrar for Colorado Courage, an affiliate of the national Center for Courage & Renewal leadership program based upon the writings and guidance of Parker Palmer; Colorado Senate Chaplain, 2000 to present. Awards: Phi Beta Kappa, University of New Mexico, 1974; Harvey H. Potthoff Award for Excellence, Iliff School of Theology, 1980; Man of the Year, Life on Capitol Hill, Denver, 1994; Iliff School of Theology, Alumnus of the Year, Parish Ministry, 1995. "I strongly believe that as clergy, not only do we need to provide leadership for our congregations, but we need to also be civic leaders within society. It is too easy for us to become so involved in our religious commitments that we become irrelevant to the civic needs of our communities. I believe in articulating a Christian faith that embraces all persons as loved by God. As a passionate Christian, I bless the spiritual journey of a person in his/her faith tradition as a Jew, Muslim, Buddhist, Baha'i, or Hindu. And in return, I am richly blessed by what each tradition teaches me as a Christian."

Charles S. Milligan: Fellow Iliff student, fellow Iliff professor, and pastoral associate of Potthoff's; ThM, Iliff, 1942; awarded Elizabeth Iliff Warren Fellowship 1942–1943; ThD, Iliff, 1952; PhD and STM at Harvard. He was a student under William Bernhardt and later became his replacement in Philosophy of Religion and Ethics at Iliff; was a longtime editorial worker on a great variety of publications including *The Iliff Review*; served as a member of the clergy of the United Church of Christ until his death in 2011; was very active in social causes; and was a charter member of the Potthoff discussion group and a participant until his death. He was always an extremely helpful resource for fellow faculty members, students, and others and was one of Iliff's most decorated citizens.

David Barrett Peabody: BA, MTh, and PhD from Southern Methodist University with emphasis on Jewish and Christian Biblical Literature and Greek and Hebrew languages; author, coauthor, or coeditor of four books and contributor to fourteen other books, several journals, and papers. His detailed vitae may be found on the NWU website. He has been a full-time faculty member at NWU 1984 to present; worked closely with Dr. Potthoff in the Religion Department and as guest lecturer in his courses 1984 to 1992; worked with Potthoff in the Mattingly Symposium planning and implementation; and enjoyed a close friendship.

J. Richard Peck: The Reverend J. Richard Peck is a retired clergy member of New York Annual Conference. He is a 1961 graduate of Iliff School of Theology where he took four courses from Dr. Potthoff. He is the former editor of *Newscope*, a weekly newsletter published by the United Methodist Publishing House; *Circuit Rider*, a monthly publication for United Methodist clergy; the *Daily Christian Advocate*, the "congressional record" for General Conference;

and the *International Christian Digest*, an interdenominational magazine. He retired from the publishing house in 2000 after 25 years of service. He is the former press secretary for the Council of Bishops and current editor of the quarterly magazine of the General Commission on United Methodist Men. He served twelve General Conferences in various capacities and was the staff person who drafted legislation for the Connectional Table at the 2012 General Conference. He also served as the staff person for the General Council on Ministries that wrote legislation creating the Connectional Table at the 2004 General Conference. He is the author of *Walking Humbly Doing Justice* (Abingdon Press, 2002) and *Caring for God's Earth* (Abingdon Press, 2002), and he was editor of the *2000 United Methodist Book of Resolutions*. Peck says, "I thank God for the life and teachings of the Reverend Dr. Harvey H. Potthoff. He helped shape my theology and my life."

Amy E. Phillips: MS, Finance, University of Colorado, 1993; BBA Finance, University of Colorado, 1985; BA, Environmental Design, University of Colorado, 1985; holds the Chartered Financial Analyst designation; Research Assistant on *Harvey H. Potthoff: A Life in Process.*

Richard L. Phillips: BS, Northwest Missouri State University, 1957; ThM, Iliff, 1960; EdD, Syracuse University, 1965; UM Clergy, Rocky Mountain Conference, 1959–1999, retired; Baker University faculty 1966–1975; President and Executive Director, American Youth Foundation, 1975–1980; Dean of Hendricks Chapel, Syracuse University, 1981–1998, retired 1999; author of *Hendricks Chapel: Seventy-Five Years of Service to Syracuse University* (Syracuse University Press, 2005); published articles and wrote a chapter on Dr. Howard Ham for the book *An Intellectual History of the Iliff School of Theology: A Centennial Tribute, 1892-1992,* edited by J. Alton Templin. Phillips is now retired and living in Lakewood, Colorado.

J. Alton Templin: ThM, 1953; ThD, 1956, both at Iliff; PhD, Harvard; faculty at Iliff 1967, retiring in 1997 in Historical Theology and Church History; Iliff Alumnus of the Year 1989; published *Ideology on a Frontier: The Theological Foundation of Afrikaner Nationalism, 1652-1910* (Greenwood Press, 1984) and edited *An Intellectual History of the Iliff School of Theology* (listed above in the sketch on Richard Phillips); and has many publications and articles to his credit, including extensive writings about Harvey Potthoff with whom he was colleague and close friend (starting when they were Iliff students) for many years. He remains active as a part of the Iliff community of retired faculty and a member of the monthly Potthoff discussion group.

Thomas C. Wood: MD, FACP. Born 1938 in Denver and attended Christ Methodist Church. When his parents died in a 1950 accident, he established a close relationship with Harvey Potthoff, his pastor at the time; studied at Dartmouth College, Denver University, University of Colorado School of Medicine, then University of Washington School of Medicine. After Thomas's marriage and the birth of his two children, Harvey became an integral part of the Wood family as surrogate father and grandfather. Wood had a private medical practice in Anchorage, Alaska, in internal medicine and nephrology from 1971 until retiring in 2006; continues as a consultant for a community medical clinic for the indigent and underserved of Anchorage.

Introduction

Why a biography of Harvey Henry Potthoff? Why now? Why by me?

Harvey Henry Potthoff was a theologian whose teaching of well over thirty-five years influenced many hundreds of students in the Iliff School of Theology (IST) in Denver, Colorado. In addition to his teaching, he was very influential within United Methodist circles nationwide. Harvey's writings, both published and unpublished, are extensive. All of his books, almost all of his speeches, more than 919 sermons, much of his correspondence, and many other source materials are archived in the Ira J. Taylor Library, IST.

Following his retirement from Iliff in 1981, he taught for eleven years at Nebraska Wesleyan University (NWU) in Lincoln, Nebraska, where his institutional and community impact were equally great. In both locations, his influence among professionals and with lay people in churches, primarily in Methodism, reached many thousands of people and continues to grow as his former students continue their respective careers. Harvey's work, scholarship, and extensive pastoral ministry as a churchman are equaled by few modern theologians and none of them in quite the same way. His theology is divided almost evenly between philosophical theology and pastoral theology.

Dr. David Peabody has written Chapter 11. He wrote from personal interaction with Potthoff as a colleague for eight years and from extensive NWU and IST holdings. There are other important guest chapters also. There is no lack of information about Potthoff and his teaching and scholarship on which to base this biographical work. His writings range from dealing with the scriptures to death and dying issues; indeed, as the saying goes, he covered the waterfront. Interestingly, Potthoff's first writing job was sports reporting. He himself was a good athlete.

Perhaps the most unusual aspect of Potthoff's theology is a lifelong effort to unite process thought based theology with scripture, church history and tradition, preaching, and pastoral theology. He reflects his heritage in this. His father and grandfather were German Methodist pastors in the United States. Most modern theologians, at least in the Christian tradition, do not focus on the implications of their philosophical theology for churchship or the practical matters of piety, spiritual life, preaching, worship, scripture, church policy, and polity. Even so, Potthoff does not take a second seat to any theoretical theologian in his precise development of what is often called philosophical theology.

Potthoff worked a great deal in ecumenical and interfaith circles, and knew and appreciated the great diversity he encountered in that work. His students and friendships included almost all faith groups, including rabbis, Roman Catholic and Orthodox Catholic priests, and other adherents of Christianity from fundamentalists to humanists. In addition to working with professionals from other religious traditions, his circle of friends and acquaintances included physicians, writers, musicians, visual artists, and scientists. His keen interest in both science and religion was lifelong, and he included many scientists in his teaching, often as guests in the classroom.

Harvey, both before and after his early church pastorate in Denver and following his year at Harvard with Alfred North Whitehead, was a model minister to many. In fact, over half of the tributes sent in for this biography focus on his impact as a pastor to students and to individuals who never studied under him yet felt his influence in their work and their lives. That group includes fellow faculty members and many other colleagues. For many, this impact was far greater than his work in philosophical theology.

This book's subtitle, *A Life in Process*, has a double meaning that I think would suit Harvey just fine. The first has to do with the centrality of process philosophy (Whiteheadian to be sure, but not totally so) in Potthoff's understanding of reality and the development of his philosophical and pastoral theology. A second but equally important meaning has to do with the flow of Potthoff's own life, a very full life always seen by him to be ever changing, always new as it was lived with vitality to the end. (A special thanks to David Peabody of NWU for suggesting this subtitle for this biography.)

Harvey never married. There were stories about a romance when he was young that ended due to the woman's accidental death. His interest in marriage must have died with her. It is clear that he had a very full life as a single man. His teaching career, writing, speaking, church work, activist work in social and professional matters, and friendships filled his amazingly productive life. He was a key planner of many social events with colleagues, students, and friends throughout his life. He loved spirited conversation and good food, and loved treating people to Denver, Aspen, and Lincoln restaurants, plays, music, and athletic events as well as other important cultural and political events.

There are, as we will see later, critics of Potthoff's theology and even a few critics of him as a person. The great scholar and author Peter Gay, in the preface of his biography of Sigmund Freud, quotes Freud: "Biographers are fixated on their hero in a quite particular way." In the same paragraph Freud goes on to say that the resultant biography may thus be bound to be an exercise in idealization which often results in "lies, to concealment, to hypocrisy, to embellishments."[1] While it is true that the writer and editor of this biography is a fan and friend of Harvey and his work, I have, because of this cautionary warning by Freud and Gay, done my very best not to fall victim to exaggeration or reporting only the positive as I crafted this work.

Chapters written by guest writers make up much of this biography. The guest writers reflect Potthoff's career and person as well as his theology and churchmanship. The reader will find my introduction to each writer in the "Contributors" section in previous pages.

Now to the "why me" of this biography. In 1957 I graduated from Northwest Missouri State University and came to Iliff to begin my theological studies. My college majors were general science and agriculture, not standard preparation for the study of theology. My first course with Dr. Potthoff (as all students called him) was the 1957–1958 year, and I understood only a part of what I experienced at that time. Even so, I was so impressed by his knowledge and the power of his teaching and his presence as a person that I read some of his works outside of the classroom assignments and took as many of his courses as I could during the next two years. Several years later, I began to grasp the depth of what this liberal and process thought theologian was doing in his writing, church work, teaching, and pastoral work.

Aside from my appreciation of Dr. Potthoff as a teacher and theologian, while I was an Iliff student, Dr. Potthoff adopted me in some special ways, as he did many students over the years. I was invited to be in a small handball group that played each week at the Denver YMCA. My wife, Ethel, and I were frequently his guests to concerts, athletic events, and meals. We discussed academic and church issues, and I often sought his advice on such things as going on to a doctoral program before I even considered going to Syracuse University.

While I was away from Denver as a student and pastor, and then as faculty member and administrator, Harvey and I visited as often as possible when we were both in Denver. After his retirement from NWU and his move back to Denver, I spent even more time with him. In his last years and in the early years of my own retirement and return to Colorado, I visited him almost every week whenever we were both in residence. It was somewhat like *Tuesdays with Morrie* but not quite the same. Usually we discussed theology, and often in the last months his questions and concerns were about the "new spirituality" cropping up everywhere. He was greatly troubled by it. Crystals, tattoos, and "spiritual but not religious" were outside of his traditional assumptions about being spiritual.

It is only partly because of my bonds with this amazing man and theologian that I became his biographer. As early as 1992, when Harvey retired from NWU, I thought someone should undertake writing his biography, and that feeling became stronger after his death in 2002. The finger did not point to me at first. There were others who could have done justice to this project but could not or would not undertake the research and writing. All agreed that a biography should be written, and it became my privilege to do so.

No introduction to this book could be more helpful than Potthoff's own words. They are from an adult Christian education publication.

Today we begin what will be for many a new kind of study. We are going to discuss theology and theologians. We are going to discuss the place of theology in the life of the church. We are going to consider the meaning of theology for the individual Christian. We are going to investigate some of the exciting things that are going on in theological circles today.

Perhaps you are one of those persons who is somewhat frightened by the word "theology." It sounds very formal and suggests something that belongs only in theological seminaries or in discussions by highly trained persons.

There are many people who are almost afraid to approach the subject of theology, because it seems far removed from them.

At the outset, then, let us make it clear that theology is for everyone who is sincerely interested in religion and especially in Christianity. If you have ever asked, "What is God?" or "What is man and human nature?" or "What is the meaning of Jesus Christ for my life?" or "What do we really mean by salvation?"— then you have asked theological questions. You are on the way to being a theologian![2]

So, let us get on with Harvey's story!

INTRODUCTION

NOTES

[1] Peter Gay, *Freud, A Life for Our Time* (New York: W. W. Norton & Company, 1988), xv.

[2] Study booklet, *Adult Student*, March 1962, Methodist Publishing House, page 24.

1

THE EARLY YEARS, PART I

by Amy Phillips

Pre-World War I Le Sueur, Minnesota, was a small community of around 1,700 people, best known for a large canning plant and the fact that Dr. William Worrall Mayo, founder of the Mayo Clinic, had been an early resident. Harvey Henry Potthoff was born into this midwestern German-American community on April 23, 1911. Harvey had three sisters: Laura, nine years older than Harvey; Florence and Julia, six and five years older; and one brother, Carl, seven years Harvey's senior.

Harvey's father, Henry, emigrated from Germany as a child. The Potthoff family settled near St. Paul, where there was a large German immigrant community. Henry Potthoff attended German Wallace College[1] in Berea, Ohio, where he met Harvey's mother, Florence, whose father was a minister of the German Methodist Church.

World War I had begun by the time Harvey was three. Years later, in an autobiographical lecture to Iliff students,[2] Harvey recalled the significance of being a German immigrant family in the sociopolitical climate of America at that time. "I remember as a boy, the discussions as to whether we ought to join the English-speaking people, and my father always thought this union should take place, but the first sermons I ever heard were in German. ... Not everybody was terribly enthusiastic about the Germans in those days." Harvey expressed still having sympathy for his parents during that time in American history: "With a real German heritage which they treasured, and yet knowing they were now in America, where the thing to do was to be American ... I sometimes I think they may have been overly protective of us, but they surely did the very best that they could." All members of Harvey's family played a major role in his life, and he said, "I think theologically I learned something from all of the family and their wonderful kind of way about what grace incarnate really is."

Growing Up with His Father as His Minister

Harvey described the family's religious orientation as German Pietism and spoke of it as a major influence on his theological foundations. With his father as their minister, the family practiced a deeply devotional faith, which he characterized as "an experiential relationship with the living Christ stressed, a belief that there should be progress in the Christian life, an emphasis on certain private virtues, and devotion involving the dimension of trust. ...'If thou but suffered God to guide thee,' things would come out alright. That was pretty much the theme." He described internalizing a "dipolar" approach to Christianity, in which a Christian trusts God, but a Christian also assumes responsibilities, as exemplified in one of his favorite hymns recalled from the family's times of singing around the piano, "Be Strong":

We are not here to play, to dream, to drift
We have hard work to do and loads to lift.
Shun not the battle; face it, 'tis God's gift.
Be Strong.

Harvey stated in "Empirical Theology and the Vision of Hope",[3] "There is no doubt that hymns were a formative factor in my theological journey."

When asked by a student attending his autobiographical course whether there was tension in his theological development between his early upbringing and liberal thought, Harvey said that he didn't really experience a philosophical crisis in this regard, because "the kind of Pietism which I experienced put quite a stress on feeling, and was not so strong on a rigid orthodoxy. As a matter of fact ... German Pietism ... rose within the Lutheran Church and in part was a reaction against a certain kind of [deductive] rationalism, or an emphasis on orthodoxy per se. ... I think I've not been overly hung up on some of these theological changes as being something terribly threatening. And I think that's grounded in the nature of the religious experience in which I was nurtured."

Dr. Potthoff spoke of growing up in a time and in a tradition of much more formal and reverent religious practices than he observed in his years of teaching, and the meaning those impressions had on his theological underpinnings. He recalled visits from the Methodist district superintendents to his father making a lasting impression on his memory. His father and the superintendent would be wearing their Prince Albert coats. Regarding the formal dress, Harvey noted that "it was quite a thing." Formal traditions relating to church sacraments and protocol left a lifelong impression on Harvey. "There was always communion on the Sunday that the district superintendent was there. So my associations with the communion service are with occasions that you took seriously. Meaningful." Even late in his career, Harvey admitted that he "winced inside" at a poorly done communion service.

One of Harvey's famously funny anecdotes gives some insight into the family's traditional devotional practices, including keeping the Sabbath day holy:

> *And how do you keep it holy? Well, anybody ought to know that. You go to Sunday school, and then you go to church, and then in the evening if you're young you go to Epworth League, and then Sunday evening service, and in the meantime, you do absolutely nothing worldly. You can't play games, you can't buy anything unless it's medicine, you certainly wouldn't have a Sunday paper. But there was one thing you could do ... it was OK to make fudge.*

As his minister, Harvey's father put him through his paces in catechism. When it came to the challenge of standing before the congregation and reciting the answers to questions of religious doctrine, Harvey might have had the inside track. But the pressure was on, because "he didn't give me any clue as to what he was going to ask!" Harvey must have done all right, because his catechism certificate from the Main Street Methodist Episcopal Church in Winona, Minnesota, dated May 29, 1921, and signed by his father, resides in the Iliff Archives.[4]

Family photo used with permission, courtesy of Kay and Pat

Harvey (the youngest) and his four siblings:
Florence, Laura, Harvey, Carl and Julia

Family photos used with permission, courtesy of Kay

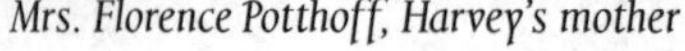

Mrs. Florence Potthoff, Harvey's mother

Rev. Henry A. Potthoff, Harvey's father

Harvey cited the Epworth League's youth camps and conferences as other important early influences on him, and on Methodism. He believed that the Epworth League and study programs of what was later called the Women's Society of Christian Service "were among the most liberalizing influences of the church."

Community

The family lived in various small towns in Minnesota, including Le Sueur, Winona, and Jeffers, where Harvey graduated valedictorian from Jeffers High School. Harvey showed his academic maturity early on, as his high school valedictorian address demonstrates.

Today Decides Tomorrow

Members of the graduating class and friends:

This great age of advancement in which we live, calls for a spirit of progress. Therefore, I am certain that the class of 1928 could have chosen no motto more appropriate than "Today Decides Tomorrow." This motto is a challenge for action. It is a motto for youth!

I think it is a significant fact, that preceding every great triumph, in any phase of life, whether it has been on the battle field, in the science laboratory, or in the halls of legislature, there has been a period of preparation, in which the foundation of the forthcoming achievement was laid. And in proportion to the effort that was put into the laying of that foundation has been the magnitude of the final achievement.

The pages of history are filled with the stories of men and women who spent their lives in framing the groundwork of the institutions which we enjoy today. Many of them never lived to see the final product of their labors, but they died in the knowledge that they had started a work which would be a blessing to future generations. I think it was they of whom Walt Whitman was thinking when he wrote

Oh, to die advancing on!
Pioneers, oh, pioneers!

I believe that Pasteur, Washington, Lincoln, and the many others whom we call "great" have had for their motto, "Today Decides Tomorrow." For all of them spent their lives working for an ideal which they believed might someday be realized.

The thought expressed in the words, "Today Decides Tomorrow", has inspired men to deeds that under ordinary conditions would have been well nigh impossible. It was because they knew that on them depended the liberty of their posterity, that in 1776 the thirteen undeveloped but patriotic states of America dared hand to the king of England a declaration of independence and then to fight for a recognition of their rights!

And finally when freedom was won, the men who before had sacrificed for future generations again looked toward the tomorrow. Immediately they set to work planning a government which would stand the test of time. In four months they produced the document, which in the words of Gladstone is "the greatest work ever struck off at one time by the hand of man" – the American Constitution.

How privileged are we to live in 1928. For this is one of the tomorrows of which the great men of history have dreamed and for which so many sacrifices have been made. Our debt to the heroes of yesterday is immeasurable. But we may show our gratitude to them by laying such a foundation in our today, that the tomorrow will be a day characterized by truth and strength.[5]

Valedictory – Tuesday, May 29, 1928; Harvey H. Potthoff

Family photo used with permission

Harvey's high school senior picture

Harvey noted how the support of communities was important in his development. He described the tolling of the town bell, everyone in the community knowing for whom, and the community providing a "tremendous sense of support" to the bereaved family. The Potthoff family experienced four deaths while living in these small communities, and Harvey indicated that the community support they received was extremely important. He contrasted these early experiences to life in big cities where a funeral procession goes by and few even think about it, and he wondered how those types of changes affected a person's doctrine of the church.

Education

The Potthoffs were a poor family, but Harvey noted that there was never a question that the children would receive a good education. He left home for college "with two things of abiding importance ... the knowledge that I was loved, and a sense of the Holy."[6]

Teachers played an extremely important part in Dr. Potthoff's theological development, and he cited them often, from a high school English literature teacher all the way through William Henry Bernhardt at Iliff and Alfred North Whitehead at Harvard. Even at seventy years old, he still remembered high school teachers' names and specifics of what they had taught him, even poems that his teachers and professors had him memorize all those years ago. Particularly vivid influences were teachers of philosophy, Latin, and English literature.

Harvey believed that "the world gets bigger through the vehicle of literature," and with the early influence of high school literature teachers who introduced him to the works of many important authors and poets, he went on to major in English literature at Morningside College in Sioux City, Iowa.

Poetry had a large impact on Harvey in those early days and for the rest of his life, particularly the poetry of Wordsworth. He noted Wordsworth's "Character of the

Happy Warrior" and its message of personal integrity as "one of the most important poems of my life."

Whose high endeavors are an inward light
That makes the path before him always bright;
Who, with a natural instinct to discern
What knowledge can perform, is diligent to learn;
Abides by this resolve, and stops not there,
But makes his moral being his prime care:[7]

In addition to his studies and extracurricular activities (debate team, acting in school plays, and editor of the school paper), he was a working student with part-time janitorial and other jobs. One of his jobs while attending Morningside College was as a sports writer and later the night sports editor for the *Sioux City Tribune*. Harvey recalled seeing "a side of life which I had not met in some of those German communities!" During his time at Morningside, his sister Florence died at the age of twenty-six of a heart ailment, inoperable at that time. Harvey stated that he "felt this very, very deeply."

Harvey earned two degrees from Iliff, his Masters in Theology in 1935, and his doctorate in 1941. Awarded the Elizabeth Iliff Warren Fellowship in 1935, he went to Harvard to study under Alfred North Whitehead and William Ernest Hocking.

"That Strange Knocking at the Door"

Morningside College did not contribute greatly to Harvey's theological development. In his talk, "Empirical Theology and the Vision of Hope,"[8] he explained, "My entering a school of theology following graduation from college cannot be attributed to members of the college faculty. I had many questions about religion during my college years, but unfortunately no member of the faculty and no one in the clergy, on or off the campus, stimulated my religious thinking in a significant way. As I look back on my college years they were well-nigh void so far as religious nurture (academic or otherwise) was concerned."

He began to think about a vocation while studying at Morningside. Writing? Teaching? Journalism? But there was always "that strange knocking at the door, whatever it is." Interestingly enough, although Morningside studies and faculty provided no particular religious or theological inspiration, the president of the college called him in, and "without any introduction, he said, 'Why don't you go into the ministry?'" Although not studying religion or finding much theological inspiration at Morningside, the president clearly saw Harvey's gift and way of approaching questions. Their conversation continued, and the president asked, "Why don't you go to Iliff?" to which Harvey replied, "What's that?"

Iliff

After graduating from Morningside in 1932, Harvey headed west to Iliff. This was during the Great Depression, and he traveled by bus and "had no money." He remembered a stop on that trip with a diner advertising meals for seventy-five cents, and marveling that anybody could pay seventy-five cents for a single meal.

With no money, Harvey was again a working student. He took one of two custodian jobs at Iliff and lived in a room in the basement of Iliff Hall. The pattern of certain teachers having a major influence on Harvey's theology continued at Iliff, with Drs. Lindsay Longacre and William Henry Bernhardt in particular noted as "companions on my journey of life." He preached his first sermon during this time, in an area of Denver owned by and named for P. T. Barnum of Barnum and Bailey, who had at one time wintered his circus there.[9] Harvey jokingly told his students that he didn't know "if there's any symbolic significance in this or not." The sermon was delivered in January of 1933, a time when the stock market crash still affected the economy, and the Great Depression wore on Americans. In an attempt to address the concerns of parishioners at that time, his sermon was entitled "A Question for the Ages."[10]

Harvey was then approached by the district superintendent to go to Argo Church in north Denver to start a ministry in a closed church building. They gave him some missionary money to get started, and off he went.[11] In his 1981 lecture to Iliff students, he said, "Well, you should have seen that church. It hadn't been entered for years, it was along a dirt road, all the windows were broken. I had to crawl through a broken window to get in – that's the way I entered the ministry. Got in, and the dirt on the pews was so thick I had to sweep it off with a broom. And, well, that's how things got started." Seven people showed up for the first service; by the next year, there were morning and evening services and a Sunday school of fifty people.

In that first year of ministry, Harvey didn't preach only about the larger implications and issues invoked by the liturgical calendar and well-known biblical parables. He tackled some very difficult issues of the day. In the long run-up to World War II, he delivered a sermon entitled "Our Friend, The Enemy," confronting the difficult question of the moral costs of war[12] and challenging parishioners: "The problem is an individual one concerning each and every one of us. For wars begin with the individual." He spoke of Christian fundamentalists and modernists in another sermon,[13] and in speaking on "A Century of Progress," he asked, "Do we need a new reformation?"[14] On the Fourth of July 1933, he concluded, "We need a new Declaration of Independence" to free us from a caste system, propaganda, and false patriotism, "A patriotism so true to all peoples that war could not be."[15]

Harvey's tenure at Argo Church was for one year, at which time the superintendent came to tell him he was needed at Christ Church. "He said it in a nice way, but I got the message. And I reluctantly went to Christ Church." (See Chapter 2.)

As his ministry at Argo and then as an associate at Christ Methodist Church were unfolding, his Iliff student days were revealing a very successful and impressive scholarly interest and ability. The key to this is wonderfully demonstrated in the lifelong relationships that were developing with his mentors Lindsay Longacre and William Bernhardt. Upon graduation from Iliff in 1935, Potthoff received Iliff's highest academic honor. The Elizabeth Iliff Warren Fellowship provided for a year of graduate study at any institution of Harvey's choosing. He went to Harvard to study under Alfred North Whitehead.

In conclusion, I add a personal note. I met Harvey Potthoff only once, by accident, at a Sunday worship service at University Park United Methodist Church across from the Iliff campus in Denver, around 1994. I was sitting second from the end of a pew, and there was what seemed to be a very nice older gentleman sitting next to me. When it came time to stand for a hymn, I noticed I had the last hymnal on the row. I offered to share it with the nice gentleman and will never forget his response:

"No thank you, dear, I know them all." Well, I found that hard to believe, but sure enough, he knew every stanza and every verse and every melody that we sang that day. Now, *that* was impressive. Sometime during the service, I found out his name (whether this was from signing the register or acknowledgment from the pulpit or chatting with him, I really don't remember), but I knew he was a minister. A few weeks later, I asked my cousin Dick (Dr. Richard Phillips, author of this book) if he knew Harvey Potthoff, told him that I had met him at church, and what an impression he had made on me not only with the hymns, but a presence that was very special. All of this in an hour! Only then did Dick explain to me who Harvey was, his importance to Iliff, Methodism, and liberal theology.

There are few people in my life that have made an unforgettable impression and memory in just one meeting, and Harvey Potthoff was one of them. I will never forget meeting him, and I feel privileged to be learning more about him through this project and compiling from the Iliff files his early years and his influence on theology.

–Amy E. Phillips

THE EARLY YEARS, PART II

By R. L. Phillips

Late in the research and writing of this book I was able to be in touch with several Potthoff family members. The family tree is extensive and is being well kept by individuals from at least three branches of the family. My first contact was initiated by Roy Smith of Yuma, Colorado. He had heard that I was writing this biography and contacted me when he was to come to Denver for a meeting. We visited and viewed several photographs of his side of the family; he is a great-nephew of Harvey's and is now retired. Eventually he sent me a family tree document that has been developed by another member of the family from Yuma, Ken Tiffany. Both Potthoff's mother and the Roy Smith side of the family are descended from John Ploch, who was born in Germany in 1816 and later came to Indiana.[16]

More closely related to Harvey are several relatives discovered after my meeting with Roy Smith. I was able to find an old address of one of Harvey's nieces, Pat, a daughter of his sister, Laura Louise. My letter reached Pat, and I was delighted when she responded and sent me a packet of family information and pictures. Laura had three children, they are all still living—Pat, Mary, and Jo. Pat's daughter Kay Walter has been very helpful with information and pictures. She lives near her mother in Lincoln, Nebraska. Harvey's brother, Carl, also had a family but I have no information concerning names or locations. Carl started an Iliff scholarship fund in Harvey's name. He died during Harvey's retirement years. Three of the Potthoff siblings, Florence, Julia, and Harvey, had no children.

Keepers and archivists of the family records for the Florence and Henry part of the family are a mother-daughter team, Shawn Brand and Bettina Brand Potthoff Schneider. Their extensive correspondence with me, as well as my contacts with Pat, Kay, and Roy, mostly in printed copies of emails, are contained in the Iliff Archives.[17] Shawn (daughter of Jo) and Bettina are Harvey's great-niece and great-great-niece, descendants of Laura, who married Dr. Oren Wesley Brand. The photographs of Harvey parents—Florence Amelia Baechtold (spelled Bachtold or Bechtold in some places) and Henry Anthony Potthoff—on page 6 are courtesy of Kay. Thanks to several family members,

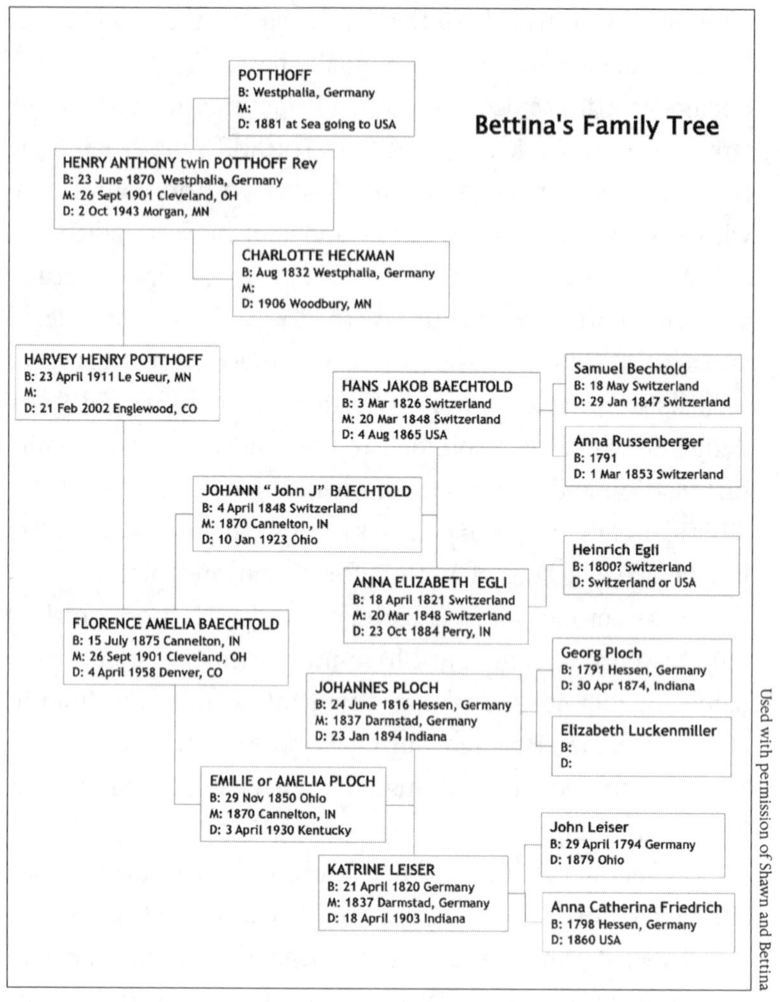

Used with permission of Shawn and Bettina

Family tree by Bettina Brand Potthoff Schneider,
Harvey's great-great-niece

the Iliff Archives now contain many pictures. The photo of the five children—Florence, Laura, Carl, Julia, and Harvey (the youngest)—is also courtesy of Kay and Pat. The family tree above is printed with permission of Shawn and Bettina; it does not include Harvey's siblings. Anyone interested in more details of the family tree and history can get the information in the Iliff Archives, including how to contact several family historians.

Family members (almost all on his mother's side) are often listed as ministers in the German Methodist tradition, medical doctors, and, in recent times, several lawyers. It is my understanding that attempts to trace Harvey's father's family have not been successful. One of Harvey's second cousins, Benjamin Schwartz, served as chancellor of Nebraska Wesleyan University from 1938 to 1946, something Harvey never mentioned in connection with his own role at NWU from 1981 to 1992. What has been interesting is to discover how important the intellectual life has been and is to the family.

Harvey's oldest sister, Florence, died while he was in college. Harvey was deeply saddened by her death. He was close to all of his siblings, perhaps especially to Carl, who was a medical doctor. Carl came to Denver to be with Harvey and their mother when she fell ill. Here is the story as told in email correspondence with Shawn and Bettina. "Florence would rotate amongst her living children. [She] was on a regular stay with Harvey when she felt ill. He took her to the doctor in Denver. They found an abdominal mass now believed to be ovarian cancer. Harvey wrote all his siblings. Carl flew out to Denver. Shortly thereafter, Carl and Harvey left the apartment to go get an ice cream cone. Florence was 'fine' when they left. Upon their return, Florence was found dead in Harvey's apartment. Her body was sent to Minnesota for burial in Morgan."[18]

In my visits with Harvey over many years, he seldom talked of personal things, even of his immediate family, other than that there was deep family love and that he was a proud member. There were many visits, letters, phone calls, and exchanges of pictures over the years, especially with his mother.

Harvey (left) and his three living siblings probably at their mother's funeral.

Potthoff's student years at Iliff were a joy to him as well as academically formative and productive. He worked his way through Iliff much as he had done at Morningside. He served Iliff and the University Park Methodist Church across the street as custodian while also serving Argo and then Christ Churches and doing limited other preaching. All the while, according to his Iliff student colleagues, he was a fun part of the student culture, played basketball on the Iliff team in the Denver University intramurals (he remarked that he was a good high school player and helped Iliff win the DU basketball championship), went on student picnics in the mountains, and attended a number of musical and theatrical events in Denver. Having established well his academic and cultural and athletic interests at an early age, these traits were to remain hallmarks of his personality for the rest of his life.

The Year with Whitehead

Harvey's reading and his work with William Bernhardt introduced him to Alfred North Whitehead as a philosopher with theological interests. His keen interest in studying with the already famous Whitehead (a process thought–oriented scholar and writer) was thus well established and the key to his firm choice to use the Elizabeth Iliff Warren Fellowship to study at Harvard. In the summer of 1935, he made the trip east.

In addition to classes with Whitehead, he took classes at the Boston University School of Theology and at another college in that area, where he had courses with Edgar S. Brightman and William Earnest Hocking, which he remembered with great appreciation in his theological and church career. Potthoff also relished attending worship services and hearing many of the great preachers in that area. Of course, he continued his attendance at musical and other cultural events.

Potthoff's studies at Harvard and related experiences in the area were important for all of his future work. There is no doubt that being with Whitehead was seminal in his thought and his future self-identification as both scholar and committed pastor. During a visit I had in Potthoff's Denver apartment in about 1994, he shared with me his two-page reflection on being in Whitehead's classes. He reported that at the end of the last class, he went right to his apartment in Andover Hall, sat down at the typewriter, and wrote his thoughts and memories. Harvey allowed me to make a copy of the document for my own keeping. Selected paragraphs are quoted below but without the many handwritten additions he added over the years.

HARVEY H. POTTHOFF

ALFRED NORTH WHITEHEAD
Andover Hall, May 21, 1936

This morning I want to write just a few of the things that I now feel about Alfred North Whitehead so that later on after I no longer have the privilege of being near him personally and feeling the inspiration of his presence I may be reminded of some of his greatness. Perhaps in that way I shall be able to feel again "my heart strangely warmed" as it has been so often during these months at Harvard while listening to him lecture and in conversation with him.

Surely Whitehead is the greatest man I have ever known. At 75 years he has a boyish interest in things—all things. Above all he seems to be interested in people. Any of his students may go to him and be made to feel [that] Whitehead is interested in him very much.

Whitehead seems to live in this world and yet above it. He watches movements far greater than those manifest in his own day, seems to seek the perspective of the years. He enjoys the moment in its immediacy and is saddened by the great loss which comes at its passage. Yet, he is always alert and anticipates with zest that which lies ahead. Never have I known anyone so alive to life. He seems to go to the depth of life.

In it all one sees his great reverence for life. Never does it bore him. Whitehead never seems to doubt the marvel and the wonder of the universe, and his whole soul is wrapped up in the effort to know it better and to be more worthy of it.

One is so strangely drawn to the man that precise formulation of the reason is difficult. It is partly his warm smile, it is partly the twinkle in his eye, it is partly his dress—a simple dark suit, wing collar and usually a large blue tie folded over, it is partly his manner in moving about, it is partly his build—short and somewhat stooped, partly his walk as he glances about as when coming into the lecture room carrying his battered old case, partly the way he pounds the desk when he wishes to emphasize some point in a lecture, partly the simplicity of his illustrations. ... but above all it is the man Whitehead who is a picture of all these things and more. He is a great human man, one feels that he has felt the deepest and finest emotions. And then his mysticism. How often in a lecture he has looked out the back window from his desk in the front of the room, and as he talked apparently become totally oblivious to those in the classroom as he has grappled with some great problem for which he almost seemed to have a solution. He himself has spoken of those moments when looking at a beautiful sunset—one feels that he almost has an answer to all the questions which disturb us.

He seems so alive to every situation. For example, he has mentioned several times that he prepares each lecture shortly before that lecture. How easily he could use notes of previous years! And then he tells us that he must wait until the lecture itself in order to get the right phrasing of things—in order to get his point over as he wants it. My personal conversations with Whitehead have been few—but all indicate the spirit of the man. The first time I met him I went to him in September, 1935 before lectures began to have him sign my registration paper. In the large philosophy committee room in Emerson Hall he welcomed me, asked my name, suggested we sit down together. He asked me where I came from, my chief interest, and other questions. He never referred to himself and quite naturally seemed to keep the conversations directed toward topics outside himself. At the end of the semester I went to him to sign my registration card for his second semester course in the Function of Reason. He smiled and said, "You did very nice work last semester."

> *Later on in the year I went into the committee room to see him for a moment. He autographed my copy of [his book]* Process and Reality *and displayed considerable interest in it, since he thought it was being printed on a new kind of paper. He showed me his worn old copy. How often he must have read it to have it worn as it was! He told me that he was chiefly interested in working out a philosophy beginning with experience. After the lectures were over I went to get my term paper. I had written on some of the implications of Whitehead's philosophy for religion. He told me that it was a very nice paper and that he liked the paper especially for its sincerity. "That's what I liked about it," he said. He had written a note at the end of the paper saying that he felt it was a fair abstract of his position on the matter.*
>
> *All in all, Whitehead has attracted me as no other person ever has. I think that is true of many of his students. He shows in his life just how beautiful and interesting life can be. My own life is so much richer for having known him. I hope that I shall always be able to preserve some of the glow coming from his personality.*
>
> *After his last lecture in May, 1936 for the year the students gave him tremendous applause. It had been Whitehead's habit during the year at the close of each lecture to remain [at] his desk in order that students might come to him with questions. This day the applause continued so long that he found it necessary to pick up his papers, put them in the old brown case, and leave the room. He waved goodbye to the class as he left the room – the applause continuing until after he was gone. A great tribute to a great, great man.*[19]

Harvey allowed me to also make a photocopy of a paper he wrote for Whitehead. He was proud of his teacher's comments as well as the grade he received. The original paper in its original binder is in the Iliff Archives.[20] The title of the paper is

"The Influence of Cosmology upon Theological Concepts—for Dr. A.N. Whitehead—Philosophy 3b—Harvard University—by H.H. Potthoff—December, 1935." On the frontal or title page in his own hand, Whitehead wrote "A" "Excellent ANW."[21]

On the last page, again by hand, Whitehead wrote: "I have found this a very interesting essay. I wish, however, you might have concentrated on the contemporary situation in theology with reference to the contemporary and historical elements determining its trends. You seem quite qualified for such a study."[22]

The summer of 1936, when Potthoff returned from Harvard to Denver, his full-time fledgling career as Methodist minister was by no means the only thing that filled his time. In a real way, it marked the beginning of his multiple task approach to life that would continue for many years to come.

THE INFLUENCE OF COSMOLOGY UPON THEOLOGICAL CONCEPTS

Harvey H. Potthoff
Philosophy 3b
December, 1935
Dr. A.N. Whitehead

Excellent
ANW

A

Iliff Archives, box 31, file folder 19

Cover page of paper by HHP written for ANW with ANW's grade and remark.

Philosopher, one of world's greatest, is Alfred N. Whitehead, author of *Process and Reality*.

Iliff Archives, box 31, file folder 19

Harvey clipped this from an unknown magazine and placed it along with the paper.

Bibliography

(In addition to assigned readings)

Aall, A. Hellenistic Elements in Christianity
University of London Press; 1931

Angus, S. The Religious Quests of the Graeco-Roman World
John Murray, London; 1929

Brightman, The Problem of God
The Abingdon Press; N.Y. 1930

Dampier, A History of Science
The MacMillan Co. 1932

Taylor, A.E. Platonism And Its Influence
Marshall Jones, Boston; 1924

Shedd, W.G.T. A History of Christian Doctrine
Shas. Scribners Sons; 1863

Alexander, A.B.D. The Shaping Forces of Religious Thought.
MacLehose, Jackson and Co. Glasgow, 1920

Sheldon, H.C. History of Christian Doctrine
Harpers; 1886

Haydon, A.E. The Quest of the Ages
Harpers, 1929

Russell, Bertrand; Religion and Science
Henry Holt and Co. 1935

I have found this a very interesting essay. I wish, however you might have concentrated on the contemporary situation in theology with reference to the contemporary historical elements determining its trend. You seem quite qualified for such a study.

A.N.W.

Iliff Archives, box 31, file folder 19

ANW's handwritten comments on the final page of the paper.

NOTES

All documents referenced in footnotes relating to Harvey H. Potthoff Papers can be found in Iliff Archives, code 3.F.12, Taylor Library, The Iliff School of Theology.

[1] Now Baldwin Wallace University.

[2] I draw heavily in this chapter from a lecture Harvey gave to Iliff students on March 24, 1981 (transcribed from audiotape) from a course entitled "One Person's Religious/Theological Journey," which has been invaluable in recounting his early years and their influence on his theology. Unless otherwise noted, direct quotes from Harvey in this chapter are from this lecture. The full transcription of this lecture can be found in the Iliff Archives, box 44, file folder 7.

[3] Harvey H. Potthoff, "Empirical Theology and the Vision of Hope," Iliff Archives, box 6, file folder 7.

[4] Iliff Archives, box 40.

[5] Iliff Archives, box 5, file folder 1.

[6] Harvey H. Potthoff, "Empirical Theology and the Vision of Hope," Iliff Archives, box 6, file folder 7.

[7] Excerpt from William Wordsworth "Character of the Happy Warrior" (lines 6–11), 1806.

[8] Harvey H. Potthoff, "Empirical Theology and the Vision of Hope," Iliff Archives, box 6, file folder 7.

[9] The Barnum neighborhood of Denver is now the area between Federal Boulevard and Perry Street on the east and west, and Sixth and Alameda Avenues on the north and south.

[10] *Rocky Mountain News*, January 18, 1986. Interview with Harvey Potthoff for the Religion page by Terry Mattingly. No copy of this sermon is in the Iliff Archives. There is a sermon dated October 7, 1932, entitled "Give Me This Stranger!" based on the apocryphal "Acts of Pilate." A note in Potthoff's handwriting next to the date reads "My First!" It is undocumented as to whether this sermon was delivered or was for academic work at Iliff only. Harvey H. Potthoff Papers, Iliff Archives, box 14, file folder 1.

[11] *The Methodist, Evangelical, and United Brethern Churches in the Rockies 1850 – 1976.* Edited by J. Alton Templin, Allen D. Breck, and Martin Rist. (Rocky Mountain Conference of the United Methodist Church, 1977), 300–301. The Argo Church was one of three Methodist mission churches in the north part of Denver. They were located in an area where there were at least three smelting operations. Argo survived the other two; in part, because it was closer to an expanding Denver, but the year after Potthoff served the church it closed and was sold to another denomination. The church failed to attract enough people to sustain it and was abandoned. Ironically the last two Methodist pastors at Argo Church were both Iliff students who became members of the Iliff faculty. Martin Rist, who was student pastor of the Argo Church in 1929, received his doctorate from Chicago and served many years as New Testament professor at Iliff. He and Potthoff became great friends. After Rist's year at Argo, the church was closed until Potthoff was appointed student pastor in 1933. I (RLP) traveled to the intersection of 44th Avenue and Jason Street in February 2013 to see where the Argo Church had stood on the northeast corner of the intersection. In talking with one of the proprietors of the company just

north of where the church had been, I learned that it was torn down sometime between 1978 and 1980. As the smelters left the district, it became a warehouse area. Now there are many small appartment houses and small homes in addition to businesses and warehouses.

12 "Our Friend, The Enemy," November 12, 1933, Iliff Archives, box 14, file folder 2.

13 "The Sin of Indifference," July 30, 1933, Iliff Archives, box 14, file folder 2.

14 "A Century of Progress," August 6, 1933, Iliff Archives, box 14, file folder 2.

15 "A New Declaration of Independence," July 2, 1933, Iliff Archives, box 14, file folder 2.

16 A copy of the Potthoff family tree plus many pictures and related correspondence are in the Iliff Archives, box 43, folder 2.

17 Iliff Archives, box 14, file folder 2.

18 Email of August 21, 2012, Iliff Archives, box 44, file folder 12. Her death was April 4, 1958, at the time the author was one of Potthoff's students.

19 Harvey Potthoff notes on Alfred North Whitehead, Iliff Archives, 3-F-12, box 31, file folder 19.

20 Iliff Archives, 3-F-12, box 31, file folder 19; and Whitehead file.

21 Ibid.

22 Ibid.

2

CHRIST METHODIST CHURCH AND ILIFF FACULTY

By R. L. Phillips

In April 1934, late in his second year as a student at Iliff, Harvey Potthoff became the assistant pastor of Christ Episcopal Methodist Church in Denver. The switch from Argo Church to Christ Church was probably due to the respect and confidence that Iliff and Methodist officials had in this young student pastor and the need at Christ Church for more pastoral assistance. Rev. Floyd L. Sampson, senior pastor of Christ Church, was leaving in 1935 to join the faculty of the University of Denver as chairman of the Department of Religion. Harvey and Rev. Sampson became good friends, and Harvey "appreciated so much his pastorate and his helpfulness to me as a student."[1] After Potthoff's first year of service to the church, the congregation was so impressed with him that they asked the bishop, in the spring of 1935, to appoint him as their senior minister. This involved two almost impossible and very unusual decisions on the part of the church and the office of the bishop. The first was for such a very young minister, still a student, to even be considered for such a large church appointment.

By the time Christ Church made its request, Harvey had been awarded the Elizabeth Iliff Warren Fellowship and had committed to studying under Alfred N. Whitehead at Harvard for the next year. When Harvey explained that he had accepted this opportunity, Christ Church requested that Potthoff be appointed to be their senior minister when he returned the next summer. This led to the second rare decision within the denominational structure and methods of operation: the request for a year's delay was granted! The Methodist Church has what is called the appointive system. Pastors are appointed to churches by the area bishop in consultation with the Conference Cabinet, made up primarily of district superintendents and with the individual church in question.

In the summer of 1936, Potthoff returned from Harvard to Christ Church as the senior pastor. "The people knew him and loved him. They felt he was well prepared to become their pastor."[2]

Christ Church was one of the earliest Methodist churches in the Denver area and, at the time of Potthoff's appointment, was in new (1927) facilities. The church was deeply in debt due to the new building and "nothing had been paid on the debt of that church when I came as the pastor in 1936."[3]

There were very hard times after the Great Depression. Intense concern and work on Harvey's part necessitated a multitask approach to ministry.

Potthoff's insight into his ministry at Christ Church and how his experiences there influenced his ministry and his evolving theology were expressed in a 1981 speech with the subtitle, "Reflections on a Personal Journey." At the time of his appointment, the church was

> *. . . located two blocks from the University of Colorado Medical Center—a medical center devoted to research, medical training and treatment. Three other hospitals were nearby. Thus, associated with the church were doctors, nurses, medical students, technicians. People in these fields were on hand for services as well as family members of out-of-town patients. I quickly learned that if I was going to use illustrations of a medical nature I had better have the facts straight.*
>
> *I also got the point that in every congregation would be some persons dealing with life and death on a daily basis. Many of the persons in services were hurting and hurting badly. Ian McLaren's words seemed to make sense, "Be kind to every person you meet. He is having a hard time." [It became a Potthoff theme song.]*
>
> *One day I had an appointment to meet Dr. Franklin Ebaugh, head of the Department of Psychiatry at the medical school ... He was late for the appointment; he was seeing a patient. When he finally arrived he began the conversation by saying, "I wish you theologians would come up with a doctrine of forgiveness which takes into account what we now know about human nature." Some time later I wrote an article entitled Some Reflection on the Doctrine of Forgiveness. It might just as well have been entitled The Functional Significance of the Doctrine of Forgiveness in a Naturalistically-Oriented Theology.*
>
> *I spoke of forgiveness as life's permission to go beyond the past, and the grace to create a new present by transforming the past and anticipating the future. My experience in parish ministry clearly had theological overtones. Ministry provided grist for my theological mill.*

> *As I look back on the sermons I preached, I am impressed with how many of them involved the attempt to interpret and re-interpret life situations theologically. This entailed the attempt to make sense of God-talk, to help persons discern the spiritual dimension of their experience, and to say some things which were not being said by journalists, psychologists, sociologists and positive thinking cults. I assumed, and still assume, that some people go to church for something not available elsewhere. ...*
>
> *I endeavored to draw on potential resources in empirical theology in addressing life questions and situations. My pastoral experience fed into my theological journey. I tried to be a theologian-in-residence [an advocacy he maintained in his teaching] and aimed at nurturing a theological community of faith—with down-to-earth experience providing basic data.*[4]

In a subsequent speech, Harvey added more of his thoughts on how being a pastor developed his theology.

> *I think that in a very real sense I hammered out some of the most important elements in my theology, in the context of a parish ministry. In a real sense, my theology is and has been what might be called an ecclesiastical theology—the theology of the church. A pastoral theology. Closely related to and drawing on what some people would call philosophical theology. When I talk about theology of ministry, I'm talking about something which I think is at the heart of my concern.... I'm simply saying it has been my way of doing theology and this has been a focus of concern. The experience of preparing and officiating in worship services, the experience of preaching, the experience of leading in an education program, the experience of pastoral work, the experience of administration; all fed into my theologizing and all provided data for theological work ... there were several*

challenges at Christ Church to which our congregation was called to respond, and these challenges really helped to give focus to what I tried to do as a pastor, and gave real direction to the form of my theologizing.

During the time Harvey was the senior pastor of Christ Church, the church faced several challenges: the Depression, theological tension between fundamentalism and the early liberalism, World War II, being situated near a major medical center and trying to provide a ministry to both medical staff and patients and families.

Well most of the challenges that I've referred to had to do with the situations in the world out there, so to speak, but every pastor knows that there are all those private human dramas that are going on, issues of life and death, the perennial problems of being human. People turning to the church for a living faith, for Courage, for a living and meaning in living, and how does the church respond?[5]

Potthoff was the consummate pastor, deeply involved in all aspects of church administration and was a part of many church activities. Church finances are very important in the life of a church, and Potthoff was very mindful of that fact. During his pastorate, there was a celebration on Sunday, December 25, 1946, of both the 75th anniversary of the organization of Christ Church and the burning of the church mortgage.[6] This was a huge milestone in the history of the church. Potthoff's energies were focused on the financial survival of the church during his first years, a survival that was seriously in doubt when he became the senior minister.

HHP photo in Iliff Archives 3-F-12

Potthoff at his desk in Christ Church around 1940

Not only did Potthoff take part in many Christ Church programs, he was also involved in developing new programs. He brought together a group of young adults at the church on Friday evening, September 26, 1942, for a social meeting. During the evening, a new organization was formed, called the Wesley Fellowship. The group met on Sunday morning for a short business meeting and for lectures and discussion. In addition there was a monthly meeting for programs and entertainment.[7]

The first seminar series at Christ Church was held in the fall of 1947 and became a distinctive feature of the church's total program. Potthoff was on the planning committee of the first seminar, and "anyone interested in the subject of a particular discussion, whether he was affiliated with Christ Church or not, was invited to attend. There was a question and answer period at the conclusion of each meeting."[8] Discussion leaders came from many fields. Potthoff was a discussion leader in the first seminar series of six discussions on the basic theme, "How to Meet and Master Adversities."

One of the powerful influences of Potthoff's youth was the Epworth League, and he was very involved in the Epworth League of Christ Church. Dorothy Lagger (a former member of Christ Church) writes:

While Wilma [Dorothy's sister] and I were members of the church, we both sang in the choir and attended the Epworth League meetings Sunday evenings where Wilma played the piano for our hymn singing. I have a photo of a Sunday afternoon meal with all the League members in the Wormwood cabin at Lyons, CO owned by church members. Since Dr. Potthoff is not in the photo, I am assuming that he was the cameraman.

A picnic spot on Genesee Mtn. was often the destination for the League on a Sunday afternoon where a hot meal was prepared after a lively softball game. Since we had no car, getting to go to the mountains was a real treat.

Many times after the service at the church, Dr. Potthoff invited those who were interested to come to his parsonage owned by Mrs. Lord, a church member who was in her eighties at the time. Peter Gay was always one who came, and we listened to Dr. Potthoff's recordings of great symphony music.

Other times after the service we would go in Dr. Potthoff's car to a restaurant on S. Broadway for chili/mac, a combination of chili and macaroni. None of the League members had cars but Dr. Potthoff used Mrs. Lord's old buick that held seven or eight people.

Dr. Potthoff was noted for playing a very vigorous game of handball with several young men in the church including my husband and his brother.

Even after we had all left Christ Church, contacts with Dr. Potthoff continued. He officiated at baptisms and weddings of family members and always attended the family Christmas Eve meals at Wilma's house.

In The Christ Church Story, *one line reads "that because he had no family, Dr. Potthoff had lived in Mrs. Lord's house." The fact is that the whole church became his family, and he was loved by everyone.*[9]

It has long been observed by many that due to his being single and so completely committed to his ministries, both at Christ Church and always the whole church, that Harvey was actually married to the church.

In his later writings and sermons and speeches, it is very clear that he relished his time at Christ Church and that his memories were precious. That remained true to his last days.

Iliff invited Harvey to teach part-time in 1937, which he did until 1952. This was during his doctoral student days at Iliff, which culminated in receiving a ThD degree in 1941. So, the master of multiple tasks was pastor of a large church, seeking a graduate degree, and teaching at the graduate level part-time, all at the same time. In 1952 Potthoff was invited by Iliff to become a full-time faculty member as Professor of Christian Theology. "Although Dr. Potthoff regretted leaving Christ Church and the people he had served for 16 years, he felt he could better carry out his Christian work through the field of teaching."[10] The position at Iliff would also mean he would have more time to write and give lectures as he pursued what had become a focus on youth and education from his very first years as a student and then pastor.

HHP photo in Iliff Archives

HHP after graduating with his doctorate

"The Official Board regretfully accepted 'Harvey's' resignation, for each member realized how sorely he would be missed by the congregation. He had endeared himself to men and women, alike, through his generous help to others in time of need. For sixteen years, he had been their guide and counselor, pastor and friend. His had been the longest pastorate in the history of Christ church, and the teen-agers had known no other minister. Their parents had enjoyed his insightful and profound preaching. Nevertheless, all felt proud that their pastor had been chosen for such a significant position."[11]

In this period of its history, the Iliff faculty was few in number, and all of them knew Potthoff well as student, pastor, and teacher. The entire faculty respected his academic skills and interests. His mentors Lindsay Longacre and William Bernhardt were longtime and experienced faculty members who were held not only in great respect but had considerable administrative clout. They were undoubtedly the key to his coming aboard part-time and then in 1952 full-time. From 1937 until 1981, Harvey was the central figure in theology at Iliff, truly a remarkable as well as memorable tenure. It must be added that throughout this period of time he was also a very active member of the Colorado Conference of the Methodist Church and its successor, the Rocky Mountain Conference of the United Methodist Church.

As he prepared to retire from Iliff on March 29, 1981, a "Harvey H. Potthoff Day at Christ Church" was celebrated. Obviously, not all who would have liked to be there could be there. The following are excerpts from letters sent to Potthoff by some who could not share the day with him. The letters, as well as photographs, are contained in a scrapbook presented to him by the congregation of Christ Church.[12]

Greetings from the Beautiful Oregon Coast. We will be with you in spirit, sharing the wealth of blessed memories spanning four decades of your significant leadership, fellowship and inspiration:

The Indomitable "Ma" Lord, Christ Church Forum, Wesley Fellowship, Building Campaigns, Christian Social Concerns, Christ Church Seminars, Hospital Visits, Iliff At Aspen Summer Seminars, Picnics at Maroon Bells, Morning Breakfast Walks, Touring Skaggs Hall and the New Iliff Campus. These are only a few of the joyous recollections for which we are happy to add our word of deep appreciation,

Love and Blessings!

Franklin and Adena Wherry, March 21, 1981

Word has reached us out here in Sacramento that you are about to retire. That we greatly doubt, believing that instead it will in reality be merely a change of schedule and a reordering of specific activities and occupations.

We look back on our years with you at Christ Church, Denver as some of the very best church years of our lives. Unfortunately our move west deprived us from sharing in your many contributions to church activity in the Denver area.

Our best wishes for the future.

– Sincerely,

Lewis and Anne Tuthill, March 21, 1981

What a great chance to say 'Thank you' for being you!

I wish I could be there to enjoy the festivities with you.

When your name comes up, I think of so many ways in which you touched my life, but it would take at least 50 pages.

You helped me in my singing career in a way I am sure you were not aware of. I have passed on your advice for dealing with extreme nervousness when singing in front of people to my public school students as well as private students.

You always had time to listen and to suggest people to be their "best selves."

You presided at our wedding with your usual dignity and warmth.

You have continued touching my life with your study books which our prayer group uses. I thank God for your presence in my life. Blessing on you.

Helen Wheeler Holzinger, March 23, 1981

Many years ago when my first husband, Fred Keck, and I lived in Denver, we went to Christ Methodist Church to meet you and hear you preach. We found what we were seeking and soon after joined your church. Since you have lived as you preached, you became our spiritual guiding light, and you have always come when we called to help us as only you can. You conducted a beautiful memorial service for Fred. Many told me that this was the finest memorial service they had ever heard. My thanks to you.

When you left Christ Church to go to Iliff we were comforted by the realization that if you could teach young men to preach Christianity as you do, your influence would be more widespread than your work as pastor of any one church.

Congratulations on your retirement and may your future days be filled with true happiness.

Lovingly,
Lora Keck Chandler, March 9, 1981

We are using this means to convey our best wishes to you on your day.

Our minds go back to how much you have been involved in our lives. Yours was the only letter welcoming me to Iliff even before I got to Denver. Time and time again your thoughtfulness and generosity was expressed toward us. And these memories—from the Queen City Dixie Land Band to the fabulous eating places and experiences "in between"—are impressed in our minds forever.

Whenever I am with former students your name always comes up as one who has had a great influence on them.

Be assured always of our sincerest concern and love.

Yours,
Pat and Bill, March 24, 1981

During my brief encounter with you at Denver I was very impressed with the way in which you encouraged your students and all the people of the church to "think." You have provided us with an important legacy. Your thoughtfulness engenders the thoughtfulness of others. Your faith enhanced the beliefs of those who were beginning their pilgrimage. I want to thank you for your guidance and friendship.

I remember many times of helpful conversation in class and in private.

May the richest blessings be with you on this day. You have helped me think, and celebrate, and minister with a depth which would have not been possible without your participation in the life and thoughts of people like me.

My fondest regards,
Steve Ailes, March 23, 1981

... I use this letter to convey my best wishes as you mark your retirement from the Iliff School of Theology and from the active ministry of the United Methodist Church.

My wife and I and our son Roland, enjoyed our association with you and Christ Church during our few years in Denver 1941 to 1944 and we were unhappy that circumstances made it advisable to return to St. Louis and terminate the wonderful relationship we had established.

We have carefully preserved the splendid letter, dated August 15, 1944, you sent to us when we left Denver. You wrote such nice things about us that warmed our hearts and helped to ease the pains of parting ... the warm personal regard you felt for us in Denver and which you so beautifully described in your letter And in the same vein, the love and genuine affection the Eckmans felt for you so long ago still remains a cherished memory with me.

Very sincerely,
Irvin A. Eckman, March 23, 1981

There are some very special people in this world and you are right at the top of the list.

Thank you for those years of inspiration and help when I was a member of Christ Church. May all the years of your retirement be full of joy.

Sincerely,
Grace Davis, March 29, 1981

Louise Larrick's friendship with Dr. Potthoff began at Christ Church. Louise and her father, Herbert Gottschalk, began attending in 1944. Potthoff performed her marriage ceremony and later baptized her son and nephew. During Potthoff's years at Nebraska Wesleyan University, Mrs. Larrick became interested in, and was a financial supporter of, the Mattingly Symposiums that Harvey facilitated at NWU.

Mrs. Larrick sent me copies of letters she received from Potthoff thanking her for her support of the symposiums. His letters always included comments on such things as how well the symposiums came off, the excellence of the speakers, and expressions of appreciation from those attending. Potthoff also included personal notes about his classes and summer plans. In one letter, he says of leaving NWU after eleven years: "My Wesleyan experience has been great and I will miss much and many in Lincoln. But for everything there is a season."[13]

Harvey looked back on his years at Iliff with deep appreciation just as he later did with his many roles at NWU. I cannot repeat often enough the sense of good fortune that he carried within himself. The reasons will become evident as the reader digests the contents of the following chapters.

From 1952 to 1981, Potthoff continued to thrive both at Iliff and in the church at large (see Chapter 6 by J. R. Peck). Chapters 3, 4, and 5 explain in some detail the theological thought, both philosophical and pastoral that was the core of Potthoff's teaching and church work.

So much praise for his Iliff days as faculty member makes it is easy to forget that he worked in a context of an institutional reality, as part of a mix that became so instrumental in the Iliff experience of students for more than four decades. The fit of the mix I was able to experience firsthand from 1957 to 1960 and, in many ways, beyond those years. Faculty members William Bernhardt, Martin Rist, Walter Williams, Charles Milligan, Howard Ham, Alex Bryans, Gordon VanSicle, Oliver Reed Whitley, and others joined with Potthoff and made all the difference in our education. These men and the men and the women later added, or their replacements, were a team committed to the education of mostly young and eager students looking to church ministry or related endeavors. Not all of them locked on to Dr. Potthoff as the key to their education, but each and every one of them were the beneficiaries of a rich and wonderful faculty mix. To observe that these faculty members complimented each other is an understatement. I am sure the same can be said by the students of the 1950s and right up to the first decade of this century and beyond. We all benefit from contexts as well as from individuals. But, alas, this book is basically about Harvey Potthoff even if not exclusively. *He, like all of us, was standing on shoulders!*

Upon leaving Christ Church in 1952, Potthoff rented an apartment at 2125 South Josephine Street only two blocks from Iliff. This was to be his Denver home, which he maintained while at NWU for nine months of each year. He lived there until moving in 1994 to the Meridian, a retirement complex not far from Iliff.

Potthoff's home on South Josephine became familiar to dozens of his students over the years who experienced there discussions, music, and more discussions. His entertainment there usually did not include meals; if so, it was pizza or catered. During that part and almost all of his life, he ate three meals out every day!

His apartment in the Meridian continued to be a gathering place for colleagues, friends, and former students until very near the end of his life. He relished treating visitors to meals in the Meridian dining room.

My discussions at the Meridian with Harvey often turned in the direction of his heartfelt memories of how truly rewarding his career was. The reflections found in Chapters 13 and 14 will confirm many of the reasons why this was the case for a very appreciative man. Even while noting this, I never had the feeling that he was living in the past. He focused on what was going on now and what the future held, particularly in theology.

From 1952 to 1981, and in courses he taught after retirement, Potthoff's involvement and his status and reputation at Iliff and in the wider Methodist circle just grew and grew (see Chapter 6) and became more and more diverse. He edited *The Iliff Review* for some years; served as interim president at times; directed various academic programs; started a program in Aspen, Colorado; and became pastor/minister to a great many on the faculty, staff, and student body. His services on committees beyond Iliff spread from Denver to the Boulder area, to the state of Colorado, and the very large Western Jurisdiction of the Church. That he earned and deserved the moniker "Mr. Iliff" is beyond question.

During these years, his attending cultural and athletic events, serving as a guest preacher in hundreds of churches, writing, delivering papers, and doing workshops continued apace. The breadth of his reading in theology, liberal studies, and related fields was extensive. He loved travel and whenever possible accepted trips north, south, east, and west for both guest appearances and for vacation time. He once told me he tried to accept all invitations if he saw that he could be helpful in any way to the intended audience.

He became a favorite of chaplains in the military services for doing workshops and for dealing with both popular and controversial topics and issues concerning armed forces personnel. Such service found him traveling from Hawaii to New York, from Japan to Alaska, and points in between.

He was legendary for including students in his life; one way for me was in his YMCA handball group. Personally I have never known a person who better filled the designation "a man for all seasons"!

A compilation of all the courses taught by Potthoff at Iliff can be found in Appendix E.

NOTES

[1] Transcription of Lecture #1, Tape 2, "One Person's Religious/Theological Journey," given March 24, 1981, page 1, Iliff Archives, box 44, file folder 7.

[2] Hoffman, *The Christ Church Story*, 52.

[3] Transcription of Lecture #1, Tape 2, page 2, Iliff Archives, box 44, file folder 7.

[4] From Harvey's speech at the Highlands Institute, Highlands, North Carolina on 6/18/1991, entitled "Empirical Theology and the Vision of Hope: Reflections on a Personal Journey," pages 8–10, Iliff Archives, box 6, file folder 7.

[5] Transcription of Lecture #1, Tape #2, March 24, 1981, from his course titled "The Theology of Harvey Potthoff," Iliff Archives, box 44, file folder 7.

[6] Hoffman, *The Christ Church Story*, 53.

[7] Ibid., 145.

[8] Ibid., 169.

[9] From an email from Mrs. Dorothy Lagger, December 3, 2011, Iliff Archives, box 43, file folder 5.

[10] Hoffman, *The Christ Church Story*, 55.

[11] Ibid., 55, 56.

[12] Christ Church scrapbook, Iliff Archives, box 42.

[13] Louise Larrick's letters, Iliff Archives, box 43, file folder 6.

3

THE THEOLOGY OF HARVEY H. POTTHOFF

By Richard L. Phillips

This chapter is a companion to Chapter 4 by David Conner. (It is not intended to correct or modify his in any way.) There is some overlap in the issues covered. This chapter has a somewhat different approach and covers some different aspects of Potthoff's theology during a long and diverse career. It also spells out some of the terms and concepts central to his thought and writing. David and I are in agreement about all of the major issues as he has expressed them, and I endorse his chapter with enthusiasm. It should be helpful to the reader to know that these two chapters were a part of the plan from the beginning, and one of the chapters should not be viewed as a response to the other.

Either of these chapters can be read first. David's deals with the backdrop of Harvey's work both intellectually and culturally, and may be more appropriate to be read first by those who have some theological background. The present chapter may be best read first by those readers who are relatively new to such issues.

In both his writings and speeches, Potthoff often referred to his theology as a process thought based empirical, naturalistic theology. It is important to understand just what these terms mean if one is to grasp his thinking and his theological positions. Technically, *theology* means the study of God (or the whole of the God question) but is often expanded to what some German scholars call uber-theology (theology dealing intellectually with all things about religion); for Potthoff, it did expand to the totality of concerns of religious scholarship and faith.

Process Thinking and Theology

Potthoff was introduced to the idea of process thought before he went to Harvard to study with Alfred North Whitehead. Process thought is the chief reason he wanted to study with him. After his year with Whitehead, this way of understanding reality became foundational for Potthoff's theology. I tell some of the story of his year with Whitehead in Chapter 1.

So, what is process thought? First, process thinking affirms an understanding of reality (the universe or cosmos in its totality) that is dynamic rather than static. It affirms that what we experience as real is not set for all time but is in process. This means our knowledge of things is always subject to correction because reality itself is changing, that is to say, is forever in flux or process. This includes the understanding that truth itself is in flux, that what may be true about some level of reality today may need to be modified later. Tomorrow, new information and insights about reality will be forthcoming! This is not the same as saying nothing is true or dependable in life. There are many aspects of reality within a process orientation that are seen as dependable and can be understood and treated as if they are conclusively true. In other words, there is much stability on which we rely day in and day out, and we need have no concern about that stability suddenly disappearing (gravity, for example). So, even a process thinker can live each day in the comfort and assurance that reality is sound and will support us in our human endeavors. Potthoff finds the basis of human hope and many other theological concerns to be compatible within a process view of reality (see Chapter 5).

In an unpublished lecture he delivered to a faculty group at Nebraska Wesleyan University, Potthoff wrote: "There have long been philosophers who in seeking to give an accounting of how things are have spoken of flux, change, movement, becoming. They might be called 'process philosophers.' Heraclitus (535-475 B.C.) held that the universe is in a state of ceaseless change: '...you could not step twice into the same rivers, for other and yet other waters are flowing on.' Process themes are found in Stoicism, Buddhism, Socinus, Hegel, Schelling, Bergson, Alexander, Smuts, Peirce, James, Dewey and others. Process thought holds that becoming is more fundamental to reality than is being, that relatedness is more basic than independence or absoluteness."[1]

In arriving at an understanding of process thinking, I turn to what I have found helpful. David Conner writes about the massive change stemming from the discoveries of Charles Darwin and many of his contemporaries and soon many successor scientists. In fact, Darwin's discoveries and conclusions during his voyages on the *Beagle* were first arrived at reluctantly. He saw that they would result in a very major shift in the way we view and understand the biological world, even us humans. Darwin delayed the publication of *The Origin of the Species* because of the uproar he knew it would create. Additionally, as a clergy educated Anglican, he was very sensitive to what impact his findings would have on the clergy and laity of the time. So, what changed due to the work of Darwin and other thinkers of his time and times both before and since? After receiving his theological degree at Christ Church at Cambridge, Darwin decided not to become a parish priest. There is some debate about whether he was ordained as a Church of England clergyman. While on the *Beagle*, he performed and was treated as if he were a member of the clergy.

Prior to Darwin's time, the biological world was almost always thought of in stable or static terms. God had created all of the animals of the world just as they are, and they will be just as they are now for all of existence. The idea that biological reality is dynamic rather than static was a new, unfolding idea—one that was denied and resisted by many, including many in the scientific community of that time. Even today, there are many people who either do not believe in any form of biological evolution or refuse to believe that their views of the world need to change in any substantial way because of it. Some do conclude that evolution can be accepted in the animal world but not in the human species. Even so, the biological sciences now operate on the principles of biological evolution in all of life as they were very accurately developed by Darwin and those who followed. This is true, for example, in the medical professions that now impact our lives so basically and importantly on a daily basis. Not many of us today even think about getting demons cast out in order to get over the flu or a bowel obstruction or a ruptured blood vessel! Of course, we could use "demons" as a metaphor for natural causes!

Back to the point: process thought and evolutionary thought share a similar history. Both, based on careful observation of reality, have moved from a basically static view of things to a dynamic, changing view of our world, and of course that world includes our selves.

Potthoff came to believe that these discoveries, along with other discoveries inherent in all of modern scholarship, lead one to different understandings than do traditional views of reality, and they are very important for our religious views. Potthoff was not alone. From the mid-1800s, such discoveries resulted in many theologians and scholars, who studied scriptures and religion, changing their worldview in a way parallel to what Harvey thought essential if religion could be relevant in the lives of people with an understanding of such newer views of reality. Conner has described well some of those changes in Chapter 4.

Advances in biblical scholarship were very important in this unfolding thinking about how we view faith issues. Discoveries in archaeology, sociology, linguistics, and literary and historical analysis, as well as the continuing advances in sciences like physics and chemistry, have added greatly to the weight of evidence about the nature of the Bible and of natural (cosmic) reality, including our human makeup.

Potthoff believed we must be open to changing our understandings of our faith based on what he called the "newer views of the universe." He never doubted that this move was going to be resisted by many scholars and as well by many church members. He was fond of responding to students who demonstrated concern about apparent conflicts by saying that when science and religion seem to be in conflict, we should be willing to adjust our theological thinking as well as challenge scientific conclusions. Harvey did not have any appreciation for what some call scientism—scientists or the general public believing that science has all the answers and only through science will we be made whole. He believed science must be treated with respect and with care and be subject to correction, but not to ever be revered as the sole source of truth. Harvey did extensive work on the relationship between religion and science.

Empirical, naturalistic theology—what does that mean? *Empirical* essentially means the development of knowledge based on human experience, both personal and social, and including, but not limited to, science. That is to say, the development and testing of hypotheses about what we can productively use as valid knowledge in reaching understandings and conclusions about any given aspect of reality. It is important to note that trial and error should be seen as a commonly used scientific method. Over the history of humankind, much of our know-how and insight have been arrived at by years, even centuries, of trial-and-error learning. This is true concerning our understanding not only of the natural world but of the values we have developed for ethical and moral behavior—for everyday things like knowing what foods not to eat, what is necessary sanitary practice, and on and on! Every day, children learn what not to do based on trial-and-error behaviors.

Potthoff was convinced that Christianity could be understood and adjusted and adapted to the new views of reality and be just as helpful, meaningful, and spiritually productive as it had been in a prescientific understanding of the Christian faith. He was also convinced that the ancient wisdom in the Bible had as much to say, and in some cases even more meaningful things to say, to us in this day and age. Later in this chapter, there is a focus on this topic. Harvey spent his professional life researching, teaching, preaching, writing, speaking, and being a Christian minister doing his best to fulfill his theological conclusions. His chief guideline in doing so was reflected in his response to a classroom student question, as best I remember it, "In the practice and understanding of the faith, one must commit oneself to a rigorous intellectual honesty." That is not an easy task, and in his wisdom he also taught that it is not necessary to question or challenge the faith of others at every turn, especially in a context where it would only be hurtful. Harvey was always the "pastor" to others in such matters.

Naturalistic theology is the affirmation that the information we use in understanding and practicing our Christian faith is to come from the natural world alone. This is thus a rejection of a two-part view of reality. It also brings human reason and our reasoning powers into a very important position in any concept of authority for belief. The belief in a supernatural realm in addition to the natural realm is the key issue here and is one of the most important points in understanding Potthoff's theology and that of others like him. It is for many Christians a catch point. It represents a major shift of understanding and thus a barrier to change. Limiting one's understanding, thinking, and practice of the faith to a non-supernaturalistic viewpoint is a drastic change for many. Millions of today's Christians have never even heard of the possibility of making such a shift.

Even so, the Bible was written from a non-supernaturalistic

viewpoint. It is in fact written from the natural world view of that time. The division of knowledge into "natural" and "supernatural" did not come into existence until the advent of empirical and scientific developments in more modern times. It was then that many in religion grasped the supernatural as a necessary source of knowledge not to be challenged by scientific methodologies or conclusions; God, they advocated, operated outside of nature. To be sure, there are many biblical passages that can be interpreted as implying a supernatural reality or realm. However, in the Bible, God appears to operate totally within, and knowledge of God was derived from the real, natural world just as in Potthoff's view. Even the traditional "seventh" heaven ideas were seen as part of the natural world, usually thought of as being part of expanded circles of reality.

For the more recent history of the faith, the assumption of a supernatural realm as the source of revelation, salvation, the abode of God, and, for many believers, the final destination of human souls in one form or another has been the norm. Potthoff is often seen as non-biblical in his theology, but that could not be further from the case. In naturalistic theology, there are not two sources of knowledge, the natural and the supernatural. Even so, for Potthoff and others who hold his views, knowledge comes not only from scientific methodology but also from experience and reason. Some things we know as true, like love, are not normally thought of as scientifically verifiable. Additionally there is transcendence in naturalistic thought; often the whole of something is more than (transcends) the sum of its parts. Understanding Potthoff's use of the Bible is thus seen by many today as more compatible with biblical times and thus a natural rather than a supernatural viewpoint. Two scholars who have contributions in this biography, Dr.

Howard Bailey and Dr. Alton Templin, are far better historians than I, and both agree that supernaturalism emerged in recent centuries.

Process thought and empirical methodologies necessitate that we accept a lack of certainty in our conclusions. Potthoff is known for stating his insight over and over that many Christians (and presumably persons in other religions as well) will and perhaps must cling to a pattern of belief that yields absolute certainty. Some persons could never feel at home where such certainty, in either this life or what is to come, is not a part of their view of reality. This is probably true even for some secular people, many of whom assume a supernatural realm in some of their views about reality. How much tolerance do humans have for living in a world where flux is at the very heart of reality? At the same time, today millions of persons in the world with such a worldview demonstrate the ability to "live and move and have their being" and find meaning in a world of ultimate flux. Potthoff wanted a Christianity that can make a modern version of the historic faith meaningful to such Christians. Over centuries, Christianity has made major adaptations to different cultures, which have included important theological changes from the first century on, and Potthoff thought such adjustments are possible now. Making such an adjustment could, he hoped, save the church for our times and the future, especially for persons who live in keeping with a contemporary and ever-changing world view.

Many, if not most, of today's staunch opponents of religion, especially from the world of science, do not see a divorce from supernatural thinking as a possibility for Christianity. Their criticisms of Christianity often assume that all Christian belief and practice is and must be supernatural in nature. Potthoff in his day and with his theology wanted to prove them wrong. At the same time that he rejected supernaturalism, Harvey did envision some types of transcendence. A good example would be the position that a human being is something that transcends the mere physical and chemical makeup of the human body. His ideas of transcendence were of course other than supernatural in nature (more on this matter later).

It is revealing to read *Evolutionary Philosophies and Contemporary Theology* (Westminster Press, 1969) by Eric C. Rust, a Southern Baptist professor then at Southern Baptist Theological Seminary. Dr. Rust came to many of the same conclusions reached by Potthoff during basically the same time frame. He did not find process thought, belief in biological evolution, and so many of the other well-established conclusions of the scientific community to be a threat to the Christian faith. He, unlike so many of his peers, believed we can hold a modern scientific world view and still understand and appreciate the Bible and the traditional faith. He saw viewing mythology, metaphor, poetry, and other symbolic understandings as legitimate ways of dealing with such things as virgin birth, physical resurrection, and miracles as "truths" seen from the eyes and minds of prescientific searchers for the divine (see the quotation below). There were, for Rust, limits. He saw the heart of the gospels communicating an ultimate truth about God and Christian foundations—he held that there is ultimately in this revealed *truth* certainty. He advocated a type of transcendence that had supernaturalistic elements. Thus he falls into a category Potthoff often referred to as a partial eminence and a partial supernaturalistic way of understanding the faith.

The following quotation is from Chapter 8, "Theistic Faith in a Secular Society," in Rust's book (pages 202–203):

> It is very evident to all serious Christian thinkers that any realistic presentation of the Christian standpoint must take note of the data provided by contemporary scientific investigations, including the facts which underlie the evolutionary viewpoint and the models by which scientists seek to understand such facts. Furthermore, the importance of [Biblical] history in the Christian faith needs to be matched by the deeper understanding of history which has emerged in the last century. Finally, the secular society, which in a very real sense is the result of the Christian emphasis on this world, has resulted in a radical challenge to traditional Christian theological conceptions, especially because of the value placed upon this world and its processes, both at the level of nature and at the level of human history. To speak to such a world intelligibly, theology must find a philosophical bridge, a natural theology or Christian philosophy which provides some point of contact with preoccupations and attitudes of "secular man."

I have cited Rust's work here for two reasons. First, to help the reader realize that conservative positions (as in the Southern Baptist Church) can and often do incorporate scientific views of reality. Second, it becomes clearer why Potthoff was interested in and able to have working and common-ground interactions with more conservative theologians. Potthoff was aware that many with more conservative Christian beliefs shared with him, in part, the need for a new day: a theology based on the knowledge we have seen generated in so many fields of study in today's world.

Before examining other aspects of Potthoff's theology, I turn to some important guidelines in his life, teaching, and ministry that he both repeated to others and lived by.

While Harvey made no secret of his theological position, he always looked at other theological positions, even very traditional and otherwise different ones, to understand two things. The first was to discern how that theology functioned in the life of that believer (as in the functional analysis methodology of William Bernhardt that Harvey embraced) and to try to see a positive value (or positive function) in the other's belief. The second was to see and to advocate the value and worth of the individual holding another belief. One of his favorite quips was that people are better than their particular theology. As a result of this, he often worked to bring people of very different belief systems together to discuss and work toward what could be common goals.

A key guideline in Potthoff's life that he always communicated to his classes, including the last class he taught by special request at Iliff in 1981,[2] was that "I, Harvey Potthoff, do not ask you to accept my theology but rather that you examine the information and then make up your own mind, develop your own theology just as you must develop your own ministry whatever it might be."[3]

Another important insight is that Harvey's theology, though very solidly developed by the time he began preaching at Christ Church in Denver, did undergo additional development—evolution, if you will—as the years went by. He saw change as important and that each of us must change as our insights mature and as the world around us changes. He believed that change was a strength in one's belief and not a weakness, and that it was also a sign of wisdom. Of course, changing for the sake of change or of momentary convenience was not at all recommended. Integrity and honesty in life were to be hallmarks for all conduct!

Harvey often quoted John Wesley, the primary founder of Methodism. Harvey thought these quotes applied to our theological and religious differences today. He found the following brief quotations of Wesley helpful; they are contained in a single page from Potthoff's notes:[4] "If we cannot always think alike, may we not always love alike? Indeed we may." Wesley then added, "Is your heart as my heart? Then give me your hand" (see 2 Kings 10:15). My observation at such points is that Harvey allowed positive relationships to reign over belief in theological matters, though the theological issues were very, very important to him. His treasuring of relationships was one of the most basic character traits of his personhood.

Conner, in his chapter, describes Harvey's earlier identification with early liberal Christianity, which was already long established when Potthoff came on the scene. Harvey saw great problems with what he and others found in this early liberalism. One of the chief characteristics of Harvey's developing theology was his diligent work toward what he wanted to call a neo-liberalism—without the baggage or problems of early liberalism mentioned by Conner. It is helpful to know that the term *liberal*, in this context, means "open to new information," and that is certainly the way Harvey used and understood the term. Social and religious conservatives and liberals of today, and especially those persons against any form of liberal thinking, need to be aware of the meaning of the term. *Liberal* in its meaning does not of necessity oppose traditional or conservative thinking.

Potthoff saw his theological work divided between two chief concerns, which go under the category of theology. The first is philosophical theology. This side of theology has been the primary focus of most theologians. The second is called practical theology or pastoral theology. Harvey saw each as equally important, and this is without a doubt because he was an avid, indeed devout churchman, as well as a scholar. Pastoral theology issues occupied more of his time during the latter half (or more) of his career for a very good reason. If empirical, naturalistic theology was to be an alternative underpinning for Christian understanding of the faith, these two aspects of his theology must have a workable marriage. In order to be viable, Harvey believed philosophical theology must be transferable to the practice of the faith: use of the Bible, prayer, worship, piety and spiritual life, hope, forgiveness, meaning, church policy and polity, and all the rest that goes with being both human and Christian in productive and internally satisfactory ways. As a result, he worked endlessly on the marriage of the two. Many of his writings—especially his unpublished papers, speeches, and sermons, but also many of his publications—tried to establish the practical utility of his basic theology. This task was never finished, yet there is much that he did accomplish in articulating and demonstrating in his own ministry and teaching that this marriage is possible. (Special attention will be given to this matter in Chapter 5.)

David Conner mentions in Chapter 4 that Harvey did not write, as many theologians (such as Paul Tillich) have, a systematic theological treatise. But that is not to say that he was not systematic in dealing with the very wide range of topics that were theological in nature. One need not get very far into the study of Potthoff's theology to realize that he was very systematic in dealing with all of the standard philosophical and pastoral concerns in any Christian practice (see Chapter 5).

Potthoff and the Bible

We turn now to a very important and sometimes poorly understood aspect of Potthoff's theology. First, it must be clear that Harvey loved the Bible. He used it extensively; quoted it in his writings, preaching, and teaching with great regularity; and had many favorite passages that he used repeatedly. All of this was natural for him. He grew up in a devout, Bible-studying family and spent his formative years in a basically conservative (but not fundamentalist, he says) family and in churches in which his father was the minister, as had been his maternal grandfather. Both were clergy in the German Methodist Church, which later united with other Methodist denominations.

Potthoff's approach to the Christian and Hebrew scriptures was different in very significant ways than the traditional approaches. Traditionally, the Bible has been *the* primary authority for the development of theology. For Potthoff, it was a two-way street, and understanding this point is basic to grasping the essentials of his theology. One's theological understandings must become the basis for biblical interpretation, and when world views change, then it becomes necessary for some reinterpretation of the biblical material. Traditionally, biblical content is the basis for the development of one's theology and the basis for evaluation of that theology. For Potthoff, the sharing of the traditional approach together with the empirical naturalistic theology he espoused and developed was essential. So, for him, the Bible remained a necessary authority for theological development. What must be added is an up-to-date world view together with the results of contemporary biblical and historical scholarship. We then have a complexity of things for authority on how we are to understand and interpret the Bible and to use it responsibly. In Potthoff's theology, the heavier burden is on modern scholarship. Love the Bible, but interpret it carefully, incorporating scholarship, history, and a current understanding of the nature of reality.

Perhaps Harvey's greatest appreciation of the biblical material, as might be expected of a college literature major, was of the poetry in the scriptures. The Psalms, the wisdom literature, and many other parts are full of great and very spiritual poetry—poetry that has meaning through its use of analogy, metaphor, mythology, and symbolism. The four Gospels were also very formative and remained central throughout his life. Harvey found that parts of the scripture which did not themselves use metaphor could be understood today to have deep insight and spiritual meaning when *seen as* metaphor. Understanding the biblical book of Revelation, for example, is not possible without using such a principle in biblical interpretation. Explaining the Bible (Hebrew and Christian) and theology using metaphor became a favorite tool for Harvey's use of and understanding of many aspects of the scriptures. Metaphor is a very old biblical concept and practice, and Harvey used it to see meaning and importance in the Bible even when the biblical writers were speaking from an ancient world view.

To reject the Bible due to its antiquity was for Potthoff a tragic mistake. Its wisdom is in its constant search for the divine within life, its searching exploration of the nature and activity of God in all things, its insights into the human being and human society, and more. Therefore the Bible is not to be abandoned by modern Christians. It has been in all of Protestant Christianity a primary, treasured source of wisdom and spiritual life. For Martin Luther it was, as he rejected the tradition and authority of his church—the only source of authority for the faith and for most Christians today the primary source! Luther later gave a greater role to reason. That is most evident in his leaving out many books of the Bible when he translated the scriptures into the then German language. He decided they were not worthy of inclusion in the Bible. It is worth noting that Luther is given credit in his translation work with the formulation of the modern German language.

Potthoff recognized that the Bible has within it many mistakes. Our world is not flat; it and its companion orbs in the universe are not recent creations; human nature is not evil, even though prone to doing evil things; and even the biblical writing does not speak with one voice about the history and events and faith positions it records. That includes the history of Jesus as recorded in the Gospels, Acts, and the New Testament letters. In fact, Harvey came to the conclusion, along with almost all biblical scholars, that the books of the library we call canon or the Bible were not dictated by God but represent humans searching, over a long period of time, for God and for wisdom about life and all other matters and certainly for human self understanding, both individual and group. It is in such ancient centuries of endeavor that the development and the focus of the scriptures become, and remain for Potthoff, *sacred.*

Appreciation of the Bible is enhanced by this understanding of its nature for not only Harvey but for millions of others as well. To use the Bible responsibly, for Potthoff, was to use it through the eyes of a contemporary, not via an ancient world view. We must understand that ancient view as best we can.

Biblical studies for Harvey did not start in college, nor did he take courses in religion, and only at the very last did he even think about the ministry. When he became a student at Iliff, he studied Bible under Dr. Lindsay Longacre, Hebrew Scriptures professor, and while a doctoral student at Iliff under Dr. Martin Rist, professor of New Testament. Rist was certainly one of the most brilliant men under whom this writer has ever studied. He was a product of the Chicago School—a tradition that David Conner documents in his chapter. Rist and Potthoff remained colleagues at Iliff for many years, until Rist's retirement, and they remained lifelong and very close friends. In fact, their letters exchanged after Rist retired demonstrate that Harvey had become and remained his chief counselor and friend, including during some troubled times for Rist before his death.

Potthoff did not write extensively on the Bible, but he did write two important documents. One is a 1965 book, *Acts: Then and Now,* in which he focused on the work of Paul as it is recorded in the book of Acts, and then projected Paul's work and letters to discern its relevance to the church and to Christians today. Acts documents Paul's work with young and troubled churches recorded in his letters; many are now books in the Bible. This Potthoff book is a delightful example of the work Harvey put into his favorite task of making the biblical material relevant to the contemporary church and faith.

The second very important document is an unpublished paper in two chapters: "The Biblical Jesus" and "The Historical Jesus."[5] These fairly long chapters are not dated but were written early in his career. The latest source he cited was a book written in 1941. The first chapter compares representations of

Jesus as recorded in the four Gospels and in Paul's letters. The second chapter outlines the picture of Jesus in the different expressions of Christian faith and denominations. The views in all cases do differ greatly, such as between the Gospels, between the four Gospels and Paul, between Luther and Calvin, and between Roman Catholic and Methodist. Both chapters show his depth of insight into biblical scholarship and reveal his primary resources.

Harvey often mentioned, usually in notes to himself, his soul mates in biblical scholarship: Albert Schweitzer, Edgar Goodspeed, Lindsay Longacre, and of course Rist. Schweitzer's book, *The Quest of the Historical Jesus* (1906), was one of his favorites. In that book, Schweitzer traces much of the scholarship that made the middle and late nineteenth century such a productive time for biblical scholarship. Potthoff kept up with scholars and publications in biblical studies his entire career. Such scholarship is the basis for both understanding and use of the Bible.

The Authority of Scripture

In Chapter 6, Rich Peck documents Potthoff's work as a member of a national Methodist working task force on theological guidelines in Methodism. Harvey was one of the working members and was a key to the full expression of what is called the Methodist Quadrilateral. Some call it the Wesley Quadrilateral, but it is not fully developed in the writings of John Wesley. It has to do with the authority issues in the development of theology, education, and church policy. The United Methodist Church doctrinal statement that Potthoff worked on commends the use of four criteria for theological authority: scripture, tradition, reason, and experience. Many see Harvey in his theology as placing reason and experience as the most basic of the four. This is not true because he was very supportive of, and found great meaning in, both scripture and tradition in church matters. He was quite a traditionalist in many ways. Harvey placed scripture very high, in this author's estimation. For Potthoff, each of the four criteria for authority has critical value for the church, and current understandings of the Christian faith and I found no evidence that he ever ranked them.

To summarize, Harvey did not think any expression of Christianity should abandon the Bible as a necessary theological centerpiece of the faith. That said, it is also true that he wanted current biblical scholarship and theological insight to play an equally important role in the understanding and expression of the faith. So, again, all four—scripture, tradition, reason, and experience—are elevated to primary roles in his view, something he often repeated in his writing and his speaking.

Potthoff on God

In Chapter 4, David Conner deals extensively with Harvey's thinking and position on the question of God and the answers that come out of his empirical, naturalistic theology. I have no quarrel or issue with David's content and will only add briefly to this topic.

As his primary source, David often quotes Potthoff's *God and the Celebration of Life*. There are a number of other sources the interested scholar or layperson would do well to explore. It would probably necessitate a trip to the archives or the Iliff library to find some of them. Potthoff's later writings do not make any major changes in his views, but do add to his ideas regarding different contexts and situations inherent in church-related thinking and practice. Examples of such papers by Potthoff are "Theological Uses of Process Philosophy," "Some Introductory Comments on Process Theology," and "Theology and the Vision of Greatness." (See these and others listed in the appendixes of this book.)

I quote from an article published in *The Iliff Review* entitled "God and the Newer Views of the Universe." This title is one of Harvey's phrases used again and again to tie together his theology and a current world view now pervasive of our times and our thinking about reality. Harvey was, for several years, the editor of *The Iliff Review*, which is no longer in existence. It featured articles in diverse areas of religious interest, many of them by Iliff faculty.

This quotation from the article expresses the hopes Harvey held for his theological efforts: "The time has come for a recognition in Christian circles that there is need for a new theological approach more thoroughly empirical in character than the earlier liberalism. There is need for a neo-liberalism which moves out from a concern in the religious phase of human experience to investigative, experimental studies of the nature of man and the universe; and from these studies to a systematic organization of knowledge, which is the heart of metaphysics, so conceived, to the formulation of a theological framework articulating the intellectual phase of religion—wherein man is enabled to see events in relation to a divine scheme, giving them changed meaning."

In the above quotation, he reveals that the task he wants to accomplish is still very much before him and also other scholars, particularly in the discipline of theology.

He goes on to say, "this newer form of liberalism has something important to say in carrying on and adding to the Christian tradition some of us believe most deeply."[6] His work often focused on the efforts he was making to articulate and apply such an understanding of the divine and of reality to questions of religious importance and to meaning in human life. (See Chapter 4 for more.)

Among many papers, there are two in which Potthoff expressed his theology in very clear terms. The first was delivered to a conference of Methodist educators in Cincinnati, Ohio, in 1965: "The Reality of God: The Meaning and Experience of God's Continuing Revelation." This paper was an outgrowth of the national Methodist work on theology mentioned earlier, which bore the same title. There is no question that it is one of his best efforts at theological self-disclosure. It is so complete and so well developed that I was tempted to make the greater part of it a chapter by itself. "Potthoff on Potthoff," it might have been called, but space is also an issue. I refer the reader interested in more of Potthoff's writings in this and other areas of theology to a little booklet he and others put together, published by Criterion Press (an Iliff in-house press) at the time of his retirement in 1981: *Selected Papers of Harvey H. Potthoff*. The archives hold a copy[7] and so does the library. It is a compilation of his writings, mostly previously published in *The Iliff Review*, and contains the Cincinnati paper referred to above but under the shorter title "The Reality of God."

A friend who attended the Cincinnati conference told me that Harvey shook up some folks but that the paper was also very well received. For obvious reasons, the prevailing image of Harvey's theology was never an easy sell to the average Christian gathering. There were several neo-orthodox supporters at the conference, but some had a hard time realizing that many of the then current scholars of neo-orthodoxy agreed with much of Potthoff's theology and his biblical views. This, I believe, is why Harvey often found it hard to escape the negative connotations of the "liberal" label associated with early Christian liberalism. Neo-orthodoxy was, in part, a rebellion against early liberalism. Potthoff agreed with the neo-orthodox criticism of early liberalism. He did not favor what he viewed as a retreat to basically orthodox theology while at the same time neo-orthodox scholars tended to accept modern biblical scholarship and an essentially modern world view.

If the neo-orthodox movement was in part a rejection of early liberalism, there is another twentieth- and now twenty-first-century movement called fundamentalism, which Potthoff saw (and most mainline theologians see today) as a rejection of the main features of a modern or contemporary world view. Some fundamentalist and conservative thinkers do accept a contemporary world view, but hold the belief that there is another realm, the supernatural realm, in addition to the world studied by science.

In this paper, Harvey dealt with God's continuing and continuous revelation. He was clear that this happens, and we can know about it not from some supernatural realm, but from the dynamics of nature, including human life, and our experience of the here and now. He strongly advocated the central importance of reason and experience in the theological endeavors of us humans. It seems so clear and logical that if God is currently revealed in our world, as in biblical times, we humans must surely have perceptive brains to detect and know something about the divine. Of course, that also depends on what we believe about the nature of nature and of God.

The second paper, entitled "Some Introductory Comments on Process Theology" (unpublished), is from the speech given at Nebraska Wesleyan University. I quoted it early in this chapter. In this paper, Potthoff deals specifically with the doctrine of God. It reflects his more recent thinking about the nature of God.

> There is no one process [position concerning the] image of God. However, process theologians do not talk about a god of the gaps, an external planner and intervener, a guarantor that everything is going to turn out right. Process theologians are inclined to identify the divine with the creative, redemptive, whole-making, calling forward dimensions of reality. ... The human being is seen as potential, co-creator, decision-maker, steward, seeker of meaning—for whom the highest art is the art of loving.[8]

Potthoff advocated a theology that could be both credible and relevant for today and tomorrow. He believed a process thought base to be necessary in achieving this.

Within this thinking, Harvey favored the concept of whole-making in his understanding of the divine. (For more on that aspect of his theology, see Chapter 4.)

I turn now to some very exciting current news from the world of science, which has some relevance to Potthoff's God concept.

Theoretical physicists have been seeking for decades to confirm the Higgs boson hypothesis as the basis for the building activity of nature itself. The particle, proposed in 1964, was first announced in a 1965 publication by Scottish physicist Peter Higgs. The popular press has referred to the assumed particle as the "God particle," even though scientists have not. David Conner and I both think Potthoff would not use the term "God particle" to designate its possible existence. Harvey owned a book on theoretical physics by Heinz Pagels titled *Perfect Symmetry* (1985), which mentions the hypothesis about the assumed existence of the Higgs field. David now has the book that belonged to Potthoff and has shared this information with me. David was in a class in the Iliff-at-Aspen summer courses when Pagels was invited by Harvey to speak to the class.

HHP photo in Iliff Archives

HHP photo he usually sent out for guest appearances

March 2012 brought news that researchers in Geneva, Switzerland, were very close to confirming the existence of this tiny speck of reality which is thought to be a fundamental aspect of creativity and all ongoing development in nature. This particle may help answer the question of why the planet is dynamic and not permanently static/unchanging.

In May 2012, I paid a visit to Syracuse University and went to the Physics Department to talk with two scholars involved in particle physics research. Each was informed about efforts in Switzerland to verify the Higgs boson particle and believed its existence would soon be verified. Later I talked with another researcher in Denver who affirmed, "We have already seen the Higgs boson particle." What is not clear is just what the existence of this long hypothesized particle at the very base of reality really means or will mean in our understanding of reality. The scientific communities, and to some extent the nonscientific communities, are now studying such questions as to what this will mean for philosophy, metaphysics, and theology.

On July 4, 2012, both BBC News and NPR News announced that the lab in Geneva had confirmed the existence of the Higgs boson! The Large Hadron Collider at Cern (European Organization for Nuclear Research) in Geneva had been working for some time to confirm the existence of the particle and announced the confirmation (with a great degree of certainty) amid great celebration in the scientific and particle physics communities. Professor Stephen Hawking was present for the announcement ceremony and spoke words of congratulations for a discovery he once predicted would not be verified. Dr. Higgs was also present and was, of course, delighted with the confirmation of his 1964 hypothesis. The research team estimated that the particle is about 133 times heavier than the protons that lie at the heart of every atom.[9]

As stated above, this particle may help answer the question of why the planet is dynamic and not permanently static/unchanging. The possibility that it may be a basis of creativity is what, many years ago, gave the news media cause for calling it the God particle. The confirmation of the hypothesis would surely please Harvey, first because he believed creativity was the underlying, inherent characteristic of nature. Additionally, he would be pleased because it relates so well to his position that God is the "Wholeness Making Reality." His understanding of the nature of the divine is very much supported by this important scientific discovery. Potthoff would also be pleased due to his friendship with Heinz Pagels and the confirmation of Higgs's scientific endeavor.

David Conner and others assure me the "Wholeness Reality" in Potthoff's theology is not to be seen as the same as the Higgs boson. Potthoff's concept of the divine is broader than any single bit of matter, important as it might be. David and I both have an educational background in science, he much more so than I, and so share a special interest in this matter as it concerns science and religion.

David and I agree that the existence of the Higgs field and Higgs boson could conceivably be given a religious interpretation. For a naturalistically inclined theologian, it is not hard to see and experience a sense of sacredness in contemplation of the particle. In my own mind, this particle is very supportive of Potthoff's understanding of God being immanent and the creative force in nature. In another book, Pagels wrote: "[W]hat I [myself] embody, the principle of life, cannot be destroyed. ... It is written into the cosmic code, the order of the universe."[10]

Christology

I now turn briefly to the theological issue of Christology. It is frequently mentioned in Potthoff's writings, but he does not have a treatise on this important theological issue. Of course, the term *Christology* relates to the meaning of Jesus as the Christ and its place in Christian theology. Potthoff is clear about what Christology means within his naturalistic theology. As in so many areas of Christian tradition, he interprets Christology very differently than do various more orthodox positions. He did understand this and saw the use of the term *Christ* to be appropriate in many settings, including prayer, and he wanted it to be used with theological integrity and consistency. Potthoff's Christology is contained in his position that Christ as the *anointed* one is the disclosure and mediator we have revealing to us the basic nature of God. God as creator and sustainer and the *love and concern* God displays toward creation, especially the human, is revealed in Christ. Christ also reveals to us the sacredness of the works of God. For Potthoff, Jesus as the Christ points us to the nature of God.

It is important to note that Potthoff did not favor using "Jesus Christ" as if the two words were the first and last names for Jesus. Neither did he consider Jesus as the Christ to be another god somehow alongside God. Potthoff's is a "theo"-centered faith; that is, a God-centered religious faith. He found the practice by some Christians of actually praying to the Christ (or to Jesus) to be an incorrect understanding of the meaning of the term *Christ* and the role played by Jesus during his life. For Harvey, the Christ was to be viewed as the "anointed" one of God. He preferred when using the term that it be stated as "Jesus the Christ." Jesus was especially anointed to reveal the divine, not to be another god. He also saw Jesus as teacher, actively ministering religious activist, savior, healer, and a man of his own times. Jesus the Christ was interpreted by Potthoff in non-supernaturalistic terms. For Harvey, Jesus's ministry as a healer of the God-human relationship is perfectly valid in naturalistic theology.

Inherent in Jesus's life, teaching, ministry, and death, the very nature of God is revealed. This is best summarized for Harvey within and by the term *love*. The New Testament uses many metaphors in dealing with Jesus as the Christ, which Harvey finds spiritually helpful. Here again it must be repeated that he did not ever, in my experience or research, look down upon anyone who held a different view of Christology.

Returning to Dr. Potthoff's God-related conceptualizations, it is helpful to turn to his own words from his *God and the Celebration of Life*:

> There are two points of crucial importance at which the concept of God as the Wholeness-Reality differs from many God-concepts. First, as developed here, God is not understood as being a guarantor that specific things are going to happen or that all situations are going to come out in a certain way. Rather, God provides the conditions by virtue of which there are possibilities (as well as limitations) in situations. By virtue of the reality of God, there is the possibility of meaning and hope for man in a given situation, but there is no guarantee that he will realize it or that events will turn out happily. A second difference between the idea of God as the Wholeness-Reality as discussed here and some other ideas of God is found in the locus of hope and expectation.
>
> Traditional religious views have frequently looked for hope outside the world and outside the changing events of experience. Deliverance from limitations and change has been sought. The suggestion is here being made that we need to orient our living and aspiring in line with the fundamental character and movement of things as they are—in their relatedness, interplay, and becoming. Life in this age cannot be organized productively around the static and the other-worldly. We need to seek orientation and guidance in the

> context of our existence, in the discernment of long-range dependabilities and directions, in patterns of process and behavior which are disclosed in the nature of life itself. This approach may lead to chastened expectations, and to a reconsideration of what constitutes appropriate human hoping. On the other hand, it will nurture expectations more in harmony with the fundamental structures and processes of reality as experienced. In this view, the hope which God makes possible is not a hope despite the limitations inherent in existence, but through these limitations.
>
> The image of God as the Wholeness-Reality draws no sharp line between sacred and secular. The secular is sacred in its wholeness. The image of God as the Wholeness-Reality recognizes that at the heart of life, and supremely in man, is the persistent urge for expression and fulfillment. Life is for living; in the depths of our experience we know it and seek it. And if life is worth living, it is worth living well.
>
> The deepest resources for significant living are not encountered by turning from the pain and wonder of responsible existence-in-relationships. They are encountered in recognizing the rational character of all existence and in seeking such growth in and toward wholeness as is possible. Life itself mediates courage for living. God is where the whole-making, whole-seeking is. Life is holy in its wholeness.[11]

Potthoff did not see his theology as something that would please many, let alone most, Christians in today's world. To some extent, he saw his work as a theology for the future.

He deeply believed it was and is a theology appropriate for today's educated clergy and laity—and for persons who have abandoned a supernaturalistic world view and persons who want the church in their personal life but without having to accept an antiquated view of reality. So many traditional theological assumptions are contained in what religion scholar Sophia Fhas called "the old story of salvation." Harvey passionately believed the new story has just as much power for our religious lives. He was fond of Fhas's work.

In an article in *The Iliff Review* entitled "Theology and the Vision of Greatness," Potthoff has this to say about his theology as it fits the times.[12]

> Not only difficult times, but new times affect men in different ways. Some seek the security of the past—the fixed answer enshrined in authoritative book or creed. Others seek to push ahead in the faith that revelations of the divine are unending, waiting on those who seek; that life carries within itself resources for the meeting of the emerging new, the challenge at hand. It is the latter the centuries recall with greatest appreciation. These are exciting times in which to live—demanding and exciting.

It is in just such a spirit that Harvey approached faith and life in general.

Theological Shifts Do Happen

There is no question but that the Potthoff theological thinking was dominant at Iliff during his long tenure on the faculty. Even so, it was never the only theological position at the school or represented in the curriculum. Additionally, Potthoff, well beyond any theological orientation, was for most of his Iliff faculty service known as Mr. Iliff and treated that reality with reserve and dignity, never with a hint of arrogance. Both the variety of roles he played and his winsome personality did mean that everyone knew and had some experience with Dr. Potthoff!

Given his rather comprehensive roles, one might expect little Potthoffs came off some sort of theological production line. There is no doubt that some of that took place. However, there were many students and fellow faculty members who did not emerge from the Iliff experience as theological images of Potthoff. Some in fact, for a variety of reasons, were never attracted to his theology or his dominant role in the academy. Some of the input from former students contained in Chapter 14 will verify this. In addition, there were students who changed their theological positions during and after their Iliff years. The purpose of this section is to document this with two Iliff graduates: Vernon Goff and Richard Leach. What follows is the result of my mini-dialogue with each.

Vernon Goff is now retired in Omaha, Nebraska after a long career as a United Methodist pastor. He came to Iliff as a fundamentalist, having served as a youth evangelism minister before his arrival. His use and understanding of the Bible was solidly in the fundamentalist tradition, and he held it with some fervor.

During his Iliff years (which overlapped mine), he changed, and what follows is his own account as he reflects on the Iliff experience. We have had telephone conversations and email exchanges in addition to the content quoted below from a

June 21, 2012, email. He has given permission for me to include it in this book.

Vernon Goff

Memories of Dr. Harvey Potthoff

Having received degrees from Taylor University, Iliff School of Theology and The San Francisco School of Theology, I have had numerous contacts with professors of Theology. No one stands out as more exceptional in my memory than Dr. Potthoff. My contacts with Dr. Potthoff were within the framework of the normal course work for a theological degree from Iliff and special Summer seminars provided by Iliff-at-Aspen.

My approach to academics has been more on the level of assimilating and digesting than on the intellectual level of memorization and quotation. My background was strict fundamentalism seasoned with sufficient intellectual curiosity to permit a sampling of theological and philosophical thought outside the "fundamentalist box." The teaching method utilized by Dr. Potthoff was one of personalizing a belief system that made sense in relation to human life as experienced in the modern world. The "Potthoff method" suited my need for a bridge from fundamentalism to a theology in harmony with the world as I understand and experience it.

I had never given serious thought to Dr. Potthoff's contribution to my theological journey until Dr. Phillips asked if the title of my book, *Making God Talk Make Sense*, was directly related to the teaching of Dr. Potthoff. My response was "no," not directly. Serious consideration to the question, however, has brought me to the conclusion that the answer is actually "yes," indirectly. Dr. Potthoff taught with a spirit of compassion which insisted on a theology that was centered in the "love" aspect of Christianity rather than on the fear and judgmental aspects of "the old time religion."

Dr. Potthoff taught from a perspective which held that every human being is of value and experiences challenges that can be met best with a faith grounded in compassion and love rather than in fear and judgment. He appealed to the higher nature of human beings as basic to a moral life. He appealed to the hopeful nature of human beings as they express their lives in a manner which they believe to be consistent with the intent of their Creator.

Although I did not give credit to the contribution made to my theological journey by Dr. Potthoff at the time of my own writing, I do so now. Dr. Potthoff was a man of gentle and loving nature who lived the theology he thought and verbalized. I am grateful not only for what he taught me in class, but also for what he taught through his manner and spirit.

[Both Vernon's book mentioned above and his ministry are solidly in the theological tradition that Potthoff studied, taught, and lived.]

A Mini-Dialogue with Dr. Richard Leach

Richard Leach and I are very close friends. We both go by the name Dick, so I will identify us as "DL" and "DP" in what follows. We studied at Iliff at the same time, and our families maintained a close relationship following the seminary years. These included visits in our homes, parishes, and academic institutions, and we have maintained our relationship to this day. DL's first wife, Marge, died of cancer many years ago, and after some years passed, he married Wanda, a delightful person and an active United Methodist clergywoman now pastor of a church in Hot Springs Village, Arkansas, where DL has taken up a busy life as a retiree. The bulk of his professional life was as a member of the faculty of Lakeland College in Wisconsin. His doctorate is from Iliff.

We continue to correspond but have not been together since an Oklahoma visit in their home about ten years ago. This background is important for what follows. DL has given his permission for inclusion of his communications in this book.

While at Iliff, and for years following, we both held Potthoff in high esteem and basically functioned within the same theological pattern, but were not necessarily theological twins. Additionally, we were both very close friends of Harvey. DL served as Potthoff's assistant while at Iliff. He, Marge, and family had many interactions with Harvey, and the relationship went back to DL's student days at Dakota Wesleyan University where DL's father served on the faculty.

At the time of the 2002 memorial service for Harvey, DL came to Colorado and stayed with us, and that was a wonderful reunion as well as a shared tribute to our friend. The following quote is what DL submitted to *The Iliff Review* for the 1981 tribute issue at the time of Potthoff's retirement. During the time we spent together for the memorial service, I detected no change in the position here articulated.

> From DL: In an era when fundamentalistic and neo-orthodox ways of thinking have generally had their

way in Protestant Christian thought, Harvey Potthoff has offered refreshing alternatives. He has stressed the interrelatedness and interdependence of all forms of human knowledge. He has courageously stood against those who would isolate and compartmentalize Christian truth. He has helped keep the church in touch with other disciplines in the learning community, so her theology could contribute to and benefit from several modes of inquiry.

His dynamic view of the divine nature has contributed to evolutionary and process thought on the one hand and opened doors of wisdom from philosophical quarters on the other. This has stimulated many of us who would have been "at ease in Zion." For us, Harvey Potthoff has been a twentieth-century Abelard in constructive theology, keeping us from living in the past and bringing us to grips with inescapable realities of the present.

Furthermore, he has helped keep alive the mystic dimension of Christian theology in times when it has been largely smothered or pushed into non-Christian expressions. Those who took his classes had rich exposure to the saints of the church, who, like Brother Lawrence, had rapture in the midst of the ordinary, or others who knew the anguish of the "dark night of the soul." Harvey Potthoff put us in touch with a strand of our catholic heritage too often ignored.

Finally, he has developed a distinctive free-church understanding for United Methodist ecclesiology. His doctrine of the church as "the community of those being saved" is a much needed corrective to static

> purist and sacerdotal notions. It is indispensable to a dynamic view of human nature and to the church as a community for growth in grace. In closing, I am personally indebted to Harvey Potthoff. He is the friend and mentor who first engaged my mind in serious and critical theological inquiry.
>
> – *Richard D. Leach, Associate Professor of Philosophy and Religion, Lakeland College, Sheboygan, Wisconsin*

As work on this biography got under way, I requested DL send in any additional reflections he might like for me to include in this book, perhaps along with the 1981 one quoted above. To my great surprise, the following brief and very different response that separated him from the Bernhardt/Potthoff theological understanding he once favored came back in the mail. The following quotation came in a letter to me dated October 23, 2007, almost exactly five years after the memorial service for Harvey.[13]

> *As for the functional analysis of religion and the doctrine of absolute immanence: no thank you. My disenchantment with both began while preparing Easter sermons and discovering the credibility of the accounts of resurrection and the birth of the church in scripture. The gospel and epistle accounts made more sense as reported, than did reinterpretations along the lines of subjective states of ecstasy on the part of the disciples. Also as a pastor, dealing with people's needs was more than [Bernhardt's] metatechnology, it involved uncovering and applying the truth in God's Word. Furthermore, I found that the absolute rejection of the supernatural was no less dogmatic and far more problematic than historic Christian affirmations. … The philosophies of*

religion espoused by Bernhardt and Potthoff ... are fascinating distractions from what Christians have always believed.

I, DP, include these quotes and those below because I believe the reader of this biography needs to have a sample of the basic and informed arguments against, as well as for, the Potthoff theology. In subsequent letter exchanges, DL has clarified his new and current position, specifically in a letter of January 6, 2012, which he has given me permission to use in this substantive exchange, a mini-dialogue if you will. A copy of his whole letter is in the Potthoff archives at Iliff along with materials accumulated as a result of research and writing.[14]

In this recent letter, DL also pays Dr. Potthoff and me a tribute: "I remain grateful for the stimulus of Harvey Potthoff's process theology and for the close friendship I enjoyed with him during my Iliff years and thereafter. I commend my good friend and classmate Dick Phillips for his energetic efforts to compile the Potthoff biography. I predict the outcome will not be disappointing."

Now, below, are four brief but precise paragraphs from DL just as they appear in the letter. The first is unnumbered and is his introduction to the following three points.

Dealing with the Iliff legacy in general and Dr. Harvey Potthoff's influence in particular has been a major undercurrent of my [DL's] adult intellectual life. What transpired between my affirmative remarks of 1981 ...are the following realizations. [DP's responses follow each numbered item.]

DL #1.

The dramatic change in the apostolic post-crucifixion mind-set from withdrawn dismay, distress, and despair to confident, confrontational commitment is better explained by the New Testament accounts of Jesus's historical resurrection and Pentecost than by Dr. Potthoff's theory of shared subjective ecstasy. The latter is neither compelling nor convincing. It is the revision, not the former.

DP # 1

There is no doubt that HHP (Potthoff) saw the scriptural reports of the dismay following Jesus's death in the same way DL has in this first point. HHP's position is admittedly revisionist in nature, but the theory did not originate with him. That the biblical record itself has an element of "subjective ecstasy" also seems not just to be a Potthoff (and others') invention, such a response is also to be found within the persons within the Gospel accounts and between the Gospels themselves. Both Potthoff and DP do, even so, find a non-supernaturalistic interpretation of the post-crucifixion events both compelling and convincing, and, of course in keeping with the view of reality HHP has articulated. I would argue that each of the events contained in the Gospels has such a diversity of historical claims (some even contradictory) that any one of them can be seen as "revisionist" in nature. As for the spiritual value, I do not find belief in a more historical understanding of the texts (which I once shared) nearly as rewarding as the interpretation by Potthoff and most other naturalistic theology. The position that the biblical material is pure, or nearly pure, history seems rather untenable based on the content of the Gospels themselves as well as almost all of current biblical scholarship. I do not know for sure how DL would respond to the fact that the biblical texts do not come from a supernaturalistic viewpoint but from a view that God is very much a part of the natural world. Belief in a supernatural realm did not develop until several centuries later.

DL # 2

The substance of classical Christian thought developed in the formative early centuries of the Church carries more historical weight than Iliff's nineteenth- and twentieth-century "advance in doctrine." Faith grounded in Biblical-Reformation-Wesleyan essentials is more durable than the shifting philosophical-cultural sands of liberalism.

DP # 2

Here I would submit DL gives more credit to Iliff than warranted, the trend in scholarship ("advance in doctrine") is much older. I think that the shifting sands of a process understanding of reality applied to Christian thought do result in major adjustment to any historical affirmation about the developing faith. DL and Potthoff are/were, I am sure, aware of this based on the issue of supernaturalism, which seems to guide one and was rejected by the other. It must be remembered that the reformers and Wesley were operating within a basically prescientific (somewhat modified to be sure) world view. When a non-supernaturalistic world view fully impacts theology, it is not possible to understand or use the biblical material without major reinterpretation. As noted earlier, this does not mean for me or HHP that the scriptural accounts are of no value; they contain much very valuable and helpful information and new understandings of the messages and claims can be just as valid as the old. It does, I agree, require a greater acceptance of uncertainty in life, and not all Christians find living with "shifting sands" to their liking. Finally, the Iliff School of Theology "advance in doctrine" is not really an Iliff product. It existed before and during HHP's years and has increased in general Christianity since. I know DL does not think it is confined to Iliff, but the statement itself seems easily interpreted in that way.

DL # 3

The absolute rejection of God's transcendence and the supernatural by Iliff's Naturalism involves the reductionist fallacy. Theological epistemology cannot rightly be limited to empirical verification which necessarily excludes one-of-a kind events such as creation, exodus, incarnation, resurrection, and Pentecost. These are more fruitfully examined by effect than cause in this methodology.

DP # 3

First, it is only fair to say that HHP does not give up all understandings of transcendence as is pointed out earlier in this chapter. Transcendence can and does have a variety of meanings. But DL is on target with this part of his observation. Again I note that DL has given too much credit to Iliff. Naturalistic theology is by no means an Iliff or Potthoff creation. For me also, HHP's theology can in part be seen as built on "reductionist" thought. (I assume here the reductionism in theology DL is referring to is the position that, in general, religion is the creation of human culture.) Even so Potthoff's theology is for me always affirmed as "constructive" as in being built (or constructed) by taking into account current understandings of physics, chemistry, biology, biblical studies, Christian theology, historical methodology, and philosophical insights including from other fields of study, all of which are seen as always open to adjustment. Most science today has given up the notion of absolute certainty. A high degree of functional certainty is of course affirmed by science.

In process thought, the "static" understanding of nature is given up. One must induce from the evidence in nature the philosophical and theological positions which make the best sense and to continually adjust hypotheses about any such philosophical or metaphysical or empirical starting point because views of reality do change (e.g., the Higgs boson).

Finally on this #3 - HHP affirms, as do I, that events such as creation, exodus, incarnation, resurrection,

> and even Pentecost—and a host of other such events—can be very fruitfully understood by a process thought methodology, and with some thoughtful effort can have rewarding spiritual value. HHP spent much of his career building a thoughtful basis for just such value. At the same time, HHP has never limited the avenues to insight about religious or general human insights to empirical verification. There are always other avenues to valid understandings: emotion, experience, and reason, even imagination, have their weight as well as other avenues to knowledge.

This mini-dialogue deserves to have a future, and very likely the two of us will see to that. But, alas, too late for inclusion in this biography. Neither DL nor DP see our close relationship coming to a close by the above-mentioned differences. For two similar situations in Christian life, I first point to the book by Marcus J. Borg and N. T. Wright, *The Meaning of Jesus: Two Visions*. Borg, the contemporary liberal, and Wright, the traditionalist, see the same issues in very different terms which are very similar to our differences, but at the same time they remain close friends. The book is a HarperOne paperback (2007) and would be a very revealing read for any interested person. Each position is well stated and carefully documented. Additionally, Potthoff's deep and abiding friendships with Roman Catholic priests, rabbis, and orthodox, conservative, and even fundamentalistic thinkers—all of whom find themselves taking radically different positions on important theological issues—demonstrate that such friendships as ours can last.

While it is speculative on my part, I now quote HHP from a note card he had attached to one of his lectures. He habitually did this as updates and reminders of what he wanted to communicate in a sermon or lecture or speech. My speculation is that the content of this self-reminder would be one way HHP would respond to the above mini-dialogue. It is preserved in the Iliff Archives with some of his sermons.[15] [Capital letters are HHP's.]

> There have been many instances in Biblical history when people OUTGREW THEIR PREVIOUSLY HELD CONCEPTS OF DEITY. ... Experience led them into an awareness that they lived in a larger world than they had realized—that they had relationships they had not dreamed of—that the world is more complex than they had supposed. TO BE FAITHFUL TO BIBLICAL HISTORY IS TO KEEP REMEMBERING THAT people need to integrate their religious ideas and beliefs with all their other knowledge and experience.

For Potthoff, this demanded never-ending changes in views and understandings, even of the Bible and church history and tradition. He also affirmed that this does not leave us with nothing on which to base and practice the faith! See Chapter 5 on his pastoral theology.

I end this mini-dialogue with an apology to Dick Leach. I earlier warned him that the problem with including this in the book is that I would have the last word. Of course on the issues themselves, none of us has the last word, but DL certainly deserves another word!

NOTES

[1] Lecture titled "Some Introductory Comments on Process Theology," Iliff Archives, box 11, file 34, page 1.

[2] Lecture series to Iliff students entitled "One Person's Religious/Theological Journey," on March 24, 1981, Iliff Archives, box 44, file folder 7.

[3] Original recordings of "The Theology of Harvey Potthoff," as well as written transcriptions of parts of the lecture series, are in the Iliff Archives, box 34.

[4] Iliff Archives, box 6, file folder 8. The paper does not have a title. It was probably part of a lecture.

[5] Iliff Archives, box 4 file folder 15. While never published, two copies of these two chapters are preserved in the archives: one is the original typing by Harvey, and one a more readable photocopy of that very yellow document.

[6] "God and the Newer Views of the Universe," *The Iliff Review*, Fall 1959.

[7] Iliff Archives, box 2, file folder 7.

[8] Iliff Archives, box 11, file folder 34, page 9.

[9] Paul Rincon, "Higgs Boson-Like Particle Discovery Claimed at LHC," BBC News, July 4, 2012, http://www.bbc.co.uk/news/world-18702455.

[10] *The Cosmic Code: Quantum Physics as the Language of Nature* (New York: Simon and Schuster, 1982), 349.

[11] Harvey H. Potthoff, *God and the Celebration of Life* (Chicago: Rand McNally & Company, 1969), 195–196.

[12] *The Iliff Review*, 1959, page 12.

[13] Iliff Archives, box 44, file folder 15.

[14] Ibid.

[15] Iliff Archives, box 18, file folder 12.

4

HARVEY POTTHOFF'S PLACE IN CONSTRUCTIVE THEOLOGY

By David E. Conner

It must be understood from the start that Harvey Potthoff's theology is a theology generally intended to be used within the Christian church and by persons who embrace the Christian faith. In other words, unlike many other contemporary theological efforts, Potthoff's theology was not created chiefly in order to enter into learned dialogue with other theologians. Nor do any of his writings betray an attempt to gain recognition through the sophistication of their erudition. Rather, Potthoff's theology typically avoids the abstruse terminology and complicated argumentation that frequently haunt many theological articles and books today. There are two or three reasons for this.

An obvious one is simply that all of Potthoff's books were written at the request of publishers who intended them to be read by a lay audience. There is not a single instance when

Potthoff created a book proposal or a manuscript and then submitted it to publishers, as most scholars do today. Each book was planned from the start to be accessible to pastors and laypersons and relevant to practical issues of the religious life.

A second consideration is that, though thoroughly committed to critical scholarship, Potthoff was first and foremost a churchman—a pastor and a denominational leader who was, as it turned out, also a theological educator. His primary professional goals centered on the vitality of the church and on the spiritual resilience and depth of faith of the church's members. This has been one reason why Potthoff sometimes displayed a less-than-wholehearted interest in the academy of religion, whose members quite often evidence little if any sympathetic interest in the church.

A third consideration is perhaps this: that Potthoff's intellectual orientation was deeply pragmatic, not only by training but by natural inclination. Potthoff had an intuitive appreciation for the philosophy of William James (1842–1910) and for James's well-known interest in the "cash value" of ideas. Moreover, Potthoff's initial years of theological education were spent under the tutelage of William Henry Bernhardt (1893–1979), himself a graduate (PhD, 1928) of the celebrated Chicago School of empirical theologians. One of Bernhardt's foremost interests was the development of a "functional philosophy of religion"; that is, an analysis of religion that dwells not upon the analysis and development of theological systems of ideas but on the contributions, whether positive or negative, of specific religious beliefs to the actual hopes and behaviors of human beings.

In the Chicago way of thinking that Bernhardt conveyed to Potthoff and others, God, Christ, Spirit, salvation, the sacraments, and other religious notions are approached not as an intellectually orchestrated body of concepts but as convictions that actually influence the ways in which people think and live. This is not to say that Bernhardt neglected logic and coherence as he framed his own theological arguments—far from it—but that he sought finally to understand religion not as a cognitive enterprise but as an experiential reality that functions in certain ways in the lives of human individuals and their social units. Certainly in his own theological work, Potthoff did not follow Bernhardt in every detail, but Potthoff's overall perspective did reflect the empiricism and functionalism that Bernhardt's methods exemplified. Generally speaking, Potthoff integrated this functionalism and empiricism into a pragmatic theology that is firmly rooted in the life of the church and in the religious feelings and needs of human beings.

Unfortunately, the fact that Potthoff's theology is grounded in actual religious experience is liable to lead to several mistaken conclusions. One such error would be to assume that Potthoff's work is merely an example of what is often called "practical theology"—theology that aims primarily to relate itself to topics such as worship and liturgy, psychology of religion, pastoral care and counseling, church polity and administration, and the interpretation of the sacraments. A second and related mistake would be to suppose that Potthoff's sensitivity to the practical needs of the church means that he sought to avoid weightier theological problems. The fact that Potthoff attempted to write in accessible, nontechnical language does not imply that his work lacks genuine depth. Plato, Augustine, Luther, and Hume relied largely on ordinary language and labored to make their ideas as understandable as possible, but have not therefore been accused of being simplistic or unscholarly. A final error would be the inference that Potthoff's theology must be essentially *confessional*; that is, that it simply accepts on faith such traditional Christian affirmations as the lordship of Christ, the authority of the Bible, or the validity of specific Christian doctrines or creeds. In actuality, Potthoff's work is not dogmatic but unfailingly *philosophical* in character. Though Potthoff's theology does acknowledge its place and function within a specific religious tradition, it seeks to base itself on experiences and assumptions that could be shared by persons of other faiths or of no particular faith at all.

If truth be told, from the perspective of our present intellectual milieu, Potthoff's theology appears to be circumscribed not so much by its desire to function within the church as by *the content of the philosophical and cosmological assumptions upon which it is based.* In order fully to understand this statement, it is necessary to take account of two major intellectual movements that were in progress during Potthoff's formative years. One is the *evolution of classic liberal theology in American Protestantism*, and the other is *the revolutionary new worldview that arose from the discoveries of nineteenth- and twentieth-century biology and physics.* Both had a profound impact on Potthoff's outlook. We now turn our attention to these two well-known sources of intellectual ferment.

Liberal Protestantism was certainly not a recent innovation when Potthoff was in school during the 1920s and '30s. In fact, it is customary to trace liberal Protestant theology all the way back to the German theologian Friedrich Schleiermacher (1768–1834), and liberal theology has existed robustly in North America at least since the middle of the nineteenth century. However, liberalism was in the throes of transformation throughout the period of Potthoff's theological writing and research. These developments exercised a decisive influence on his theological perspective. Therefore, as we consider Potthoff's work, it is important to be aware of liberalism's basic beliefs and methods.

It is often thought that theological liberalism arose mostly as a response to the scientific discoveries of geologists such as James Hutton (1726–1797) and Charles Lyell (1797–1875) and of astronomers such as Nicolaus Copernicus (1473–1543) and Galileo Galilei (1564–1642), but of course most emphatically because of the findings of the great biologist Charles Darwin (1809–1882). Each of these scientists advanced ideas that at certain points contradicted a literalistic or common-sense interpretation of the Bible—thereby, in the opinion of many, seeming to cast doubt on the authority of scripture as a whole.

But we have a much more accurate view of the situation if we recognize that, even without the aid of scientists, religious scholars themselves were already gainsaying biblical literalism. The most notable example from the nineteenth century is probably the Graf-Wellhausen hypothesis, named for Julius Wellhausen (1844–1918) and Karl Heinrich Graf (1815–1869), who in 1876 published studies in which they analyzed the linguistic styles and theological contents of the Hexateuch[1] and concluded that the first five books of the Bible were not written by Moses, as had been believed for centuries, but were an amalgamation drawn by one or more editors from at least four sources whose varying historical accounts and theological convictions were often not in agreement with one another. Furthermore, criticism of biblical literature on historical and literary grounds precedes the discoveries of Wellhausen and Graf in work such as that of Wilhelm Dilthey (1833–1911) in literary studies and hermeneutics; and Dilthey's efforts were in turn based on the work of Schleiermacher. For that matter, recognition by religious scholars of the Bible's inconsistencies and historical inaccuracies goes all the way back to the Reformation and much further. For example, the Jewish scholar Philo of Alexandria (20 BCE–50 CE) objected to the Bible's crude anthropomorphisms, noting that God does not literally have a face and hands or a back (cf. Exodus 19:9, 14–22; 24:1–2; 31:18; 32:16; 33:18–23). Progressive religious thinkers were critiquing scripture on rational-empirical grounds even during the time of Christ.

It is important, then, to understand that theologians were not simply forced under intellectual duress to adopt more modern, plausible worldviews because of the discoveries of geologists, biologists, and astronomers. Moreover, it is not merely inaccurate but prejudicial to caricature theologians as provincial pedants of narrow scholarly compass whose work is restricted to arbitrary, anachronistic traditions and who are either unwilling or unable to engage in open-minded self-criticism. Sadly, this caricature persists even today, not only in the company of militant atheists but among many natural and social scientists, numerous philosophers, and more than a few ordinary people. Potthoff was vividly aware of this stereotype, and used to joke that many people think of a seminary as "a building with ivy creeping around on the outside and old men creeping around on the inside." More seriously, throughout his adult life, Potthoff steadily undertook, as Schleiermacher had done over a century earlier, to counteract such a stereotype of religion by portraying and exemplifying religious faith as something that is (or at least can be) intellectually defensible, psychologically healthy, and socially responsible.

The historical-critical or "liberal" approach to the Bible

that I have just noted may be thought of as the fountainhead from which the other ideas and methods of modern liberal theology were spawned. The major premises of theological liberalism were, in the main, embraced and advanced by Potthoff throughout his career. Though the ideas and methods of liberal theology are already familiar to many readers, it will be helpful to summarize them here for the benefit of those who are not. In terms of *content*, then:

(1) Liberal theology holds that the literature of the Bible does not possess some unique or unassailable authority because it was supernaturally inspired. Rather, the Bible is an historical collection of writings that were produced by human beings in search of the divine in order to address their contemporary circumstances and interests. Liberals believed, therefore, that the Bible should be studied using the same general methods that are applied to other historic writings.

(2) The conclusion that the Bible can be (and in fact *must* be) subjected to the standards of scholarly inquiry is related to another characteristic liberal attitude, namely, that *all truth is of God and from God* and that *human reason is a gift* that may rightfully be used to discover new truths not only about the natural world but about the Bible, God, faith, etc.

(3) Liberalism's higher level of confidence in human gifts and abilities led liberals to be skeptical regarding the traditional doctrine of original sin. Many liberals simply rejected the orthodox religious teaching that human nature is "fallen."

Potthoff himself often noted that, though infants are born in a state of utter self-absorption, it is in human nature to grow and to mature, so that human beings are neither essentially good nor essentially evil, but characterized by *potential.*

(4) The miracles described in the Bible had been under attack ever since the Enlightenment. Scottish philosopher David Hume (1711–1776) had delivered a particularly telling blow. The theological liberals' acceptance of Biblical criticism led to a reinterpretation of religious miracles as mere historical artifacts that were the logical consequence of the biblical authors' prescientific worldviews. Though not all liberals categorically denied the existence of miracles, liberals characteristically ceased to regard a belief in the miraculous or the supernatural as a crucial aspect of faith. For many liberal theologians, and especially for those of the Chicago School, God was no longer viewed as a supernatural being and was associated instead with certain creative, renewing tendencies in nature and/or in human society. The Chicago method came to be referred to as *empirical theology* because, instead of thinking of a divine being and then attempting to verify that being's existence, God was identified with certain experiential realities—such as universal creativity or social transformation—whose existence itself was more or less self-evident.

(5) The liberals' increased confidence in human reason led to a new hope in social reform and

moral progress. Sin, they argued, arises in human life not because of Adam and Eve's disobedience in Eden but mostly because of social problems such as ignorance, poverty, oppression, abuse, injustice, mental illness, and so on. The liberals reinterpreted the New Testament image of the kingdom of God in terms of actual social transformation: better education, the reduction of poverty, progressive legislation, and so on, all inspired essentially by moral suasion and exemplified especially in the teachings of Jesus.

(6) The liberals developed a keen interest in the relationship between religion and science. Theological liberals felt that one lesson of Darwinism was that opposition between science and faith leads ineluctably to a diminishment of the credibility of faith—unless one were willing simply to deny science altogether, which the liberals viewed as tantamount to a rejection of reason itself. Liberals therefore undertook various attempts to reconcile science and religion.

These are the major *contents* of liberal religious belief. *Methodologically*, it is clear that the liberals promulgated a new reliance on the powers of *reason* and on the validity of knowledge gained from human *experience*. In distinction from liberalism, orthodox Christian theologians had taught that reason and experience can be theologically instructive, but only up to a point. Reason and experience, the Church had said, can lead us to such general ideas as the affirmation that a Creator exists and that human beings are morally and spiritually insufficient to save themselves. Only *special revelation* can reveal the saving power of Christ, the existence of the Holy Trinity, the indispensability of the sacraments, the meaning of eternal life, and so on.

For centuries the church had maintained that there are two sources of such revealed truth: scripture and the authority of the church. It was further held that both of these sources are conveyed and interpreted by the ancient church councils (Chalcedon, Nicaea, etc.) and, for Romans Catholics, by the Vatican. (Luther and other Protestants naturally rejected papal claims and appealed to the authority of "scripture alone.") In contrast, for liberal theology, *reason* and *experience* were elevated at least to equal status with scripture and tradition—and it could be argued that reason and experience were, *de facto*, of greater authority, since they were employed by liberals as criteria by which the claims of the Bible and the Church were accepted, revised, or even rejected.

These liberal theological ideas and methods are more than just a prologue to our consideration of Potthoff's theology: they are part and parcel of what he believed, taught, and wrote. To be sure, Potthoff did not simply accept the canons of liberalism at face value, nor did he espouse liberalism in a way that was doctrinaire, defensive, or uncompromising —attitudes which, in fact, he viewed as being distinctly *non*-liberal. Furthermore, as I have stated, during Potthoff's period of theological activity, liberal theology was itself in flux. In many quarters, it was being vociferously attacked, and even its staunchest defenders were recognizing the need for revision. Potthoff himself was acutely aware of this and joined with other liberal theologians in acknowledging that the historic formulations of liberal theology were in many instances insufficiently nuanced or even in need of thoroughgoing reformulation. Nevertheless the fact remains that in order to grasp Potthoff's theology, one must understand the liberal religious orientation in which he was brought up and educated and which he sought to defend and then develop.

I have said that a second intellectual development that circumscribed Potthoff's thinking was the revolutionary new worldview that arose from the discoveries of twentieth-century physics. To be sure, Potthoff was influenced also by Darwin's impact on biology, but Darwin's ideas had been engaging liberal theologians for at least two generations prior to the time when Potthoff began his work. Quantum physics and relativity theory were more current. Considering Potthoff's grounding in liberal theology, it should not surprise us that he was fascinated with the advances in physics and cosmology that were gaining increasing public attention during the first three or four decades of his life. Though he did not, as some do, view science as the ultimate arbiter of truth, Potthoff himself had a consistent concern to take contemporary science into account as he articulated his theological position. The scientific advances now under consideration extend in their meaning far beyond the realm of technical science. If we are to understand Potthoff's theology, it is necessary to consider, if only briefly, the impact of the theory of relativity and quantum mechanics on our understanding of the universe and of our very existence itself.

By the early part of the nineteenth century, scientific opinion had settled in favor of the idea that light consists of waves rather than particles, and that light is carried by a medium known as the "ether," just as sound is carried to our ears by the air. But in 1887, using an ingenious instrument called the interferometer, Albert Michelson and Edward Morley showed experimentally that *the speed of light does not vary, regardless of the direction of its travel and despite the varying motion of the earth's surface through the supposed ether.*[2] This result was completely enigmatic, for it contradicted all contemporary understandings of the transmission of waves. It was as if the motion of the ether did not matter or that no medium even existed.

In 1905 Albert Einstein (1879–1955), until then an obscure Swiss patent clerk, published a paper in which he accounted for the negative results of the Michelson-Morley experiment mathematically. In order to explain his mathematics, Einstein proposed that two assumptions must be adopted. The first was that "the laws of physical phenomena are the same when stated in terms of either of two reference systems moving at a constant velocity relative to each other." The second was that "the velocity of light in free space is the same for all observers, and is independent of the relative velocity of the source of light and the observer."[3] These two postulates contradicted the assumptions upon which classical understandings of waves and motion were based; nevertheless, Einstein's hypotheses agreed with experimental observations. The physical predictions of Einstein's equations have since been thoroughly validated and are universally accepted.

However, the *philosophical* implications of Einstein's theory are not so amenable to experimental testing and are still being debated even today. This topic is beyond the scope of our discussion, but for present purposes, relativity offers two major ideas that we must take into account. One is that *space and time may no longer be thought of as absolute realities that pertain uniformly to all phenomena throughout the universe.* The other is that *the idea of perspective or point-of-view ("frame of reference") is now woven into the very fabric of scientific investigation and, by implication, into the essence of knowledge itself*. Though it may not seem obvious at first, both of these conclusions have major implications for theology.

This is because, historically, the monotheistic religions have taught that God exists beyond the realm of nature—that is, "super-naturally." In an attempt to describe the supernatural state of God's being, Augustine of Hippo (354–430 CE) argued in his great classic, *The Confessions*, that God exists outside of space and time, that is, nontemporally and nonspatially.[4] Augustine believed that God created space and time in one eternal moment, as it were, as a way of providing for the transient, changeable nature of physical existence. Augustine based his ideas on the teaching of Plato (424/423–348/347 BCE) that space and time are "receptacles," like universal containers in which all physical things exist. The Platonic theory that space and time are absolute—that they apply in the same way to all events everywhere—was accepted by virtually all scientists, until the time of Einstein.[5]

After Augustine, the notion of space and time as absolute receptacles became important not only for scientists but for theologians, for the receptacle-theory of space and time gave classical theism an obvious way to describe the supernatural status of God. God, theologians said, dwells in timeless eternity, whereas we mortals and the physical world exist fleetingly, as finite creatures living within space and limited by time.[6] For classical theologians, these ideas were not a minor technicality but a fundamental assumption, providing a way of thinking about God's unsurpassable goodness (as changeless perfection), God's omnipresence (being present everywhere at once), God's unlimited foreknowledge (seeing all of history from one eternal moment), and God's absolute constancy or incorruptibility (being literally beyond the processes of time and decay). The claim that God is beyond space and time also gave theologians a handy way to defend the traditional distinction between natural theology (derived from the physical world) and revealed theology (based on revelation from the realm of the eternal).

But with the coming of the special theory of relativity, *space and time ceased to be physical absolutes whose boundaries God might conveniently be said to transcend.* Rather, space and time are now seen to be inseparably interwoven as "space-time" and as malleable—or, more accurately, as pertaining to physical phenomena in various ways, depending upon the frame of reference of the observer. In fact, for certain physical phenomena, time seems not to apply at all. Radiant energy (light, radio waves, etc.) itself does not experience the passage of time, so that relativity theorists might say only half in jest that eternity is now inhabited not only by God and the angels but by electromagnetic radiation.[7] The point is that space and time are not absolutes, but vary depending on one's perspective. The concepts and assumptions used by Augustine and other orthodox theologians to describe theological transcendence are no longer applicable.

This radically undermines the historical ways in which the realm of the supernatural had been understood. Traditional religious supernaturalism, which, as we have noted, had already been under attack at least since the time of Hume, appears in the wake of relativity theory to be simply implausible. In order to understand Potthoff's theology, it is necessary to see that he, along with numerous other theologians, came to regard theological supernaturalism as patently untenable, an anachronistic position to be summarily rejected. Relativity theory seemed to suggest instead that *what had historically been referred to as "the eternal" is in reality inextricably intermingled with the temporal and the physical.* For Potthoff and others, this suggestion proved to be extremely fertile ground for theological exploration and construction.

During roughly the same years when the theory of relativity was being developed and tested, quantum mechanics emerged. Scientists had observed that when individual chemical elements are heated to the point of incandescence, only certain wavelengths of light are emitted. When this light is passed through a prism, narrow bands of color appear, separated by wide areas of darkness. Classical physics could not account for this. In 1900 the German physicist Max Planck (1858–1947) proposed that atoms exist only in specific states (or "quanta") of energy, which may be calculated as multiples of simple whole numbers (1, 2, 3, 4, etc.). In 1913 the Danish physicist Niels Bohr (1885–1962) theorized that the electrons orbiting the nuclei of atoms are each limited to certain energy states—a "ground" state when the atom is most stable, and various "excited" states when the electron has absorbed energy (either by being heated or by being exposed to radiant energy). But the electrons cannot absorb or emit just any amount of energy; each specific electron is restricted to discrete amounts ("quanta") of energy which are peculiar to that particular electron and which are, as Planck said, limited to multiples of whole numbers. As quantum theory expanded, it was discovered that the atoms in every element spontaneously organize themselves into a system of energy levels, with a unique pattern of organization that is identical in every atom of that specific element. These consistent patterns of organization are what give each element its unique chemical properties.

As with relativity, there are philosophical implications pertaining to quantum theory, implications that are too complex to be considered here. Again, however, there are two conclusions derived from this branch of science that are relevant not only for science but for theology, and especially for liberal theology. These are (1) *that nature manifests a previously unrecognized ability to transmit and utilize information*, and (2) that *this information is used spontaneously to create patterns of organization that lead to the emergence of increasingly complex systems in which the whole is greater than the sum of the parts*. Both of these ideas are immensely suggestive for the theological doctrine of creation, and both were especially important in the thinking of Harvey Potthoff. It is not that Potthoff was an authority regarding the natural sciences as such. He was fascinated with science, but his interest was from the standpoint of a nonspecialist. However, Potthoff's appreciation for scientific cosmologies was greatly deepened because he had the good fortune to study with the mathematician-philosopher Alfred North Whitehead (1861–1947), probably Potthoff's favorite teacher and certainly the most eminent. Whitehead was noted especially for his work in the field of philosophy of science.

An eminent British mathematician and logician, Whitehead was invited to join the philosophy department at Harvard in his mid-sixties. In the ensuing two decades, he produced major works on the relation between science and philosophy and then on a cosmology or theory of reality that he referred to as "the philosophy of organism." Whitehead's system is heavily indebted to (and perhaps chiefly motivated by) the discoveries of relativity theory and quantum mechanics.[8] Whitehead's seminal book *Science and the Modern World* contains entire chapters devoted to each of these two subjects. In 1935 Potthoff completed his seminary degree and received the Elizabeth Iliff Warren Fellowship, which enabled him to study for a year at Harvard with Whitehead. In this way, Potthoff became steeped in the assumptions underlying modern physics even without having studied physics as a subject unto itself. Potthoff's personal recollections of Whitehead are recorded elsewhere in the present volume. In order to adequately appreciate Potthoff's theology, we must examine Whitehead's overall system of ideas—ideas that continued to guide and influence Potthoff's theology throughout his life, and that are drawn from the discoveries of twentieth-century physics.

Whitehead recognized that atoms and particles cannot behave as they do unless they have some means of transmitting and receiving information. He certainly did not believe that atomic particles have minds or that they "think," nor did he believe in a divine Being who controls the world by imbuing nature with mathematical patterns or laws. Still, the mathematical patterns are evident, not as some sort of overlay or construction contributed by the human mind but as an observable fact. *Holism,* the emergence of increasingly complex groupings of simpler parts, is manifest not only in biological evolution but in chemistry and physics. This holism suggests that patterns are used throughout nature in ways that are implicitly constructive or purposive.

Whitehead also recognized that *perspective or viewpoint* must be acknowledged as being intrinsic to natural processes, as illustrated both in quantum theory and in relativity theory—in quantum theory, as the impact of the methods of the observer on experimental results, and in the language of relativity, in the ubiquity of *frames of reference*. This suggests to many persons that an element of subjectivity is built into nature itself.

Finally, Einstein had discovered that matter may no longer be regarded, as Newton had stated, as inert stuff that has no motion or energy unless acted upon externally; rather, matter has energy mysteriously locked within it—in fact, energy in very large quantities, as we now know only too well.

In light of these and related considerations, Whitehead developed a metaphysical system that is based on several convictions.

(1) Reality is composed not of inert substances or internally static matter, as Aristotle had said; rather, reality is constituted of *dynamic events*. Whitehead wrote, "the process itself is the actuality, and requires no antecedent static cabinet."[9] We now can see that Whitehead's views on this point are close to contemporary string theory, which holds that subatomic particles are composed of vibrating "strings" of energy.[10]

(2) The processes that constitute reality are influenced not only by mechanical or physical interactions ("efficient" causes, after Aristotle), but by the purposive use of information ("final" causes). This implies that each "actual occasion" (Whitehead's term for the most fundamental units of reality) experiences a level of purposiveness and is ultimately self-caused (*causa sui*). Each occasion is a dipolar unity of the physical and the informational (or the mental).

(3) The purposive use of information allows single "occasions" to interact with one another in such a way as to form larger systems or wholes, which Whitehead called "societies" of occasions. This is exemplified in the actual world even in the formation of subatomic particles, but also in molecules and cells and in the evolution of increasingly complex life forms. Thus for Whitehead, reality is dynamic, relational, constantly evolving, and holistic or organismic. There is a primitive type of experience or subjectivity or "feeling" that pertains to every tidbit of reality, and nature is characterized throughout by a kind of aliveness.

Having said this, it is important to clarify several points at which Whitehead has often been misunderstood. Whitehead was not a *vitalist*; he did not believe that there is a separate principle of vitalism that causes matter (which would otherwise be inert) to come to life. Whitehead was not a "panpsychist"; *psyche* is a Greek word associated today with "soul" or "personality"—highly evolved modes of human experience that do not pertain to all of nature. Whitehead did not believe that the universe is conscious or that the universe has a mind, nor did he believe that all physical objects have feelings. He regarded many objects, such as rocks and clouds, simply as aggregates or agglomerations of items whose unity is simply physical and spatial, not sentient or intentional. Whitehead was not a Platonist; though he believed that information and patterns are present in nature, he did not believe that ideas or "forms" act on their own or that they are the preeminent form of reality. Lastly, Whitehead did not equate "process" with "progress." The processes of which reality is constituted may and quite often do result not in wholeness and upward evolution, but in destruction and tragedy.

Nevertheless, despite all these caveats and restraints, Whitehead's view of the universe does seem to encourage a hopeful perspective on things. His philosophy reveals an organismic tendency both in individual entities and in nature as a whole. Superficially, the world may seem to be in the grip of "the clashings of senseless compulsion"—that is, to be controlled ultimately by the chance collisions of material particles—and yet, Whitehead says, we are confronted by the obvious facts of wholeness and growth. Material systems do evolve in such a way that they acquire an ability to counteract entropic dissipation and disorganization.[11] Life emerges and becomes more complex; civilizations arise; and our own experiences testify to "the tendernesses of mere life itself."[12] Whitehead recognized that the materialistic-mechanistic assumptions of the Newtonian worldview stubbornly persist not only among many scientists but, perhaps most of all, among professional philosophers,[13] but Whitehead argued compellingly that Newtonian materialism cannot account either for the discoveries of relativity and quantum physics or for the plain facts of human experience. Harvey Potthoff joined Whitehead in these convictions and constructed his theological vision in the context of an outlook that is essentially Whiteheadian.

However, Potthoff did not attempt simply to convert Whitehead's philosophy into religious terminology—a project that certain other theologians may be said to have undertaken. Whitehead himself had written a good deal about God, but Whitehead's God is not the transcendent Being of traditional monotheism. For Whitehead, God is a universal structure that serves to coordinate information or patterns so that the information or patterns that are applied are relevant for specific occasions as they come into being. In other words, Whitehead's idea of God is associated with the spontaneous emergence of patterns or organization throughout nature. Whitehead believed that some principle must be operative in the creation of the order that nature manifests.[14] During the mid-twentieth century, Whitehead's use of the term *God* was studied by many liberal-minded theologians who soon began to advance a school of thought that became known as "process theology," which focused initially on the idea of God but soon broached other theological topics also.

Potthoff's own concept of God is presented most definitively in his *God and the Celebration of Life*.[15] In this book, Potthoff acknowledges his agreement with many of the themes of process theology but adds that his way of affirming the reality of God "differs from the approach of some of the process theologians in associating God with the wholeness of reality rather than with some abstracted phase or function of reality or with some 'entity' or 'being'." In *Process and Reality*, Whitehead had described God as the only "non-temporal actual entity." In the statement by Potthoff just quoted, Potthoff distances himself not only from Whitehead's nontemporal actual entity but from Henry Nelson Wieman's concept of God as "the source of human good,"[16] which seemed to Potthoff to be a somewhat artificial and anthropocentric construction—that is, an "abstracted phase or function or reality." Instead of basing our ideas about God on some previously articulated concept, Potthoff states that "The deepest religious conviction is grounded in experience,"[17] and he cites the experience of *wholeness* as being both a key to understanding reality and a source of religious feeling.

> The fundamental interrelatedness of things leads us to think of reality in terms of parts and wholes. . . .
>
> The concept of wholeness does not imply a static, completed structure of some sort, nor does it necessarily imply all there is. It refers to reality in its related diversity and eventfulness, in its amazing interplay of parts, dimensions, levels, and wholes. It refers to that character of reality by virtue of which all parts of the known universe are sensitive to all other parts and are mutually affected by each other. Reality manifests a sensitized relatedness of the parts, and in this sense is a functional whole. ...
>
> The concept of wholeness suggests reality in its depth and breadth and height; in its being and becoming; in its vastness and intensity; in its potentialities and qualitative richness; in its never-ending interplay of persons, events, and situations; in its creation, disintegration, and re-creation; in its flux and in its long-range dependabilities; in its impartiality and integrity; in its endings and new beginnings; in its mysterious uniting of fate and freedom, tragedy and triumph, death and life, creation and redemption. Realistic and enduring hope is ultimately grounded not in some segment of reality but in the character of reality in its wholeness.[18]

Potthoff concludes this description of the experience of wholeness with the proposal that God may be spoken of variously *"as the ground of wholeness, the character of reality in its wholeness, the dynamic reality making for wholeness."*[19] By denying that "wholeness" refers simplistically to "all there is" and by emphasizing that wholes are just as real as their parts, Potthoff differentiates himself from Bernard Loomer,[20] taking a theological position that may be viewed as standing somewhere between Loomer and Whitehead. "In this holistic approach, power and value, process and structure, limitation and potentiality, integration and disintegration, part and whole, life and death are held together *in patterned process* by virtue of the reality of God."[21] In his interpretation of wholeness, Potthoff is very close to the religious sensibilities of Friedrich Schleiermacher, "the father of empirical theology," who asserted that our experience of God derives from our "feeling of absolute dependence"—that is, our direct sense of the ultimate reality upon which all of our experience depends.[22]

Potthoff recognizes that his own concept of God is not as detailed or precise as Whitehead's, but he sees this as an improvement.

> A certain vagueness and imprecision inevitably attend the word "wholeness." We prefer words which point to the concrete, the specific, the tangible, and the measurable. However, it is our preoccupation with the concrete, specific, and tangible which gets us into so much of our difficulty as human beings. Creative living also involves attention to another dimension of reality. It is a dimension which gathers up such elusive realities as sources, relations, patterns, potentialities, qualities, and goals. The word "wholeness" functions in pointing to the dimension of comprehensiveness. It refers both to the totality and the part-whole structure of reality.[23]

Potthoff acknowledges that his focus on holism raises the question as to whether there is ultimately an all-inclusive whole with definable characteristics. He responds that "[t]he only answer at this time is: We do not know."[24] Though orthodox theology commonly affirms that there is a single divine power that creates the universe and sustains its orderliness, Potthoff holds that "such a belief can neither be verified nor falsified."[25] In an address to a denominational conference on Christian education, Potthoff stated:

> At this stage of human history we are not in a position to speak of God with finality or even, perhaps, in the sense of affirming that God is metaphysically **One.** However, I do think we can speak with some assurance of **patterned process** in the light of which man may reinterpret events and experiences, come to an appropriate direction of expectation, discover a potentiality for meaning and becoming in himself and in his universe, and be encouraged in an attitude of hope in an affirmation of the human venture. ... It is my own judgment that insofar as man comes to be related to what is fundamental and enduring in the nature of things (here referred to as patterned process) in such ways that there emerge religious meanings and values (the life of faith), the language of trust and devotion—including the affirmation of the reality of God—is appropriate.[26]

Potthoff often questioned the plausibility of conventional personalistic notions of God. It is noteworthy that he chose to do this even at a national meeting of Methodist teachers and editors, most of whom must have found his ideas on this topic either perplexing or unpalatable.

Potthoff's appreciation for a certain amount of vagueness and imprecision in theology, along with his stated denial that we can responsibly answer certain theological questions about the unity of God, amounts to an open endorsement of a level of mystery in theological discourse. In point of fact, Potthoff includes an entire chapter in *God and the Celebration of Life* entitled "An Appropriate Agnosticism"[27] in which he advances an essentially Jamesian notion of the provisional nature of knowledge.[28] While Potthoff does not develop these themes specifically as a response to Whitehead, he clearly is taking Whitehead's idea of God into account and constructing his theology with an awareness of the methods and conclusions of process theologians.

Potthoff's "dynamic reality making for wholeness" may sound abstract and academic, but he does not leave the concept at a cerebral, theoretical level. One of Potthoff's earliest published writings is an article entitled "Some Comments on the Doctrine of Forgiveness," first appearing in 1944.[29] This article, written when he was in his early thirties, reveals Potthoff's lifelong genius for reinterpreting traditional Christian doctrines in terms of a naturalistic worldview, with results that are not merely more credible intellectually but more deeply applicable existentially and pastorally. Potthoff begins by speaking of the profound need that all human beings have for forgiveness. It is a truism that every human being, over the years, encounters failures, mistakes, and missed opportunities. Virtually everyone accrues various reasons for feeling regret, sorrow, or shame. Some respond by muddling along in the hope that time will heal all wounds, some respond with evasion or denial, some pursue therapy, and so on. Potthoff notes that there is good reason why the heart of the Christian message has focused on forgiveness. Even so, he observes:

> [I]ncreasing numbers of people are finding it difficult to discover very much meaning for themselves in the traditional doctrine of forgiveness. The basic human problem remains; the proposed solution has lost reality.
>
> The basic difficulty is clear. The whole structure of thought involved in the traditional view is raised upon the basis of a supernaturalistic worldview. Man and nature are here; God is there. Man and nature are evil; God is good. Nature is devoid of resources adequate for man's salvation; God in his heaven is sufficient. Man is estranged from God, but God is not part and parcel of the stuff of the world with which man deals; instead, he is a God removed whose condemnation of sin is an otherworldly condemnation and whose salvation is an other-worldly salvation. That such a God actually exists is seriously doubted by increasing numbers of people. That such a salvation is a particularly meaningful salvation may be doubted with equal seriousness. The consequences of failures, mistakes, missed opportunities are present consequences; the values we would find are present values; the oneness with God we would achieve is a present oneness; and the forgiveness we seek is a present restoration with the divine factor in the universe, bringing in the living present the lasting fruits of real religion—a sense of peace and a sense of importance.[30]

Potthoff writes that the word *God* may most meaningfully be understood not as referring to a supernatural Being in heaven but by identifying God with the healing, hope-conferring aspects of our own experience. "We may apply the term 'God' to those aspects of reality in terms of which we achieve religious values." Potthoff continues by observing that when people truly experience forgiveness and renewal, the experience comes by regaining rapport with a God who is resident in nature, not by appealing to a supernatural being beyond ordinary experience. But is there anything *within* nature that offers forgiveness and redemption? Potthoff's answer is that if we take a long-range view,

> we may make the following affirmations with considerable assurance: (1) In nature we find "certain uniformities in the behavior of things." A more popular, although sometimes a somewhat misleading, way of putting it is that the universe is law-abiding. (2) Activity and change are fundamental characteristics of nature. (3) Creation and growth are fundamental aspects of nature. In these three statements we have the basis of a naturalistic doctrine of forgiveness.[31]

In passing we may notice the thoroughly Whiteheadian character of all three of these affirmations—the metaphysical persistence of process, the dependability of structure and pattern within process, and the ever-present possibility of emergent wholeness. But Potthoff has no reason to mention Whitehead, and he certainly would not have wanted to burden the article with a discussion of philosophical technicalities. Instead, he moves on by describing the meaning of forgiveness itself.

> It is possible for man to draw upon and relate himself to those aspects of nature engaged in creativity and growth and so to enter into their life. In so doing, he finds the real heart of forgiveness; he achieves a measure of rapport with deity, for one of the functions of God in some situations is that of creation. We may say, then, that forgiveness is not erasing the past; it is outgrowing the past. It is organizing the materials of today into a meaningful kind of life, sustained and encouraged by those ever-present aspects of reality which further development.[32]

In our bodies, Potthoff notes, there are innate tendencies toward healing. There are innate tendencies toward healing in the mental and moral areas as well. This healing activity is operative in human experience, and yet the factors that make it possible were not invented by us. They are extra-human. The possibilities and processes related to healing are possibilities and processes that we associate with God.

> Such, in brief, is the direction which the formulation of a naturalistic doctrine of forgiveness may take. By virtue of the dependability of nature, the fact of change, and the creative phase of reality which finds expression in growth and healing, the individual may hope for at least a measure of release from the shackles of past failures, mistakes, and missed opportunities, in the sense of moving on into a finer quality of experience. ...
>
> One cannot be insensitive to the tragedy of someone whose life has been impoverished through

> mistakes of some kind. But sometimes we see that individual gathering the redeemable fragments of his broken experience, and setting out to make the most of the rest of his life. In time he finds himself living a meaningful life, meaningful to himself and to others. Life is not just as it was before; perhaps it is quieter and deeper and simpler. In one way or other things have worked out so that his life has found significance in the light of the more enduring realities. When we see this take place, we might well put off the shoes from our feet, for the ground whereon we stand is holy ground. We are in the presence of divine forgiveness.[33]

Potthoff concludes that "any credible doctrine of forgiveness must grow out of the credible doctrine of God." The God we need is not a supernatural being but "a God of dependability, of change, of creation, of growth, of healing." Ultimately, "from such a God no person can ever become completely estranged, and in such a God there is always a measure of hope."[34]

One central emphasis in Potthoff's doctrine of God, manifest in his concept of forgiveness, is the achievement of an appropriate balance between *subjectivity* and *objectivity*. We have noted that for Whitehead, there is at least a small element of subjectivity woven through the "mental pole" into each "actual occasion," each tidbit of reality. Whitehead's affirmation of subjectivity grows partly out of relativity's affirmation that no frame of reference is absolute, and also out of quantum theory's recognition that the methods of the observer cannot help but influence the outcome of experimental measurements. But the *subjectivity* of each actual occasion is also *objective*, forasmuch as one entity's subjectivity becomes a fact (an event with a definite outcome) that then has influences on future occasions.[35] The subjectivity is itself an objective fact of nature. As James said, "We have every right to speak of it as subjective and objective both at once."[36] Without referring to Whitehead or to James, Potthoff applies this ontological intermingling of subjectivity and objectivity to a concept of God, recognizing that all of our ideas about God must in some measure be subjective, though also objective. Potthoff's position here is a radical departure from the traditional attitude of monotheistic religions that alleged truths about God are purely *objective*—for example, that it is objectively true (true regardless of one's perspective or personal history) that God is a supernatural Being who is eternal, omnipotent, all-knowing, and so on. For Potthoff, God is not a being "out there" to be studied dispassionately, like a planet or an atom whose mass and temperature may be tested in a laboratory. God is rather associated with the renewing, hope-conferring, motivating experiences that arise in the dynamic matrix of life's events. There is, therefore, always an element of *interpretation* attached to our experience of God.

> My suggestion is that serious God-talk must proceed in a di-polar fashion as we speak from both objective and subjective poles. It is the task of theology to seek to bring together the languages of designation and description, with the languages of personal confession of meaning. We must seek a merging of talk about the **fact** of God and the **meaning** of God in personal experience. The theologian in our time must seek to relate the God discerned in the vast reaches of the universe with the God discerned in the promptings

> of the inner spirit of man. The theologian must seek to relate in some meaningful way the divinity discerned in reality in its wholeness with the divinity discerned in events of revelatory-illuminating, commitment-evoking significance.
>
> The distinction between objective and subjective poles of God-talk cannot legitimately be drawn in an absolute sense. But for purposes of analysis there is justification for the distinction and we shall proceed on that basis.[37]

One incidental advantage of Potthoff's affirmation of the subjective dimension is that a major basis for the historic scandal of religious intolerance is undermined. For Potthoff, God is not merely a being whose "divine attributes" may be objectively stated; rather, the reality of God is associated with a *choice* to interpret the events of life in certain ways—a choice to affirm *subjectively* that there is an *objective* basis for hope, meaning, and inspiration in life. Thus, claims that God is simply "like this" or "like that" become, to some extent, inappropriate. The idea that God-talk always involves a personal decision to view the Sacred Reality in a certain way tends to diminish or remove the grounds for historic disputes between, say, Arians and Athanasians, Arminians and Calvinists, or possibly even between Muslims and Jews. On the other hand, this does not mean that all God-talk is based solely on personal preference. There is an objective aspect to Potthoff's "Wholeness Reality" or "Ultimate Real Other" that does tend to rule out many of the more popular, anthropomorphic notions that have historically been associated with deity.

The subjective pole of our experience of God is more than

just a way to avoid doctrinal disputes with other believers. The subjective dimension of faith, in effect, frees us from dogmatism for a more existential, applicable way of embracing belief. The traditional Christian idea of grace, for example, takes on richer meaning.

> The grace of God is believed to be mediated in and through relationships. Life-giving grace is not understood as an infused potency or favor arbitrarily bestowed by an external God. Rather, grace is the power for being and becoming more whole, appropriated in the midst of life, as man is open to the deep resources mediated in work and play and love and worship and commitment to the God who is ever working in events toward greater wholeness. ... To speak of God as grace is to speak of that dimension of God's working by virtue of which that which has been estranged, broken, and counted evil is accepted and gathered into a new structure of wholeness and meaning. Such words as healing, reconciliation, forgiveness, redemption suggest the experience of God as grace.[38]

The element of personal decision and commitment that is intrinsic to faith also opens the way to a more flexible understanding of religious language. Most religious statements about life and about God may not appropriately be interpreted with a rigid literalism. Poetry and metaphor are indispensable to faith, just as they may be in our communications with loved ones and friends. When we read "the Lord is my shepherd" or "I am the vine and you are the branches," we do not complain that we are not sheep or stems on a creeping plant. Similarly, to say that "God is good" may mean not that God is literally a heavenly being who grants benign favors but that we ourselves are affirming life's larger patterns, purposes, and meanings.

Potthoff's theology clearly is not a system of belief that fosters selfish motives. Potthoff's God is not a being who gives us special rewards for sticking to the rules or for praying faithfully enough. *Eschatology,* the traditional Christian doctrine of the "last things," is for Potthoff not about going to heaven or about some cataclysmic end of history in which sinners are punished while the righteous are saved. Rather, Potthoff asks, what is it that life allows us to hope for *ultimately?* It is both unrealistic and unhealthy, Potthoff believes, to hope for unshakable inner peace, for salvation through association with like-minded persons, for a perfected past from which all sources of regret have been annulled, for an apocalyptically fulfilled future, or for an imperturbable sense of acceptance—for we really do make mistakes. Ultimate hope, instead, must be based on the total dynamic and wholeness of which we are a part.

Our lives take on meaning finally, not because of any reward that we might receive individually but because of the holistic, healthy, caring ways in which we take part in that larger matrix which has given us life and to which our own lives make contributions. Morality, in this view, is "an art rather than a legalistic application of fixed rules."[39] The effort to live a moral life in the perspective of faith recognizes that we are parts of the goodness and purposefulness of creation. It recognizes that, as the Wholeness-Reality, God provides a basic structure of existence in which our actions are "both judged and undergirded. ... Because God is real, the seeds of destruction are in life-styles of irrationalism, hatred, and exploitation; because God is real, the seeds of renewal and hope are in life-styles of inquiry, goodwill, life-affirmation, service, experimentation, and cooperation."[40]

We have recognized that Potthoff's God is not one being among many beings, but rather an encompassing Reality, creating and deepening wholeness within and among relationships. It would be natural to assume that such an idea of God would lend itself to application in the setting of the church, an institution based fundamentally on relationships—and this turns out to be the case. Potthoff notes that there are several popular understandings of the church that are, in his view, merely ancillary.

> Some persons think the church is relevant if it simply provides settings for enjoyable social occasions. Others define relevance in terms of meeting psychological needs: for security, reassurance, renewal, recognition, a sense of personal worth. Some take a more sociological approach, holding that the church should function in giving force to social norms, celebrating the values of the group or community. There are many persons who believe the church is enacting its primary role when it is functioning as an agent of social criticism and social change.[41]

For Potthoff, however, the chief question to be addressed is whether the church has some distinctive role to play, meeting a need not being addressed by other organizations or institutions. The answer comes in terms of a depiction of life that is specifically religious and, for Christians, that traditionally involves a reasonable, faithful understanding of God as made known in Jesus Christ. When God is experienced as the Wholeness-Reality, the aspirations and hopes offered by the church are not of some other-worldly salvation.

> First, we say to the church: Give us your vision, your revelation of God and man and life. Help us see the dimensions of transcendence and depth and height in the midst of the present moment. Communicate this vision in such a way that it comes, not as a series of intellectual propositions to be accepted, but as light, disclosing the sheer wonder of the universe and human life and all that partakes in being. Give us a vision that will make us ever discontented with a life of triviality, insensitivity, mediocrity. Give us a vision of greatness which calls us out of apathy, which shakes us into the awareness that we have not been born for ease but for a measure of greatness, sharing in the divine work of creation and whole-making in human relations.[42]

In addition to a vision of life, the church is also in a position to offer a *history*, a complex of traditions and conventions through which its members relate to the past and find a sense of identity, both personally and corporately. Though often neglected by modern people who are fascinated by popular culture and immersed in technology, a heritage of shared values and purposes can be of immense value.

The church may also provide a *language*, a way of speaking about the sacred, a vocabulary that comes to be associated with what is most precious in life and about life. "We are able to talk to each other about likes and dislikes in food, television programs, public figures, and so on. Unfortunately, we are less able to communicate on a thinking, feeling, valuing, aspiring level in matters of enduring importance. We are inwardly impoverished because of this fact."[43] It is a contemporary duty of the church to reinterpret its traditional language. "Languages reflecting prescientific or frontier or pastoral or rural settings communicate with fewer and fewer persons."[44] Words, metaphors, and religious phraseology must be conveyed in ways that communicate an applicability to the deepest and most vital experiences of existence today.

Finally, Potthoff says, the church must offer *a witness.*

> Above all else, the church in this time is asked to be an authentic witness to the greatness of its vision and the greatness of its hope. In the current confusions of the world there are many witnesses to the irrational, destructive, and immature dimensions of man. The church serves the world exceedingly well when it bears witness to the God who makes for wholeness, and to man as a creature who is born for wholeness. The church serves in bearing witness to the dignity and strengths and possibilities of man.[45]

A part of the church's witness must be in its own internal life. The practices, programs, and plans of the church must be made meaningful in ways that make a genuine difference in today's world. But the most significant changes envisioned and pursued by the church have to do with the church's relation to the world beyond the church's own boundaries. "At the heart of Christian faith is the affirmation of a divine grace which goes forth at personal cost to save and heal and restore and make whole." This is a message not only for church members or for a religious elite; it is, at some level, a message for all human beings.

> Can modern man speak meaningfully of the reality of God? The answer to this question cannot come in words alone. It must come in the decision for meaning and purposefulness which men bring to their existence. It must come in the trust and devotion men reveal in their daily living. It must come in celebration of life in its wholeness, which is the worship of God. For many persons the answer will be profoundly influenced by the church's witness to the gospel with which it has been entrusted. It is the enduring function of the church to make God real to man.[46]

This, then, is a brief foray into the theology of Harvey Potthoff. Clearly it has not been possible in the present chapter to mention even in passing all of the topics into which he made significant theological inquiry. Much of importance has been left out. What is offered here is merely a summary of some of his most characteristic perspectives and ideas. But even in such a cursory examination, there is, I believe, much to ponder. It only remains now to go beyond the tasks of description and analysis to a brief assessment of Potthoff's contributions to twentieth-century Protestant theology.

I will now mention three basic criticisms that might be directed at Potthoff's writings. The first is that his work is insufficiently academic to have a lasting influence. The second is to ask whether, like many other liberals, Potthoff trusted too thoroughly or too uncritically in the criteria of *experience* and *reason*. The third criticism is that Potthoff was insufficiently responsive to the claims of *liberation theology*, which were being voiced with growing intensity during the final decades of his career.

First, did Potthoff fail to enter sufficiently into the fray of scholarly debate? The contemporaries of Potthoff who now seem to be standing the test of time—one thinks of Paul Tillich, Reinhold and Richard Niebuhr, H. N. Wieman, Daniel Day Williams, Rosemary Ruether, John Cobb, Schubert Ogden, among many others—managed to undergird a certain appeal to a wider audience with a footing of academic rigor. In comparison, by writing primarily for clergy and lay persons and limiting the extent of his conversation with professional colleagues, did Potthoff effectually limit his own significance as a theologian?

Second, did Potthoff rely too heavily on *experience* and *reason* as theological resources? Clearly such an overreliance would be objectionable to religious orthodoxy. Despite Potthoff's overt endorsement of scripture and tradition, reason and experience appear to function for Potthoff as trump cards, final adjudicators of what may and may not be said theologically. Theologians who are more traditional will feel that Potthoff gives insufficient attention to the hard-won conclusions of historical theology. Also, there are many persons of deep spiritual conviction who see scant connection between religious faith and the scientific cosmology that Potthoff cites as a basis for theological revision. The Swiss theologian Karl Barth (1886–1968) is probably the most celebrated champion of the view that the God of faith, who created heaven and earth, is categorically beyond the rational-empirical modes of analysis that we apply to ordinary objects of study. Why should we feel required to adapt faith to the criteria of science or philosophy?

There is another standpoint from which Potthoff's emphasis on reason and experience might be attacked: the standpoint of postmodernism, with its recognition that reason and experience are not the unbiased, commonly acceptable criteria that they were once believed to be. Does Potthoff make the unsustainable assumption that reason and experience can function adequately (even if not perfectly) as epistemological "foundations"? Or, does he assume too confidently that the reasoning he employs and the kinds of experience he cites are adequately representative of humanity generally, regardless of gender, race, economic status, educational level, or national background? By attempting to rely on rational-empirical techniques in order to get at what is broadly representative of human experience, has Potthoff inadvertently failed to attend specifically and deliberately to the voices of persons who, because of class, race, gender, sexual orientation, and so on, have been systematically oppressed or disenfranchised?

It is not my intention, nor would it be appropriate in the present chapter, to attempt any sustained defense of Potthoff's work. In the end, his own words can and do serve as his best vindication. However, there are several observations that may now be made.

First, the claim that Potthoff's work is insufficiently scholarly is at heart a superficial, *ad hominem* attack. We are entitled to regret, as I myself occasionally have regretted, that Potthoff seldom reacted in print to the more creative and thought-provoking views of his theological contemporaries. His students knew that his opinions on these matters were well informed, up-to-date, and succinct. But in any case, Potthoff's reluctance to use books and articles to engage in technical theological argumentation is no proof that his work was thin or lightweight. I have suggested already that beneath the relative plainness of his language, we find original insight and genuine theological substance. In my view, it is the duty of responsible scholarship to discern and make use of this.

The question of whether Potthoff relied too confidently on reason and experience as theological criteria is more complex, as is the question of his reaction to liberation theology. Potthoff aimed, as other liberals before him had aimed, to construct a theology that could be relevant and helpful to all sorts of human beings. This is a worthy motive and a time-honored one; it goes all the way back to the early Christian apologists. To those who suggest that Potthoff relied too heavily on twentieth-century science, the response must be that Potthoff was in fact not naïve but quite critical in the ways that he responded to scientific ideas. Also, it is significant that many who now disparage the applicability of science to religion continue in actuality to accommodate their thinking to scientific discoveries. For example, theologically, Karl Barth claimed to reject science and philosophy in favor of scripture, but he nevertheless declined to defend the antiscientific contentions of Biblical literalism. And finally, the postmodernist protest that the supposedly objective authority of reason and experience is actually specious does not apply very well to Potthoff, for he characteristically mingled his theological assertions with an open acknowledgment of the limits of human knowledge, and he affirmed that theological mystery is not merely unavoidable but of positive value.

On the other hand, it is my feeling that Potthoff's wish to appeal to nonsectarian, objective criteria did lead to a certain diminishment of attention to traditional Christian affirmations and symbols. This diminished attention was not severe, but it was noticeable. For example, he did not write a great deal about the authority of scripture, about the meaning of the sacraments, or about the person and work of Christ.[47] Perhaps he did not feel that such topics lent themselves to development in the light of his own methodological criteria or to inclusion in his agenda of naturalistic reinterpretation. Given a forced choice between scientific-philosophic plausibility and fidelity to traditional Christian formulations, he tended to side with the former. Siding with contemporary methods of inquiry can benefit theological construction in many instances—but not always. It is possible that Potthoff's emphasis on the *subjective* pole of theological construction could have opened the door to a fuller examination of subjects such as Christology and Biblical inspiration, which may appear at first to be too tradition-bound to be included in philosophical theology.

Moreover, it is not as if Potthoff lived in a time when no one was yet aware of the latent intellectual hubris that lurks in the idea that one's own methods are adequately objective or unbiased. Reinhold Niebuhr never tired of pointing out that "neutral reason" is never really neutral;[48] Freud compellingly exposed our tendency to use reason to create rationalizations; and Whitehead himself noted trenchantly that "there is not a sentence which adequately states its own meaning."[49] Potthoff characteristically was well aware of the dangers of overstatement; but I am not convinced that he fully appreciated the ways in which the liberal method of relying on reason and experience tends to attach normative value to the ideas and experiences of white, middle-class, male intellectuals, while neglecting other modes of expression and experience. Potthoff did often say that, if it were possible, he would revise his writings to accommodate the use of inclusive language.[50] Like any good liberal, Potthoff never deliberately excluded persons on the basis of race, class, or gender. But neither did he deliberately *emphasize* or *elevate* the experiences of women or persons of color with the goal of compensating for the errors of the past. He appeared never fully to embrace "the epistemological privilege of the poor."[51] Ironically, to some degree, his liberal agenda of objectivity and impartiality ruled out the seeming favoritism of giving a preferential hearing to the voices of the oppressed or the disadvantaged.

These omissions and oversights may be unfortunate, but they are not fatal. Is Potthoff's theology limited by the conditions and assumptions of its own time? So were the ideas of Irenaeus, Aquinas, Calvin, Edwards, Barth, and Tillich. Each of these great thinkers could occasionally be provincial, short-sighted, and even narrow-minded; but when we encounter them at their best, we can only marvel at the ways in which they transcended the limitations of their own era. Considering the overall scope, originality, and applicability of Potthoff's theological work, it would be wise simply to correct problems where we can detect them while focusing our more concentrated efforts on gaining from his theological strong points. Those strong points are impressive.

1. In a day when most theologians offer us an unsatisfactory choice between noncommittal modes of intellectual analysis and recycled, predictable forms of confessionalism, Potthoff reminds us that we not only can but must embrace our own religious tradition without being insular or doctrinaire.

2. Potthoff's work refreshes our appreciation for what is most vital in the tradition of liberal Protestantism—an openness to novel and diverse points of view; a willingness to reformulate old ideas on the basis of new discoveries; an opposition to what is most oppressive, rigid, stultifying, and authoritarian in religious practice and belief; and the conviction that God is not a power over and above us but is instead revealed in our own best qualities and achievements.
3. As a Whiteheadian, Potthoff offers a functional-empirical alternative to the rational-conceptual-scholastic methods that prevail among the majority of process theologians.
4. Potthoff had a keen insight into the ways in which the subjective and the objective must be integrated into a unified religious vision. His God is both undeniably real and yet always claiming some level of personal interpretation and commitment. Potthoff's notion of a dipolar unity of subjectivity and objectivity mitigates the contentious claims to objective truth made by historic orthodoxies and frees contemporary believers to embrace metaphor and symbolism in their religious language. Potthoff offers a viable middle ground by taking into account both postmodernism's insight that none of us can transcend her or his own perspective, and the earlier modernist conviction that there are some facts of existence, culminating in an Ultimate Real Other, that we must *all* struggle to speak about and respond to.

5. Potthoff's concept of God as the "Wholeness Reality" offers us a way to think of God that is detailed enough to withstand intellectual scrutiny and yet humble and open enough to acknowledge the value of religious mystery. Potthoff takes us beyond conventional theological personalism in a day when personalism is increasingly being questioned by thoughtful laypersons. It is remarkable that Potthoff advanced an original, naturalistic alternative to personalism not from the standpoint of an unsympathetic academician safely ensconced in the walls of a university, but as a church leader who spoke both as a scholar and as a pastor, and as the most well-known representative of a denominational seminary.
6. Potthoff creatively integrated twentieth-century cosmology and process philosophy into a *pastoral* vision—a vision of moral responsibility and ethical motivation, a vision of redemption and renewal, a vision of grace, compassion, and hope. He never deviated from the conviction that theology exists first of all not as an academic field of study but as a tool of faith whose true purpose is to challenge, inform, and deepen the spiritual dimension of human life. In this conviction, Potthoff now appears to be a near anomaly. In today's academic milieu, it is difficult to avoid the impression that the main concern of most theologians is to gain the respect and recognition of other theologians. Potthoff's life and work remind us that theologians have a much higher and richer calling—to testify

> in accessible, compelling terms to the reality behind what Whitehead called "a vision of eternal greatness, incarnate in the passage of temporal fact."[52]

In all of this, Harvey Potthoff gives us not only an achievement to applaud, but an example to follow.

HHP photo in Iliff Archives

David Conner and Potthoff in earlier days taking a walk in Estes Park where David was serving a church.

NOTES

1 For scholarly reasons, Graf and Wellhausen included Joshua, the sixth book of the Hebrew scriptures, in their studies; thus the term "Hexateuch." Because the death of Moses is described at the end of the book of Deuteronomy, the "books of Moses" are commonly viewed as including only the first five books, that is, the "Pentateuch."

2 Since the earth spins on its axis and revolves in its orbit around the sun, it seemed obvious that the surface of the earth must be moving through the universal ether.

3 Irving Kaplan, *Nuclear Physics* (Reading, MA: Addison-Wesley Publishing Co., 1962), 113.

4 Augustine, *The Confessions of St. Augustine*, trans. John K. Ryan (Garden City, NY: Image Books, 1960), Book 11, chapters 11–16.

5 The philosopher Immanuel Kant (1724–1804) should be given great credit for recognizing, in his *Critique of Pure Reason*, that we have no objective means of analyzing the actual nature of space or time, for our impressions of space and time are preconditions of all our modes of understanding; that is, we have no means of looking at space or time "from the outside." Space and time are unavoidably part of the way we experience and think, and therefore we have no neutral standpoint from which to scrutinize them.

6 The Apostle Paul seems also to have absorbed some of the Platonic outlook when he exhorts us to "look not at what can be seen but at what cannot be seen; for what can be seen is temporary, but what cannot be seen is eternal" (2 Corinthians 4:18 NRSV).

7 The equations of relativity show that for radiant energy, time does not pass at all. From our perspective, light traveling to Earth from distant stars takes a finite amount of time, but from the "perspective" of the photons themselves, time does not pass. Neither perspective overrules the other; rather, both are accurate. This is one of the so-called paradoxes of relativity.

8 It is equally possible to arrive at this organic conception of the world if we start from the fundamental notions of modern physics, instead of ... from psychology and physiology. In fact by reason of my own studies in mathematics and mathematical physics, I did ... arrive at my convictions in this way." Alfred North Whitehead, *Science and the Modern World* (New York: The Macmillan Company, 1925), 219.

9 Alfred N. Whitehead, *Adventures of Ideas* (New York: The Macmillan Co., 1933), 356.

10 Lee Smolin, *The Trouble with Physics: The Rise of String Theory, the Fall of a Science, and What Comes Next* (Boston: Houghton Mifflin Company, 2007), especially Part II.

11 I am aware, and Whitehead was aware, that living organisms do not actually contradict the second law of thermodynamics, for they manage to obtain energy from their environment. My point here is rather that the concept of entropy in chemistry and physics does not necessarily require, as some theorists have suggested, that disorder and "heat death" are the eventual culmination of all physical processes.

12 Whitehead, *Adventures of Ideas*, 218.

13 "But the Hume-Newton situation is the primary presupposition for all modern philosophic thought. Any endeavour to go behind it is, in philosophic discussion, almost angrily rejected as unintelligible." Whitehead, *Modes of Thought* (New York: The Free Press, 1966; originally published in 1938), 135. More recently, instead of openly espousing materialism, many philosophers have claimed to reject metaphysics altogether, based on the contention that metaphysical philosophy is either methodologically unfeasible or, at any rate, obfuscating and pointless. However, many of these same philosophers continue to argue from premises that are at least implicitly antiholistic, on the basis of assumptions that are tacitly metaphysical.

14 The conceptual problem now under consideration is illustrated in the early work of the quantum physicists. For example, prior to the publication of Niels Bohr's first paper on quantum theory, Ernest Rutherford (1871–1937) wrote to Bohr: "There appears to me one grave problem in your hypotheses which I have no doubt you fully realize, namely, how does an electron decide what frequency it is going to vibrate at when it passes from one stationary state to another? It seems to me that you would have to assume that the electron knows beforehand where it is going to stop." From Robert Nadeau and Menas Kafatos, *The Non-Local Universe: The New Physics and Matters of the Mind* (New York: Oxford University Press, 1999), 33; emphasis added. The point is that the recurrent subatomic patterns that we human beings describe in terms of the Schrödinger equation must somehow be available in advance to electrons as they organize themselves in each atom, since it is very hard to imagine that these patterns are somehow created de novo by each electron from moment to moment. Whitehead's idea of God may be understood as an attempt to refer empirically to the consistent functionality by which such patterns of organization spontaneously emerge within nature.

15 Harvey H. Potthoff, *God and the Celebration of Life* (Chicago: Rand McNally & Company, 1969).

16 Henry Nelson Wieman, *The Source of Human Good* (Carbondale: Southern Illinois University Press, 1946). Wieman believed that "creative interchange" or "creative transformation" is the basic source of human growth and redemption; thus he equated creative interchange with God. Potthoff viewed Wieman's position as being too human-centered and critiqued it as an abstraction that arbitrarily emphasizes certain processes simply because they are of positive value to human beings.

17 Potthoff, *God and the Celebration of Life*, 185.

18 Ibid., 188, 190, 191-192.

19 Ibid., 192. Italics original.

20 Bernard Loomer, *The Size of God: The Theology of Bernard Loomer in Context*, ed. William Dean and Larry Axel (Macon, GA: Mercer University Press, 1987). Loomer drew heavily upon Whitehead's ideas but eventually proposed the pantheistic idea that "God should be identified with the totality of the world, with whatever unity the totality possesses," page 20.

21 Potthoff, *God and the Celebration of Life*, 193.

22 Potthoff taught a course on Schleiermacher's theology and often referred to him appreciatively.

23 Potthoff, *God and the Celebration of Life*, 191.

24 Ibid., 189.

25 Ibid., 190.

26 Potthoff, "The Reality of God," *Selected Papers of Harvey H. Potthoff*, 140. This paper was first delivered as an address to the Methodist Conference on Christian Education, Cincinnati, Ohio, Nov. 10, 1965, and published in *The Iliff Review*, Spring 1967.

27 Potthoff, *God and the Celebration of Life*, 99–107.

28 William James, one of the founders of pragmatism, associated truth not with a universally valid set of verbal propositions but with those beliefs that allow us to function most effectively in specific situations. James also allowed that a willingness to act on an idea is sometimes the criterion that allows that idea to become true. Thus the "will to believe" may be part of the creation of truth.

29 Potthoff, "Some Comments on the Doctrine of Forgiveness," *The Iliff Review*, Winter 1944; republished in *Selected Papers of Harvey H. Potthoff* (Denver: Criterion Press, 1981), 7–16.

30 Potthoff, Selected Articles, p. 9.

31 Ibid., 11.

32 Ibid., 12.

33 Ibid., 13. Cf. Exodus 3:5.

34 Ibid.

35 Alfred North Whitehead, *Process and Reality: An Essay in Cosmology*, Corrected Edition, eds. David Ray Griffin and Donald W. Sherburne (New York: The Free Press, 1978), 88.

36 James, *Essays in Radical Empiricism* (Mineola, NY: Dover Publications, 2003), 10.

37 Potthoff, "The Reality of God," *Selected Papers of Harvey H. Potthoff*, 139.

38 Potthoff, *God and the Celebration of Life*, 208.

39 Ibid., 254.

40 Ibid., 257.

41 Ibid., 263.

42 Ibid., 266.

43 Ibid., 269.

44 Ibid.

45 Ibid., 272.

46 Ibid., 272–273.

47 It is true that Potthoff includes two chapters in *God and the Celebration of Life* about the central importance of Jesus for Christianity. Nevertheless, my point at present is that he did not seek to explore the ramifications of his naturalistic philosophy for Christology, as he had done rather thoroughly pertaining to the doctrine of God. In my view, Whitehead's notion of God's immanence can be extremely suggestive for theologies of the Incarnation, and Whitehead's idea that God supplies an "initial aim" for every concrescing occasion might usefully be associated with more subtle interpretations of the "Moral Influence Theory" of the Atonement. I believe this association might have been made even while maintaining Potthoff's empirically oriented desire to avoid a Whiteheadian scholasticism and to minimize references to Whitehead's metaphysical neologisms. Instead of reinterpreting Christology in the light of naturalistic metaphysics, Potthoff offers a beautiful but brief description of the historical Jesus and concludes that the real question behind Christology reverts to questions about the nature of God. See *God and the Celebration of Life*, Chapters 9 and 10, and especially pages 139–141.

48 "The fact remains, nevertheless, that reason is not capable of defining any standard of justice that is universally valid or acceptable. ... The natural law of the eighteenth century was supposed to be descriptive rather than prescriptive. ... But its real significance lay in its specific content. The content of this law justified the bourgeois classes in their ideals, just as the older law justified the feudal aristocrats. In short, it is not possible to state a universally valid concept of justice from any particular sociological locus in history." Reinhold Niebuhr, "Christian Faith and Natural Law," *Theology*, February 1940; reprinted in *Love and Justice: Selections from the Shorter Writing of Reinhold Niebuhr*, ed. D. B. Robertson (Philadelphia: Westminster, 1957), 48–49. The point of Niebuhr's comments about definitions of justice would, I submit, obviously apply also to definitions of God.

49 Alfred N. Whitehead, "Immortality," the Ingersoll Lecture for 1941, in *The Philosophy of Alfred North Whitehead*, ed. Paul Arthur Schilpp (Evanston, IL: Northwestern University Press, 1941), 95.

50 Most of Potthoff's published work predates the general acceptance of inclusive language by the academy.

51 This phrase refers to the fact that persons who are oppressed or subjected to injustice quickly gain a perspective from which systemic inequities and disparities are much more obvious than they are to persons who are comfortable with the status quo. The phrase is useful but unfortunate in its use of the word *epistemology*. The point is that the poor have a more immediate and more accurate knowledge of injustice.

52 Whitehead, *Adventures of Ideas*, 41.

5
POTTHOFF AND PASTORAL THEOLOGY

By Richard L. Phillips

Both David Conner and I have noted that Potthoff did much thinking, speaking, and writing concerning the very comprehensive subject matter in this chapter. It is fair to say that he saw almost all topics related to religion and life in general as legitimate subject matter for inclusion in pastoral considerations. In his teaching about ministry in the church, for which the bulk of his students were preparing, he consistently placed pastoral concerns above the concerns of philosophical theology. At the same time, he never stopped his advocacy that in a church the pastoral role should always be paired with and include the minister serving as "theologian in residence."

Preaching was, for Potthoff, a key activity in the church setting, and he never failed to advocate that sermons should always bring theological issues into focus for the church members. In his early years of teaching at Iliff, he taught courses in preaching and pastoring skills, interests he held his whole life. He also saw education as a primary activity of the pastor and believed it should take place from the pulpit as well as in many other church settings.

Potthoff's concern, in his published and unpublished writings as well as in speeches and sermons, turned often to his long and solid efforts to see pastoral and church work in general as compatible with his process thought based empirical, naturalistic theology covered in Chapters 3 and 4. How could he advocate integrity and theological honesty if he believed otherwise? This list of pastoral concerns is long. Included are all the traditional and many not-so-traditional ones; it is not exhaustive nor in prioritized order. It is not possible to cover them all individually in this chapter.

Pastoral concerns that require sensitivity, insight, and skill:

-worship	-teaching	-doubt
-hope	-wellness	-education
-morale	-illness	-belonging
-forgiveness	-health	-despair
-social concern	-justice	-salvation
-aging	-wholeness	-loyalty
-diminishment	-recovery	-maturity
-dying/death	-value	-life style
-scripture	-morality	-soul
-prayer	-sharing	-loving
-music	-faith	-spiritual life
-mystery	-Jesus	-responsibility
-serenity	-Christology	-meaning
-quality of life	-study/learning	-churchship
-paying back	-loneliness	-sharing
-appreciation	-struggle	-helping ministries

-conversing	-social activity	-weddings
-visiting	-environmentalism	-funerals
-receiving/giving	-work	-church holidays
-reconciling	-play	-sexuality
-eating	-frustration	-secular holidays
-maturity	-limitations	-rewarding

Harvey wrote articles and books, preached sermons, left us notes, and gave major speeches and seminars on these and more such pastoral concerns. He often worked several of them into the same offering. Such is the case in all of his books—including *Loneliness: Understanding and Dealing with It; A Whole Person in a Whole World; God and the Celebration of Life; Acts: Then And Now;* and *A Theology for Christian Witnessing*, to name just a few. Appendix A documents some 919 sermons he preached. They are in his original typing with hand notations, and there is at least one on all major pastoral issues. He wrote many booklets and study guides for the church, and they are filled with pastoral themes. His speeches and papers contain the same, and many are noted later in this chapter. Again, all of these, including an amazing number of papers that are unpublished, are in the archives and are listed in the appendixes of this book.

There really was no human concern or condition that Potthoff did not see as a theological and a pastoral matter. Later are several examples of his dealing with pastoral concerns under specific headings. Harvey's exploration of pastoral topics is consistent from issue to issue. Once the reader is familiar with the goals he held for one important pastoral function, the carryover to other concerns is easily achieved. As a result, it is not necessary to deal with each of the concerns listed above. Doing so would be a book and not a chapter!

There is no question in my mind that Potthoff saw living the Christian faith within his "contemporary world view" more productive of a richer and more diverse spiritual life than the more traditional world view which he had known in childhood. He also realized that care must be taken to make clear *how* it can be just as religiously available. He did not make the judgment that his theological position should or must be accepted by all Christians. Harvey believed we must not miss the richness of the spiritual life of our neighbors who harbor a more traditional world view. John Wesley again as quoted by Potthoff: "If we cannot all think alike, may we not all love alike? Indeed we may." Wesley then added: "Is your heart as my heart? Then give me your hand."[1]

Worship

No survey of Potthoff's work can miss the great importance he placed on worship. For him, worship is the primary way we relate ourselves to the essence of our being, the indebtedness we have to others and to cosmic reality. The creative source of our very existence is what we try to feel, to appreciate, and to acknowledge in worship. It is along with other things a time of saying thanks for it all, to lift our spirits and our hearts in just such thanksgiving. To lift up the very values we treasure most—*that* is what worship is all about! Potthoff planned his own services so that every aspect of the worshipping experience spoke to and related us to the divine, to God. Worship should be a whole human response to God as the "Wholeness Making Reality," one of Potthoff's favorite terms for God, the very depth of his theology.

No part of worship is unimportant, be it the music, the

scripture readings, the prayers, the sermons, the congregational responses, or the passion from the pulpit. He did not hesitate to use the term *God* in worship, or in preaching, prayer, writing, or speaking—while at the same time fully realizing that there were those who would place on this term for the divine reality, different meaning and see it from a different world view. Potthoff lived comfortably with that realization. He saw beauty in all sincere and serious worship. He also found some weaknesses in many forms of worship and yet always believed there is great potential whenever people gather. Fulfillment of human potential realized through worship was one of his goals for any worship experience, indeed for a ministry of any kind.

Congregational singing was very important to Potthoff. He found in the great hymns of the church much important theology and pastoral wisdom, even when some more modern interpretation was needed, as when a supernaturalistic world view was evident. As an ardent appreciator of poetry since his college days, Harvey had little trouble understanding that good poetry (as many hymns are) can have great spiritual value for today.

The sacraments of the church hold a special place in worship and in the Christian tradition. Baptism, Communion, and Marriage are key developments of the early church, even though each of them was several centuries in the making before reaching a form from which the current practices are derived. Potthoff held that the celebration of life in what we call funerals and memorial services had such high importance that for him, they attain as much pastoral importance as the three cited above. In many of the more orthodox traditions, all four still have sacramental status, meaning sacred status.

Sacraments for Potthoff are some of the church's key symbols. "Human beings are so constituted that we find value in using symbols. ... A symbol is a tangible reminder of something great, which may be more or less intangible—yet real. ... [T]he communion service is a symbolic service calling to mind some saving truths of our faith.[2] In what follows, the reader should not miss the opportunity to compare the use of these symbols in Potthoff's theology with (where the reader has such personal memory) how they are developed in most of the more traditional Christian practices. For Harvey, it is important to see the divine at work in a variety of theological understandings. Potthoff has a clear purpose; he is here making a sermonic effort to overcome what for many has become a lack of perceived meaning in the sacraments.

First, Harvey observes that we come together and approach the "table" in a worshipful manner. As a community, we are all level at the foot of the table, a divine symbol related to our humanity be we different in race, gender, economic status, age, or education. In this way, we are expressing the spirit of Christ. As his followers, we are seeking to "carry his spirit into life ... to be one in him."[3]

"The bread is a symbol of strength—life-giving strength. As a sacred symbol we see it coming out of the earth itself ... the resources, natural and spiritual, for the maintenance of life."[4] Potthoff goes on to say that the symbolism relates to and speaks to our inner life of faith, which also sustains us. This part of the sacrament feeds our faith and hope and trust for what we face ahead, including being broken as we all are at times in each of our lives.

"The cup—in a material sense—is a very little thing. As a religious symbol—it says so much! ... It is a reminder of

Him who gave His very life on Calvary."[5] It is testimony, for Potthoff, of a life of service and sacrifice to a confused, hungry, bleeding, and often indifferent world. It speaks of the divine concern for the human spirit, for hope in life. It points us to the importance of not only Jesus's sacrifice but the sacrifices we are called upon as Christians to make in our own lives. It lends a divine perspective on blood, sweat, and tears as they are required of us. The chief Christian symbol, the cross, speaks to us of the importance and the centrality of sacrifice in the living out of our lives. Of course, each of the symbols—the table, the bread, the cup, and the cross—are dealt with in more detail in this sermon and in his other writings.

The whole of the communion service reminds us that "we are the debtors ... to the ... men and women before us for the blessings you and I enjoy today."[6] For Potthoff, the service is a devotion, a love, and a gift in which we are uplifted and healed. In this sermon, he has drawn many more meanings from the symbols than I have here explored. He finishes the sermon affirming that the truths communicated through symbolism are "as deep as life itself" and that they can as such be real to us.

For Potthoff, worship should be anything but routine. Worship is the key event in a Christian's spiritual life. For Harvey, it should be the power drink of the week. It should enrich, inspire, re-create, educate, and activate! In his senior years, he expressed, in our personal conversations, some real disappointment in the trends he saw in diminished attention to worship on the part of many clergy. His guideline for his students was that each week between sixteen and eighteen hours should be devoted to sermon and worship planning. In addition, he advocated planning well ahead to meet one's congregation at the points of their needs, interests, and problems. Months ahead is not too early for planning, but at the same time, leave room in any sermon planning for real-life unexpected events that demand to be addressed from the pulpit from a Christian perspective.

Worship is always, even if only two or three are gathered, a matter of relationships. "Christian faith assures us that life finds its deepest meanings through relationships—with the good earth, with other persons, with significant causes, and most profoundly, with God."[7] Worship should always have such a comprehensive makeup. Above and beyond all else, worship should point to God. Theologian Paul Tillich often envisioned God as the "ground of being." Harvey liked that but always thought there was a little more that needed to be said about God. He liked the Pauline phrase in thinking about God, "in whom we live and move and have our being." It is a favorite Potthoff biblical quote in many of his writings. For him, it adds the realization that God is an active and current participant within and with us and all of nature. He understood humans as co-creators with God and believed it made worship that much more meaningful. It also makes human activity that much more important in the scheme of all reality. Like it or not, we are all "playing God" in what we do with our own lives and interactions with others!

In bringing this section toward a close, I turn to a 1991 address Potthoff delivered in North Carolina to the Highlands Institute. The institute is engaged in writing and research about current theological thinking as it impacts life.[8]

The title of the address is "Empirical Theology and the Vision of Hope." Here I quote Potthoff on the role of worship as it impacts morale and hope (more from this address in the next section of this chapter).

Where there is reverential living and dying—there is worship and there is meaning. Experience has much to reveal about a world in which worship is appropriate. Worship is:

> Where there is a sense of wonder—mystery—awe
> Where one would be silent in the presence
> of unspeakable majesty
> Where there is a sense of "sanctity in
> existence and reverence for life"
> Where there is felt kinship with all that
> partakes of being
> Where there is a vision of "an eternal
> greatness incarnate in the passage
> of temporal fact" ... an eternal greatness
> which lures and calls
> Where there is the inner persuasion that
> human life is not so much a possession as a
> gift—a trust—to be passed on.[9]

Potthoff closes the address with this quote from Miguel de Unamuno: "Sow yourselves, sow the living part of Yourselves in the furrows of life."[10]

Worship for Harvey was a form of both sowing of self and a response to what is of great value to us and to the totality of what we each have received. He truly revered worship and did so within many forms.

Spirituality

Worship is certainly not the only place where one finds or practices spiritual awareness and feeling. The spiritual life can and should be found in one's life and faith in other contexts as well. From Harvey's point of view, it can and does happen in many settings and through many types of activity. Potthoff became very concerned in his advanced years with the fact that so many Christians, especially the young, especially those with family church backgrounds, were finding and advocating that spirituality is best found outside of the church. He and I shared as much conversation time about this as any other issue. He was not pleased with what was happening. Especially troublesome were the "spiritual but not religious" trends so much in the news and in popular and even scholarly books.

For Harvey the current scene did not provide real quality or depth, and had little aesthetic value or appreciation of the experience of the mystical; it was a very weak spirituality in his view. As was his style, in trying to deal with his frustration, he wanted to go back to a basic definition of "What is spirituality?" He observed over and over, if we cannot find a solid definition, then it just might be that anything and everything would qualify! The shallow, the frivolous, the one-minute attention spans to which we seemed, to him, to be rapidly drifting toward were going to be very difficult, not only for religious practices but for the social and political aspects of our lives as well.

Harvey saw the church as the vessel of the Christian faith. It had been, and for him it should be, the principle vehicle for the spiritual life. Crystals, pierced jewelry, spastic dancing, drugs, and even just plain feeling good were not going to fill the spiritual need of humans as far as he was concerned. Where can the church go with this? He never found an answer he liked. He passed from the scene with no resolution to his frustration about current trends in spiritual resources and practices. Through our conversations, I came increasingly to understand the churchman mind-set and church loyalty at the very base of his being. I think his basic concern was that the church just might be losing the battle to be relevant in people's lives! Relevance and meaning were criteria for effective theology, for pastoring, and for being the church. He spent his life on a pilgrimage to be sure the church was just that. Success for Harvey's hope is far from certain.

One resource for what was happening not only to spirituality but in much of Christian practice was the great philosopher and psychologist Harry A. Overstreet. Harvey preserved the June 1953 issue of the journal *Pastoral Psychology*, with an article by Overstreet, "The Foundations of Our Spiritual Life."[11] Its appearance came at the very time Potthoff was early in his full-time Iliff career and working hard on the details of his theology. It is not possible to be sure, but it does appear that he not only appreciated and used Overstreet's observations but also used much of his terminology in matters of current perceptions of religion in society, especially regarding the issue of religious maturity, including spirituality. He obviously used and underlined the content of the article. The issue also has a paper on loneliness (another important pastoral concern) by Ina May Greer, which Potthoff took very seriously.

Overstreet's article expresses how he summed up the tenor of the times: "The feeling of 'I don't know' has bitten deeply into the life of today. In some cases it has led to an outright denial of all that once, as religion, had seemed true and dependable; in others, to a troubled questioning of old religious assumptions; in still others, to vigorous efforts to rethink the whole scheme of things."[12] Harvey's position exactly! They were together in solid membership within the "rethinking" effort.

Overstreet's observations on maturity seem to have had great influence on Potthoff. Overstreet again, this time quoting theologian-psychologist L. J. Sherrill: "[A] person's religion is inevitably on the same level of maturity as his personality."[13] Here he affirms that an immaturity in religious matters has become increasingly widespread. He observes that Erich Fromm, a favorite of Potthoff's, sees the persistence of authoritarian-seeking tendencies to be instrumental in immature approaches to religion. For Fromm, they go hand in hand.[14] Fromm goes on to say that we should be doing just the opposite; that is, we should be inviting "individuals to grow beyond the child's sheer dependence upon a Power, obeyed but not understood, into intelligent and affectionate co-operation with the greater Life that is the source of our being."[15] Here Overstreet cited another of Potthoff's favorite sources, Gordon Allport with this brief quotation: "We [must] begin increasingly to realize that much of what has hitherto been called religion has been little more than immature and undisciplined wishing ... such that man's religion could remain, egocentric, magical, wish-fulfilling, and [with] no questions asked."[16]

Potthoff's positioning in theology, pastoral work, and certainly in spirituality may have been well developed before the 1953 Overstreet article cited above. They may have been developed at the same time, but they certainly reflect the same desire for religion to take on a much more mature mantle in the second half of the twentieth century than what was happening in midcentury. Potthoff and Overstreet are also kindred spirits in the persons they select as great resources!

Practices in spirituality can and must be based on maturity—all matters of religion should always be, Potthoff advocated. What would he have to say now, over a dozen years after our visits on the matter? Harvey firmly believed the key source of spirituality needs to come, for Christians, from the churches and the ministries therein. Of course, as stated elsewhere, Mother Nature is also a legitimate and wonderful source of spiritual experience; after all, God is the whole making reality! For Harvey, growing from immaturity to maturity, one must increasingly see and experience the wholeness of our personal makeup as well as the cosmic makeup. I close this section with Potthoff's own words.

> *My image of Christian spirituality (informed by scripture, tradition, experience and reason) is best defined within a holistic model. The God of Christian faith, I believe, is a God present to and in the world of our experience making for wholeness. With Father Goldbrunner I believe that "Holiness is wholeness." The Christian goal is a wholeness centering in spirit.*[17]

Hope and Morale

In Christian theology, the understanding of hope as a foundational issue in the religious life was and is widely acknowledged. This was true for Potthoff just as it was in the Middle Ages for the Roman Catholic scholastic scholars such as Anselm and Aquinas. Obviously Potthoff saw hope issues in a "this worldly" context and did not accept hope as forever and only related to a supernatural world view. In more traditional theology, the ultimate hope was of course seen as otherworldly salvation. As with all issues of pastoral concern and theology in general, Harvey saw hope just as well served through process, naturalistic thinking. His thinking on immortality (traditionally an important element in Christian hope) comes later in this chapter. For Potthoff, hope in all of life, both religious and secular, is of great importance and as such is a theme repeated by him over and over. (He wrote several papers on hope, which can be found in Appendix B.)

Potthoff finds hope and morale to be essentially the same thing and deals with them as such. There is no morale (life spirit, purpose, appreciation) where there is no hope, and vice versa. In other words, if our hope is gone, we have no basis for morale. Morale of course has to do with values and any sense of purpose to be found in a day or a lifetime. When a sense of value is missing in life, hope dies. He wrote and lectured widely on topics associated with the two terms.

An unpublished, undated paper by Potthoff entitled "The Future: Is Hope Possible?" is located in the archives.[18] There are hints that it is lecture content from the mid-1970s. Most of this paper is made up of brief quotations from well-known persons with very little commentary by Harvey. A few of the familiar names are: Erik Erikson, W. F. Lynch, J. L. Adams, Erich Fromm, Bertrand Russell, John Gardner, Kenneth Boulding, Nikolai Berdyaev, Carl Sandburg, Rene Dubos, Margaret Mead, Albert Camus, Alex Pope, Dag Hammarskjold, Norman Cousins, Gibson Winter, Martin Luther King Jr., Reinhold Niebuhr, Julian Huxley, Loren Eiseley, Pierre T. de Chardin, Gardner Murphy, Gordon Allport, Viktor Frankl, William James, William E. Hocking, Arnold Toynbee, A. N. Whitehead, L. H. DeWolf, Rudolf Bultmann, Philip Phenix, Douglas C. MacIntosh, Jurgen Moltmann, B. F. Skinner, and Maurice Strong, as well as the Psalms and, of course, himself. I mention the names here because they represent persons whose contributions help us better see into the inner who of Harvey. The paper is a valuable read!

Here is an example from this paper, a quotation from Harvey: "The difference between hoping and despairing is the difference between inner life and inner death of the spirit. The hoping person exhibits a readiness for the next step, a movement toward what might be but is not yet. He exhibits the quality of wakefulness. Whereas the person of despair lives with a sense of being trapped, the person of hope feels that somehow there is a way out and that there is the potentiality for meaning in his situation."[19]

A second example, this time from Norman Cousins: "The capacity for hope is the most significant fact in life. ... What we don't have, but can regain, is confidence in ourselves, in our history, and in the ultimate power of ideas."[20]

A final example from Viktor Frankl: "A human being is not one thing among others; things determine each other, but man is ultimately self-determining. What he becomes—within the limits of endowment and environment—he has made out of himself. In the concentration camps, for example, in this living laboratory and on this testing ground, we watched and witnessed some of our comrades behave like swine while others behaved like saints. Man has both potentialities within himself; which one is actualized depends on decisions but not on conditions."[21]

In dealing with hope and all other pastoral concerns, Potthoff always pushes us toward a holistic view of reality—that is, not to consider issues from a theological (or any other) perspective alone but to get a broader perspective. Here is a very good example.

> Science can tell us much about the universe in which we live and move and have our being. It can tell

> us much about the human creature. But science has little to say about many matters of 'ultimate concern'—matters having to do with values, right and wrong, meaning. There are dimensions of human experience about which we need input and insights of other disciplines: ethics (to speak of morality); aesthetics (to speak of the experience of beauty); theology (to speak of the experience of the holy). The human being is a creature who hopes. But if our hopes are to be more than wishful thinking, we need a wisdom which is more than knowledge, a wisdom which flows from the whole of human experience.[22]

Indeed Harvey wanted to see things in a larger context, and sadly he did find much "wishful thinking" as well as selfishness in so many religious expressions. Potthoff was always a stick-to-reality type person.

In Potthoff's address to the Highlands Institute, "Empirical Theology and the Vision of Hope," given relatively late in his life, he said, "Nature affords morale-enhancing resources. We look to empirical theology to discern such resources, to interpret them, and sometimes to suggest ways of appropriating those resources."[23] Potthoff did not think the discovery was always easy, but to be a good pastor, it was essential.

In times where the broader perspective of nature, beyond the human, was called for, Potthoff often turned to the poets. He quotes the poet Thomas Hardy on this point; "Let me enjoy the earth not less: Because the all-embracing might: That fashioned forth the loveliness: Had other aims than my delight."[24] A broader perspective for Harvey involved seeing that "re-interpreting situations in the light of a larger scheme makes considerable sense."

In a naturalistic theology, precious hope and spirited morale are real possibilities. Nature itself has its own built-in therapy. In the next section, we will see that the expectation of forgiveness is seen as possible on the same basis. For example, the same natural forces that sometimes make us ill are the forces that in turn make for healing and wellness. The underlying nature of reality is in this way of thinking our best friend. William James said, "All is not vanity in the universe, whatever the appearances may suggest." Potthoff in this context reflects on Kass who, as Harvey expresses it, argues "if life is to be taken seriously, is to be saved from boredom and tedium, is to have meaning—then look to this life and look to nature."[25]

A year or so ago, I attended the funeral of the grandmother of my step-nephew. She died at an advanced age, and there were few there. One member of her family in paying tribute to her quoted from one of her poems that resulted from the rather rich existence she had led in her long and art-filled life. "There is absolutely no reason to ever be bored. Everything, absolutely everything is interesting!" That approach to "everything" is at the heart of Potthoff's theology of pastoring. Religiously put, everything has a sacred stamp upon it. The human soul runs deep!

"What, then, are the factors or processes involved in the coming of hope?" Potthoff responds to his question with the following:

> I would suggest that where there are creative processes whereby possibilities are realized, chaos

> gives way to a measure of order, brokenness issues in a measure of wholeness, tragedy issues in a measure of meaning, destructive contacts give way to creative community—there is a basis for hope. To discern and to relate to the processes of creative synthesis or creative organization and re-organization is to move toward creative hope.[26]

In summary of the issue of hope in Christian pastoral work contained in the Highlands "address," Potthoff has this to say: "Hope is perhaps the primary fruit of functioning religion. Realistic hope is the fruit of mature religion. On this assumption we may say that the word 'God' in its religious meaning refers to the source or ground of hope."[27] Fanciful and unrealistic hope is a sign of immature religion for Harvey, and he wished to eliminate such characteristics from any quest in one's practices wherever he could. If he was on any lifelong campaign, it was to foster *mature* religion.

Harvey does not tell us what to believe, just as he does not tell us how to do pastoring. What he does tell us is to understand the world, the sanctity of the person, the situation, and the limits of our own skills. Appropriate techniques in dealing with the pastor's role in hope-related issues are never random. They are prescribed by our deeply held God concept. We must discover and know both our God concept and our self. From these understandings, ministry develops. It is never just handed over by some teacher/mentor, even though a good foundation may be taught. Whoever claimed ministry was to be easy? Not Potthoff!

Forgiveness

Forgiveness must be possible in both everyday life and in religious life if naturalistic theology can be accessible for pastoral purposes. With this in mind throughout his writings on hope and other pastoral issues, Potthoff has built a solid case for a theology of forgiveness and the practice of a forgiveness-focused ministry. Like the issue of hope, forgiveness is a key, if not the key, issue in the entire history of the Christian faith. After all, the story of traditional Christian salvation is a story of God's forgiveness.

We all make mistakes, some make very serious mistakes, and thus, in process-based theology just as in traditional theology, we all stand in need of forgiveness. Few of us would deny the importance of forgiveness between human beings because of our shortcomings and what are often called sins toward one another. Many books have been written, many sermons preached on the importance of forgiveness in our human relationships. The benefit of genuine forgiveness extended to aggrieved (real or imagined) persons in marriage, play, work, family affairs, community life, etc., is that it is one of life's great healing therapies. Sometimes the therapy takes effect immediately, sometimes it develops only slowly. Therapy has, as in all healing, both short- and long-term success. Forgiveness is for Potthoff a very real and very important part of salvation. How so? The root meaning of our word *salvation* (salvus) is "healing." Indeed the understanding of traditional, more orthodox concepts of salvation has to do with the healing that needs or must take place between God and God's "fallen,"—"made in the image of God"—children. Just as in traditional Christianity, so also in any naturalistic

Christian understanding forgiveness must be realistically and spiritually available.

For Potthoff, the key to forgiveness is to be found in the nature of nature itself. The world, the cosmos has a kind of built-in forgiveness within it. When nature repairs the damage and recovers from destructive forces such as earthquakes or floods (and other things seen as bad, if not evil, from a human perspective), such eventual natural recovery can be understood as "forgiveness" (even when reality is altered) from a broader-than-human perspective. From this we can assume the same dynamic is true of our species and that after forgiveness, there is the realization that a person also may be altered, hopefully in positive ways.

Potthoff would not for a moment say that nature's built-in "healing" and "forgiveness" are going to be very comforting to people who have suffered devastating illness or loss of a child or companion, including of course loss of hope/morale or when in serious need of forgiveness. What he does believe is that a perspective broader than the human perspective on values can help humans deal with what for us are life's, and nature's, devastating experiences. He believes we have in nature the basis for working out understandings and practices that serve well in times of great need and can help us rebuild our lives, even if never back to quite the same as before, but nevertheless to a state of relative wholeness.

As early as 1944, Potthoff had developed a very comprehensive treatment of the doctrine of forgiveness, which is still helpful today. He writes: "The immortality of influence looms large among the significant facts [events] ... more than one individual is handicapped by results flowing from yesterday's irrevocable record."[28] We cannot, he says, pretend the harmful deed was never done; we cannot erase it and should not even try. What we can do and can help to happen is to grow beyond into a new future. Forgiveness is the key provider of this hope. And the beginning of forgiveness is a two-step process: First, to recognize the deed in question calls for self confession and then to find a way to ask the aggrieved for forgiveness (even if the aggrieved is self) and then to receive some measure of forgiveness. Implicit here is the self-understanding of who the self at its most fundamental reality really is. Potthoff is fond of noting that arriving at this point in one's awareness involves, indeed demands, some understanding of what the human is—of having a solid doctrine of *man*. Potthoff wished he had been alerted much earlier to the use of more gender-neutral language, which he tried to use in his later writings.

In the 1944 article, Potthoff says three understandings are the building blocks of a naturalistic doctrine of forgiveness. First, the steady dependability of nature. Second, the fact that nature is also dynamic, that tomorrow is different than today, ever changing, and that the change itself gives hope for forgivenesses large and small. The third aspect of nature is "creation and growth." When these factors enter our lives, we know that it is possible that we can become, *will* become new persons, and that the "real heart of forgiveness" is at hand.[29]

The article concludes with eleven comments, each a paragraph in length, designed to guide the church and pastoral processes with the hope of establishing the fruits of forgiveness in individuals' lives. Discovering the value of the human soul is basic. The power of pastoral work lies here, and a quote by Potthoff from the great minister Phillips Brooks ends the article: "The power is the value of the human soul, felt by the preacher and inspiring all his work."

This brief review of Potthoff's eleven ways the church and pastoral technique can be ready to deal effectively with issues of forgiveness will end this section.

1. Be sure the church is geared up to deal with difficult forgiveness matters.
2. Tie the doctrine of God with a fully compatible doctrine of forgiveness.
3. Treat forgiveness realistically, not on the surface only, and treat persons seeking help very seriously.
4. Always be sincere.
5. Try to move persons away from a theology that holds to the concept of "unforgivable sin."
6. Take your time, keep person focused on the point—too much talk may indicate other kinds of problems.
7. Move persons away from thinking they can "pay back" and thus get over the problem/guilt, etc.
8. Help the individual find something to be gained or learned (even theologically) from the error/questionable action.
9. In sermons and other settings, use ideas and phrases that may be lightbulb experiences for the individual in question but are not addressed directly to the person.
10. It is not sufficient to simply say that forgiveness is possible.
11. Respect and appreciate the inner person with whom you are dealing.[30]

Potthoff does not consider these eleven items exhaustive, only a set of suggestions for beginning to deal with matters of forgiveness. They do illustrate the depth of his pastoral concerns and his belief in the church's ability to minister effectively in this area.

Aging, Death, and Dying

Locating this pastoral topic here reflects Potthoff's career-long emphasis on these life span realities shared by all humans. Sermons, articles, book chapters, workshops, and college courses were developed concerning all these topics within any setting he thought potentially fruitful. He saw ministry here as central not only for the aging persons who tend to be more and more concerned with these issues, but for all human concerns at any age. It was, for him, a way of working the depth of theology and theological understandings into some of life's key realities. He often started his approach to the topic with the observation that we are aging from the very moment of birth, indeed even before birth. Harvey habitually begins dealing with topics of almost any kind with a statement of the obvious, his way of getting the reader/listener thinking about the matter at hand, a kind of warm-up, if you will.

This is a good place for one of Harvey's favorite quips. He often started a speech on such matters with the observation that there was much to say on this (any) topic and he felt "like the Egyptian mummy who was pressed for time!" He paused here because for many audiences, there was need for some take-up time.

In 1996 Iliff published some study guides under the banner *Reflect—A Series of Faculty Reflections on Contemporary Issues*. One of them, "Good Aging: A Christian Perspective," is written by emeritus faculty member Potthoff and records some of his latest thinking on the topic.[31] It had been a career-long concern; as early as his 1930s and 1940s pastorate at Christ Methodist Church in Denver, he had started preaching sermons on this topic.

Perhaps his most extensive treatment of the several issues involved was developed at Nebraska Wesleyan University late in his working life. He developed a very popular undergraduate course, which he taught several times (see Chapter 11). Lecture notes from a 1989(?) class at NWU titled "In a World Where Death Is a Fact," partly typed and partly in his handwriting, develops his ideas and contains quotes from other theologians and many different scholars on the topic of aging and death.[32] It is evident that he took pains to spell out the issues for undergraduate students even more carefully than his similar content did for graduate seminarians and members of the clergy.

A quick summary of the content is of value both from the standpoint of exploring his treatment of the topics involved and for revealing even more about Potthoff himself. As was his scholarly approach to all theological topics and concerns, Harvey used a holistic framework. He quoted Matthew Arnold's sonnet tribute to a friend "whose even-balanced soul; From first youth tested up to extreme old age; Business could not make dull; Nor passion wild; Who saw life steadily and saw it whole."[33] Potthoff used the quote often in other contexts, and I reflect upon it because it was also the life Harvey himself exemplified and pursued with steady intentionality. It also exemplifies his habitual treatment of the most serious of issues with emotionally based content (often quoting poetry) as well as his penchant for the give-me-the-facts philosophical approach.

Potthoff saw death as the definer of life. If there were not death, there would be no life as we know it. He also used Douglas Steer's idea of death as the illuminator of life. Harvey, as he did with all serious topics theological or otherwise, pushed the student to pursue a broadly based awareness of the knowledge of our own mortality, the mortality of those who are nearest and dearest to us, the mortality of those who make up the communities that have meaning for us, the mortality of all living beings. If we deal with death realistically as natural to our species, we must see it as personally real and as therefore basic to any working out of a philosophy of life. To fail to do so is death-denying posturing that is both unrealistic and immature. For example, it often leads to making no provisions for one's dying, which in turn creates major problems for the survivors.

Pastorally, for self, clergy, and others, individual persons can be helped to deal with the reality of death through a variety of ministries. These ministries identified by Potthoff, among others, are: the ministry of memory; the ministry of presence (most clergy know this as a most basic pastoral must); the ministry of friendship and family; the ministry of beauty; the ministry of one's own inner strength; the ministry of dignity in adversity; the ministry of hope; the ministry of fresh self-recommitment to life; the ministry of the awareness of wonder, preciousness, and trust; and the ministry of meaningful living. About this last one, he quotes Robert Butler, former director of the National Institute of Aging: "What we fear most is not really death but a meaningless and absurd life."[34] Potthoff himself observes that being forced to face the fact of death in turn "forces us to face the question, what gives life meaning?" It is never too early for an undergraduate college student to pursue a course of living that will yield a meaningful life. For Harvey, this is the key to developing meaningful aging and meaningfully facing death. For him, meaning in life does not just fall together as we live; it is something at which we each must intentionally work if we are to be mature humans and have mature religion, two of his emphases in his extensive and diverse ministry.

It deserves brief mention here that Potthoff uses much content in this lecture from the scientists who deal with the natural phenomenon of the death of all that partakes in being. Harvey's own thinking is based on death as natural and rejects the idea that death is the result of sin committed ages ago. He uses much biblical content that assumes that death is natural. Death as a punitive invasion by God into reality he attributes to errors of biblical content written and understood from a prescientific world view. Affirmation of his position on such matters is, as is so characteristic of Harvey, done in a gentle way and often includes the use of both poetry and humor. Potthoff believes that all death is a proper basis for sorrow and grief, but this is most especially true of early tragic death that robs the sharing of life for both the person who has died and those who survive.

The understanding of aging is critical in the adjustment to life's many ups and downs as well as the approach of the end of life. In "Good Aging: A Christian Perspective," Potthoff weighs in on some major twentieth-century interpreters of the Christian faith. He names Albert Schweitzer, Karl Barth, and Dietrich Bonhoeffer as examples of those who see ethics as the main underlying basis for living as Christians. David Conner relates that Potthoff rejected the nineteenth-century notion that Christianity is merely ethics expressed in poetical or metaphysical trappings. With William Bernhardt, Potthoff did not believe religion could be reduced to ethics. The word and concept of love is the underlying heart of each interpretation. Schweitzer especially was a soul mate for Potthoff. From Schweitzer, Harvey quotes, "The essential element in

Christianity, as preached by Jesus, is ... that it is only through love that we can attain communion with God." Schweitzer was not talking about love of God or one's understanding of God; he was talking about the love he called the "reverence for life." When asked why he went to Lambarene, he replied, "I wanted my life to be my argument." Earlier, another soul mate, John Wesley, spoke similarly in his theological concept and goal of "being perfected in love."

Potthoff holds that good aging and good dying result from good living; good living results from living a full, rich, whole love-filled life, lived to the full measure of what is possible given one's circumstances. Death can then be embraced as a friend, not as an enemy! Of course, Harvey didn't believe in being eager for death, except in certain very specific circumstances. For him, there is good in the Dylan Thomas poem, "Do not Go Gentle into that Good Night." And he not did go gently but was very grateful for several medical interventions that restored a measure of health to his life.

So, in conclusion, what about what is next—any afterlife? In many places, Potthoff takes the position expressed in the phrase, "We just don't know." We have no empirical evidence at all that there is a conscious afterlife. We know about the hope of the ages for a conscious afterlife; it has been there for many and is the case for many today. I have not discovered any absolute denial of such an afterlife or any specific affirmation thereof in his writings. In place of that, Potthoff does often speak of immortalities of many kinds and that the certainties of many of them must be enough for us, given what we cannot with certainty know what other ways we might survive death's certain blow. For him, life's deeds are in themselves immortal. Life's less-tangible accomplishments are as well.

Having biological successors, while not the fortune of all, is certainly a very real kind of immortality. For the writer, the artist, the speaker, the teacher, the administrator, the friend, the custodian, and indeed the enemy—in these we also find the building blocks of immortality. There is life-affirming spiritual value in such immortalities as well as the meaning found by many in an otherworldly afterlife.

Potthoff quotes a poem by Robert Browning Hamilton:

I walked a mile with Pleasure
She chattered all the way,
But left me none the wiser
For all she had to say.

I walked a mile with Sorrow
And ne'er a word said she,
But oh, the things I learned from her
When Sorrow walked with me.[35]

Potthoff's approach to the subject of immortality is solid in both scholarship and in the use of biblical material and his wonderful world of poetry. His 1941 doctoral dissertation bears the title: "The Doctrine of Immortality in the Philosophies of Edgar Sheffield Brightman and Alfred North Whitehead." His copy of the document is in the archives with many hand inserted notations.[36]

Prayer

Potthoff was not given to confrontational approaches on any subject. Even so, a colleague of both Harvey's and this

HHP photo in Iliff Archives

Pastor Potthoff at podium in an updated photo

writer's recently related Harvey's reaction to a prayer that had been delivered by a minister whose service of worship he had just attended. At the door, Potthoff is reported to have asked, "Who or what did you think you were addressing in that awful prayer?!"

Potthoff believed in prayer and believed that any prayer should be intellectually and spiritually honest from the prayer's theological perspectives. Additionally, Harvey wanted to place limits on prayer content, personal or public. One should never pray for personal gain or special treatment from the divine. One should especially never utter a prayer that implies or asks for anything that would damage or harm another person or persons or even nations. One might offer prayers of thanks for one's personal skills, such as strength and agility, the intellectual ability for a level of mental function, and perhaps gratitude for the blessings of situations in which one finds oneself. If one does not hold to a personal, supernatural God theologically, then one should not pray as if God is a person who can reach in from someplace beyond nature to the natural world and change the gearing of reality. One might well pray that one's strength and wisdom be sufficient to deal adequately with reality, including tragic situations. Prayers themselves, especially public prayers, are often put into metaphorical forms and are to be understood by looking for the relevant meaning(s), even if they are not always so interpreted by all listeners.

Prayers from church tradition—and there are many great ones—can with care, given one's specific context, be used in both worship and pastoral work. Prayers should always be a fit within the overall context, be they silent or public. As an example, in an address to an audience of mixed clergy in Denver, Potthoff prays an ancient prayer: *O God, keep our hearts sound, our lives pure, our thinking straight, and our spirits humble—that we may be true interpreters of thy life to our fellow men.*[37]

A broader perspective on prayer typical of Potthoff is that, in a world where the sacred is everywhere and God is considered the creative agent of all reality, we are at prayer all the time. How we live is a prayer, how we react in relationships of all types is a form of prayer, even what we think is a prayer. In Judaism, by tradition there are 1,000 ways we pray. One of my favorites is that we are at prayer in study; that is, studying. One's conjugal relationship with one's spouse, even that is a very precious form of prayer—it certainly had to be for Abraham!

Some prayers are indeed timeless. Harvey used at the end of many services this benediction: "*May the peace of God, which passes all human understanding, That peace which the world can neither give nor take away, Dwell in your hearts this day and ever more.*"[38]

Early in his career, he closed a Communion service with this prayer: "*Grant, Our Father, that these truths—as deep as life itself—*

shall be real to us. ... We pray, seeking more of the spirit of Christ." Of course, the truths he is talking about are the table, the bread, the cup of communion, and the cross (see pages 145, 146).

Another Potthoff benediction prayer example: *We thank thee, our Father, for all those persons who have made, and who are making, this world a better place—by their presence in it. Grant us the privilege of so living, that we may enter the fellowship of those whose influence lives to bless. And so, direct us in all our doings, by thy most gracious favor, and further us with thy continual help—that in all our works, begun, continued and ended in thee—we may glorify thy holy name. Amen.*[39]

My own experience with Potthoff's benedictions has been that he always focused on the benediction as a blessing, which is indeed the meaning of the term benediction. It is not just a closing touch to a service or event.

One more example of a Potthoff benediction. His format, in a poetic meter, was a common way for Harvey to write his prayers.

AS WE GO FORTH FROM THIS PLACE OF WORSHIP
INTO THE WORLD OF WORK AND HUMAN
RELATIONSHIPS AND
RESPONSIBILITIES OF MANY KINDS ...

MAKE US MINDFUL THAT THIS IS INDEED THY WORLD

Thou art our dwelling place.....
There are resources adequate for our needs.....
And there are tasks which await our caring
and our service....

May we be responsive to the beauty about us.....
the wonder of life.....

And as we make our way through the days of this week
may something of the grace of our Lord Jesus Christ be
manifest in us. Amen.[40]

Loneliness

The emphases Potthoff placed on the issues associated with the subject of loneliness are among the most important of Harvey's pastoral contributions to both the theory and the practice of being a pastor-teacher. His major book on the topic, *Loneliness: Understanding and Dealing with It,* was, without doubt, one of the most used and praised of all of his writings. It was published in 1976 and went through three printings due to its many uses and popularity. It was popular as a personal help book, as an adult study book in a great many churches, and as a text in educational settings. He received many letters from readers from all parts of the United States and some from international locations, thanking him for the benefits they received from reading it.

He started dealing with the subject in sermons and in educational efforts at his first full-time parish at Christ Methodist Church in the 1930s and 1940s, and much later in his interim pastoral duties at University Park UMC in Denver in 1994–1995, his final pastoral assignment in the Conference. (To be sure, retirement did not stop any of his pastoral activities; only his health the last weeks, and his death on February 21, 2002, could end that approach to life.)

Potthoff's articles in *The Iliff Review* on loneliness are

preserved in the archives. Also in the archives is a commercial printing done by Christ Methodist Church of an eight-page paper "Understanding Loneliness," delivered by Potthoff on a Sunday evening in 1955.[41] This became the base of his expansion of the topic in articles and the book on loneliness.

Potthoff conducted seminars and workshops on the topic in a wide range of Methodist circles, including conferences, schools, and churches and in other contexts, both secular and religious, as well. One result was that it increased his popularity as a guest preacher on this and many other theological and pastoral topics. By the time he retired from Iliff and went to Nebraska Wesleyan University in 1981, he saw himself as not only interested in the topic but as something of an authority on the topic. In preparation for going to Nebraska, he experienced a new level of awareness about loneliness.

In the autobiographical section of his June 1991 address to the Highlands Institute, he records this experience.

> Several weeks before I left Denver for Lincoln a social psychologist at the University of Denver, who has done considerable research on the experience of loneliness, informed me that his studies indicated that the most acute loneliness is experienced, not necessarily in the late years of life, but in adolescence, and often in the first year of college. He said, "You are going to be meeting a lot of lonely people." [42]
>
> Taking him at his word I re-read Erik Erikson on the identity crisis. Early in my stay at Wesleyan I offered a course entitled "Loneliness And The Search For Meaning." ... I supposed 10 or a dozen students might sign up for such a course offering and also for a class

on "Aging, Dying And Death In Religious Perspective"
... but 102 did.

Thus, early at NWU, Potthoff became a very popular professor! We all experience loneliness in life, often even when we are with other people and when we are busy with daily and professional tasks. It can be mild in nature or severe, even debilitating. The focus of his writing and teaching about the topic was not on any specific population or circumstance in life, but focused on a reality that in some very important ways extends to all of us. By including meaning in life as a companion topic, which he saw that it was, he dealt with two major pastoral issues together.

The issue is closely tied with one's self-perception and increases Harvey's conviction that "know thyself" is the very heart of overall awareness of life and life's issues. Each of us has a need to feel good about ourselves, and there are ways we can achieve that both through self-help and pastoral assistance. It ties in closely with death and dying, discussed earlier in this chapter. To live well is to age well, meaning in life is a product of living a full, whole life; To deal effectively with loneliness is to see one's life in its wholeness and not just in terms of the inevitable ups and downs of daily and week-by-week living. Potthoff believed that loneliness can lead to depression and even suicide, and in such extreme cases pastoral help is not enough. Getting professional medical help could become a must and that should not be seen negatively. Feeling lonely should not be a cause for guilt and certainly not panic, but at the same time, it is important to have a conversation with oneself and ask, "What should I be doing about my feelings of being alone?"

A great deal could be added here about Potthoff's awareness, concern, teaching and writing about loneliness. Little more needs to be said here, in part because his work is so available to interested persons. My purpose is to document the very serious depth with which he dealt with the reality of loneliness. His remedy in a word is "intentionality." Actively find those things in life that have meaning, that make sense, and bring some joy to you; then engage, pursue, attend to, and get involved in such things on a regular and, in at least some cases, a deeper-than-surface level. Attending the symphony as an experiment can lead to new interests, new meaning. Hiking; going to the theater, public events, or lectures; traveling; meeting new people; getting involved with things that "touch who I am"; and a host of other avenues—even something as simple as going to dinner with friends—are open to us all. We must *decide* to get with it! Loneliness often leads to escape behavior. Avoid that!

Potthoff as a Pastoral Being

Throughout this biography, there is much content about the pastoral effectiveness that characterized Potthoff in a variety of contexts. This chapter closes with a look at Potthoff as what so many who knew him saw as a supreme example of a pastoral presence, a pastoral being. It is my judgment that Harvey's success as a pastor is due to a combination of at least three factors.

The first is that serving as a pastor, counselor, and mentor were built in to his true nature. Potthoff was a natural! It surely helped that coming from a family with clergy members made for a pastoral contextual reality from his earliest days.

Second is that Harvey had over the years many excellent pastor role models who motivated him in that direction. Such tributes and admiration as he heaps on mentors William Bernhardt, Lindsay Longacre, and A. N. Whitehead, and widely known clergy such as Phillips Brooks and Harry E. Fosdick, set a proper example for his own pastoral work. Medically related professionals like Erick Fromm, Jim Galvin, and Potthoff's own brother provided other valuable models. World-renowned figures such as Albert Schweitzer and colleagues of many years like Charles Milligan and so many other of his peers at Iliff were dear to him. He celebrated their accomplishments and their part in his life. At the end of his career at Nebraska Wesleyan University, there were many examples added to his experience. Harvey did not suffer for lack of footsteps worthy of following, and he often expressed thanks for them in his writings, through conversations, and with invitations to dine. In his tribute to Whitehead (see Chapter 1), written on his last day of classes with the legend, he expressed the desire to be like Whitehead in some very important personal and professional ways.

Third is what I call Potthoff's penchant for intentionality. He planned his life carefully in areas of his professional life and his personal life. Intellectually he experienced and came to believe deeply in the importance of pastoral effectiveness, availability, and commitment, all very early in his working life. Believing in the critical importance of being able to be a pastor to people in life's large and small troubles, he consciously and constantly committed and recommitted himself to excellence in this dimension of ministry. His commitment is verified by the fact that he hated to turn down an invitation to preach or speak if he thought he could contribute something he saw as important. He did "not think of himself more highly than he ought to think" but at the same time he knew when he had something of value to offer. The fact that he experienced considerable success as a pastor could only have added strength to his commitment to function in so many of those roles.

And why was there considerable success? Harvey's personality was a very winsome one. Persons with and without significant problems were drawn to him. To visit, to dine, to exercise, to travel, and perhaps most of all to visit about important and relevant issues were always present whenever in contact with our Dr. Potthoff! Additionally, Harvey dug deep to uncover the inner person. As he so often asked people, "What makes you tick? What is it that is important to you?"

I now relate a personal need for Potthoff as a pastor. While a very young clergyman, I confronted a situation that could have done damage to my reputation and ultimately my status in the Rocky Mountain Conference of the United Methodist Church. One day on my way home from the Denver church I was serving as an associate pastor, I came upon the wife of my clergy colleague. Their parsonage, adjacent to the church, had a fenced-in lawn. She was crying and in great distress. Confronted with the need to engage in a pastoral role, I explored the situation, and it was obvious I needed to take action. I consulted (over a three-day time span) with her family physician (a member of the church) and my wife, Ethel. Then the three of us in two vehicles removed her and her children from a potentially dangerous situation and spirited them off to a safe haven.

Following that, I returned to my role with the church and the clergy colleague (who did not know for many days what had happened, other than receiving a note from his wife that she was "gone" and would soon be in touch). Later, with no additional involvement from me, a permanent resolution (divorce) was reached. It was a messy situation, with several weighty aspects to it. The physician's involvement was a great help and done with a genuine depth of knowledge and empathy. At the end of that church year, both my clergy colleague and I made a career shift.

Early in this pastoral action, I recognized the kind of rumors that were possible given the critical church-related nature of the situation. I needed awareness and some trusted backup to guard against what might develop and potentially harm me personally and perhaps my career. Within the local church, I knew that the physician involved was a backup of unquestioned merit. Then I scheduled a meeting with Harvey, told him the whole story, and asked for his help in being sure key members of our denomination knew the facts of the case. His pastoral ear was at its best! Near the end of our time, I asked him who in the local and administrative church structure should know the whole story. Potthoff, with his vast and intimate knowledge of related church matters, suggested that I talk specifically and in person with two of the key members of our church's connectional system and to let them know that he could be called about the matter.

I followed his advice completely and have been very grateful for it. Other than discussing the matter with personal friends who came to know about the situation, I have never heard anything or had any negative results whatsoever, now about a dozen years into my retirement! So, yes, I knew Harvey as my pastor as well as teacher, mentor, and friend.

Harvey was a pastor to his barber Elmer Wells, to a good many waiters in the area eateries, to his colleagues, to his students, to bishops, to death row prisoners, and to hundreds and hundreds more. As pastor, his skills and reputation are equal to that of his teaching, preaching, lecturing, parenting, and social involvement. In fact, there are many, many who love him for his pastoring skills but who know nothing of his theology, as well as those who know of it but do not share it.

As this biographical research and writing were under way, I communicated with a 91-year-old woman whose family came to love Potthoff's work as minister of Christ Methodist Church so many years ago. I am sure her feelings are similar to so many of the laywomen and men who have come to know and deeply appreciate him through his pastoral work—and often, I am sure, are only minimally aware of the theological base for his work. That might even be true of some of his former students! Again, when it came to being a pastor, he was a natural!

Harvey's involvement and support of youth and student ministries were well known. In his eighties, he wrote a paper titled "The Theological Assumptions We Bring to Campus Ministry."[43] He had always been popular as a guest speaker on campuses and took special interest in his students, former and current, who had gone into campus ministry. He firmly believed youth and campus pastoral attention were the foundations of the church's future, especially because of their potential to bring people into church ministry. Campus ministers were especially successful with invitations for Potthoff to come as a special guest on campus. He believed that an ongoing pastoral presence with youth and college students was in every way foundational to an ongoing church.

In addition to his position that youth are the future of the church, he saw they are in need of being recipients of good pastoral attention from qualified clergy. This is, unfortunately in my thinking, not the position many clergy take toward campus and youth ministry. It is so often seen as an unwise financial burden for the churches and as an escape from real ministry on the part of such ministerial practitioners. Potthoff did not agree! He supported such ministry with his presence and his pocketbook! These two ways of support are in all contexts very solid evidence of genuine interest and pastoral concern. I know this from long experience both with Harvey and my service on college campuses! Rather than see youth as immature consumers of time and money, he saw them as he saw all humans: filled with potential. Where there is human potential, there is hope and thus the need for a pastoral function.

Former students and colleagues have sent reflections concerning Potthoff for this book. They are placed elsewhere (see Chapters 13 and 14), and many of them add testimony to Potthoff's pastoral skills.

NOTES

1 From notes on Wesley, Iliff Archives, box 6, file folder 8.

2 October 7, 1945 sermon, "The Table, the Bread, and the Cup," Iliff Archives, box 17, file folder 16.

3 Ibid.

4 Ibid.

5 Ibid.

6 Ibid.

7 Harvey Potthoff, *A Whole Person in a Whole World* (Nashville, TN: Tidings, 1972) 19. Also Iliff Archives, box 2, file folder 4.

8 "Empirical Theology and the Vision of Hope," 1991 address, Iliff Archives, box 6, file folder 9. (The Highlands Institute was re-named the Institute for American Religious and Philosophical Thought in June 2012. The Highlands Institute is used as the name of the Institute throughout this work.)

9 Ibid., 30,31.

10 Ibid., 32.

11 Iliff Archives, box 2, file folder 4.

12 Harry Overstreet, "The Foundations of Our Spiritual Life," *Pastoral Psychology* (June 1953), 39; found in the, Iliff Archives, box 2, file folder 4.

13 Ibid., 40.

14 Ibid., 40.

15 Ibid., 40.

16 Ibid., 40.

17 Potthoff, "A Christian Spirituality of the Whole Person," circa 1975, Iliff Archives, box 4, file folder 13.

18 Potthoff, "The Future: Is Hope Possible?," Iliff Archives, box 31A, file folder 26.

19 Ibid., 3,4.

20 Ibid., 5.

21 Ibid., 9.

22 Course lecture, "The Image of the Human Being: Scientific and Theological Perspectives,", Iliff Archives, box 7, file folder 9, page 12.

23 "Empirical Theology and the Vision of Hope," Iliff Archives, 1991 address, box 6, file folder 9.

24 Ibid., 23.

25 Ibid, 22.

26 One-page item probably used by Potthoff in a lecture, Iliff Archives, box 31A, file folder 26.

27 "Empirical Theology and the Vision of Hope," 1991 address, Iliff Archives, box 6, file folder 9.

28 Potthoff, "Some Comments on the Doctrine of Forgiveness," *The Iliff Review* (Winter 1944), 22; *Selected Papers of Harvey H. Potthoff*, Iliff Archives, box 2, file folder 7.

[29] Ibid.

[30] Ibid.

[31] Potthoff, "Good Aging: A Christian Perspective," Reflect –A Series of Faculty Reflections on Contemporary Issues, Iliff Archives, box 2, file folder 4.

[32] NWU course lecture "In a World Where Death Is a Fact," Iliff Archives, box 6, file folder 9.

[33] Ibid.

[34] Ibid., 8.

[35] Reflect–A Series of Faculty Reflections on Contemporary Issues, Iliff Archives, box 2 file folder 4.

[36] 1941 doctoral dissertation, Iliff Archives, box 1, file A.

[37] "The Minister Looks At His Own Spiritual Life," Iliff Archives, box 18, file folder 22.

[38] 1996 sermon "Reflections of Sixty Years in Ministry," Iliff Archives, box 19, file folder 26.

[39] 1956 sermon "The Immortality We Cannot Escape," Iliff Archives, box 18, file folder 22.

[40] 1984 sermon "The Experience of Being a Worldly Christian," Iliff Archives, box 18, file folder 25.

[41] "Understanding Loneliness" printed by Rhea Lithographing & Envelope Co., Denver, Iliff Archives, box 1, file folder A.

[42] Highlands Institute address, Iliff Archives, box 6, file folder 7, page 8.

[43] Potthoff, "The Theological Assumptions We Bring to Campus Ministry," Iliff Archives, box 6, file folder 9.

6
ON THE WORLD STAGE

By J. Richard Peck

The Reverend Dr. Harvey Potthoff (HHP) not only helped shape the theology of hundreds of students preparing for ministry in several denominations, he also helped shape the theological stance of the United Methodist Church and helped establish the structures of the denomination following the 1968 merger of the Methodist Church with the Evangelical United Brethren Church.

Eight-time Delegate to General Conference

HHP was elected an astonishing eight times as a delegate to General Conference, the top legislative body of the denomination. Every four years, when clergy members of the Rocky Mountain Conference cast their ballots for delegates to the quadrennial gathering, Harvey Potthoff's name was on the top of most ballots. The first elected clergy member usually chaired the delegation, and from 1952 to 1976, he served as chairman of the Rocky Mountain delegation.

"One of the paradoxes of my life came when I was the first clergyperson elected to the 1980 General Conference," said Bishop Calvin McConnell. "It was the first time Harvey was not the first clergyperson elected."

McConnell said it was difficult to take Harvey's place because of all he had done for the Western Jurisdiction and the denomination. "He was as gracious as he always had been," said the bishop. "He told me, 'I know you'll do a good job.'"

General Conference begins its work by breaking into legislative committees. In those committees, members consider hundreds of petitions sent in from individuals, local churches, annual conferences, boards, and agencies. Chairpersons of those ten to fourteen committees must organize subcommittees and processes to handle hundreds and sometimes thousands of suggested changes in the *United Methodist Discipline*, the book of laws, and the *Book of Resolutions*, which records the church's stance on current social justice issues.

HHP served as chairman of a legislative committee during two General Conference sessions, and had to deal with complex and frequently controversial proposals and people with opposing viewpoints.

During the 1972 General Conference, HHP also served as chairman of the Fraternal Delegates Committee, and he introduced representatives from other faith communities to the legislative body.

The Rev. George Beazley, chair of the Consultation on Church Union, told delegates to the 1972 assembly about the "overwhelming hospitality" he received from HHP.

Potthoff personal photo in Iliff Archives

Potthoff at the microphone at a session of a General Conference of the Methodist Church

HHP was a two-time delegate to the World Methodist Council. He attended a session in London in 1966 and a session in his hometown of Denver in 1971. He was also a delegate to the 1968 World Council of Churches meeting in Uppsala, Sweden.

The Board of Education

The former Methodist Church and the United Methodist Church created a Curriculum Resources Committee to guide authors of curriculum materials and to approve specific materials. HHP served as a member of that committee from 1958 to 1972, and he chaired the section that approved all adult materials.

He also served on the Methodist Board of Education from 1960 to 1968, and he continued on the board for another four years following the 1968 merger with the Evangelical United Brethren Church. During that time, he served as president of the Methodist Conference on Christian Education, from 1963 to 1965.

He also served on the Education Legislative Committee during the 1970 General Conference, and he helped the group understand the role of the Board of Education.

It was a crucial time for the board as it established a guide for curriculum writers in the newly formed denomination. HHP played a key role in developing the 1964 *Design for Methodist Curriculum*. That design reminded curriculum writers that the Good News of Jesus Christ "comes alive and is seen by the learner as relevant only when he sees the gospel in connection with his persistent life-long concerns."

In 1965 HHP was asked to comment on the new curriculum design at the 1965 Methodist Conference on Christian Education, meeting in Cincinnati, Ohio. He was assigned the topic "The Reality of God—The Meaning and Experience of God's Continuing Revelation."

"Let us note at the outset that the gospel is defined not simply as an intellectual proposition or the affirmation of a static, transcendent Being, or as the memory of something that happened in the past or simply as the promise of something in the distant future," said HHP. "It is the good news of God's whole continuous creative and redemptive action."

HHP noted the failures of early liberals, and he spoke of neo-orthodox avoidance of problems raised by natural theology.

"And now," he said, "we are feeling the sometimes stinging criticisms of analytical philosophers who keep insisting that much of theological discourse just doesn't hold up in the light of the canons of logic."

Time for New Theological Spadework

"This is probably not the time for a major theological synthesis," HHP further stated at the 1965 conference. "It is a time for theological spadework in a new setting. We have evaded the challenge of new understandings and world views too long on the pretense that this really is not important for theology."

HHP started the theological digging by asking curriculum writers to speak of the reality of God from both the "cosmological and the existential poles."

In looking at God from the cosmological pole, HHP said, "God is not to be identified with everything that is, but God does sustain a relation of immanence to all things. ... It is God in whom we live and move and have our being."

In looking at God from the existential pole, HHP noted, "Man is not only an observer of an order of things; he is a participant in it. ... Theology needs to keep coming back to the data of first-hand religious experience."

HHP told the Christian educators that they were not only responsible for talking about God, they were to create settings in which "visions may be kindled [and], revelation may be experienced."

Revelation for HHP is not something that happens *to* someone, it is something that happens *in* someone: "The lights come on; there is disclosure; there is illumination involving new self-understanding and commitment."

He encouraged teachers to provide settings in which people are encouraged to ask ultimate questions in ways that are real to them. He wanted students to understand that God is continuously active, and it is the responsibility of teachers to help students discern where and how God is present.

Finally, HHP suggested that it was not a good time to talk about God in the usual way. "But it is a good time to be there in Christian integrity, in direct service to those in need, in Christian social action, in conversation with the world."

Author of Curriculum Materials

HHP not only established a theological base for curriculum writers, he also wrote many books used by adult Sunday school classes across the nation.

In 1969 he penned *The Inner Life* and *The Christian in Today's World*, two units in the *Foundations Studies in Christian Faith* series. In *The Inner Life*, class participants were asked "to experience God in the depths of one's inner life, in the fellowship of other persons of faith, and in the world of action."

William Northcutt, an Atlanta attorney and chair of the Education Commission at First United Methodist Church in College Park, reviewed all the study books of the curriculum series. "This letter is written to express appreciation for *The Inner Life*, the seventh in the New Day Series," Northcutt wrote in a June 1969 letter. "I consider *The Inner Life* the best."

"It has only been in the past six months that I have truly understood what the passages of the Bible have meant, and understanding myself has been my biggest problem," wrote Nancy Harman of Wauwatosa, Wisconsin, in a May 1970 letter. "Your book has been such a help and I do feel you deserve a word of thanks from someone who is trying very hard to understand."

"I am a better person for having spent the last three months with you," wrote James Paris, a Sunday school teacher in Piedmont, Alabama, after teaching The Inner Life to a young adult class.

Surprisingly, HHP took the time to respond to each appreciative letter, writing full explanations in response to simple questions.

Alice Propst, a teacher of a class of adult women in Fayette, Alabama, asked what was meant by "a life of continuing rebirths."

"I was trying to express an idea which has been part of Methodist thinking since the time of John Wesley," responded HHP. "[Wesley] spoke of 'the new birth' as 'a change from the love of the creature to the love of the creator; from earthly and sensual to heavenly and holy affections.' He spoke of a new creation in which through the power of God 'hatred, envy and malice' are replaced by 'a sincere, tender love for all mankind.' However, Wesley also thought of the life of the Christian as a 'growth in grace.' One does not fully arrive in the Christian life in what is sometimes called the new birth. Wesley wrote of 'a gradual sanctification, a growing in grace, a daily advance in the knowledge and love of God,' which normally continues through most of the earthy life of the believer. ... When I wrote of continuing rebirths I had in mind that the Christian life is a life of growth in grace and love."

I doubt Alice Propst anticipated receiving such a full explanation from the busy author.

A Complaint

Sherman Gibson, an attorney in Kansas City, wrote an angry letter to Bishop McFerrin Stowe, complaining about HHP's book, *The Christian in Today's World.*

"You can file this in your 'letters from aroused laymen' file," began Gibson, who was teaching a class based on the book. "[HHP's] primary message comes through loud and clear, to wit: 'The only way the church can become relevant in today's world is to go social action.'"

The attorney noted that HHP wrote that the followers of Jesus thought the world was flat and they were affected by a flawed world view. "Now, Bishop, it has finally filtered through to us middle-western Christians that some changes need to be made in the church. ... A glowing social challenge coupled to an abstract God offers me only an excuse to spend my church allocated time on politics or any place where I can evade this obvious sellout of the church of John Wesley."

The bishop referred the complaint to Horace Weaver, executive editor of adult publications at the Division of Curriculum Resources.

"If I understand your major gripe, you are fearful that the United Methodist Church may take action in the areas of human relationships—public housing, unemployment, population explosion, taxes, etc.," wrote Weaver. "If that is your conclusion then we must admit that there is some truth in what you say. We are concerned that the mission of Jesus Christ toward those who are hungry, naked, imprisoned and poor should have some effect on us who go by his name 'Christian'."

"I think there is no point in my commenting on Mr. Gibson's letter," HHP told Weaver. "We certainly write for a diversified audience."

Theological Study Commission

The 1968 conference that united the Methodist Church with the Evangelical United Brethren Church named HHP to the "Creedal Study Commission." That commission was later renamed the "Theological Study Commission on Doctrine and Doctrinal Standards."

Delegates to the Uniting Conference authorized the group to "study Part II of the Plan of Union and other pertinent references in the *Discipline* and in the history of doctrine in the Methodist and Evangelical United Brethren Churches and to bring to the next General Conference a progress report concerning doctrine and doctrinal standards in the United Methodist Church."

The 24-member commission elected as chair Dr. Albert Outler, noted Wesleyan scholar at Perkins School of Theology. Other notables on the commission included Dr. Harold DeWolf and Dr. J. Robert Nelson of Boston University School of Theology, and Dr. John Cobb, professor of Theology at Claremont School of Theology.

"Harvey was one of the avowed theological liberals on the commission," said Dr. Robert Thornburg, secretary of the commission and former chaplain at Boston University. "In discussion of theological methodology Harvey and John Cobb argued that the quadrilateral must begin with experience."

In an email to me, Cobb wrote, "My belief is that all of us begin with our experience. Reason orders and clarifies that experience and contributes to its enrichment and development. This kind of reflection leads us to see how profoundly our experience is shaped by our tradition. As we reflect about our tradition, we see that it points to the Bible as its authoritative source."

Outler and Nelson argued that theology must begin with scripture.

Peacemaker

"Harvey frequently played the role of peacemaker between participants, and he was extremely polite," said Thornburg. "I didn't agree with him on much, but I very much admired his civility and the way in which he always tried to move the process forward rather than getting us caught in a doctrinal backwash."

Noting the dominating role of Outler, Thornburg said, "Harvey always urged patience, and he was more polite than Albert deserved."

In an interim report to the 1970 special session, Outler introduced Potthoff and other members of the commission who were delegates to the General Conference. In that report, Outler thanked Iliff for hosting two of their four sessions, and the commission called for the addition of no fewer than three and no more than five bishops to be added to the commission. The Council on Youth Ministry also called for the same number of young people. Both motions were approved.

After agreeing to include John Wesley's Articles of Religion in the *Discipline*, delegates asked the commission to send a letter to the Vatican noting that seven of the articles have anti–Roman Catholic references, but the denomination offers "goodwill and Christian brotherhood to all our Roman Catholic brethren in the avowed hope of the day when all bitter memories (ours and theirs) will have been redeemed by the gift of the fullness of Christian unity."

Thornburg recalled a session right before the 1972 General Conference when the commission was to give its final report. "(Bishop) Bill Cannon wanted to scrap the entire section three dealing with theological method," said Thornburg.

"Albert and I walked the streets of Kansas City that night, thinking all our work was going down the tubes. However, the following morning Bill came back and apologized for his actions."

In the unusual step of voting by written ballot, 925 of the 946 delegates to the 1972 General Conference supported the new doctrinal statement.

Author of Anthology of Affirmations

After accepting the statement prepared by the Theological Study Commission, delegates to the 1972 General Conference, meeting in Atlanta, established a twelve-member group of scholars to produce what Dr. Outler described as "an anthology of appropriate doctrinal affirmations of various sorts and from various sources old and new that may be deemed consistent with Doctrinal Standards of the United Methodist Church."[1] Outler said the study would provide "stimulus and guidance for theological study and cooperative worship throughout the church."[2]

The committee agreed that the anthology would be divided into three sections: Section I would deal with major historical and ecumenical developments to illuminate Methodist understandings. Section II would deal with central affirmations and the distinctive emphases of United Methodists. Section III would deal with guides for formal and informal celebrations and encourage readers to develop their own affirmations of faith.

Bishop Cannon was named editor of the entire anthology. Bishop Wayne Clymer was named chairman of Section II, and HHP was asked to be the principal writer of that section.

HHP divided Section II into three parts.

Part 1 showed how the gospel becomes real to individuals when it is confirmed in their experiences. HHP affirmed Outler's description of John Wesley's technique of arriving at truth through Scripture, tradition, reason, and experience. HHP also quoted from Wesley's sermon, "The Catholic Spirit," in which the founder of Methodism noted that the Christian faith could be expressed in various languages, doctrines, affirmations of faith, hymns, forms of worship, and various forms of service and witness.

In Part 2, HHP noted affirmations from the United Methodist tradition, including:

Wesley's *Sermons and Notes*
Articles of Religion
Doctrinal Statements in Official Courses of Study
The Social Creed of 1908
The Korean Creed
Edwin Lewis's affirmation of faith in the *Book of Worship*
The Evangelical *Articles*
United Brethren *Confessions*
The Evangelical United Brethren *Confession of Faith*
Foundations of Christian Teaching in United Methodist Churches
Part II of the *1972 Discipline*: Doctrine and Doctrinal Statements

Part 3 of the anthology discussed ways in which theologizing must continue in the future. HHP called for the use of scripture, tradition, experience, and reason in the effort to deal with contemporary issues within a Christian framework.

Upon reading HHP's manuscript, Bishop Clymer, said "I think it is an excellent statement and I have very little in the way of critical suggestions. ... I feel confident that your manuscript will be well received."

The bishop was correct. The manuscript was not only well received, it became part of the authorized United Methodist curriculum for study in all United Methodist churches.

Honored for Service

In 1995 the General Board of Higher Education and Ministry honored HHP with the Francis Asbury Award for fostering United Methodist ministries in higher education. The award was named for Asbury, who, in 1791, challenged all Methodists to "give the key of knowledge in a general way to your children, and those of the poor in the vicinity of your small towns and villages."

James Noseworthy, director of annual conference relations for the Nashville-based board, wrote to HHP: "In 1937, you began teaching at Iliff School of Theology while serving as pastor of Christ Methodist Church in Denver, becoming a full-time professor in 1952. After 44 years of personal and scholarly ministry to individuals preparing for ordination, you became professor of Christian theology emeritus. In 1982, at an age when most persons retire, you accepted the position of Mattingly Distinguished Visiting Professor at Nebraska Wesleyan University. Your anticipated one-year appointment grew into 11 years of service to the university and to the students.

"Your more than 58-year teaching ministry is matched by your skills as a distinguished scholar and church leader. You are the author of eight books, more than 25 scholarly articles and over 35 different church school curriculum materials. ... I congratulate you and express our sincere appreciation to you for your ministry."

Candidate for the Episcopacy

HHP was not only elected a delegate to eight General Conferences, he was nominated as Rocky Mountain Conference's "favorite son" candidate for the episcopacy at the 1964 Western Jurisdictional Conferences in Portland, Oregon.

Dr. R. Marvin Stuart of Palo Alto, California, took the lead on the first ballot with 64 votes and held the lead through the next three votes. HHP held on to second place with 41 votes. Ninety-four votes were needed to elect.

"We tried to get HHP elected, but neither he nor Marvin Stuart could get the number of votes needed," said the Rev. Taylor McConnell, who was serving as program director for Rocky Mountain Conference at the time. "I then visited with the delegates of the Washington Conference, and we agreed both conference delegations would support Marvin," so HHP withdrew. Stuart was elected on the next ballot, and he was appointed to the Denver area.

In 1968 there were no vacancies in the Western Jurisdiction, but most people thought HHP would be elected bishop at the 1972 assembly in Seattle.

In a 1971 letter to members of Rocky Mountain Annual Conference, the Rev. Ben H. Christner, a pastor in Greeley, Colorado, called on annual conference members to name HHP as a nominee for the episcopacy.

"While serving in the conference, he has led in the causes

of development, growth and services of our institutions," wrote Christner. "He has assisted in the training of our men and women as ministers of the churches, teachers in our colleges, and in other special service of our church; he has labored in the ecumenical and social uplift programs interdenominationally in the city of Denver and this region."

Christner also noted that HHP had preached in conference churches, led youth camps, served as chair of legislative committees at General Conference, and served as a member of the Adult Publications Division.

"With all this and more, he has remained your friend and my friend and as kind, helpful, and approachable as when we first saw his smiling face and shining countenance," he concluded.

Following Rocky Mountain Conference action supporting HHP for the episcopacy at the July 1972 Western Jurisdictional Conference, Dr. Jameson Jones, president of Iliff School of Theology, wrote a letter to HHP. Jones expressed appreciation for HHP's presence on the Iliff faculty and concern about finding a replacement if he were elected.

"There is no way that you can be replaced on the faculty of Iliff," wrote Jones. "I shudder over the prospect of trying to replace you because I know how far short we would fall."

Responding to Jones one week before the July Jurisdictional Conference, HHP celebrated his twenty years as a full-time faculty member at Iliff and encouraged Jones to "do nothing that would assist in the process toward election and nothing to hinder the process. That, in essence, is in line with the stance I have tried to take in the difficult process of assessing personal feelings and trying to be open to the call or calls of the church."

On the first ballot at Jurisdictional Conference, HHP led with 46 votes; followed by the Rev. Jack Tuell, pastor of First United Methodist Church in Vancouver, Washington, with 43 votes; and Richard Cain, a faculty member of Claremont School of Theology, with 34 votes. Melvin Wheatley, a pastor in the California-Pacific Conference, had 26 votes, and Wilbur W. Choy, chaplain of the California Senate, came in twelfth with 12 votes. A total of 92 of the 138 ballots were required for election. On the sixth ballot, HHP's total increased to 58 votes, but Wheatley's total increased to a leading 62 votes.

As balloting continued, HHP was always near the top, but after Tuell and Wheatley were elected, it appeared there would be no one from an ethnic minority named to the episcopacy in the jurisdiction.

At that point, HHP and Cain discussed the situation and decided they should withdraw in order to support the election of Choy. HHP drafted a withdrawal speech.

"As our Jurisdictional Conference has moved on this week, it has become increasingly clear that we are struggling to find our way into the new day and the new future which is coming to us," said HHP. "A part of that new day and new future involves recognition of our common humanity and our oneness in Christ. We need in new ways to be a united church."

Speaking for both Cain and himself, HHP said, "It is evident that the mind of this conference has been moving toward recognition of the need for a more truly representative episcopacy. We affirm that movement and that need."

Cain and HHP withdrew their names from further consideration, and Choy was elected.

HHP was never elected to the episcopacy, a blessing to all Iliff students who attended the seminary after 1972.

Jurisdictional Committee on the Episcopacy

HHP served as member of the Western Jurisdiction Committee on the Episcopacy from 1952 to 1970.

Composed of one lay delegate and one clergy delegate from each annual conference in the jurisdiction, the committee does most of its work during Jurisdictional Conference by appointing bishops to their episcopal areas.

These appointments are critical to the success of both the annual conferences and the bishops. Bishops are not allowed to serve in their own annual conference in their first quadrennium.

In the process of making the appointments, the committee consults with each bishop and conference leaders to determine the best matches. During the quadrennium, the committee also reviews and evaluates the work of the bishops, passes judgment on their character, and reports findings to the jurisdictional conference.

Caught in a Buzz Saw

For the most part, the work of the jurisdictional committee is without controversy.

That changed in 1968 when the *Los Angeles Times* announced that 60-year-old Bishop Gerald Kennedy had appointed himself as pastor of First Methodist Church of Pasadena. The newspaper noted that Kennedy would continue to head the Southern California-Arizona Annual Conference with 800 clergy and nearly 300,000 members.

"It is believed to be the first time in the 230-year history of the denomination that an active bishop has assumed full pastoral leadership of a local congregation while remaining as bishop," wrote Dan Thrapp, the *Times* religion editor.

Thrapp reported that Kennedy would preach three Sundays a month at the 2,676-member church, reserving the other Sunday for appearances in one of the other 500 churches of the conference. "I will not be a part-time pastor, nor will I become a part-time bishop," Kennedy told Thrapp. "Maybe I'm crazy," Kennedy joked. "But they asked me and I accepted."

Four years earlier, *Time* magazine had named Kennedy "among the four or five most dazzling preachers in the United States today." *Time* described his pulpit language as "unchurchy, larded with wit and timely references to the secular world around him. Yet his message is always related more to eternal truths than to the morning's headlines."

"I never quite adjusted myself to being without a congregation," said the bishop.

The September 13 church newsletter announced that Kennedy would become senior pastor and would move into the church's parsonage. That announcement led to a nationwide firestorm with HHP, who was now serving as chairman of the Western Jurisdictional Committee on the Episcopacy, at the center.

"I'm not so concerned about breaking precedent as I am about what this action by Bishop Kennedy may be saying about the episcopacy," said Rev. Gene Albertson, a superintendent in the Oregon Annual Conference. "There is some question about such a change in the duties of the episcopal office coming about without proper study and action by the General Conference. What does the action say about the appointive system when a bishop 'accepts' the 'invitation' of a local church to be its senior minister?" Albertson urged HHP to take action opposing this dual appointment.

Rev. Tuell, a member of HHP's committee, said Kennedy's action "raises some rather grave issues which our committee needs to face."

Tuell (who was later elected bishop) noted that the *Discipline* does not provide for such an appointment since the bishop is not a conference member (bishops become members of the Council of Bishops following their election). He also said the action contradicts the "appointive philosophy" of the church. "The whole import of this article is that the church issued him a unanimous call, and he accepted it. If he can do it, can everybody else do it?"

Tuell also observed that cabinets have been pretty hard on ministers who take on extra jobs to earn extra income. "Does this apply to bishops as well?" he asked.

The Rev. Randall C. Phillips, pastor of the 2,000-member Wilshire United Methodist Church in Los Angeles, penned an editorial criticizing Kennedy's decision. "It is a time we need a bishop full time in the field, moving into as many churches as possible to keep morale high," he wrote. "I feel Bishop Kennedy's action creates more unrest in a ministry already concerned with how appointments are made." Phillips concluded with a recommendation that Kennedy reconsider his decision or resign from the episcopacy.

HHP Responds

In response to the controversy, HHP called an October 18 meeting of his committee with the College of Bishops. During that Los Angeles meeting, Bishop Marvin Stuart of the Denver area, said he had discussed the matter with Mary Kennedy, the bishop's wife.

"I shared with her the strong reaction and criticism to the appointment in Pasadena," said Stuart. "I told her I concurred in much of this criticism."

Stuart went on to suggest that Kennedy should not appoint himself pastor of the Pasadena congregation; instead, he should agree to preach there two or three Sundays a month and the church should give an amount that they would normally pay their minister of preaching to the Fund for Reconciliation or the Conference Benevolence Fund.

"Mary's answer to all these suggestions was 'that sounds good to me, and I think Jerry will accept them,'" reported Stuart.

Kennedy agreed to most of Stuart's proposals in the immediate future, but asked to be released from the obligation to travel through the connection and from episcopal supervision.

HHP and Kennedy made a joint announcement saying "no appointment of the bishop to that pulpit is involved. Bishop Kennedy has agreed to preach two or three times a month in that pulpit until he can retire as a bishop. The pair said Kennedy will not be identified as senior minister and will not be responsible for pastoral or administrative work. The bishop would receive no financial remuneration from the Pasadena church and the Kennedys would continue to live in their Hollywood home."

Request for Judicial Council Ruling

Acting on behalf of the Committee on Episcopacy, HHP asked the Judicial Council, the highest court in the denomination, for a ruling on the constitutionality of a disciplinary paragraph giving the committee the right to release "a bishop, at any age, and for any reason deemed sufficient from the obligation to travel through the connection at large, and from episcopal supervision."

In an October 28, 1968 ruling, the Judicial Council said the committee did not have the right to release a bishop from such responsibility, and the disciplinary paragraph granting that authority was unconstitutional. Eight of the nine members of the court argued that action by a jurisdiction would conflict with the guaranteed life tenure of bishops.

"To say that a bishop may be retired 'at any age, for any reason deemed sufficient by his Jurisdictional Conference' is to leave the Jurisdictional Conference without guidelines or objective standards to maintain uniformity in the retirement of bishops," the court ruled.

"Such a grant of authority would empower the majority of members of a Jurisdictional Conference to terminate the active service of even the youngest bishop without regard to health or any other standards for retirement," said the council.

Leon Hickman, a member of the Judicial Council, submitted a minority opinion on February 1, 1969, in which he argued, "No one is in a better position than a Jurisdictional Conference to make such a determination. The bishop serves within its geographical territory, it elected him and it passes quadrennial judgment upon his work."

Kennedy Responds

Following the ruling, Kennedy wrote HHP: "The only thing I want to make clear is that I have no intention of following this [retirement] route for myself and I think that was made clear when the Episcopal Committee met. I do think we are wise in having this clarified, but I want to make sure that the Judicial Council does not get me personally involved in this particular discussion of the issues being raised.

"I am terribly sorry I have caused you so much trouble as I know you are a busy man," concluded Kennedy. "I think if I had to do it all over again, I would be tempted to say it just isn't worth troubling so many people about a matter that is not primarily their responsibility."

Request for General Conference Action

The Western Jurisdiction Committee on Episcopacy petitioned the 1970 General Conference to amend the relevant paragraph to read, "A bishop, at any age and for any reason found to be in the best interest of the bishop and of the church by his jurisdictional conference, may, either on his request or on initiative of the Jurisdictional Committee on Episcopacy, be released by that body from the obligation to travel through the connection at large and from residential supervision."

The committee argued that adding the guideline of "the best interest of the bishop and of the church" would address the Judicial Council concern that there was no guideline for such a decision.

The committee asked the legislative body to rule that a bishop affected by the ruling would receive a pension in an amount determined by the Council on World Service and Finance.

In a final request to the 1970 assembly shaping the structure of the denomination following the 1968 merger of the Methodist Church with the Evangelical United Brethren Church, the committee suggested that bishops who had served for twenty years be allowed to retire regardless of their ages.

The provision for a jurisdictional conference to place a bishop in a retired relationship continues in the *2012 Book of Discipline* (¶408.3).

Inter-jurisdictional Committee on Episcopacy

Only slightly battle-scarred from his service as chair of the Western Jurisdictional Committee on Episcopacy, HHP was elected chairman of the national Inter-jurisdictional Committee on Episcopacy from 1976 to 1980.

This committee is responsible for discussing the possible transfer of bishops across jurisdictional lines, but HHP did not have any difficult decisions in that office as there were no requests for such transfers.

A Continuing Legacy

HHP may be best known for shaping the theological views of thousands of students, people who were privileged to hear his lectures, and students using his thirty-five church school materials.

His role in helping delegates elect an ethnic minority to the episcopacy in the Western Jurisdiction and his peacemaking role on the doctrinal study committee may not be known to many, but the results of his efforts can be seen in the current Council of Bishops and contemporary doctrinal statements.

Thousands of curriculum pieces have been developed since HHP helped write the guidelines for curriculum writers, but the same guidelines are used today by Church School Publication staff members and the writers they recruit and train.

Few people know of HHP's hidden role in resolving the very public issue of Bishop Kennedy's announced acceptance of an invitation to become a pastor of a local church. No bishop since that time has suggested a similar action. HHP not only provided Bishop Kennedy with a graceful way of backing out of the announced appointment, he created legislation that would address future situations.

There are, no doubt, hundreds of untold situations in which HHP established harmony out of discord. His ability to use humor and reason in stressful situations provides an example for all us today.

Through former students and leaders of the United Methodist Church, HHP continues to call the church to accept and address scientific findings while encouraging members to experience God in both the routine and the miraculous.

I thank God for the life and teachings of the Rev. Dr. Harvey H. Potthoff, who helped shape my theology and my life.[3]

NOTES

[1] *Daily Christian Advocate*, proceedings of the General Conference of the United Methodist Church, Atlanta, Ga., April 1972, page 761.

[2] Ibid.

[3] Editor's note: In writing this chapter, Dr. Peck relied upon the extensive archives of The Iliff School of Theology, his personal files as an author and editor of many national Methodist publications, various United Methodist publications, and his own recall of events and personal conversations.

7

ILIFF-AT-ASPEN AND FRASIER IN BOULDER

By Richard L. Phillips

Potthoff was involved in some very bold moves by both Iliff and the Rocky Mountain Conference of the United Methodist Church. Frasier Meadows Manor came first, but Iliff-at-Aspen was directly related to Iliff, so I deal with it first. Both could be seen as extensions of Harvey Potthoff, both involved extensive organizational action and effort.

Aspen

Over the years, there were Iliff summer courses that took place in locations off campus. Because of Harvey's fondness for and involvement in Aspen summer events like the music festival, and due to other arts prominent in that lovely mountain community, he dreamed of it as a perfect setting for summer courses. There is where he focused his summer teaching for a number of years.

Gregg Anderson, the Methodist chaplain and senior pastor at the Aspen Chapel of the Prince of Peace, reports that there was a program in the summer of 1972, in part sponsored by Iliff and the Aspen Theater Institute. Gregg took that course and suspects that it was the seed or precursor of Iliff-at-Aspen. His early help with the program was critical in the initial development of this new educational extension by Iliff.

As the program unfolded, Gregg became very impressed with Potthoff, seeing him as the thread that held the Iliff-at-Aspen program together. As a result of his interaction with Potthoff, Gregg, while still serving as chaplain at the Aspen Chapel, went to Iliff and studied for and received his M.Div. degree. For a time Gregg served as the resident director of Iliff-at-Aspen.[1]

By all accounts and records, the birth of Iliff-at-Aspen was Harvey Potthoff's idea, its existence a genesis based on his own planning and work and as the primary person giving administrative attention. Until his retirement in 1981, Potthoff taught at Aspen, including the summer before going to Lincoln. While teaching at Nebraska Wesleyan University, Harvey returned to Denver in the summer. He taught in the Iliff-at-Aspen program in the summers of 1986,'88, '89, '90, and '91. After his permanent return to Denver, he taught in Iliff-at-Aspen in '92, '93, and '95. Iliff-at-Breckenridge, a Colorado mountain community much closer to Denver, came into existence as a spinoff of the Aspen program. Harvey taught in that short-lived program in both 1984 and '85.

By his planning and effort, and with Iliff's permission for credit, Potthoff co-taught one of two Aspen courses offered in the first summer, 1973. With his close friend and colleague Dr. James Galvin, head of psychiatry at the University of Colorado Medical School, Harvey team taught "Religion and Psychiatry in Dialogue." They had worked together often. You can read a reflection by Galvin in Chapter 13. Galvin was the medical doctor who worked with those of us who took a summer program during our Iliff years called Clinical Training. The course was held at the Psychiatric Hospital on the University of Colorado Medical School campus on Colorado Boulevard not far from Iliff. I took the course in the summer of 1959, one of the finest in practicum experiences. In addition to working directly with patients—from the admission procedure to attendance at staff meetings to patient therapy sessions—the summer also included an internship at one of several Denver-area facilities. Here again, Harvey was the generator along with Galvin of a very effective educational program.

The second 1973 course at Aspen, Culture and Religion, was taught by Iliff faculty member Dr. Chester Pennington. Each course was offered from August 6 to 17 and was held at the Aspen Chapel. Many activities outside of the classroom were planned, and often classes featured guest speakers from the area. The results were successful enough that another summer would follow. Each course that first summer cost $50, and each was for two hours of graduate credit. Help for finding inexpensive housing was provided, but students were responsible for paying for housing as well as transportation and food. Spouses of credit seekers were encouraged to audit the courses.

By the summer of 1974, the success of the program called for expansion. That year, there were four courses taught over two sessions extending from July 22 to August 16. In addition to Harvey, other Iliff faculty members offered courses, and again many guests were involved as well as much team teaching. Potthoff's offering was "Theological Issues Today." That was a direct result of the intense interest in the directions theological studies and writers were headed in that decade. David Conner had been enlisted as the student registrar of the program and reported that forty-three persons were involved in the summer of 1974, in addition to faculty, and that twenty-five had participated in 1973.

In the fall of 1974, there were meetings to evaluate and bring recommendations for the program and its future. Iliff president Jameson Jones asked a committee of those who had taught in the Aspen program to work with others at Iliff to formulate a statement. Following an Estes Park working retreat in September 1974, Aspen-related faculty members Milligan, Pennington, Potthoff, and Wilbanks sent a memo to the entire Iliff faculty and administration.

> *We have had a conversation in which we shared our perceptions of the program, tried to identify some of the policy matters which must be faced, and formulated a few suggestions. Our attempt is to draw the entire Iliff faculty into a discussion of Iliff at Aspen.*
>
> *The Aspen Idea: What is not well known is that Aspen is the home base (at least part of the time) for: Aspen Center for Environmental Studies, Aspen Center for Physics, Aspen Institute for Humanistic Studies, Aspen Music Festival, Aspen Music School, Aspen Theatre Institute, Ballet West, The Center for the Eye (photography workshops), Given Institute Of Pathobiology, International Design Conference and now Iliff-At-Aspen.*
>
> *Iliff should have some sort of presence in this think-tank,*

cultural center. That presence might take any one of several possible forms. [Included as part of] our thinking was providing an educational opportunity for ministers and laymen, capitalizing on the Aspen resources, stressing interdisciplinary work, presenting the theological disciplines in ways which would indicate their relation to concerns being expressed in the various Aspen centers.[2]

The conclusions of the committee report were: (1) we have something significant going on; (2) the courses have limited potential for academic credit and should focus on clergy and laity, if credit is available assignments should be mailed out well in advance due to lack of library resources at Aspen; (3) regular Iliff students may attend, but should not be encouraged to take Aspen courses due to costs and the projected purpose of the program; (4) whatever Iliff does, it should not "get in the way" of the program we now have going. Many more details are contained in that report.

As a result of the work of the committee, the focus of the program continued to be the encouragement of dialogue between religious and secular concerns, the relating of theology to the many aspects of culture, and the interplay of religion and civilization.

It is easy to see that the committee was responding to some rather serious academic concerns on the part of the overall institution. The program did continue for many years, with the basic conclusions above being the guiding concerns. Other recommendations included limiting class size, charging those who audited the course the same fee, and arranging for exclusive use of the primary class center—the Aspen Chapel—due to problems of competing for space and issues regarding noise. Gregg Anderson was and, in 2013, still is the senior minister at the Aspen Chapel, and he played a role and worked diligently in the Iliff program as host for many years.

Dr. Ed Everding of the Iliff faculty became involved early in the program and served in several ways, in addition to teaching classes over the years. In an email to me in 2011, Ed reported: "In the early stages of Iliff-at-Aspen, Harvey would be the administrator as well as the presenter. He helped arrange for coffee and doughnuts for session breaks. He would provide resources (e.g., books) that he would transport from Iliff. He would assist in the registration of participants. He also helped locate reasonable housing and provided information about restaurants in and around Aspen." As the years went by, more and more of the routine duties were done by volunteers, and by 1978 Iliff's director of Summer School helped with the administrative duties. Ed became the director of Iliff Summer Sessions, which included Aspen. He asserts that the Aspen program's "mission is compatible with Iliff's and HHP's: To promote open and progressive theology, spiritual enrichment, and peace through interfaith engagement."[3]

Iliff-at-Aspen became a popular assignment for Iliff faculty members, and over the years many of them taught there. Harvey's classes are listed below by year and title. The 1973 and 1974 classes were noted earlier; '75 Clergy-Physician Dialogue; '76 Modern Cosmology and Religious Faith and Theology of the Body; '77 Aging: An Inter Disciplinary Approach; '78 Aging and the Life Cycle; '79 Religious Faith and Mental Health; '80 Religious Faith and the Search for Meaning; '81 Process Theology and the Issues of Life; '86 Emerging Images of God; '88 A Dialogue on Science and Religion; '89 Aging Diminishment and Death in Religious Perspective; '90 Humor and Struggle: Ingredients of Faith; '91 A Modern Theology of Earth; '92 Spirituality, Old and New; '93 Process Theology and Life's Meaning; and '95 On the Edge of Theology; and at Breckenridge, '84 The Search for a Contemporary Spirituality and '85 A Theology of Wholeness. All these courses, especially the last half of the listing, reflect Potthoff's central interests during his later years as both teacher and pastor.

There were several other important players at Aspen over the years. Chaplain Gregg Anderson, as host and for some time the resident director, was certainly an important one. Another was David Conner who, while still an Iliff student in Denver, came to the Aspen program regularly and served in several ways. In his essay, Anderson relates some interesting aspects of the program.

> *There was a woman who became connected with the Chapel during the summers named Harriette Line Thompson. She lived in Charlotte, NC, was an active United Methodist, and spent her summers in Aspen helping the Aspen chapel. She was also a concert pianist. She became an essential host for Harvey and the Iliff programs. Harvey and Harriette became quite a team as the summers went by. Harriette had the most positive energy anyone could imagine and this coupled with the wisdom and wit of Harvey was a winning combination. Harriette still resides today in Charlotte at the age of 89. She is running in the San Diego marathon next month. This is just one example of the energy and life of Harriette.*
>
> [She is also typical of the kinds of people with whom Harvey liked to associate.]
>
> *In addition to the seminars, each morning began with a brief worship service led by clergy in attendance with music by*

Harriette. Harriette also provided wonderful refreshments during the breaks and was always available to give advice about the best restaurants in town and other activities such as the Aspen Music Festival.

Harvey not only taught [in the program] exceptionally, but he was very social and organized social events during the week.

Harvey loved the Aspen Music Festival and attended quite often and encouraged participants as well giving them the daily line up each morning. Each week included a dinner at the old mining town of Ashcroft, 30 minutes from the Chapel up Castle Creek Road. The long time, if not forever, curator and preserver of Ashcroft "ghost" town was a colorful man named Stuart Mace. Having the class meet at Ashcroft on Wednesday nights for a tour of the town, a fresh trout dinner and stories by Stuart with spiritual anecdotes by Harvey was a time many people most remember of the whole week.

There were also the Thursday after-class picnics at the multi-A-frame home on the Roaring Fork River of Bud and Justine Woods in Woody Creek. Bud was a retired Chaplain and Colonel of the Air Force. He was also a trustee of Iliff School of Theology. With that and the Aspen connection Harvey and they became very close friends and hosted these great picnics on the deck of their home one foot from the energy of the rolling Roaring Fork River that begins at the top of Independence Pass and the Continental Divide and flows through the Roaring Fork Valley.

Iliff at Aspen was mostly attended by clergy and spouses from all over the United States. The subject matter was typically creative and progressive themes. This was because Harvey was creative and progressive. It was a great institution and it would be wonderful if it could ever be resurrected, but it would take a reincarnated Potthoff to do so. Perhaps that person may come along some day.[4]

HHP photo from Tom Wood used with permission

President Jimmy Carter and Potthoff visiting on a mountainside at Aspen

Interaction with important scientists, cultural and political figures, and artists was easily arranged at Aspen, at least for a person of Potthoff's skills. They ranged from physicist Heinz Pagels (see Chapter 3) to President Jimmy Carter to singer John Denver to astronaut and NASA scientist Charles R. "Rick" Chappell and far too many others to mention here. Charles Milligan reports that Carter spent more time visiting with Harvey than anyone else present. The mountainside picture of Carter and Harvey captures one of Harvey's treasured memories of that summer. Pagels lectured regularly in the Aspen courses. He and Harvey became close friends. Gregg Anderson reports that Pagels's widow, Elaine, a biblical scholar, still speaks at the Aspen Chapel every summer.

The following paragraphs were submitted by Rick Chappell, who became a close friend and frequent guest in Potthoff's classes both at Aspen and NWU. Rick's content here treats his teaching and interaction with Harvey in several ways, but the focus on Aspen leads me to include all of the content here. Harvey and Rick planned for some time to write a book on the relationship of science and religion. Their schedules kept that from happening, but the project would have had some real value both educationally and as part of the Potthoff legacy. (For information about Chappell, see Contributors section of this book.)

> I have the most wonderful memories about all of my times of being with Harvey—in Montgomery, in Lincoln, in Aspen, in Sitka, in Huntsville, and in Denver. He and I always had fantastic discussions on all sorts of topics, but especially on the interplay between science and religion in the public discourse. My grandfather had been a Methodist minister in North Carolina, Tennessee, and Oklahoma and both of my parents were college teachers. Hence, the academic/religious environment was very comfortable for me. When Harvey and I first met at the symposium at Huntingdon College in Montgomery, our interaction that night surfaced a compatible and rewarding discussion that eventually led to our desire to write a book. As a lifelong Methodist and a scientist, I was very comfortable with the partnering role that science and religion play in our lives. With his deep theological understanding and his interest in natural science, Harvey and I found a strong common bond.
>
> Our discussions continued because of Harvey's kindness in continuing to invite me to participate in different lecture and workshop events. Our initial interaction in Montgomery in March of 1987 had been

arranged by Dr. Allen Jackson, an Iliff graduate who had known Harvey in Denver. Following this event, Harvey invited me to come to Nebraska Wesleyan to give a talk to the students about the solar-terrestrial system and our role as stewards while we are passengers on spaceship Earth. The interactions with Harvey and with the students there were again magical and encouraging.

Then Harvey asked me to be part of a summer workshop in Aspen that he had organized through Iliff for many years. That was my first real contact with Aspen, Colorado, a place that I am continuing to visit as often as possible more than twenty years later. The workshop was held at the Prince of Peace Chapel on the outskirts of Aspen and was attended by about twenty delightful people, many of whom were devotees to Harvey over a long time. In the discussions during that workshop, the topic of science and religion was examined from both points of view, and Harvey and I soon realized that we were very *sympatico* and reinforcing regarding our views of how the cohesive study of the Creator and the Creation were important and completely understandable in a nonthreatening way.

Because of his long history with Aspen, Harvey gave my wife, Barbra, and me the insider's view of that magnificent place and the people who live there. Harvey introduced me to his friends, Bud and Justine Woods who had lived in Aspen for many years. Bud asked me to speak at the Aspen Rotary Club, which led to an initial meeting with the Windstar Foundation leadership and then with John Denver. My subsequent friendship with John Denver led to the creation of the Aspen Global Change Institute, an interdisciplinary scientifically based group that is still in operation today.

We were able to visit with Harvey on at least two occasions in Aspen and, through his knowledge and connections to the place, soon began to feel like permanent residents. It is one of the most inspiring and interesting places that I have ever had the opportunity to visit, and I still return as often as possible, usually in the summer when the wildflowers and the vistas are amazing. Aspen is in my heart, and it is there because Harvey gave it to me. It is a place where big thoughts are easy to come by; the ability to be high up on the mountainside and to look out for fifty miles or so, gives an openness to creativity that is not felt to that degree in many other venues.

From the initial Aspen workshop also came the invitation to Harvey and me to give our science and religion discussion at a meeting of Alaska doctors in Sitka, Alaska. The group was very interesting to be with, and the immensity of the Alaska frontier was very eye-opening and inspirational. It was a long way from north Alabama and was an amazing foothold on the vast wilderness that is Alaska. After I checked into the small hotel ... and opened the drapes, I saw a lot of very large birds flying around the harbor that seemed to be vultures. After closer examination, it became evident that they were bald eagles! The eagles and the humpback and Orca whales in the outer harbor were also incredible. That place was just another adventure that I got to experience because of my fulfilling relationship with Harvey.

Although busy, Harvey was generous with his time. He even traveled to Huntsville, Alabama, to give several talks related to science and religion. I had been telling my friends and colleagues in Huntsville about Harvey for so long that I wanted all of them to get to meet him. He obliged me by traveling from Denver and spending several days.

The last time that I saw Harvey was at the retirement home in Denver where he moved toward the end of his life. Barbra and I were traveling to Aspen again, and we drove from the Denver airport to Harvey's place in order to visit. Harvey showed us around, and then he and I talked in his apartment. He seemed to be happy, and all whom we passed in the halls and lobby were anxious to speak and talk with Harvey. He was beginning to show some signs of age and was still concerned about his sister's well-being. We talked about the book some more, and both of us wanted to see it progress, although we were being tugged in different directions because of the other responsibilities of life.

Harvey Potthoff is one of those very special people who are grounded in the Word and in their knowledge of the world and of people. He always engendered enthusiastic discussion, and encouraged the full spectrum of ideas to come forth. He had a smile and a lightness about his demeanor that brought forth good comfortable discussion. But then he could bring things together through his broad foundation of

> understanding of God and of life. I still see him in my mind's eye when certain topics come up, and I always see him in the small Victorian streets of Aspen's west end, or at the Prince of Peace Chapel, or at Toklat where he introduced me to Stuart Mace, or on the Roaring Fork from Bud and Justine's deck, or in the Brand Building where we stayed when in Aspen. The majesty of the mountains pay tribute to the majesty of Harvey's influence on our lives.[5]

Dr. Everding reports that the Iliff-at-Aspen program was canceled, probably due to financial realities. Transportation, housing, food and faculty and guest expenses simply became too great for the program to underwrite. Its final summer appears to have been in 1995. It was a sad day for Potthoff and a very popular program.

Frasier

The Frasier Meadows Manor (now Frasier Meadows Retirement Community) was a project of the Colorado Conference of the Methodist Church (now the Rocky Mountain Conference of the United Methodist Church). Harvey Potthoff was tapped as one of the persons to lead the effort and became the first president of the Board of Trustees. The best sources on the history of the facility and its operation are two books, one a memoir by Ben Christner, ThD,[6] and the other edited by Eileen Metzger.[7] Dr. Christner, a Methodist minister, was asked to be the first director and Dr. Potthoff to lead the board. Metzger, a personal friend of both of these men and of mine, was a longtime resident with her late husband. She continued as the manor's historian until her death. Christner directed the project from the time of the first planning. He was involved in all phases, and Potthoff was his chief partner until Ben's retirement as Executive Director.

Located in Boulder, Colorado, the senior continuing care residential facility received its name from Mr. and Mrs. Elmer Frasier of Frasier Farms sometime after they donated twenty acres for the building of the facility and after the completion of the first phase of construction. After several possible names were considered, the name Frasier Meadows Manor was a unanimous decision of the board. In the process of the creation and planning of the Manor, Potthoff and Frasier became very close friends, and both worked diligently to bring hopes to reality. The Frasier family were active members of the First Methodist Church in Boulder.

Harvey continued to be involved with the Manor until his last years of life. In 1995, having earlier been a part of the groundbreaking celebration for the most recent of the residential facilities (Frasier North), Harvey was present for the dedication of the new wing of the Manor. He was honored several times over the years for his work and support of the project, recognition that continued until only a year before his passing. He was very proud of the Manor and his involvement with it. Many of us expected Harvey to become a resident of the Manor after retirement, and at times he seemed headed in that direction. In the end he felt he needed to be near his many friends and colleagues in Denver and close to his great love, the Iliff School of Theology.

I was on the Board of Trustees for five years (2000–2005), and my parents, Helen and Bud Phillips, were residents of the Manor for approximately the last fourteen years of their lives.

As a result, I have lived a good share of its history and am or was acquainted with all of its leadership from the very start. My family lived in Boulder and were also members of the First United Methodist Church there. We even have a family story or two about our relationship with the Frasiers in those years.

I was a student at Iliff and in attendance at the dedication of the first residential building in 1960. The south wing of the main building was completed and dedicated in 1964. Since then, there have been five major additions, many smaller specialty units, and many renovations. The campus has grown and is now a major and very comprehensive home for the retired.

Potthoff was serving as the president of a Colorado Conference organization known as Methodist Homes as the idea of the facility was under development in the early 1950s. The focus of the group was centered on providing residential living for aging persons. It was a time of cultural change in how the aged were accustomed to live during their final years. Nationwide, Methodist homes for this purpose were in existence or were being constructed as early as the end of World War II, especially in California and in and around Chicago. These established residential communities became resources and examples of what might be done in Colorado.

Harvey's Annual Conference roles were many, and his work in the greater church as well as his teaching at Iliff were greatly respected. It was no surprise that he became the leader of the first Board of Trustees of the Manor; he was elected on February 23, 1956. His bishop at the time was Glenn R. Phillips (not related to me), who had been involved as a pastor in California with similar projects and was a real driving force in the planning and building of the Manor. Phillips is the one who tapped Ben Christner, pulling him from a church pastorate to be the first full-time director of the Manor. Ben and Harvey were great friends, both great workers, and—together with many, many helpers from the members of the board, the Conference, and volunteers—are the ones who, along with full Conference support for the project, brought it to reality. Financial hard times aside, there was great joy associated with bringing the Manor from dream to reality.

There was early concern about how well the facility would attract residents. Christner believed a building must be ready to view before people would buy an apartment. As it turned out, that was not necessary. Here is how Ben tells it:

> Oh how well I remember receiving the first application for admission and the $500 check accompanying the same. It was from Mr. Robert Spencer, editor of the Fort Morgan Times. As conference lay leader he had been a trustee from the beginning: in fact one of the trustees of Methodist Homes and Institutions and a member of the site Committee in securing the gift of the twenty acres from the Frasier Meadows addition. He said to me at one of the meetings, 'Would it help you, Ben, if I turned in my application for Admission? I would like to be the first founder.' On his next trip to Denver he had the Application for Admission paper and we signed it and had it notarized. This was on April 9, 1957. As we returned to my office, the morning mail was delivered and there on my desk was a letter from Mrs. Sonia Richardson of Washington, D.C. Enclosed with the letter was a check for $500 asking for the Application for Admission papers and

> stating that she would soon be in Boulder visiting her daughter and we could complete the papers then. At the meeting of the Board of Trustees May 22, 1957, the Admissions Committee submitted the Application for Admission papers for R. B. Spencer and for Misses Florence and Grace Bedell of Boulder. ... By the time of the groundbreaking June 8, 1958 we had nine regular founders.[8]

Ben looked back in his account of the earlier work and had this to say when remembering those who were so instrumental in the project:

> Five of the original number stand forth in my mind and love. These are Bishop Glenn Randall Phillips, Dr. Harvey H. Potthoff, Mr. John N. Adams, Mr. Elmer Frasier and Mr. Willard Bozert. Much might be said of each. Suffice it to say, by their abilities, dedication and love to the work and responsibilities of the Corporation and project we were able to visualize, plan, promote and build Frasier Meadows Manor. Many others now love and carry on in this most desirable and worthy program.[9]

In her history of the Manor, Eileen Metzger has words of praise for all of the early leaders and the roles they played in the planning and administration of the facility. Eileen and Ben are in total agreement in their sense of appreciation and praise.

Christner retired from the Manor in June 1968. Later, he and Mrs. Christner returned as residents. She died in 1986;

Ben died in 1990 and has been honored in many ways since.

In the middle of the first decade of the twenty-first century, the name was changed to better reflect the purpose of the facility and its function. "Manor" was dropped from the name, and the necessary legal filings were accomplished to change the name to Frasier Meadows Retirement Community.

Photo from The History of Frasier Meadows Manor by Eileen Metzger.

Reverend Christner, Potthoff, and Bishop Phillips at the groundbreaking for Frasier Meadows Manor on June 8, 1958

FMRC is a highly regarded continuing care facility in Colorado. Special units in addition to the independent living apartments include: Health Care Center, Personal Care, Assisted Living Units, Residents' Workshop, Alzheimer's Wing, Phillips Chapel, Adult Day Care, Pool and Rehab Center, Resident's Computer Lab, multiple dining rooms, a library, and many lounges and work areas. Residents, from the very first, are involved in many aspects of the operation, serve on the board, and are key players in major decisions regarding the facility.

At the fortieth anniversary celebration, Dr. Alton Templin, historian of the Iliff faculty, delivered a paper on the history of the Manor. His final paragraph of the paper relates: "Dr. Potthoff, the first Chairman of the Corporation, was present—

then nearing his 90th birthday. This whole project was a fitting tribute to him as well as the other two major leaders: Bishop Phillips and Dr. Ben Christner."[10]

One year after Harvey's death, the Frasier community celebrated his many years of service from the Manor's genesis to that day. Charles Milligan and I both spoke at the February 2003 event; it was a very warm and comprehensive occasion. The trustees drafted the following tribute in preparation for the events.

FRASIER MEADOWS MANOR

TRUSTEES TRIBUTE TO

HARVEY H. POTTHOFF

JULY, 2002

Whereas Dr. Harvey H. Potthoff, in his 91st year of life, died earlier this year after a lifetime of ministry and service to the United Methodist Church, The Iliff School of Theology, Frasier Meadows Manor and a great variety of other organizations and causes, and;

Whereas Dr. Potthoff was among the first to promote the idea of a Methodist retirement community in Colorado, and:

Whereas he served as the first President of the first Frasier Meadows Manor Board of Trustees and as such was one of the key founders of Frasier Meadows Manor, and;

Whereas he continued his keen interest and support of FMM throughout the remainder of his life, visiting and speaking here often, and;

Whereas the FMM Library has a holding of most of the H. H. Potthoff writings spanning many years and many topics;

Therefore, be it resolved that theTrustees of FMM do honor and praise and express undying gratitude to The Reverend Doctor Harvey H. Potthoff, and;

Direct that February 2003 at FMM be designated Harvey H. Potthoff month. During said month it is recommended that the reading of his works be encouraged and that programs featuring his diverse and remarkable ministry be generated through the efforts of the CEO, the FMM Chaplain, the FMM Historian and the Board of Trustees.

From the Iliff Archives

Ed Putzier, a current and longtime resident, sent me an email in August 2011. He had edited the institution's newsletter for several years. He was present for the fiftieth anniversary celebration and reported that the following message from Dr. Potthoff was printed in the program for the day.[11]

> All who were deeply involved with the planning in those early days were of one mind ... the dream for an attractive and efficient physical facility in a beautiful setting where persons might live safely and comfortably in a community environment. For a setting in which persons might savor their vintage years, recalling memories of journeys traveled, nurturing inner appreciations of heart, mind, and spirit and making new journeys of the inner life.

One final note regarding Potthoff and Frasier. On one of the anniversary celebrations while I was on the board, Harvey was our guest, and the event ended with a luncheon in the Sky Lounge, a fifth-floor assembly room with a magnificent view of the mountains west of Boulder. Harvey and I went to one of the windows to take in the view, and he related this brief, heartfelt story.

> Following the dedication of the first unit, Elmer Frasier and I stood right here at this window. He said to me, "It is good, isn't it Harvey?" "Yes, it certainly is," I replied.

NOTES

[1] Gregg Anderson, *Origins of Iliff at Aspen*, Summer 2012, Iliff Archives, box 45, file folder 14.

[2] Aspen memo, Iliff Archives, box 12, file folder 29.

[3] Everding email of August 31, 2011, Iliff Archives, box 45, file folder 15.

[4] Gregg Anderson, *Origins of Iliff at Aspen*, Summer 2012, Iliff Archives, box 45, file folder 14.

[5] Chappell email of December 11, 2011, Iliff Archives, box 43, file folder 6.

[6] Reverend Benjamin Heater Christner, *Thou Art the Man*, published and distributed by Frasier Meadows Manor, 1982.

[7] Eileen Metzger, ed., *The History of Frasier Meadows Manor: Boulder, Colorado 1960-1997*, published in 1997 by Dorothy V. Nightingale and Gregory G. Rowley with support from Ada Johnson and Johnson Publishing, Boulder, Colorado.

[8] Metzger, *The History of Frasier Meadows Manor*, 13.

[9] Christner, *Thou Art the Man*, 203.

[10] Templin speech in 2011 about Harvey Potthoff and his part in the conception and implementation of Frasier Meadows Manor retirement home, Iliff Archives, box 45, file folder 18.

[11] Ed Putzier email, August 2011, Iliff Archives, box 45, file folder 18. {Thank you, Ed; but for your email, I would not have found this quote.}

8

POTTHOFF AS FAMILY MAN

Dr. Tom Wood

Harvey Potthoff has been described in many ways—a man of letters, teacher, colleague, friend, pastor, preacher, theologian, and author. In addition, he was a confirmed bachelor and, yes, a father and grandfather. How could this be? This story has many facets, each of which incorporates the preceding descriptions of Harvey Potthoff, our surrogate father and grandfather.

Our journey began at Christ Methodist Church in Denver, Colorado, about the time I was seven or eight years old and a member of the "Junior Choir," which displayed its year-long effort to learn all the verses of "Fairest Lord Jesus" each Easter Sunday. Sitting in the choir loft below the beautiful stained glass window of Mary at the sepulture exclaiming "Raboni" and then looking at Dr. Harvey Potthoff in his colorful festive vestments behind the pulpit, I could have never foretold of the many events that were to influence our life together. My parents, Gerald and Virginia Wood, and my younger brother,

Nick, attended this church regularly until I was eleven. My memories consist of Sunday school, taught by a rigid and stern physician, a general practitioner, who was always able to find Bible chapters and verses much more rapidly than his students. There were only occasional brief interactions with the minister, Harvey Potthoff.

Our lives changed radically one night in September 1950. I was still a pre-teen boy when my parents, paternal grandmother, and her good friend Mrs. Clarkson, were all killed in a head-on collision with a truck one rainy night near Brighton, Colorado. My father had purchased a new car, and had sold our old car and was delivering it to its new owner. The others were going along for the ride, and the opportunity to ride back to Denver in the new automobile. I was at our home, babysitting my younger brother. Our mother had led the woman's Bible study at the church earlier that day.

Police officers awakened us in the middle of the night and told us our parents had been involved in an automobile accident. Next came my uncle, an attorney, who told us the true consequences of the tragic accident, and arranged for other family members to stay with us over the next few days. These were days of sadness and confusion; what would happen to my younger brother and me, to our dog, our home, our family and friends? Our other grandparents had all died before we were old enough to know them. Except for my uncle and his new wife, no other relatives lived in Denver.

Some of those questions were answered after the funeral, at which Harvey Potthoff presided. "Tom," he said, "you will never be alone." I didn't understand the meaning of those words for many years, nor did I know that Harvey had befriended another young boy, who had escaped the Holocaust with his parents and settled near the church in Denver. That young boy, Peter Gay, a German Jew, was to become an emeritus professor at Yale, celebrated author, and director of the New York Public Library's Center for Scholars and Writers. I know that he, too, always felt the love and friendship of Harvey Potthoff throughout his life.

After our parents' death, my brother and I were cared for by a succession of older women, ill-prepared for the rigors of raising two young boys, as were my uncle and aunt, who two years after the accident, moved us into their home. During the next four years, we rarely saw Harvey, either by circumstance or design. My brother and I each went to separate boarding schools, returning "home" for only a few days for holiday vacations. While I was at school in Colorado Springs, Harvey was periodically invited to lead a vespers service at the school, and this was always preceded by a dinner with him at a restaurant in Colorado Springs. This allowed me to leave the school briefly, enjoy a special meal, and catch up with Harvey's activities, and he with mine. One time, we celebrated Easter together after he led the sunrise service at the Garden of the Gods, an experience I will never forget. These years in high school were difficult, however. During the school year, I was being taught classical studies such as Greek and Roman history, and on my vacations, I worked as a cowboy on remote ranches in Wyoming. Contacts with Harvey, in person, were infrequent, as were letters and telephone calls.

Things changed when I started college in New England. My freshman English class included study of *The Dartmouth Bible*, an abridged version emphasizing the prose and poetry of many biblical verses. I also joined the Dartmouth Christian Union, a college organization under the guidance of Dr. George

Kalbfleisch, a progressive, philosophical scholar. I began talking with Harvey every week or two, discussing my studies and involvement with colleagues who were also interested in seeking answers to difficult theological and ethical issues. Many weekends I served as a lay minister for three small New England churches, two Congregational and one Baptist! These churches had congregations of fifteen or twenty, woodstoves, and pump organs; I picked up the organist, an elderly lady, on the way to the first service. Harvey was always available to answer questions and give guidance. We also began to communicate more regularly by mail.

After my graduation from Dartmouth, I returned to Denver to complete courses, which would qualify me for admission to medical school. While being very supportive of my personal decision to enter medical school, I always felt he was disappointed that I didn't follow in his footsteps and enter the ministry. We did get together much more frequently to talk, since I attended the University of Denver and Harvey had his Iliff office on the same campus. We had many dinners together, some with Iliff faculty members, and he began introducing me to them as his surrogate son. For some reason, they all seemed to already know all about me!

Medical school was very demanding, leaving little time for socializing. I did teach a Christian education class to adolescents attending Christ Methodist Church. Harvey again offered me assistance in preparing lessons and offering suggestions for course materials. While he wrote many books for adult education, he did not compose any specifically for young people. He always enjoyed participating in our class, when invited, and even attended a campfire meeting with us near Evergreen. He always believed that listening to young people and addressing their concerns was of utmost importance.

During my four years of medical school, I also worked for a surgical organ transplant team which performed many of the first kidney and liver transplants. In my opinion, this was the dawn of bioethics. Many questions were asked and continue to be discussed. How do we distribute scarce resources? Should we operate on a healthy individual and remove an organ, thereby exposing him to harm? Who is responsible for payment of the costs, and should treatment be limited to those who have the capacity to pay? Are doctors playing God?

These questions were of great interest to Harvey, and because of his interest in science and its relevance to theology, gave us new subjects to discuss. We often remembered Albert Schweitzer's quotation, "Ethics is nothing else than reverence for life." These questions were reviewed many times when we participated together in classes at Iliff, Aspen, and at the annual meeting of the Alaska State Medical Association in Sitka, Alaska.

In 1962 I met a lovely young woman at a Christmas party and we quickly fell in love. She was attending college in Oregon but transferred to the University of Denver so that we could continue our courtship. Harvey quickly included her in all of our social events and in 1964 performed our wedding in Colorado Springs. The day before the wedding, Harvey and I had long discussions about the meaning of love and commitment. He told me he loved me as a son, and I told him I loved him as a father. After the wedding ceremony, each of us had a new awareness of our self and our relationship to each other.

My senior year in medical school left little time for anything—including sleep! One night was spent on call at the University Hospital, the next at Swedish hospital where I "moonlighted," and the third at home with my new wife. We were all able to attend an occasional dinner, symphony, or play together. Harvey's schedule was equally hectic and included his teaching duties at Iliff, guest services at small rural churches, writing books for adult Christian education, and early planning for the construction of Frasier Meadows Manor. We did have a large celebration together with other members of our families, when I graduated from medical school.

The year 1965 found the United States at war in Vietnam, and I served my first postgraduate year in the Army, stationed at Letterman General Hospital in San Francisco. Harvey visited us once for a few days, and we returned to Denver once during a Christmas break. We otherwise had to communicate by letters and an occasional phone call, which was to define our relationship for many years. Birthdays were special, and I could always anticipate a telephone call and card from both my younger brother and from Harvey. I would do the same for their birthdays. While we were all separated by both time and distance, there was always the presence of love.

We went from San Francisco to Alaska for two more years of Army duty, this time an assignment with a nuclear missile unit defending the entire northwest coast of the United States. Telephone calls were a rare extravagance at eight cents a minute, but postage remained relatively cheap. We had a new daughter, Karen, and two years later a son, Bob. We kept in touch with Harvey by mail, and he started referring to the children as "his grandchildren."

We returned to the Lower 48 in June 1968 for three more years of postgraduate training in internal medicine. Telephone calls to Harvey as well as letters were easier to accomplish, and he visited us in Seattle. Kathie was the major correspondent because of my schedule, but we all participated and rejoiced when Harvey visited us or when we traveled to Denver to visit Kathie's family and Harvey. Phone calls, letters, and occasional visits were to be the pattern of our busy lives for the next forty years.

I returned to Anchorage, Alaska, in 1971 and have remained here ever since. It was then that I truly realized how much we meant to each other. Harvey sent us a copy of his new book, *The Inner Life*, with the following dedication:

TO
DR. AND MRS. THOMAS C. WOOD
AND THEIR CHILDREN
KAREN ELIZABETH — ROBERT COWAN
WHO ADD SO MUCH
TO MY INNER LIFE

In 1972 Kathie and I adopted an Inupiat son when he was only two days old. Harvey and Kathie's mother both visited us for the baptism of all three children, Karen, Bob, and Paul. We had a wonderful time with "Grandpa Harvey" and Grandmother Francis; this visit was especially meaningful to all of us. We constituted a family.

Courtesy of Tom Wood, used with permission

An Alaskan hike with grandchildren Karen and Bob

HHP photo in Iliff Archives

Christmas in Denver, 1972: Bob, baby Paul, Tom, Karen, and Kathie with Harvey

Once again, our lives were controlled by our chosen fields of interest. Letters were sent and received regularly, and we were able to talk with each other more frequently. Our children were an important part of all our lives, and Harvey made several visits to Anchorage to celebrate major holidays or to go sightseeing with us. He camped at Denali National Park, sleeping in a sleeping bag and under a tent on a frosty fall night—but not before introducing us to the warming effects of Amaretto! On another occasion, he attended the Alaska State Fair with us and took a picture of our new malamute puppy, Willowah, smelling a fireweed plant. He subsequently had an artist make an oil painting of the photo and gave it to us as a Christmas gift. It now hangs in my son Bob's home.

As our children grew up, Harvey took each one on a trip. This, of course, was very special to each of them from the standpoint of spending time alone with their grandfather, and experiencing new cities. Karen and Harvey attended the Aspen Music Festival, and later, Paul and Harvey traveled to Washington, DC. Harvey also attended some hockey games when the boys were playing in tournaments. He always had several pucks on his desk, awards given to Bob and Paul when they scored a hat trick. They always seemed to skate better when Grandpa Harvey was watching the game. They were very proud to be able to give him the special pucks. In his own way, Harvey reciprocated, giving Paul his woolen letter sweater and Bob a set of antique golf clubs.

When Karen and Becky (Nick's daughter) graduated from Dartmouth in 1988, Harvey was there with the rest of the family. Whatever else he may have planned, milestones involving family members always seemed to take priority. The graduation also gave Harvey and Nick an opportunity to reacquaint, since Nick's education and work were always on the East Coast. Unfortunately, he never enjoyed the same relationship with Harvey that I did.

Nick got married in 1991. By now, it was family tradition to have Harvey perform the ceremony, and the children and I all went to New Jersey to celebrate the occasion. Several days before the wedding, we all attended the Yankee-Twins game at Yankee Stadium, viewing the game from the raucous right-field stands. There may have been only a single Minnesota fan there that evening, but Harvey unabashedly cheered every good play the Twins made. The Yankees, of course, won the game, Harvey learned some new vocabulary words, and we all had a good time.

When Harvey taught at Nebraska Wesleyan, he developed a passion for "Big Red" football, and along with the Denver Broncos, we had a new area of interest to discuss. His years in Lincoln were very rewarding to him, and he freely admitted to the pleasure he derived from starting the Mattingly Symposium and in being honored by the planting of an Amur cherry tree on campus. I, in turn, shared the honor I had received by being asked to address a medical conference in Khabarovsk, Russia.

On one occasion when Harvey was visiting Alaska, we went to my old homestead cabin on Crooked Lake. We had gone there together on other occasions, but Harvey seemed preoccupied and more pensive than usual. It turned out that this was the day that a death row prisoner was to be executed. For years earlier, Harvey mentored Wili Otey and another death row inmate in an effort to add substance to their remaining lives. We spent the day quietly, awaiting the national news on whether or not the governor of Nebraska had commuted the death sentence, He had not. I cannot remember another time when we needed each other for support. Words were unnecessary to express our sorrow.

Wood family photo used with permission

Christmas in Alaska, 1986: Harvey and Tom Wood

Harvey returned to Denver and soon moved into the Meridian. We initiated regular Sunday evening telephone calls, a tradition that was maintained throughout the remainder of his life. I did visit him whenever possible and became friends with many of his friends, who were also residents there. He seemed content with his apartment and a lovely view of Pikes Peak, and the ability to interact with friends who "remained involved."

For a brief period of time, he could read, think, and write without impending deadlines. When an unanticipated need arose, however, he accepted the temporary senior ministry at University Park Church. For his office there, he took with him the beautiful stained glass window that had been presented to him and of which he was very proud (see cover photo). Harvey always obtained meaning in his own life by being meaningful to the lives of others.

Harvey received special recognition when he was honored by Iliff with the naming of the Potthoff Seminar Room. I was unable to attend, but my son Paul represented the family, driving a used car nearly 2,500 miles from Anchorage to Denver. Pictures taken at the ceremony show Harvey and Paul together, each expressing pride and love in their smiles. This was a very important event in both of their lives.

Each of Harvey's adopted grandchildren wanted to express their feelings for Harvey in this chapter.

First, Karen Wood DiBari:

> I remember when we first called Dr. Potthoff, Grandpa Harvey. It was a surprise for him staged by my Mom and Dad when I was five or six years old. I have a fuzzy memory of his face when we said, "Hi Grandpa Harvey"—he was obviously very pleased. Grandpa Harvey is how we knew him, and I regarded him as my one living grandfather.
>
> When I was twelve or thirteen, Grandpa Harvey took me on a trip to the Aspen Music Festival. We went to several concerts, including one featuring cellist Zara Nelsoza. Memories from that trip include riding

the chairlift, visiting the Maroon Bells, Leadville, and Baby Doe Tabor's house. We had dinner with Grandpa Harvey's friends at their home on the Roaring Fork River.

Grandpa Harvey came to my college graduation from Dartmouth and visited me when I was in graduate school at the University of Montana. I gave him an exclusive recital in the University Theater—I had been working with a pianist on Brahms's Cello Sonata in E Minor. During that visit, we drove up to see the National Bison Range and the St. Ignatius Mission. The mission has a painting of an Indian Jesus that fascinated him. We also talked about while the church is filled with beautiful murals and stained glass inside, it offers no windows to enable a view of the spectacular Mission Mountains.

Whenever I visited Grandpa Harvey in Denver, he'd take me to very nice restaurants. He loved good food! I remember going to the Brown Palace and having black-bottomed pie. He took me to see *Die Fledermaus*. Before the opera, I bought him a cappuccino—he'd never had one before.

One time, I attended an adult education class he was teaching. It was fascinating, more like a history class than the Sunday school classes with which I was familiar. He loved books and liked to go to the Tattered Cover in Denver to find gifts. He said he'd tell his favorite clerk about the interests of the people he was buying gifts for, and the clerk would suggest appropriate titles.

Grandpa Harvey seemed to really enjoy his later years. He made strong friendships with very interesting people at the Englewood Meridian, and I admired how he would lead a book discussion and keep his mind active. He never tired of asking "big" questions, but he also greatly enjoyed watching sports on television and telling silly jokes and making puns.

When John and I asked him to marry us, Grandpa Harvey was enthusiastic. He was a bit alarmed when we planned out the ceremony ourselves. When we provided an outline, though, he relaxed and the ceremony went well.

I'm grateful to have had Grandpa Harvey in my life. He was a loving grandfather to Bob, Paul, and me and made me feel that I was an important part of his life. I never questioned that he regarded me as his granddaughter.

– *Karen*

Next, Bob Wood:

The first trip I took with Grandpa Harvey was a weeklong trip to Denver between my sophomore and junior years in high school. We went to museums, the Denver Mint, and saw many other sights in Denver. We went to a restaurant called "Turks," which Grandpa Harvey and my dad had frequented many years before. Turks was originally a restaurant on the first floor and a gambling house on the second, and there was a stairway hidden in one of the stalls in the ladies room. We also went to see *Joseph* by Andrew Lloyd Webber, who also wrote *Jesus Christ Superstar*.

Grandpa Harvey took me to Boston and Washington, DC, right after I graduated from high school. We spent a lot of time in museums, ate lobster several times, and saw the sights in both cities. We also visited Harvard, where Grandpa Harvey had studied, and had dinner with Larry McCargar, a prior student of his who was a professor there.

During my time in college, Grandpa Harvey flew me to Lincoln and we went to a Cornhuskers football game. He also flew me to Denver twice for Thanksgiving break. On one of these trips, we went to see the magician David Copperfield. Our Thanksgiving dinners were always at the Wellshire Inn and always included Dr. James Galvin.

The last time I saw Grandpa Harvey was when I was in my early thirties. My girlfriend and I flew to Denver to visit him for a few days. On this trip, I had the pleasure of taking him out to the Wellshire Inn. It was a small gesture after all he had done for me, but he sure made a big deal of thanking me!

In addition to our travels together, Grandpa Harvey and I stayed in contact throughout my adult life. He was a good source for me when I was trying to determine what my long-term goals were. When I lacked confidence in myself, he would buoy my spirits and tell me how much potential I had. Sometimes he would tell me stories about successful people he had known (there were many) and about the struggles they'd had in life. He was always full of unconditional love, and I am grateful to have had him in my life. I know I am a better person because of his influence and love.

– Bob

And finally, Paul, his Inupiat grandson:

I remember Grandpa Harvey as he was the only grandpa I had growing up. When I was younger, I knew Grandpa Harvey as a spiritual man and as a minister in the Methodist Church. To be honest, I really did not understand what that was all about. Of course, as I got older, it made sense in a way that I was able to understand.

Many of my memories of Grandpa have been around hockey. He had come to a lot of my tournaments, especially those in Colorado. One time, he came to see me play in Waterloo, Iowa. I always gave him a puck when I scored a hat trick.

After I graduated from high school, he took me on a trip to Washington, DC. During this trip, we went to the Ford Theatre where Lincoln was shot, to the changing of the guard at the Tomb of the Unknown Soldier, and to the White House. We went to many museums there as well.

I miss Grandpa Harvey a lot. I love you, Grandpa.

– *Paul*

Why did Harvey choose us to be his family, and why did we incorporate him as a surrogate father and grandfather? Why did this unlikely scenario develop in the first place, and why did it persist for more than sixty years? And why does he still remain a presence in our lives, ten years after his death? His later books on loneliness and solitude may offer us some insight into his feelings, although he was always involved with others, and cherished his students both at Iliff and Nebraska Wesleyan. More important, I believe was his reverence for Albert Schweitzer and Albert Einstein. He frequently quoted both "My life is my argument" (Schweitzer) and "Only a life lived for another is a life worthwhile" (Einstein). Didn't Harvey Potthoff's life fulfill these lofty ideals? And weren't I and my family the beneficiaries? We, in turn, returned his love without reservation. He inspired us as a mentor, guided us through various successes and failures in our own lives, and always offered his love no matter what the circumstances. It was always willingly received.

I was never alone.

– Dr. Thomas C. Wood

Wood family photo used with permission

Bob, Kathie, Paul, Karen, and Harvey at a family gathering in Alaska

9

BEYOND FRIENDSHIP

Charles Milligan and Alton Templin
Richard L. Phillips, editor

Many of the Iliff faculty members who shared faculty status with Harvey Potthoff certainly fit the beyond-friendship designation. Even so, Dr. Charles S. Milligan and Dr. J. Alton Templin stand out as measured by overlapping years together, by common interests, and by depth of similar scholarship.

Both were Iliff students while Harvey was teaching part-time at Iliff and was the senior minister at Christ Methodist Church. Each worked with Harvey in a variety of ways. Milligan was an associate pastor at Christ Church with Harvey for a time before going on to Harvard. Templin had a series of similar relationships with Harvey before also going to Harvard for additional graduate study. Each continued to be in regular contact with Potthoff while away from Denver.

Milligan joined the Iliff faculty full-time in 1957, retiring in 1988. He remained very close to Harvey in the years during their careers, their retirements, and until Potthoff's death in 2002. Templin returned to Iliff full-time in 1967, retiring in 1997. He also was close to Harvey for the remainder of his life. Milligan remained a valuable and active member of the Potthoff Discussion Group until the time of his death in 2011 at age ninety-three. Charles was to write a chapter for this biography and had gathered some of the materials he had planned to use. His widow, Nancy, gave me the folders of these materials.

Some of that information is part of the content of this chapter; all of it is now in the Iliff Archives.

Templin remains an active member of the Potthoff Discussion Group, which meets for lunch and discussion of prearranged reading material on a monthly basis. Alton has made many helpful contributions to this biography (for which I am very grateful) in addition to the content in this chapter. Like Charles, he introduced Harvey on a number of occasions and wrote some short biographical sketches, which are now part of the Potthoff archival holdings. Alton and Charles knew Harvey for more years than any of Harvey's other faculty colleagues.

Templin joined the faculty at Iliff in the area of theological history seven years after I graduated. Alton later paid me the honor of inviting me to write a chapter on Dr. Howard Ham in the book Alton edited (*An Intellectual History of the Iliff School of Theology*, 1992, published by the Iliff School of Theology). Dr. Ham had been both a student and later a colleague (1951–1960) of Potthoff's and had been one of my Iliff teachers and later my doctoral advisor during my graduate work at Syracuse University. Ham died a few years ago, or he would have shared in this biography of Potthoff.

Charles Milligan wrote several papers on varied aspects of

Potthoff's theology, and they are in the Iliff archival holdings. He also put together some pages of biographical information that he used to introduce Harvey at various times. He was the editor of the 1981 "Essays in Honor of Harvey H. Potthoff" in *The Iliff Review*. Charles and Alton were key participants in the 1981 retirement events honoring Potthoff; beyond Iliff, they were also colleagues in church and social service, and they were social companions.

I am certain, from Harvey's standpoint, there was no closer friend in the career they shared over their many years at Iliff than Milligan. Potthoff often wrote and spoke of Charles as one of his soul mates. In the last months of Harvey's life, Milligan was one of the friends who visited and assisted him in a great variety of ways. Milligan was joined in such supportive and pastoring roles by many others, including Templin. Taking Harvey to appointments, out to shop, being a confidant and a spiritual companion are among the many roles Milligan played.

To understand the respect and trust Harvey had for Charles and Alton, one has but to listen to the audiotape recording of their analyses, along with Potthoff himself, of Harvey's theology in sessions of the last course he taught before retiring from Iliff in 1981.[1] Having stated that, it must also be observed that they did not all agree on all matters of philosophical or practical theology, but they were always on very parallel pathways.

Charles Milligan was a person of such varied interests, such depth of scholarship, and such important social and community involvement—as well as being an avid churchman and treasured family man—that his life was in many ways parallel to Harvey's. They were as close both professionally and personally as any two faculty colleagues I have ever

HHP personal photo, Iliff Archives (cropped by Mary Sue Alexander)

Charles Milligan on the left, Alton Templin the right, photo late '80s or early '90s

known. The materials in the library and in the archives on Charles are quite voluminous and indicate his tremendous breadth of interests. As a resource for his peers and students, Milligan's peers at Iliff are few in number. Names that must be mentioned who were with him at Iliff, in addition to Harvey and Alton, are William Bernhardt, Martin Rist, and Howard Ham, all wonderful teachers and brilliant scholars. In his later years, many others should undoubtedly be added to this brief list.[2]

Charles S. Milligan

(Introduced and edited by R. L. Phillips)

No individual was more qualified to write about Harvey than Charles. They were the closest of friends. Harvey saw in him both depth of scholarship and outstanding skills as minister and as teacher. The following content, extracted from Charles's written materials, is a sample of his reflections and analysis of Potthoff as theologian and person. I have taken care not to duplicate too much of similar reflections contained later in this chapter from Alton Templin, himself a wonderfully able scholar and productive member of the Iliff community in a number of important roles over many years of service. Harvey, Charles, and Alton all served as editors of the *The Iliff Review*.

The bulk of the following content is from the papers (there are twenty-one, which include the remarks Milligan made at Potthoff's memorial service) that Milligan had put in a folder in preparation for writing a chapter in this biography. One paper, "The Intellectual Life of Harvey Potthoff," was written and given as an address by Charles in February 2003, a year after Harvey died and about eight years before Charles's death. It is obvious that he intended this to be the chief candidate for inclusion in the chapter he was to write. The reader and I are both very fortunate that Nancy Milligan passed his folder of materials on to me so we could all experience these reflections. What is reproduced here, with his original footnotes and only slightly reduced in length and with few editorial insertions, is a tribute to both of these scholar-friends.[3] Now to Milligan's own words.

* * *

Our friendship spanned sixty-four years and included an incredible number of hours in simple conversation. It was not difficult to discern those things that were obviously of great importance to him. One such example was of his eighth- or ninth-grade teacher in Le Sueur, Minnesota. What she opened up to him was discovery of the beauty and the thought and the music of the poetry of Wordsworth. Harvey said, "It opened up a whole new world to me." It may surprise you to know that in this early stage, Harvey's favorite Wordsworth poem was "The Character of the Happy Warrior." That tells us something about this *appreciative* quality and having a solid intellectual ferment in it. His approach had an almost scholastic, line by line, exegesis of the poem.

So this is my suggestion of the first thing to be noted about the intellectual life of Harvey H. Potthoff: his *appreciative side*. And that ran throughout his life. One reason that he was such an interesting person is that he was such an interested person. Furthermore, he was not only interested—*awake to the presence of*—but open to receiving from it. That was his appreciative approach to life, wherever and whatever.

In connection with that, it is useful to be reminded of favorite authors, writers about whom Harvey was enthusiastic. One of these was Bernard Meland of Chicago. I still remember coming out of church one Sunday around 1940 and him saying, "You know, this Meland fellow has some interesting things to say." I had not heard of Meland, so this made me curious. No religious philosopher that I know of wrote more insightfully about the neglected appreciative functions of our intellect, which Meland called, "appreciative awareness," which he said "gives a kind of nobility to the human venture."[4]

Harvey did not discover deep appreciation as a result of Meland's work. A schoolteacher had already done that in Le Sueur. Meland and no doubt others had illumined the appreciative quality as one of the essential attributes of mature religion. It is impossible to grasp accurately Potthoff's theology if you are not aware of the appreciative approach to life which undergirds and permeates it.

Of course that applies to people as well as things. When new faculty members joined the Iliff faculty, Harvey invited them to dinner at either the Wellshire or the Burnside Hotel. My wife and I were sometimes included as old-timers. After conventional inquiries, he would ask, "What is new in your field of specialty?" And that would be followed by many more questions inviting the newcomer to unload out of the newcomer's store of accumulated knowledge, about which not everybody had been eager to hear in detail.

Now to Harvey's underlying life-view, cosmic-view. Every theology has a few underlying and undergirding presuppositions. You find them in the early years, in the middle years, and in the later years. I mention but three. There well may be two or so more, but these will suffice to orient his continuing outlook on life and the world.

First, Evolution. I do not mean this merely in the biological sense, but also in the way one sees activity and process everywhere. The 1920s saw a plethora of important books in the Western world on creative evolution. This marked a basic shift from nineteenth-century thought, which was dominated by Hegel and his theory of thesis and antithesis. This new extension of Darwin's theory can be summarized as viewing historic process being one of experimentation in which there is challenge again and again, confrontation and struggle again and again. This involves new ideas, interaction between humanity and environment, requires cooperation and symbiosis, inevitable loss and defeat, as well as the emergence of the genuinely new and creative consequences.

That is quite distinct from Hegel's rather mechanical synthesis and belief in automatic progress, and certainly a far cry from Hegel's view of the state as embodiment of the divine.

This means an understanding that processes of change come about by growth, not by quantitative manipulation and compromise. This is the way character development occurs, the way religions develop, the way civilizations mature, the way significant human institutions and bondings flower, whether that be marriage or friendship, church or action group, neighborhood or cluster. In that orientation, Whitehead's philosophy of organicism, where organic involvements are the basic metaphor, struck a responsive chord in Harvey's soul. There "deep calleth unto deep." So, Harvey wrote:

> The time has come to seek an understanding of the meaning of God in relating to a dynamic, relational, and evolutionary world, and to rethink the doctrines of God, [humanity], salvation (and related doctrines) in terms which reflect contemporary perceptions of the way things are.[5]

Significant change is to be understood in evolutionary terms.

A second undergirding principle was what he called the **one-order theory of reality.** In other words, we have no basis for bisecting reality into two or more realms, as Plato did or as medieval thought did, in positing a natural realm and a supernatural realm, each with different rules and laws. "This one order is regarded as being highly complex (possibly involving levels) but with an interrelationship of parts. There is both continuity and creativity in the order of nature. ..."[6]

Many religious philosophers as well as theologians were naturalistic in the one order theory of reality. Bernard Loomer, for example, called this "the universal web" in which all things are in some way or other interrelated. That would be a metaphysical presupposition, a nondualistic conception of all reality.

In Dr. Potthoff's theology, there is another side to that one-order theory, an epistemological application corresponding to the metaphysical one. All truth, all knowledge, is to some extent interrelated and interdependent. This becomes clearer when we see it as a denial of *absolute* compartmentalization of knowledge.[7] In various ways, we find him saying this: "Relevant theology always seeks to set forth doctrines of God and [humanity] consistent with available knowledge."[8] This does not mean that theology derives its significance and illumination from physics and chemistry, but that it may not with impunity ignore or contradict established truths of the physical world. Again Harvey: "A major task of theology is that of setting forth groupings of ideas which provide the intellectual framework for a religious interpretation of [human beings] and the system of events of which [we] are a part."[9]

It is important in this connection to point out that the one-order theory of reality does not mean that there is a pervasive oneness or sameness beneath the differences and contrasts we find in nature and human nature. Quite the contrary: the fecundity, the creativity that is stirring within all things has almost run amok with diversity. The variegated realities are not superficial or epiphenomenal "appearances" of an underlying really real substance. Every new discovery seems to bring out new forms of this incredible yeasty ferment of particular differences. The DNA tiny twisted ladder, for example, which contains the informational memory and directionality of individual lives is astonishing in the fact that no two are identical; even so, continuity pervades throughout each species. Continuity does not mean uniformity.

Harvey was profoundly affected by this vision of interrelatedness, amid extravagant diversity and particularity what W. H. Auden called "the happy eachness of all things." Harvey's great mentor, Alfred North Whitehead, referred to God in some functions as "the Principle of Concretion." You might expect such a physical universe as this to grind out replicas of things and peoples and events. But what we have are concrete events, this particular happening and that—particular, definite, concrete, somewhat unique things and events and cabbages and kings. It is a crude image, but one way of imaging the principle of concretion is as if the great cosmic thrust passes through a divine screen that would not permit any reality to be merely a duplicate of others. Creative emergence is not an assembly line.

These undergirding presuppositions of course underwent transformations and developments over the years, and that was especially the case with the **one-order theory of truth.**

The third basic stance was not in the form of being a presupposition, but rather a trait of character. This is a character trait that took me years to perceive. I am going to call this the spiritual roots of German Pietism. The Potthoff father and grandfather were ministers in the German Methodist Episcopal Church, a branch of the Methodist Episcopal Church. The pietist movement began with Philipp Jakob Spener in

Frankfurt am Main in the seventeenth century and emphasized a vital personal Christianity—not individualist isolation—but deep personal faith conjoined in community with fellow Christians. It influenced the Moravians, the hymns of Gerhardt, and German Methodism among others also in Scandinavia and Switzerland.

Harvey did not talk much about this, but I am convinced that it had been bred into him in terms of the inward genuineness of his faith, his quiet unassuming dignity, his habitual kindness, his whole resonance to Jesus of the parables and the Sermon on the Mount. Perhaps a short way of indicating the spirit here is to say I see a kindred spirit at work in harmony with what we find in Meister Eckhart and Zwingli, in Schleiermacher, Albert Schweitzer, and Dietrich Bonhoeffer.

And what is the connection with Harvey's intellectual life? I find it in his avoidance of the debate format and debate style, his strong distaste for any exhibition of arrogant hostility in theological discussion, and in his inability to discuss the nature of God at length without relating it to mature human faith. And I find it also in his strong self discipline, the way his religious being was embedded in nature, intellectually as well as emotionally, his recognition that despite our wisdom, we know in part, yet we do not hide in the mystery of the unknown, but we find the holy in the known and in the knowing of it. Pietism did not have a monopoly on these splendid qualities, but the whole ensemble of them came into the mind and character of the child out of that strand of religious culture, the whole of it as the core of his being, closer than breathing, nearer than hands and feet. In his last weeks, and indeed on the day of his death, Harvey's grandfather's German Methodist hymnal was on his desk. It was from seeing that as a symbol that it dawned on me that there had all this time been that underlying nexus of meaning.

I turn now to some of the strands of development and discovery in Harvey's intellectual life. For he was a lifelong learner with a childlike delight in encountering something new or learning of an arena of life that was new to him.

The first area was in the realms of science and the interplay between science and religion. I am not going to elaborate on this, because an entire program in this series has already been devoted to that under the very capable leadership of Richard Phillips. So I merely want to acknowledge its importance in Harvey's intellectual growth over the years. Just try to imagine making a list of how much has been discovered in science since the 1920s and 1930s when Harvey was in high school and college. Even in later years, when our energy for tackling a difficult new area is waning, Harvey did that again and again.

My second example or case study is cultural anthropology. It is a beautiful example, because it includes practical application and, equally, knowledge for its own sake—knowledge born of strong curiosity. I remember Harvey expressing sharp interest in a paper on Navajo religion in 1946. I don't know whether that had any connection with his reading Clyde Kluckhohn's *Mirror for Man*, published in 1949, but in any case he read that and it had a profound effect on his thinking about the human condition as well as the grand range of religious belief and practice. Margaret Mead at the time called Kluckhohn's book "the best contemporary introduction to modern anthropology." And Stuart Chase, in reviewing the book, said, "If the statesmen of the world had the knowledge continued within *Mirror for Man,* people everywhere could sleep sounder at night." That is the effect it had on Harvey. Also I must mention the late Ruth Underhill, who was one of his special friends and undoubtedly shared her vast anthropological expertise. And also his brother Carl was for some years on the governmental medical staff on the Navajo reservation. Undoubtedly these were among the key influences during Harvey's later years.

Application? When Harvey was at Nebraska Wesleyan University in the 1980s, he ran across Nebraska Indians at some point. He began asking questions and looking into things and making connections. The result was that he persuaded the right people to invite representative Native American tribal leaders to participate in a day of special programs. Student and faculty involvement was incredible. It expanded and became an annual event throughout Harvey's years there and beyond. You will not be surprised to know that he became a trusted personal friend of the elders and had periodic contacts with them in addition to the university events.

Not surprisingly, this interest continued after he retired from Nebraska Wesleyan. His surrogate son, Dr. Thomas Wood, supplied Harvey with book after book on Native American life and ways: *The Telling of the World, Painted Prayers, The Scalpel and the Buffalo.* He became a promoter of books and generous bestower of them.

A third area of interest, which was not new to him but which flourished greatly in the autumn of life, was the system of criminal justice. In the early years, he had been a regular speaker at the Mountain View Girls Prison in Morrison. He also served as advisor and consultant in various ways. He spoke one

Sunday afternoon on the theme of applying yourself, having goals and getting a grip on them, and doing something about them. Now.

On Monday morning, Harvey's phone rang. It was Mrs. Porter, superintendent of the reformatory. She said something like this: "Thanks to you, three of our girls took your message to heart and escaped last night." Harvey, who was notoriously swift on the uptake, said, "It's reassuring to know that some of them were listening." I have to insert here that there were a lot of laughs over the years, and nobody enjoyed them more than Harvey. At Christ Church he always had a footnote at the end of the program with asterisks that referred to places in the service where ushers could seat latecomers. One Sunday, the secretary accidentally typed a *b* in place of an *s*, so the footnote read "Ushers will beat latecomers at these points in the services."

And just one more: Harvey had the habit of saying at each section of his sermon, "and now the second point is..." Apparently he decided one day that he was overdoing that. So he dropped it. After the service, a woman said as she shook his hand, "I loved that sermon. It had no point in it."

Harvey's volunteer service at the Mountain View Girls Prison in Morrison, Colorado, was very worthwhile. It was later at Nebraska Wesleyan that this interest took a remarkable turn. Somebody there saw the gift he had for relating to people in ways that release deeper meanings in their lives. That person asked him if he would be willing to visit a couple of men on death row in the Nebraska State Prison. So he did. Out of that, he formed a friendship with Wili Otey. He visited Wili regularly and got him interested in poetry. Wili began to write poetry and eventually published two collections of it in the prison press. Wili regarded Harvey as the father he had never known, and I think Harvey was prouder of the Father's Day card Wili sent than of his honorary degree. Harvey got involved in the hopeless task of trying to gain a stay of execution for Wili. They had a remarkable team doing their best, but of course they were up against an attorney general who had made killing somebody his cause célèbre.

I recently chanced upon a book, *Final Exit: Portraits from Death Row*. Boston photographer Lou Jones had gone around the country doing photographic portraits of men on death row wherever they would allow him to do that. Imagine how pleased I was to find that the first photograph in the book was that of Harold Lamont "Wili" Otey. Oh how we wish sometimes we could turn the clock back. What I would give to have run across that book before Harvey died, to show it to him.

Here you have another chapter in the intellectual venture of Harvey Potthoff that you will not find in his writings. It illustrates how lively his mind was and how he believed that the living God is hidden in the midst of existence, wherever we are, and not merely in books, and is not only to be discovered through theological vocabulary.

I turn now to observations about Harvey's calling as I think he saw it and some of the themes that he especially emphasized. In his last years, he became intrigued with the metaphor of weaving. This may have come from a prayer by Fr. W. E. Orchard: "We would stay for a moment the noisy shuttle of time that we may see the pattern in its weaving." And certainly it was furthered by a remark by Darryl Fairchild. He was a quadriplegic Iliff student whom Harvey had quietly helped in very practical as well as intellectual ways. Harvey once asked Darryl how he managed to hold up his spirit: "What's your secret?" Darryl said, "I think everybody has something he has to weave into his life. In my case, it is a wheelchair."

If there was any one event in Iliff's history prior to his own career about which Harvey spoke with excitement and pride, it was Dr. Longacre's defense of the right of Iliff faculty members to believe in evolution a dozen or more years before Harvey's student days.

Returning to the theme of calling, if there was any one quotation above all others that articulated Harvey's calling I believe it was this from Whitehead's *Adventures of Ideas*: "I hazard the prophecy that that religion will conquer which can render clear to popular understanding some eternal greatness in the passage of temporal fact."[10] That sets forth what Harvey's professional calling—whether as pastor or professor of theology—was about. Another favorite passage, which every student of Whitehead knows, was where he wrote about the religious vision.

> Religion is the vision of something which stands beyond, behind, and within, the passing flux of immediate things; something which is real, and yet waiting to be realized...[and concludes] The fact of the religious vision, and its history of persistent expansion, is our one ground for optimism.[11]

Whitehead here is connecting vision with an ultimate, long-range, far-off idealism, although there are intimations of it in the present. I bring this up in order to contrast it with

Harvey Potthoff's doctrine of the religious *vision*. I do not suggest that Potthoff disagrees with Whitehead's view, but that he adds a somewhat different emphasis. Whitehead tends to connect that with optimism. Potthoff tends to connect it with hope, which is slightly different. Whitehead's vision has to do with a "far-off divine event," or at least more ideal culmination. Potthoff's has to do with a vision tied in with empirical realities in days when ideal hopes might easily be dismissed outright.

When Harvey Potthoff speaks of hope, he also is talking about a *vision*, but it is not a premonition of a more satisfactory state of things for us. It is rather a trust "in the possibility of emerging values."[12] In contrast with the person who "sees" hope in terms of a "happy realization of [one's] wishes," it is a vision of "belief in the possibility of emergent good." Another difference between these two sorts of vision is that the former tends to see desired results as to be achieved by a power other than ourselves, whereas Harvey's view is "inclined to place greater emphasis on the significance of human thought and effort, seeing them in the context of a more inclusive divine order worthy of [our] devotion and trust." The former sees hope as "primarily a matter of expectation," whereas Potthoff sees hope as "the quality of spirit which flows from belief in the possibility of emergent good."[13]

Empirical theologies that take a process metaphysics seriously are more inclined to speak in terms of possibilities than in terms of final promises. This does not mean that empirical theologies are lacking in a positive kind of faith. On the contrary, they reflect oftentimes a more positive attitude in appreciating the possibilities in [one's] present situation, while still holding to the conviction that the divine realities we experience today are continuous with the determining realities of tomorrow.[14]

I recall in this connection a sermon that Potthoff preached around 1941. He dealt with insight and outlook, suggesting that an adequate faith for the times required both sharp insight and broad outlook. They balance each other. They supplement each other. Each restrains the other as a countervailing force, to prevent the other from going off the deep end. Insight and outlook—not enemies or opposites, but necessary supplements. Thus *vision* in the religious sense, is not only a matter of far-off ideal hopes, but a matter of every day having requisite *insight* into the hidden inner workings of life and equally a healthy, hopeful *outlook* on the world and the creatures in it. As he put it:

> What shall it profit [one who] has hope of a distant consummation but today finds little significance in the enterprise of living? The hope modern religion had best encourage is the hope of an expectant attitude—seeing the living God in the potentialities of the present situation. The hope for tomorrow may well rest upon the qualities of expectancy and sense of responsibility with which we approach today.[15]

Is it not extraordinary to discover that, in some functional terms, Dr. Potthoff was more in line with classical Christianity than either neo-orthodoxy or fundamentalism, evangelicalism or new-age? For what he was saying was that faith should make us hopeful and optimistic, but not because we therefore think we are going to get what we want, but because we can trust God to move creatively and redemptively in the lives of many, whether we live to see it or not. He was asking us to identify our hope not with me and mine, but with the human family, with generations yet to come, in ways perhaps far removed from present comforts and delights. One cannot expect that to sit well with the "me generation" or "what's in it for me and mine?" gospel. This requires a style of worship that is not primarily a performance (to please *me*) or entertainment (to distract *me*), but a vision to sustain, renew, uplift, nourish, and whereby the Eternal Thou "restoreth my soul," as the Psalm saith.

Now one further step in the Potthoff doctrine of hope. He believed, based on what he learned from psychologists like Gordon Allport, Eric Erikson, and certainly William James that the self-centered life is self-defeating. This is familiar ground, especially when related to theological doctrines of creatureliness and finitude. However, in Harvey's immanentalist view, the dimensions of tragedy and suffering are not due to sin or the punishment of a vindictive God, rather simply the given absurd attributes of the terms on which life is possible. Thus, gross inequities in addition to humanly contrived inequities befall us helter-skelter. And thus it is that a religious faith surely ought to motivate people of sincere faith to mitigate chance inequities, prevent to the extent possible their recurrence, and soften the consequences by personal intervention as well as socially organized programs. The understanding of the nature of God ought not be an additional *problem* in this area—as, for example, when it is claimed that God selects persons and times in which to inflict suffering—but is our resource for compassion, inspiration, and improvement.

Because of all this, Harvey received special delight in the habitual reading of biographies in which he found doctrine about human condition substantiated in actual lives lived out in actual conditions. For this sort of religion to have sustaining power in life, the concept of God has to be believable. When struck by the shock of brute reality, it has to carry the ring of reality.

Perhaps it is appropriate at this point to say in the simplest terms I can what the nub of Harvey's conception of God was. It would be quite wrong to take what I am going to say as Harvey Potthoff's conception of God. It is only the seed of his conception of the indwelling God.

If we look at life, our own or our friends', back in history or across the seas, we see many examples of new things coming to be, surprising things, unanticipated things. There is a creative thrust to be observed in experience. If we recall the cuts and bruises we have suffered off and on, we recall that there is in the very nature of nature a **power of healing**, of cleansing, of reknitting skin and tissue. Healing is hidden within trees and babies, dogs and fields. It is a part of the way things are.

Look where you will and you find **patterns manifest**—beauty—not only in sunsets and snow on the mountains, birds and butterflies, but the DNA double helix, Charlotte's web, the stars, West Running Brooks, the frost on the windowpane, a four-year-old's spontaneous dance. If there is anything that characterizes creation, it is above all the extravagance of patterned beauty: the beauty of holiness and the holiness of beauty. **Compassion:** the mother pheasant who will risk her life to distract the hunter from where her chicks are in the nest, the mother bear who will defend her cub, the poor young mother who will sell herself to get money to feed her child.

These are persistent attributes embedded in the very nature of things. Their existence does not mean that everything is peaceful or fair. Nature is still red in tooth and claw. Humanity remains capable of wanton destruction and selfish idiocy. But that these attributes—creativity, healing, redemptive renewal, unbearable beauty, and life-bearing compassion—are real. We do not look for arguments to prove their existence; we open our eyes and behold. These realities do not exist as isolated powers. They are intertwined. There is an interplay among them. There is a unity about this cluster of life-affirming, value-enhancing, wonder-evoking powers of goodness in which we live and move and have our being. They are real. In their unity, they inspire worship.

That depiction does not do justice to Potthoff's fully developed concept of God. It is, however, the seed, the nub of that conception. And that is real. Here is Harvey's fuller depiction of this:

> At the heart of things there is an organizing principle, a patternfulness, a purposiveness, a striving for goals. We discern it in protoplasm; we discern it in the processes of evolution, we discern it in human beings. [The human] is part of the natural processes, but in the capacity of reason, evaluation, appreciation, decision, and commitment the natural order comes to a new level of achievement. In the divine order life, mind, spirit are achievements in which natural bodily experience has

> its role. Creative becoming is fundamental in the divine pattern. Our experience of God includes participation in the divine processes of creative becoming—and this includes committed, creative participation in the body-mind-spirit pattern of existence.[16]

Now this real, believable God is not going to be satisfactory to those who want a God who plays favorites and is mostly concerned to fulfill my personal wishes and provide special protection for me and mine. But there is no problem of belief in this indwelling God and certainly no problem of responding through worship where we articulate wonder, love, and praise, as well as serving through compassion and service to the divine processes of creative becoming.

I cannot conclude this account of Harvey Potthoff's intellectual pilgrimage without saying something about his courses on death and dying. As a pastor, he of course had to deal with this, and he seemed to have a special interest in the subject and a very helpful way of ministering to people in grief or impending death. Naturally, as he grew older, this area acquired an existential dimension that added to his effectiveness in dealing with the subject. It is well known that his course on death and dying at Nebraska Wesleyan University was very popular among the students and filled a large room to capacity every term it was offered.

It seemed to me that in his last three years and declining strength, he particularly welcomed reassurance that his life had had enduring significance. I was quite touched by that, and it dawned on me that no one is capable of convincingly telling himself or herself of one's own life significance. Especially in life's sundown approach, we need that word from someone else. It is important to note that in Luther's "priesthood of all believers," he did not mean "each one his own priest," which does not work, but "each one her neighbor's priest."

Many of Harvey's teachings about death and dying are fairly standard, at least among sensitive mentors. So Harvey wrote:

> Eternal life is defined not by length of days or years, but by depth of relationship to God. That life can be real in our todays and in our tomorrows. We experience many little deaths along the way. In those very deaths our experience of eternal life can be renewed and deepened. Eternal life begins when our relationship with God is so real and meaningful that in the midst of time we have an inner relationship, which overcomes the tyranny of time.[17]

And again:

> How important it is that we mean something to each other in our living and in our rejoicing and in our grieving and in our dying. ... Sometimes the spoken word communicates more than we know. But there is also communication in the touch of the hand and sometimes in shared silence.[18]

There is one final note I want to sound in connection with Harvey's intellectual *style*. I believe the kind of truth he was dealing with was found by way of processes of disclosure.

As with the parables, the teaching begins as it were with the words *behold or hearken.* Theology in Harvey's manner casts a light upon things so that those who will ponder and open their understanding will hear and see and comprehend. They will perceive that they are standing on holy ground, though they had known it not. This explains Harvey's disinterest in debate as a technique for teaching. For that works against disclosure and discovery. The teacher and the pastor have this high calling, this privilege, of turning light on ordinary things, and calling attention to the manifestations of existence in such a manner that those who are ministered to will thenceforth see in a new way. "It makes all the difference in the world," Harvey says, "in what light we see life."[19]

He [Potthoff] loved the Bible, he did not worship it, for that would be bibliolatry. He saw it as "a lamp upon our feet, a light unto our path," not as a map or secret code.[20] And Jesus Christ he viewed as "the revealing person" in whom "the redeeming love of God is manifest,"[21] a silent companion along the trek of living.

I select but one talent among many, many others: Harvey Potthoff had this gift to enable other persons all over the map to discover hitherto hidden significance in their own lives. At Iliff, if ever there was enduring influence in the lives of students—intellectual, spiritual, and deeper appreciation—it was in the career of Dr. Potthoff.

* * *

At the end of Charles's remarks in Harvey's memorial service he quotes Henry James, saying his words are a perfect fit for Harvey: "He opened paths for our children's feet to follow. Something of him will be a part of us forever."

J. Alton Templin

Editor's note: The following content was provided by Alton Templin. He edited and reworded only slightly from papers and tributes he had previously written for and about Harvey.

Retirement Party for Harvey Potthoff, Spring 1981

When Harvey Potthoff retired [spring 1981], the faculty had a special banquet that included many tributes to him. Among those was a presentation of a Harvard CHAIR. I was chosen to be the spokesman on behalf of the whole faculty. This was my statement at the time more than thirty years ago:

As I reflected on what I might share tonight on behalf of all of the faculty, I remembered a story once told by one of Harvey's longtime friends. Everything his friends tell me about Harvey I take very seriously—although some may suggest this story is apocryphal, even made up!

Harvey Potthoff's insistence that empiricism is the best method for theology goes back a long way. From the very beginning of his career, he used experience as the basis of his theological knowledge. It seems that many years ago, Harvey was serving two small churches in his home state of Minnesota. Even then he insisted on the empirical method, i.e., that we learn through our experiences. This carried over into theology, that we develop these concepts through experience as well. In this situation in Minnesota, Harvey was serving two small churches near to each other. There was a small forest between them of little over a mile, whereas the road went around a much longer distance. Even then Harvey liked to walk, and when the weather was good, he would finish at the one church and then walk briskly through the woods to arrive at the second church with ten minutes to spare.

Ordinarily all went along very well, but one special morning he was a little over halfway between the churches when what should appear on the path ahead of him but a Minnesota black bear. For a moment, the two were both surprised and stopped to think about the surprising situation. Harvey knew he was well over halfway to his second church, so to turn and run was no real answer. Rather, he decided to walk on a detour a short way off the path, hoping the bear would not venture off the path into the thick underbrush.

Alas, the bear had different ideas, and as Harvey began to walk his detour, the bear began to follow at an increasingly brisk pace. Harvey saw he had to run for it, so he began zigzagging toward the edge of the woods. The bear grabbed at his arm, tearing his coat; then again the bear grabbed at him, catching his shirt and ripping it. Finally, as he reached the edge of the woods, Harvey sensed that the bear had stopped, not wanting to be out in the open.

Still breathing hard and still too scared to realize how lucky he was, he reached the church. Some of the people were beginning to gather, and Harvey was met at the door by one of the leaders. This gentleman, seeing the torn coat and shirt, and dirt all over his clothing, even Harvey's hair was very much disarranged—that was when Harvey had hair—asked Harvey what had happened. Harvey told him the story in brief. The layman expressed his surprise because bears were seldom seen in that part of Minnesota. Then, trying to calm the tense situation, the layman remembered some sermons he had heard and decided to discuss some of them. He said, "Harvey, you have often told us that in times of adversity, we must put the experience into a larger perspective and gain theological insight thereby. Tell me, since we learn from all of our experiences, what theological truth did you learn from this experience?" Harvey thought only a moment and, shaking his head, replied: "I learned this one theological truth—the Lord ain't so good in a bear fight."

From then on, Harvey went on to improve his preaching, improve his theology, and improve his grammar. In the process, however, he was involved in other situations which, while they may not be called bear fights, they were at least conflicts or points of tension. As you know, he was successful in all of them. Let me lift up only four situations briefly.

First, when Harvey was a student at Iliff in the early '30s, he was assigned to preach at the Argo Methodist Church, out in the north area, which is now along Interstate 70, in the warehouse section of Denver. Alas, he got to the church to find the building had been locked up for months, but as in previous trials, he thought the situation through carefully. He found a window unlocked, and he climbed in. That is how he got into the ministry in Colorado.

Second, his ingenuity helped him to the head of the class at Iliff when he received the Elizabeth Iliff Warren Fellowship, Iliff's highest honor. He used this at Harvard, as we know, to study one year under the philosopher Alfred North Whitehead. This was the beginning of another conflict. He became convinced of the importance of the Whiteheadian philosophy as the basis of theology, and became a pioneer in using process thought in theology. Alas, this was in the mid '30s and '40s when Neo-Orthodoxy was in the ascendancy—and it was dogmatic and anything but "process"-oriented. Harvey taught at Iliff part-time for sixteen years (1936 to 1952), and full-time since then, to 1981.[22] For more than half of this period, the process emphasis and the empirical method in theology seemed to be almost nonexistent. Harvey did not flinch, however, but wrote about Christian doctrine as he saw it and as he believed it was exemplified in the experiences of the people with whom he was working. Another area of conflict ended in success.

A third situation concerns finances. Christ Church moved to its present location in 1927 when they built that sanctuary with a small congregation and small resources. Then the Great Depression came two years later. By 1936, when Harvey arrived there, the (mortgage's) principal had not been paid, not all of the interest was ever paid, and foreclosure was predicted by some. There were two other churches (Methodist) in Denver in the same period, with the same problem, and indeed, one of them was lost through foreclosure. During the next few trying years, Harvey was able to keep the hungry bankers at bay, and the church put the finances in order. Harvey presided at the burning of the mortgage of the church in December 1946. Again, success in a bear fight.

Fourth, Harvey was a stabilizing influence in the faculty. He was teaching part-time when I first came as a student. He began teaching full-time when I had finished my second year. The only one here with a longer association with him is Charles Milligan. Charles died June 14, 2011, at age 93, leaving me now with the longest faculty association with Harvey.

How was Harvey a stabilizing influence among the faculty? I believe that if it were not for his gracious manner, his concern for hearing all sides of discussion, and his ability to get to the heart of various issues, there would have been more bear fights within the faculty. I do not mean to suggest this is only the case these past few months when he has been acting president. I suggest, rather, that for about thirty years his gentlemanly counsel has benefitted us all. In a real sense, he has been a minister to the whole faculty.

In anticipating his retirement, many things have already taken place. The trustees launched the campaign to raise funds to establish the Harvey Potthoff Chair of Theology. That has brought forth much response. For example, last fall the students bewailed the fact that for all these years Harvey had no chair, so they gave him the Potthoff chair. Alas, about as soon as he sat on it, the students replaced it back in the Iliff building whence it had come, and he had no chair.

The Alumni/ae gave him the same chair during the Iliff Week of Lectures, but also promptly took it away again. Then a friend of the school, not knowing what the terminology of a Chair of Theology meant, came by one day to see that real chair—again, no chair to sit on. Another person let it be known that he thought the collection of money for the Chair of Theology would be a purse or a going-away gift of money for Harvey—wrong again.

Tonight we are going to solve that problem once and for all. Harvey really needs a place to sit now as well as in the future. We might call it the Harvey Potthoff Chair of Theology, as the trustees did. Even better, on behalf of all of us gathered here tonight, we present to you The Harvey Potthoff Black Wooden Chair of Theology, with Harvard's emblem in gold, purchased through the Harvard Co-op Bookstore, commonly referred to by students as "the coop." In addition, we have a cushion in the appropriate color, Harvard crimson. If you would now, come up here. You may sit on it, and this time, don't let anyone take it away from you.

[*Addendum* added thirty years later: Harvard was well represented in the faculty that evening. Counting Harvey, there were eight with Harvard connections. Five had Harvard doctoral degrees, one had an STM from the Harvard Divinity School, and one had a BA from Harvard College. Since many of us already had Harvard chairs, it is ironic to note that while Harvey was the first among us to have been a student at Harvard, he was the last to have had a real wooden chair from Harvard.]

Harvey's Class His Final Spring Quarter 1981: The Theology of Harvey Potthoff

The final quarter that Harvey taught at Iliff before his retirement included a course entitled The Theology of Harvey Potthoff. He later taught a similar course as he was concluding his eleven-year tenure at Nebraska Wesleyan. I sat through the course to gain a more complete perspective on his theology about which I had known for many years. The format was similar to many he had conducted in the past. We met at 4 p.m. and had a break for dinner. Then at 7:00 p.m., we reconvened to continue until approximately 9 p.m. Harvey gave many summaries of his thought, read selected passages from his writings, and invited some colleagues to share their views on some aspects of the same subject. I was asked to give the final summary of his theology at the end of the quarter. Here is the summary I gave on that May evening in 1981:

As I attempt in a few words to summarize the main emphases of Potthoff's theological writing, and as these have been analyzed and discussed in this class, I should like to put his thought into a historical framework. The historical doctrines by which most of you were introduced into Christianity in your churches, and the historical doctrines which I teach up through the Reformation and beyond, were all characterized by several concepts or assumptions:

a. A supernatural world view and a supernatural creator God.
b. We were created as perfected beings at one instant in time. The human race was sinful, and we in one way or another have come up short—because of sin, we are of lesser stature than when we were created.
c. Our constant struggle has been and must be how to restore a broken, sinful relation with God who desires only the best for us, bungling and hesitating as we are.
d. We often use words like *atonement, justification, sanctification,* or *going on to perfection* against this background.

Alas, much has changed since these world views were first conceived and since they were formulated in church councils or authoritative writings of one type or another.

The significance of the theology of Dr. Potthoff is that it is conceived in a different mode. It uses different understandings of the world, of human beings, of religion, of the church, sin, and so on. To some it may sound like it is not really Christian, certainly not in any traditional sense. I believe, however, that all of you have read enough and heard enough this quarter alone to know that there is a very deep and very meaningful Christian faith expressed here. Let me suggest some of the major elements of what we have heard this quarter—at least some of the basic presuppositions which have been used. To be sure, this is a theology for the modern world, based upon modern understanding. It is certain it would have been out of place a few hundred years ago, or even a few decades ago, against the background of a different world view.

1) There are many strains of thought which we take for granted and which we must use in theological rethinking as well.

a) After Copernicus and Galileo, how do you deal with a stationary sun and a flat earth?

b) After Darwin, what do you do with the concept of a created human being—perfect and never changing?

c) After Freud, what do you do about the idea of a sinful, simple human mind or soul, never changing and never mysterious?

d) After Einstein, what do you do about heaven as up and hell as down when even space itself may be curved?

These are only a few of the newer ideas of which our ancestors had no knowledge, but which we are forced to incorporate into the realities of our everyday life. No theology will speak to the modern world which does not take all of these changes seriously.

2) Modern thought in all fields assumes that this world is the locus of our meaning and our value. This is to say that our theological understanding must emphasize immanence of God, of value, of meaning, and not transcendence or another world or realm. A traditional hymn suggested that heaven is my home and I'm not a citizen of earth, I'm only a pilgrim passing through this vale of tears. A modern theology must be diametrically opposed to this hymn, and must assist concerned people with finding meaning and value in everyday living here and now—or meaning and value will not be found unless fantasized.

3) It has often been suggested or at least assumed that religious understanding is of a higher order than ordinary human knowledge—something beyond the human capacity. The word *revelation* has sometimes been used to indicate some knowledge from outer realms. Dr. Potthoff suggests, instead, that any meaningful religious understanding for us must come through the knowable, the experiencable. Whatever is beyond knowledge and experience will have no meaning for us. [Editor's note: Even so I wish to add here that what is believed by those not of similar persuasion may provide some meaning in their lives.] All of us live in what has been called "the warp and woof of natural, historical, and personal causality."

4) In a previous age, an emphasis was made on the differences between God and man—there was an unbridgeable gap here. There has, however, been no word used more often by Potthoff, I believe, than *relational*. The God-man question is one of relation. That is, there is no objective reality or

objective truth anywhere. Something becomes real and true only as we are related to it. A religious concept, or a religious feeling, or religious insight becomes such for us only when we have some relationship with it. I am not sure how much beauty there is in a sunset or a rose until there is someone who has eyes to see—and little beauty is in a symphony until someone has ears to hear. In the same world view, the theologian Bernard Meland used the term *appreciative awareness.* All things in our living and our experience—religious and otherwise—are involved in that broad concept we use, relativity. Harvey Potthoff often uses the word *contextual* which I take to be pointed toward the same general concept.

5) Previous centuries emphasized a static human nature. Dr. Potthoff has emphasized a human nature that is changing, is becoming. Historians have always emphasized change, development, and the interrelation of various factors in creating an era. The same processes are at work in every individual human being. We are in process of becoming, of growing into a person that has never existed before. We must face problems and challenges which no person and no age faced before. This makes for uncertainty, but it is our destiny. No final word has yet been written about any one of us nor of the human race as a whole. Even that is developing and in process. The unity of a personality is an achievement, not a presupposition.

6) Our forefathers and mothers, and indeed most of the theologians we have studied, have wrapped their theology up in a tight package, with answers to about everything

worth considering. Unfortunately, Dr. Potthoff's theology is not of that sort. Given the presuppositions he uses, and the methods that apply, there are no final answers. There are always some loose ends, some unanswered questions, some more living to be done. We must be satisfied with fewer definite answers and must be satisfied with partial knowledge in many areas. Doubt and uncertainty are essential ingredients in this particular approach to faith. This is what it means to be human, and we must make commitments on the basis of what we do know, even though we have no final answers.

7) Only a theological approach, which takes seriously these commonly accepted methods of gaining knowledge, is meaningful in the world in which we live. Only with this approach can theology be taken seriously by other disciplines and only with such methods can theology be seriously related to the rest of human knowledge. A theology that presupposes a supernatural realm or super-rational approaches can have no real interdisciplinary relation to anything outside its own presuppositions. Theology in a nonrelational, nonempirical, nonscientific, nonmodern mode which is dogmatic, mythological or eschatological speaks only for itself. Dr. Potthoff takes seriously other disciplines, and his theology can be completely interrelated with them. This is perhaps its most important aspect, because now theological discussions can really be a part of the real world, not something over and beyond and superior to knowledge as a whole.

In summary, I believe this theology of Dr. Potthoff is extremely significant for our day because it is:

a. empirical
b. contextual
c. interrelated
d. evolutionary
e. naturalistic
f. pragmatic
g. historical
h. open-ended

In short, it can be meaningfully related to the modern world in which you and I live.

Harvey Potthoff as a Colleague

My Association with Harvey Potthoff's Influence

When I enrolled in Iliff in September 1950, Harvey was teaching part-time while continuing his long career as minister of Christ Methodist Church in Denver. He offered only two courses, which were repeated yearly. These basic courses were God in Contemporary Thought; and Man, Sin and Salvation. During my first two years, I enrolled in both of these courses. When Harvey was invited to become a full-time professor beginning in the fall of 1952, he began to expand his offerings. I took one or two of these newer courses during my last year. I left Iliff in August 1954 and returned for visits only once or twice. For most of the intervening years, I was living in Massachusetts, studying at Harvard, and serving churches there until 1966 when I finished my PhD degree. I was invited back to teach at Iliff in 1967 after an absence of thirteen years.

As a student, I had learned to appreciate the thoroughness of the theological work which I experienced under Harvey's leadership. When I returned to Iliff as a faculty colleague, I learned even more about his theological understanding and how that relates to the real experiences of people—parishioners as well as others. We were colleagues from 1967 to 1981 when he retired and moved to Nebraska Wesleyan University, where he taught until 1992. At that time, he returned to Denver, and we had many more associations during the years from 1992 until his death ten years later.

Harvey as a Builder of Consensus

As I sat through many faculty gatherings or committee meetings, I noticed that Harvey was skilled at forming or building consensus. Many times, after sitting relatively quietly during discussions where disparate ideas were presented and where faculty members were on different "ego trips," Harvey would often formulate a solution that would embody the concerns of divergent viewpoints. Then the meeting could move on to other matters. I believe that Harvey's skill at listening intently before speaking helped to avoid many splits and hard feelings among factions of the faculty when all could leave the meeting with the confidence that their own ideas had been heard and valued. I sensed that there was much harmony and a feeling of common purpose for the whole while Harvey was part of the discussion.

When Harvey retired and left Denver, there seemed to be less harmony among the faculty, although Charles Milligan often performed a mediating presence similar to that of Harvey. Seven years after Harvey retired, Charles also retired (1988). Consensus within the school, especially among the faculty, was further diminished, and a feeling of common purpose seemed to be lacking. Small groups of the faculty had their own agendas and different visions of what was of most importance for the education of Iliff students. About the time of Harvey's retirement and for the next several years, there were many changes in personnel. Almost all of the faculty replacements had little or no strong experience within the church, had never served as ministers within the churches, were not ordained in any denomination, and seemingly saw their task as simply part of an academic community, far removed from the strong church commitment of Harvey and his creative vision for the church.

Harvey was aware of this shift and was saddened by it, and he shared this disappointment. It was far from his main vision of an institution providing intellectual tools to lead the church and to provide ministers who would be "theologians in residence" in their own church settings. On the other hand, however, in keeping with Harvey's broad definition of ministry, many new approaches or new venues for religious concerns could exist within his larger concept of where religious needs abound and for which ministry could be not only church oriented, but perhaps also "society oriented."

Harvey Liked to Be with People

Harvey liked to be with people and had the ability to strike up a conversation with persons of diverse interests and experiences. He had an uncanny ability to draw people into a discussion and then build on their interests or knowledge. He practiced the principles embodied in his book *A Whole Person in a Whole World* (1972). This book was written for lay people and embodied basic concepts that Harvey put into action in all his discussions. In four short chapters, he gave a concise summary of his view concerning the relation of theology to real-life experiences. The chapter headings of Part 2 of this book give a good summary of topics Harvey could well discuss in a casual chat with anyone who was interested. They are:

1. About God—A Depth you may have missed
2. About Persons—A Dignity you may have denied
3. About Life—A Meaning waiting to be experienced
4. About Ourselves—Some Decisions we can make

One of Harvey's favorite settings for discussion was a dinner party where two or three couples would join him for a birthday celebration or an anniversary or for other occasions even if there were no specific theme or reason. I remember many such occasions at the Burnsley Hotel in downtown Denver or at Leo Goto's Wellshire Inn. Harvey often taught courses that met once a week over the dinner hour. The class began at about 4:00 p.m. and took a break for dinner. As many as wished to attend joined Harvey at a predetermined restaurant, where further discussion took place, not usually on the topic of the class. At about 7:00 p.m. the class would reconvene for approximately two more hours.

Although Harvey often set the place and the menu, on one occasion we decided to turn the tables on him. We planned a small gathering at our home to which Harvey was invited. Unknown to him, we also invited one of our students to help. Nobuko Miyake, from Hiroshima, and my wife went down to the Japanese market at Sakura Square to procure ingredients for an authentic Japanese meal. The planning and preparations proceeded on schedule. On this occasion, Harvey had not been in charge of the plan, but we all enjoyed discussion and food as usual.

HARVEY H. POTTHOFF

Harvey as Minister to People in Difficult Situations

Harvey's practice of an inclusive and dynamic theology led him to minister effectively with all types of people and in all situations. Two exceptional instances of this come to mind immediately. Approximately twenty years ago, one of our PhD students, Daryl Fairchild, was involved in a bicycle accident on one of the many routes in Denver developed for exercise, which also encouraged speed. At a certain intersection one afternoon, two bicycles collided. Daryl was so seriously injured that he required a wheelchair thereafter. Harvey was involved in his rehabilitation of many months. This involved a total change and reorientation of Daryl's life work. I think this was a good example of what might be called Harvey's "theology of human concern." This attitude carried over into many other associations that Harvey had with students, although most of these were unknown to the rest of the community.

A quite different situation developed while Harvey was teaching in Nebraska. He became acquainted with a prisoner on death row (Wili Otey) convicted of murder. Through his many visits to the prison, Harvey discovered this inmate had never had much vision or aspiration in life, was always despondent, felt defeated, and never had hope in anything. Through his visits, Harvey gradually helped him to see life in a different way. Evidently he responded well, and Harvey took satisfaction that he had helped to give the individual some aspiration or even hope in life. Harvey said that he believed the prisoner was rehabilitated and should be treated as such. Ultimately, however, the political climate in Nebraska was such that execution became inevitable. As Harvey later discussed this long-term relationship, he seemed to have identified with the prisoner almost as family. It seemed that Harvey was deeply disappointed in the outcome, over which he had no control. This, I think, reflected his theology of ministering to "one of the least of these."

Harvey as Minister of "Celebration"

The title of his book, *God and the Celebration of Life*, captures the spirit of Harvey's career. Since he lived in the context of a wholeness world view, a dynamic connection to all of life, and a trusting relation with whatever processes operate in our lives, for Harvey life itself was a celebration. He enjoyed it to the fullest. He strongly believed that such a life led to a helpful attitude—the opposite would be despair or defeat.

His strong emphasis on hope, however, was not a blind optimism, nor did it evade such problems as evil, suffering, disappointment, and loss. Indeed, *God and the Celebration of Life* includes a chapter entitled "Toward a Theology of Hoping." Harvey strongly believed that learning to live in and cooperate with the dynamic forces of our world could be enhanced by a religious faith that was forward-looking, intellectually grounded, and filled with ultimate meaning. His work in theology sought to instill this attitude of celebration for all to see and experience.

During the summer of 1965, representatives from several Methodist seminaries were invited to preach on successive Sundays at Christ Methodist Church in New York City. This was the church where Ralph Sockman was minister for his whole forty-five-year career. It also was the church where the Longacres were associated before coming to Denver as well as after retirement. This summer series explored various aspects of the relation between the seminaries and the life of the local church. Harvey was Iliff's representative. We were notified of this series, and since we were living in Massachusetts, we took the opportunity to spend the weekend in New York and join several others with an Iliff connection for this worship service.

After the worship, the group went to dinner and was joined by Florence Longacre, who continued living in New York several years after her husband had died. This proved to be a true celebration for Harvey and Florence, whose friendship had gone back more than thirty years in Denver. They recalled various situations and experiences in Denver, and laughed about happenings of many years ago, which we in the younger generation had not heard about before. Our weekend in New York was certainly a celebration of many wonderful and meaningful past memories for us, but especially for Florence and Harvey. During the next week, Harvey visited us at Harvard so he could walk through the campus reminiscing about his student days there in 1935–1936, another celebration. In his chapter on Lindsay Longacre in *An Intellectual History of the Iliff School of Theology*, Harvey wrote of his deep appreciation for his association in Denver and at Iliff with the Longacres.

[Editor's note: In conclusion of this chapter, let me observe that many other faculty and collegial reflections on Potthoff and his work are contained in Chapter 13 of this biography. I recommend them to the reader for more illumination on the personhood as well as scholarship of Harvey Potthoff.]

BEYOND FRIENDSHIP

NOTES

[1] Taped recordings cataloged as CST-800 in the Iliff Library.

[2] Some have made contributions to this biography; see Chapter 12.

[3] The complete paper and other items from Charles are now in the Potthoff Archives, box 45, file folder 16.

[4] Bernard Meland, "Appreciative Awareness," in *Higher Education and the Human Spirit* (Chicago: University of Chicago Press, 1953), 86.

[5] Potthoff, *God and the Celebration of Life*, 150.

[6] Ibid., 147.

[7] Harvey H. Potthoff, "The Churches Speak of Hope," *Selected Papers of Harvey H. Potthoff* (Denver: Iliff School of Theology, 1981), 35. (Explanation: The printed frontispiece says "Criterion Press," which was the official name at the time, but soon ceased to be used, because another larger firm took that title and our incorporation license ran out. I thus use "Iliff" to avoid confusion and to name the repository.)

[8] Ibid., 35.

[9] Ibid.

[10] Whitehead, *Adventures of Ideas*, 41.

[11] Whitehead, *Science and the Modern World*, 275.

[12] Harvey H. Potthoff, *Selected Papers*, 38.

[175] Ibid.

[13] Ibid., 39.

[14] Ibid.

[15] Harvey H. Potthoff, *A Whole Person in a Whole World*, 89, 90.

[16] Ibid., 99.

[17] Ibid., 100.

[18] Ibid., 18.

[19] Transcript of Charles Milligan's words at the Potthoff Memorial Service, February 27, 2002, Iliff Archives, Harvey H. Potthoff Papers.

[20] Potthoff, *God and the Celebration of Life*, 131.

[21] The question of fifteen or sixteen years of part-time Iliff teaching is something of a mystery. It appears HHP's first part-time teaching came in the spring of 1937. If that is counted as the 1936-37 school year, the total is sixteen years; if not, the total is fifteen years. The numbers fifteen and sixteen are used differently by writers in this book as well as in Iliff resources.

10

RETIREMENT FROM ILIFF

By Richard L. Phillips

As the spring of 1981 approached, preparations were undertaken for the retirement of Harvey Potthoff from Iliff. It marked forty-four years, from 1937 to 1981, of teaching at his beloved theological school. Fifteen years of part-time teaching while a pastor at Christ Methodist Church and then twenty-nine years of full-time teaching. By 1941, he had earned two graduate degrees from Iliff. One needs to be reminded that he first became an Iliff student right after his 1932 graduation from college. Such rapid advancement in the ranks from a first-year student to part-time to full-time faculty in a graduate school at that time is truly amazing.

By 1981, not only was his long service honored, but as already noted, during his tenure he had become "Mr. Iliff" in the minds of almost everyone associated with the school. His teaching ranged over a great number of areas vital to a theological education. He filled many roles due to the small number of faculty members in his early years at the school.

His retirement was rightfully viewed by everyone at Iliff, including students and Harvey himself, as a watershed in the makeup and history of the institution. It was in many ways the dominant influence that year on everyone at Iliff. Even for many alums this was true.

The year before Harvey's retirement, he and others at Iliff began working on an anthology of Potthoff's writings, mostly taken from many years of *The Iliff Review*. The publication of *Selected Papers of Harvey H. Potthoff* was available in the spring of '81, and Harvey wrote the preface. It was published by Criterion Press, an Iliff operation. Copies are in the Iliff Library and in the Potthoff archives.[1] It was first used as a text in the course "The Theology of Dr. Harvey Potthoff," which Harvey taught at the invitation of Iliff. Audiotapes of almost every session of the class are available in the library.[2] These tapes are a valuable resource for anyone wanting to do additional research on Harvey's theology. He was asked to repeat the course at Nebraska Wesleyan University before his second retirement from teaching in 1992.

A secret project was almost blown when Charles Milligan and Harvey ended up at the publisher's office at the same time, but Charles was able to fake a different reason for being there. This secret project was the Winter 1981 issue of *The Iliff Review, Essays in Honor of Harvey H. Potthoff*, which was dedicated to Harvey. At that time, Charles was the editor of *The Iliff Review*, a role Potthoff had once held. Authors of the articles are Frank Terry, William Tremmel, Peter Gay, John Cobb, Robert Coburn, and Milligan. For this issue, a staff member of the Iliff Library, Alexandra L. Happer, compiled a detailed bibliography of Potthoff's writings (see Appendix B). Also included in the issue is a section called "A Collection of Tributes," most of which are in either Chapter 13 or 14 of this volume. Harvey was both surprised and pleased with the

To Harvey:

WHEREAS: You have challenged and inspired us by the coherence of your theology and your own reverential living and celebration of life; and

WHEREAS: like your teacher, Amanda Nelson, you have helped us to imagine, to envision, to see the wonder of life and to see life whole; and

WHEREAS: In your twenty-nine years as Professor of Christian Theology at Iliff, you have been leader, pastor, and friend to generations of Iliff students, staff, and faculty; and

WHEREAS: Each of us has experienced your gracious thoughtfulness, your generosity and support, your caring presence with us and our families in times of pain as well as joy; and

WHEREAS: You understand that going on to perfection <u>really</u> means savoring life and living it well, which has more to do with things like symphony concerts, and laughter, and the Rocky Mountains, and the Queen City Jazz Band, and black-bottom pie, and sunrises, and good restaurants, and sharing all these with friends both old and new than John Wesley ever realized;

WHEREAS: We are grateful for all you have meant to Iliff and to each of us;

THEREFORE: Be it resolved, that we, the Faculty of The Iliff School of Theology, present you with this certificate of tribute, in token of our deep affection and appreciation.

--Jean Schmidt
May 15, 1981

HHP copy, Iliff Archives

Faculty tribute to HHP by Jean Miller Schmidt

honor, and again used some content from the issue in the course mentioned above.

Parties, dinners, sermons, assembly speeches, and guest appearances were taking place at Iliff and all over the area in what was a very busy year. It was busy in part because Potthoff served the last three months of his pre-retirement work at Iliff as acting president (a role he had filled at least twice before as well as fulfilling his teaching responsibilities). President Jameson Jones had moved from Iliff to another school that winter, and Harvey filled the gap. Virginia Dorjahn, retired secretary to the president, told me in a telephone interview that Harvey was wonderful to work with as president. [I often wonder if he ever slept that spring]. Virginia was one of those secretaries who could leap over tall buildings with a single bound and was a great friend to students.

A faculty event marking the retirement was held on May 15, 1981. The Iliff faculty were like family to Harvey, and he was equally dear to them. For the event, Dr. Jean Miller Schmidt, professor of Church History and Historical Theology, was asked to draft a document and speak for the whole faculty. Jean joined the faculty in 1975 as the first full-time female member of the group. Her accounts of Harvey's welcome of her and her family are heartwarming as was their continuing faculty relationship. Above is a photo of the document she drafted and presented.

The impression that all was always calm in Harvey's relationships within the faculty should not follow from the above. There are different perceptions and convictions in any faculty group, and Iliff is no exception, nor should it be. Harvey was usually quiet in faculty meetings, and when there was divergent thinking and positions on matters, he was the great arbitrator. Several members of the faculty have related to me

to

Professor of Christian Theology
Distinguished Scholar, Esteemed Colleague, Cherished Friend
Presented by Members of the Faculty of
The Iliff School of Theology
May 15, 1981

His theology has informed generations of students as leaven of wisdom in the bread of life. His vision of faith speaks:

In thoughts sublime that pierce the night like stars,
And with their mild persistence urge our search
To vaster issues... So to live is heaven:
To make undying music in the world.

HHP copy, Iliff Archives

Additional faculty tribute to HHP at retirement, 1981

that it was almost magical the way he could bring resolution before the adjournment. Churchwide issues found him playing a similar role as is documented elsewhere in this book.

Well before 1981, Harvey had become concerned about some of the directions he was fearful Iliff might be taking. For one thing, each chief executive officer brought different positions on such important matters as the institution's primary purposes, its theological traditions, its relationship to the Rocky Mountain Conference of the UM Church, the whole Methodist identity, and what to look for in faculty replacements. He argued for the Iliff Tradition which, while never set in stone, was widely understood as focus on preparations for ministry and other church vocations, a theological and biblical liberal position, and a close identification with the Chicago School, again more of an understanding in theological education and not a finely articulated pattern. While not a traditionalist in many matters, Harvey certainly did not want the Iliff Tradition to fade. His concern on this front became more pronounced during his years at NWU and after. He often spoke of the matter with me, and there was much written communication with Iliff colleagues and administrators. He shared with me some ideas that might be implemented to change what he saw as unwelcome drift on the part of the school. Even so, at the very height of his concern, his love for Iliff was front, center, and firm.

HHP photo, Iliff Archives

President Messer and Harvey, with one of his many honors

Much credit goes to President Don Messer during those years. Don and other Iliff administrators wrote letters and made visits to Harvey, including in Lincoln, in their careful efforts to assure him both of the continuation of the Iliff Tradition and of Iliff's love for and appreciation for him and the many roles he played at Iliff. President Messer was the key figure in -raising the money necessary to establish the Potthoff Faculty Chair in Christian Theology and later for the creation of the Potthoff Seminar Room located in what had been the president's office.

For Potthoff"s retirement, David Woodyard (Iliff '76), a former Potthoff student, created and presented a beautiful stained glass window to Potthoff at the Iliff Week of Lectures in

January 1981 (see cover). After keeping the window for several years, Harvey donated it to Iliff, where it hangs in the Potthoff Seminar Room window. Woodyard died in 1995.

During this extended period of time, Harvey and I had many conversations. At one time, he asked me to draft a proposal that he might submit to Iliff for the possible establishment of a biannual conference on A. N. Whitehead and process theology. I did so, but it never reached Iliff for a number of reasons. I had previously taken the position with Harvey that the money available for such an endowment would probably only support a conference every five years.

A change in the presidency brought David Maldanado to the position in 2000. Harvey's concerns had begun to moderate a bit due to special efforts by Messer and others to keep Harvey involved. Maldanado spoke with me about Harvey and the general situation. Soon he visited Harvey in his apartment, and they talked about the Iliff Tradition, and David presented some ideas of how Harvey might help. A fund for endowed scholarships won the day.

Harvey began to see a return to better days between himself and Iliff. Potthoff was often asked and taught summer courses at Iliff and at Aspen while still in Lincoln and that had helped even before Maldanado's presidency. He also taught several courses at Iliff after his retirement from NWU. He was honored to be included as a faculty colleague and so continued to see himself as intimately tied to Iliff. Many efforts within Iliff took place during Harvey's retirement to maintain this historic relationship. Such efforts were essential and successful.

In his last years, Harvey was still uncertain about the direction Iliff seemed to be taking. There were two changes that bothered him the most. One was the seeming move away from seeing the educational purpose of Iliff as preparing persons for church-related vocations. The other was the engaging of faculty members on the basis of academic criteria alone, with little concern for a church or even a theological orientation, let alone a process theology–based foundation. With this, Harvey feared the Iliff and Chicago traditions might fade, even disappear. While the fears were in part legitimate given what might be called the Potthoff tradition of Iliff education, I find today that Iliff has not abandoned its history or tradition, and the educational focus has not changed nearly as much as Harvey feared it would.

Potthoff was never of the opinion that change should not take place; change is a given. His concern regarding change related to Iliff's theologically open and liberal history, the role of process thinking (a la Whitehead), the purpose of education for the church vocations, and a faculty made up of persons committed to the value of the church relationship.

At the ordination of new clergy in the spring of 1981, the Rocky Mountain Conference honored Potthoff by asking him to give the keynote address at the service, which was held at First United Methodist Church in Fort Collins. Harvey treasured such opportunities and the chance to tie together Iliff and the Rocky Mountain Conference in this way.

Two major honors were to come to Potthoff later, and both are to be seen as a part of the recognition associated with his retirement from Iliff. First to come was the funding of the first endowed faculty chair at Iliff. Alton Templin commented on this in Chapter 9. President Don Messer and Vice President for Development John Willson noted that on April 7, 1983, the funding for the chair went over the half-million dollar goal, thus assuring the Harvey H. Potthoff Chair of Christian Theology at the school. In a one-year period, donors including alums, friends, trustees, churches, foundations, and corporations funded the chair. Many thought the goal unreachable but Messer commented that its success was a tribute to the donors' love of Dr. Potthoff and their loyalty to the school. The major donation came from the Schlessman Foundation, a longtime supporter of Iliff.

In the May 27, 1983, issue of *The Iliff Reporter*, President Messer in a front-page article "congratulated alumni/ae, friends and trustees of the School for not only matching but over-subscribing the Schlessman challenge of $220,000."[3] Willson was the director of the drive, Vice President of the Trustees Richard H. Simon headed the trustee drive, and Potthoff's former student Bishop Calvin D. McConnell was the honorary chairperson. Many other special committees were a part of the success of the drive.

Dr. Delwin Brown, a process theologian and former student of John Cobb, was brought from Arizona State University to become the first holder of the Potthoff chair in the fall of 1983. Since his tenure, many others have held the position. It is one of Iliff's most esteemed recognitions and faculty roles..[4] The current holder of the chair is the very versatile scholar Dr. Edward Antonio, a native of Zimbabwe.

Harvey was concerned that Del Brown had not visited with him about the chair. Later after Harvey's concern was expressed by the administration to Del Brown, he came to Harvey's apartment to talk with him about the chair. I know from both of them that it was helpful to each. Later, when Jean Miller Schmidt held the chair, she and Potthoff talked often. Harvey did express to me some disappointment that most who held the chair were not in any meaningful way involved with either a local church or any denominational structure. That reality was of some concern to Harvey. It also bothered him that some never came to converse with him about his career or the history of the chair's establishment.

The official celebration of the chair came during the Annual Trustees Dinner on June 28, 1983. Charles Milligan served as a member of one of the key committees and wrote in a letter: "It is a great contribution to the future of Iliff and a splendid tribute to Harvey, who means so much to so many of us. For myself it is one of the most gratifying [things] that has happened in all my years at Iliff."[5]

HHP personal photo, Iliff Archives

The chair presented to HHP in 1983 when the HHP Faculty Chair was celebrated

Peter Gay was invited but unable to attend the Trustees Dinner and the event: "[I am unable on June 28th] to celebrate the founding of a Chair in honor of my old and good friend Harvey Potthoff. I will, however, be in Germany doing some research and therefore quite unavailable—alas! But, I wish that you would be kind enough to transmit my greetings to Harvey and wish him all the best in the years to come."[6]

– Durfee Prof. of History, Yale University

President Messer remarked in a letter of April 22, 1983: "Harvey Potthoff has been deeply moved by the outpouring of love and honor evidenced by this accomplishment. He wants us to express to everyone, especially his former colleagues, his gratitude for what this accomplishment means to Iliff as well as the honor that has been brought to him personally."[7]

Much later, another great honor was the creation of the Harvey H. Potthoff Seminar Room. The room had been the president's office after the addition of Skaggs Hall. The room, Skaggs Hall 104, is prominently located on the main floor near the Iliff reception desk. This excellent space is used for classes, meetings, and seminars and—with its big round window containing the circular stained glass window presented to Harvey in 1981—is fondly called "the fish bowl." Harvey was proud the stained glass window was hung there and very pleased the room was named for him. Because of its fish bowl quality and its location in a heavy traffic pattern, Messer once told me it was not a good location for the president's office.

Photo by Ethel Phillips, composite by Mary Sue Alexander, used with permission

R. L. Phillips standing at the door of the HHP Seminar Room in 2012

Some faculty using the room have been known to feel the same!

Harvey was able to be present for the dedication on November 18, 1998. The dedication was followed by a celebratory luncheon. I happened to be in Denver at the time and was honored to be present for this event, especially to see the joy on the face of Harvey Potthoff. His remarks were quite autobiographical, and he also spoke of the Iliff Tradition in theological education.

In the litany of dedication, the following paragraph concerning the window reads: "May this stained glass window remind all of us of the ways in which we are woven together—students, staff, faculty, administrators and church leaders—each seeking to make the Iliff community a genuine reflection of the good news of the gospel. May the window serve to remind all of us of the grace given to us through the love of others."[8] The room and the window have proven to be a beautiful, functional, and appropriate tribute to Harvey. Most current Iliffians pass by the room on a daily basis.

Finally, a note about Potthoff and students. His orientation that relationships are of the greatest importance meant the lives of students and their learning was a key to Iliff's purpose and his own sense of vocation. He was not easy on students. In fact, he was very exacting academically and was always focused on their post-Iliff careers. Harvey's success can be grasped by careful reading of Chapter 14.

NOTES

[1] Iliff Archives, box 2, file folder 7.

[2] Iliff Library CST-800.

[3] *The Iliff Reporter* 36, no. 1 (May 27, 1983).

[4] *The Iliff Reporter* 35, no. 4

[5] Charles Milligan letter, April 7, 1983, Iliff Archives, box 45, file folder 16.

[6] Peter Gay letter, June 10, 1983, Iliff Archives, box 43, file folder 4.

[7] Don Messer letter, April 22, 1983, Iliff Archives, box 32, file folder 2.

[8] Dedication Bulletin, Iliff Archives, box 43, file folder 4.

11

THE HARVEY H. POTTHOFF YEARS AT NEBRASKA WESLEYAN UNIVERSITY 1981-1992

By David Barrett Peabody

Professor of Religion, Nebraska Wesleyan University

"Some people who yearn for endless life don't know what to do with a rainy afternoon."

Attributed to Harvey H. Potthoff

N*WU, 1978–1981, BP.*[1] In 1978, a family of good friends of Nebraska Wesleyan University (NWU) established an endowed chair in religion, the holder of which was intended to (1) supply complementary and supplementary courses among the university's offerings in the academic study of religion; (2) enhance the university's relationship with the Nebraska Annual Conference of the United Methodist Church, along with the broader Nebraska and Great Plains communities; and if necessary, (3) provide the Chair for the Department of Religion. Since the family wished to keep the donors anonymous, it was not until 1983 that this endowment was named, yet still not after the family of donors, but after a much beloved former chaplain and member of the Department of Religion at Nebraska Wesleyan, Lewis Edward Mattingly (1904–1985), affectionately known as "Matt."[2] Although Harvey Potthoff held this chair from the fall of 1981, it was, therefore, not until 1983 that he became the first person at NWU to occupy the chair specifically designated in 1983 as the L. Edward Mattingly Distinguished Visiting Professor of Religion.

Beginning in 1978, however, this newly created endowment at the time was being utilized to bring a variety of distinguished scholars of religion to the Nebraska Wesleyan University campus in Lincoln. One such scholar and expert in the Wesleyan and Methodist traditions was Albert Cook Outler, who was at the time of his visit to NWU in March 1981,[3] retired from full-time teaching at the Perkins School of Theology of Southern Methodist University in Dallas but had been retained on the faculty there as Research Professor of Theology. By that time, Outler was primarily focusing his attention and research on editing the sermons of John Wesley for publication.[4]

Outler's addresses related to his visit to the Nebraska Wesleyan University campus in 1981 included (1) a talk titled "The Mission Fair," which was delivered as part of the UMC Lincoln District Mission Fair (Sunday, March 1); (2) a lecture on "John Wesley's Hermeneutical Principles," delivered to a class at NWU (Monday, March 2); (3) a sermon titled "John Wesley as Folk Theologian," delivered during an NWU chapel service on the theme "Life and Myths Surrounding John Wesley"(Wednesday, March 4); (4) an address on "The Three

Wesleys," delivered to Nebraska clergy and lay leaders during Ministers' Week at NWU (Thursday, March 5); (5) another lecture (also delivered on March 5) on "Liberal Education: Value Free? or Value Prone?"[5]; (6) another sermon, on "Decisive Christian Experiences" (Saturday, March 7); and (7) a third sermon, titled "The New Commandment," based on John 13:34 and delivered at the First United Methodist Church (Sunday, March 8),[6] just across the street from the NWU campus on the site where the idea of establishing a Methodist-related college on land in that area was first formulated in 1887. Thus, the relationship between Nebraska Wesleyan University and this local church has been significant for about 125 years.

The Invitation to Harvey Potthoff to Come to NWU

Following up immediately on the significant visit to NWU by Professor Outler, the Reverend Dr. John Wesley White Jr., then President of Nebraska Wesleyan, having learned of the forthcoming retirement of Professor Harvey H. Potthoff from his longtime teaching position at the Methodist/United Methodist-related Iliff School of Theology in Denver, wrote to Dr. Potthoff, inquiring whether he would be willing to come to NWU for an entire year. His duties were to include teaching courses in religion at NWU and elsewhere in the state of Nebraska, thereby enhancing both the regular on-campus offerings in the academic study of religion, but also the so-called "town and gown" relationships between the university and the broader Nebraska community. He was also to help plan and execute a number of courses and symposia that would enhance NWU's relationship with the United Methodist Church. Dr.

Potthoff agreed to this arrangement and, finding the experience sufficiently pleasing after that first year, he eventually chose to stay at Nebraska Wesleyan for 11 years (1981–1992), "retiring" for a second time in 1992. What follows here is a selective account of those eleven years of Harvey H. Potthoff's work and relationship with the community which is Nebraska Wesleyan University, its constituencies, and its supporters.

Photo courtesy of David Peabody used with permission

David Peabody and Patsy Moore standing in front of the HHP tree

Photo courtesy of David Peabody used with permission

Harvey H. Potthoff at Nebraska Wesleyan University: Initial Contributions

Upon arrival, Harvey was greeted warmly by the administration, faculty, staff, and students. The Chaplain of the University at the time was the Reverend James A. "Jim" Stillman, who was instrumental in introducing Harvey to L. Edward Mattingly himself, whose name graced the chair that Harvey held after 1983. Chaplain Stillman was accustomed to having lunch every Thursday with Matt, so when Harvey arrived, these regular luncheons often included the three of them. Jim would also sometimes accompany Harvey to some meetings of the Iliff-at-Aspen programs, which Harvey had helped to initiate and, on some of these same trips to Colorado, Jim would take some selected students who were interested in graduate work in theology to visit the Iliff School of Theology in Denver.

Jim also once took some students with him for a summer visit to Europe and, prior to that trip, Harvey gave Jim a generous check, with the suggestion that Jim use this money to enjoy a fine meal together with these students while they were abroad. Such generosity proved typical of Harvey throughout his tenure at Nebraska Wesleyan. Any excuse for a meal with a group of colleagues and friends, particularly on special occasions, with Harvey picking up the tab, was an important and impressive aspect of Harvey's generosity, style, and character. Although Harvey was provided with an apartment in Lincoln very close to the campus, and a modest salary and travel allowance by NWU, I suspect that Harvey returned most of what he received from NWU back to the University and its constituents in both outright financial contributions to the school and in-kind gifts, such as fancy meals or concert tickets to musical and cultural events for NWU faculty, staff, and students who typically accompanied him to such events.

Harvey's first probe into what his work would be like at NWU was to formulate and execute a series of seminars for United Methodist clergy and laity. For this first series of seminars, Harvey served as the sole presenter and small group leader. He gave the general title to each seminar of "Christian Faith and Spiritual Renewal," and offered it on Fridays for clergy and on Saturdays for laity over a weekend for several months during winter-spring of 1982. He convened the first of these seminars in Lincoln on the NWU campus on January 15–16, 1982, and then convened similar seminars once a month that same year over two days in Omaha (February 19–20), Kearney (March 5–6), Norfolk (April 2–3), and Alliance, Nebraska (April 30–May 1).

His topics with the clergy on Fridays included "Christian Faith: A Way of Seeing Things," "Images of Spirituality in the Christian Tradition," "Burnout and Renewal: A Theological Perspective," and "A Theology of Meaning." Topics explored with an audience of laypersons on Saturdays included "Deepening the Inner Life" and "The Ministry of the Laity."

Mattingly Symposia

This first experiment with his new duties at Nebraska Wesleyan led to a subsequent series of symposia and conferences, which developed into events on campus that eventually came to be called the "Mattingly Symposium" series. For these, Harvey began to draw upon a wide variety of highly educated, often nationally or internationally known skilled communicators with expertise in a wide variety of fields; many of whom Harvey knew personally from earlier times and contexts in his life.

These symposia covered the topics of: "Religious Faith and Mental Health" (September 29–October 1, 1982); "The Quest for a Believable Theology" (April 20–22, 1983); "Our Wesleyan Heritage and a Festival of Wesley Hymns" (October 21–22, 1983); "The Theology and the Lives of the Wesleys" (Spring 1984, which also celebrated the bicentennial of Methodism in America, i.e., when the Methodist Episcopal Church in America was officially established at the "Christmas Conference" of 1784 in the Lovely Lane Chapel in Baltimore); "Technology and Human Values" (April 25–26, 1985); "Medical Ethics" (February 24–28, 1986, in collaboration with the Woodrow Wilson Visiting Scholars Program); "The Individual and World Community" (April 1–3, 1987, which was the first year these symposia began to carry the title "Mattingly Symposium," and the dates of this symposium also intentionally coincided with the centennial year celebration of the founding of Nebraska Wesleyan University and the annual commencement ceremony at Nebraska Wesleyan, at which time Harvey was awarded the degree of Doctor of Humane Letters, one of many honors bestowed upon him by NWU); "Share the Nebraska Tribal Experience" (March 23–25, 1988); "Ethics and Human Values in the Business Arena" (March 15–17, 1989); "A Celebration of Planet Earth" (April 18–20, 1990, which coincided with the twentieth anniversary of the establishment of Earth Day); "The World Wide Reach for Freedom and Justice" (April 24–26, 1991); and "Science and Religion" (March 4–6, 1992).

The names, titles, and institutional affiliations at the time of those distinguished persons who made major presentations at these symposia included: Monk Bryan, Presiding Bishop, Nebraska Annual Conference, United Methodist Church; Langdon Gilkey, Shailer Mathews Professor of Theology, University of Chicago Divinity School; Stephen H. Schneider, Deputy Director of the Advanced Study Program at the National Center for Atmospheric Research, Boulder, Colorado; David Thomasma, Director of the Medical Humanities Program, Strich School of Medicine, Loyola University Medical Center, Chicago; Bernard Towers, Professor of Psychiatry and Biobehavioral Sciences at UCLA; Kenneth Boulding, Distinguished Professor of Economics, Emeritus, and Research Associate and Project Director of the Program of Research on Political and Economic Change, Institute of Behavioral Science, University of Colorado; Huston Smith, the Thomas J. Watson Professor of Religion and Distinguished Adjunct Professor of Philosophy, Emeritus, Syracuse University; Reuben A. Snake Jr., Chairman of the Winnebago Tribe of Nebraska; George E. Tinker, Assistant Professor of Cross-Cultural Ministries, Iliff School of Theology; Dr. Bart Victor, Assistant Professor of Management at the Graduate School of Business Administration, University of North Carolina; Martin G. Colladay, Vice President for Public Affairs, ConAgra, Inc.; the Honorable Stewart L. Udall, former U.S. Secretary of the Interior; William Penn Mott Jr., former President of the National Park Service; Daniel Schorr, distinguished journalist and longtime news analyst for National Public Radio; Robert G. Fuller, Professor of Physics and Astronomy at the University of Nebraska, Lincoln; and John B. Cobb Jr., Professor Emeritus, School of Theology at Claremont, and Co-Director, Center for Process Studies, Claremont, California.

Harvey Potthoff, of course, did not put these symposia together by himself, but rather, in accord with his typical, collegial style of leadership, he brought together planning and steering committees of ten to fifteen people for initial meetings. Subsequently, he would invite others to join the planning and design team who were not only knowledgeable about the chosen topic, but also creative and industrious people. Initial membership in each symposium committee typically included representatives from the faculty, staff, and administration of Nebraska Wesleyan University and representatives of the Nebraska Annual Conference of the United Methodist Church, typically either the Bishop or the Bishop's representative, along with some other representatives drawn from a broader cross-section of the Lincoln and southeastern Nebraska communities. Once the topic or general theme of a symposium had been determined, others with expertise in the subject matter, or who knew good resource persons on the topic, would be invited to join the design team in fine-tuning the symposium's program, in suggesting good resource persons for it, extending invitations to prospective leaders, and in publicizing and hosting the various events that made up the symposium schedule.

Meals with Harvey

In addition to taking the lead in planning these symposia, in which Harvey himself sometimes also served as presenter, he also did much on the NWU campus to cultivate serious interdisciplinary scholarship and collegiality. Harvey loved company over a good meal. Therefore, he seemed to eat most of his meals outside of his home, and he was rarely alone in doing so.

For instance, during the lunch hour at NWU, Harvey could frequently be found eating in the snack bar of the NWU Roy

Story Student Center whenever he was not hosting a more private meal with a colleague or two—and often more than two—off campus. At that time, there was always a large square of eight-foot tables set and available in the campus snack bar where members of the administration, faculty, staff, and student body could sit together and quickly discover how rich a conversation could develop whenever Harvey was taking part.

During lunch, Harvey was almost always good for a story, a joke, or, quite frequently, a pun or play on words. For instance, Richard "Dick" Quinn remembers Harvey noting, "It was not the apple on the tree that was the problem in Eden, but the pair/pear on the ground." And, when dealing with a particularly busy schedule, Harvey would complain, "I feel like a mummy. I'm pressed for time." Harvey also once pulled out a Nebraska newspaper clipping from his wallet for all at the lunch table to see. It carried the headline, "Christian Girls Stomp Friend." It made him laugh and others curious. Although the article was actually about the girls' basketball team at the Lincoln Christian High School handily winning a game against the girls' team from the high school in Friend, Nebraska, Harvey took delight in the headline writer's play on words giving the victory a humorous twist. As a humorist and a former sports reporter, Harvey had special interest in such curious plays on words.

Amy Birky reports briefly on other gatherings for meals with Harvey.

> Retired ministers, myself, and others met periodically for breakfast here in Lincoln. The topics were varied and the conversations lively and interesting. Harvey was philosophical, open and a

good conversationalist. Herb Jackman and my husband, Gordon Birky, were also from Iliff so they had that in common. It was an enjoyable time.

Harvey Models and Influences Interdisciplinary and Team Teaching

It was also in this lunch table context where Harvey did much to bring a smile to our midday faces, and to spark and encourage interdisciplinary work among the members of the NWU faculty across its academic divisions: Fine Arts, Humanities, Natural Sciences, Social Sciences, and the Professions.

And, after arriving at NWU, Harvey took quickly to modeling such team and interdisciplinary teaching in several of the courses for which he took primary responsibility, particularly in two of his most popular courses—"Aging, Dying and Death in Religious Perspective," and "Science and Religion"—both of which he taught, or, perhaps better expressed, hosted, one evening a week for a three-hour period.

Harvey and the WILL Program

Harvey taught these and some other classes in NWU's evening program, which began its life at NWU as the "Institute for Life-long Learning," but someone quickly recognized that the acronym for this program was ILL; few would find such a program particularly attractive. This rather quickly led to a change of name to the "Wesleyan Institute for Lifelong Learning," so that its acronym then became the WILL program. Of course, the old proverbial saying, which then quickly came to the minds of many and soon became an NWU slogan was, "Where there's a WILL, there's a way." This was certainly Potthoff-pleasing, even if he was not the first to make the connection. Courses in the WILL program were coordinated at one time or another during the period 1981–1992 by Dick Quinn, Ruth Harper, or Erik Bitterbaum.

Harvey's evening class titled, "Aging, Dying and Death in Religious Perspective", was initially requested of Erik Bitterbaum by Lincoln funeral home directors, as a continuing education opportunity for them and their staff. However, the class quickly and typically also attracted from seventy to one hundred undergraduate students to the Callen Conference Center in the Smith-Curtis building on the NWU campus. Callen features about a quarter circle of several curved and raked rows of continuous tabletops on each of several curved steps in an arrangement something like a Greco-Roman *Odeion* or *Bouleuterion*. But unlike these ancient structures, Callen is also equipped with comfortable padded and rolling chairs behind tabletops that face a central podium on the floor below, which includes a control panel to the use of videos and slide presentations by a speaker.

To this class, Harvey invited many different resource persons from the greater Lincoln community, including medical doctors and nurses, lawyers and judges, religious leaders and clergy from a variety of faith traditions, journalists, poets, novelists, and artists, morticians and directors of funeral homes, plus a variety of academics and people at various ages and stages of life with varying life experiences to share in the process of aging, diminishing, and dying.

Harvey's guests for this class during 1990 and 1991 included Syd Beane, President and CEO of the Native American Indian

Center in Lincoln, contributing to the evening's topic of "Indian Perspectives on Aging, Diminishing and Death"; Rex Bevins, Senior Minister of St. Paul United Methodist Church, Lincoln, on "Protestant Perspectives on Aging, Diminishing and Death"; Naomi Brill, columnist for the Lincoln Star newspaper; Patrick E. Clare, MD, orthopedic surgeon, on "The Experience of Diminishment and Life-Threatening Disease"; Sanyi DeGrazia, son of NWU Religion Professor Louis DeGrazia, who was then a student and gymnast at the University of Nebraska, Lincoln, on "Aging in College"; Garry Duncan, Head of the NWU Department of Biology, "The Experience of Grief"; Anthony Epp, NWU Professor of French and German, who, under the title "Putting People Back into Funerals," reflected upon his own experience of personally preparing the body of his father for burial; Pediatrician Charles A. "Chuck" Erickson on "A Life Cycle (Holistic) View of Aging"; NWU Emeritus Professor of Biology Milt Evans on "What Is a Good Aging?"; Cardiologist Alan Forker; Twyla Hansen, Horticulturalist and NWU Grounds Manager and publishing poet; Richard Hartley, businessman and former cancer patient, on "The Preciousness of Life"; Kent Haruf, novelist and NWU Professor of English; Philip Kaye, NWU Professor of Speech and Department Chair, on "Keeping in Shape as a Human Being"; William Kloefkorn, NWU Professor of English and Nebraska State Poet, on "Understanding and Dealing with Loneliness"; Norman Krivosha, former Chief Justice of the Supreme Court of Nebraska and subsequently Executive Vice President and General Counsel, Ameritas Financial Services, and co-author of the article that officially outlined the history, theology, and ethics of Conservative Judaism, on "Jewish Perspectives on Aging, Diminishing and Death"; Carol McShane, RN, on "The Care of the Dying"; David Mickey, NWU

Professor Emeritus of History and eventual author of three volumes on the history of Nebraska Wesleyan University, on "The Experience of Grief"; Richard Morin, MD, specialist in Infectious Diseases and former Professor of Nursing at NWU, and his wife, Patricia Morin, then NWU Head of the Department of Nursing; Steve Olson, Funeral Director, Metcalf Funeral Home, Lincoln, on "The Role of the Funeral Director"; Richard and Donald Roe, NWU seniors, on "Aging in College"; Larry Ruth, Attorney and Adjunct NWU faculty member, on "Legal Matters Related to Aging, Diminishing and Death"; David Saperstein, Rabbi and Co-Director of the Religious Action Center for Reform Judaism, Washington, DC, on "Jewish Values in a World of Crisis"; Lela Shanks, distinguished resident of Lincoln and an activist for social justice, on "When a Spouse Is Suffering with Alzheimer's Disease"; Jacquelyn Sorensen, then NWU Head of the Art Department, on "The Experience of Grief"; Richard Swalek, St. James Parish, Omaha, on "Roman Catholic Perspectives on Aging, Diminishing and Death"; Etta Tucker, RN, Unit Manager, Intensive and Coronary Care, Bryan Memorial Hospital, Lincoln; Warren Urbom, Federal Judge, and his wife, Joyce, on "Being Kind to the Older Person You Are Going to Be"; and Betty Wallace, NWU Professor of Art, on "Keeping in Shape as a Human Being."

For the Science and Religion class, which typically attracted from thirty to thirty-five students to a more typical classroom setting, Harvey also marshaled a comparable mix of experts, which included, primarily NWU faculty members drawn from the Natural and Social Sciences, and the Humanities.

Guest lecturers for this course during the spring semesters of 1989 and 1990 included Erik Bitterbaum (Biology and Associate Provost),[7] Bill Boernke (Biology), George Coleman (Chemistry),

Glen Dappen (Biology), Louis DeGrazia (Religion), Garry Duncan (Biology), Cliff Fawl (Psychology), Denise George (Chemistry), Dave Goss (Physics), Paul Hamilton (Oncologist), Carl Jolliff (Immunologist), Ken Keith (Psychology), John Krejci (Sociology), Elaine Kruse (History), David Peabody (Religion), Bill Pfeffer (Philosophy), Leon Satterfield (English), Mary Daehler Smith (English), John Walker (Philosophy), and Bill Wehrbein (Physics), for a total of eighteen to twenty guest lecturers each semester. Some of these professors audited part or all of the course in order to enjoy the unique opportunity to hear their colleagues lecture on their areas of expertise, which was not generally possible during the regular daytime schedule, since class conflicts often prohibited such interdisciplinary visitation in colleagues' classes.

Harvey's syllabus, assigned readings, and his own lectures in these two courses served as the glue that held the class together. His role as host for each class often resembled the late-night television formats of two famous Nebraska television hosts, Dick Cavett and Johnny Carson, who typically opened their televised talk shows with a monologue, then offered some varied performances by their guests and talked informally with each guest until the close of each segment of the show. Harvey did something similar with his guests, at least in these two most popular of his classes at NWU.

Harvey Potthoff and the Regular NWU Daytime Program

Initially, Harvey brought courses to NWU's daytime program that bore some resemblance to classes he had taught at the Iliff School of Theology, although modified appropriately for a class composed primarily of traditional undergraduates, sometimes combined with a smattering of Senior College Students—i.e., nontraditional students age fifty-five and above, some of whom were seeking enrichment courses in NWU's regular daytime program and who paid a tiny amount of tuition for this privileged opportunity and others who even managed to complete college degrees in this distinctive program.

The Range of Harvey's Courses at NWU

Harvey's course offerings at NWU in all formats and time slots eventually included not only Aging, Dying and Death in Religious Perspective and Science and Religion,[8] but also courses on Loneliness and the Search for Meaning,[9] The Quest for a Contemporary Spirituality,[10] and Images of God,[11] at an intermediate level; and courses in Process Theism,[12] The Problem of Evil, Wesleyan Theology, Theology of Wholeness,[13] and Theology of Love, at a more advanced level. Other occasional courses included God in Contemporary Thought (Spring 1982) and A Modern Theology of Earth (Spring 1992).

Harvey Potthoff, Native Americans, and Their Cultures

Harvey's long and most beloved residency in Colorado, both as a longtime pastor of Christ Methodist Church in Denver and, later, as a longtime member of the faculty of the Iliff School of Theology, naturally brought him into a number of close relationships with Native Americans. He was clearly a student and an advocate of many aspects of those cultures, particularly their religious traditions. The symposium, noted above and titled "Sharing the Nebraska Tribal Experience" (Spring 1988), turned out to be one of the most successful of NWU's Mattingly Symposia, at least in terms of the number of attendees, attracting several hundred each day. Perhaps that was because this particular symposium offered an experiential and interactive program where people were not only invited to lectures about Native American spirituality and culture, but were also invited to experience Native American music and dancing, sometimes even as participants with Native American dancers or drummers and by eating traditional Native American foods, such as fry bread and honey.

For this, Harvey and his symposium committee for that year drew upon the expertise of Harvey's one-time colleague at the Iliff School of Theology, George Tinker, who at the time was an Assistant Professor of Cross Cultural Ministries at Iliff. He gave a keynote address at this symposium titled "Indian Spirituality and the American University."

In response to his experiences during this symposium, Professor Tinker wrote the following to the NWU president at the time, Dr. John White:

> I was absolutely delighted with the program Harvey Potthoff put together for us in "Sharing the Nebraska Tribal Experience." The quality of the program and the quality of participation were both first rate, and, as far as I could tell, the program was well received by both Indians and non-Indians.

And to Harvey himself, Professor Tinker wrote:

You are a marvelous person with marvelous energies and talents. Thank you for putting together such a wonderful and meaningful symposium program. It fed people and will continue to feed people in both spiritual and intellectual ways.

Enclosed are letters I wrote to Dr. White and Mr. Snake.

Most cordially,

George

Two years later, Professor Tinker came back to NWU to share the podium with Harvey at the second session of a Mattingly Symposium titled "Celebration of Planet Earth: Recognizing the 20th Anniversary of Earth Day." At that time, these good friends and colleagues, Professor Tinker and Professor Potthoff, each addressed the theme "Environmentalism as a Religious Way of Life."

Of course, Harvey also enjoyed the Native American art and artists he quickly found in Lincoln. He even became a frequent patron of at least one Nebraska Native American artist, Daniel Long Soldier, from whom Harvey purchased a number of pieces, either as gifts for others or to keep in his own growing collection of Native American art.

Harvey's Work at the Nebraska State Penitentiary

Whether the announcement of Harvey's arrival in Lincoln in 1981 prompted the following request is unknown to me, but sometime shortly after Harvey's arrival in Lincoln, President John Wesley White Jr. received a message from one or more inmates at the Nebraska State Penitentiary in Lincoln, requesting "a visit from a theologian, NOT a preacher." Although there were at least a couple of people on the NWU faculty at that time who might have been appropriate in fulfilling this request, it was Harvey who responded to the call and went to the penitentiary to visit with at least one inmate who had made the call, namely Harold Lamont Otey, also known as "Wili" Otey.[14]

After his first visit, Harvey kept a regular schedule of appointments with Wili Otey, who had been tried and convicted of rape and murder in 1977 and was sentenced to death. When first incarcerated, Wili Otey was illiterate, but in time, he learned to read and write, partly through the interventions of Harvey Potthoff and partly through the contributions of other NWU faculty members who came to know about Wili Otey and his case through Harvey.

Some of these people were then active members of the NWU Department of English, which then included Nan Graf, who was also a longtime activist and member of both Nebraskans for Peace and Nebraskans Against the Death Penalty. Naturally, Nan was particularly interested in Wili Otey's case and Harvey's relationship and visits with him. Although she did not visit Wili as often as Harvey did, she worked hard, along with her colleagues in Nebraskans Against the Death Penalty, to get his sentence commuted to something less than the death penalty.

With some help from other members of the NWU faculty in English, particularly Leon Satterfield and Nebraska State Poet William Kloefkorn, Wili Otey became sufficiently adept at writing so that he could eventually have three books of his own poetry published: *And Me, I Am Like a Leaf* (Lincoln: Bench Press, 1981), two volumes of *Singing for Mooncrumbs* (Seward, NE: Bench Press, 1985), and Yeah Clementine (self-published,

1991). He also contributed work to *Flame. African Poets in Nebraska*, edited by Mondo we Langa, previously known as David L. Rice (Lincoln: Harambee Afrikan Cultural Org., 1989).[15]

Harvey visited with Wili Otey weekly, if not more often, and came to have rather deep, especially theological, discussions with him. It would, no doubt, be fair to say that both men were deeply affected by their encounters with one another.

At a rally and as something of a last-ditch effort to postpone for a second time or commute the death penalty for Wili Otey, Bill Kloefkorn read from Wili Otey's poems and concluded, with tears in his eyes and a lump in his throat, "If these poems aren't the sign of a changed man, I don't know what is."

It was probably for the best that Harvey Potthoff had left his position at NWU and his residence in Lincoln in the spring of 1992 and didn't have to suffer through all the days that led up to Wili Otey's execution at 12:01 a.m. on September 2, 1994. On that date, Wili Otey became the first man executed in Nebraska in thirty-one years and one of the last men, if not the last man, in Nebraska to be executed by the electric chair since its use as a method of execution was subsequently replaced by lethal injection.

Potthoff on Potthoff

Prior to the beginning of the 1991–1992 academic year, Harvey announced that he intended to "retire" from Nebraska Wesleyan at that academic year's end and conceded to teach a course that several NWU faculty members—including Lois Coleman in the Department of Education and her husband, George, in the Chemistry Department, among others—had wanted to take with him since they had come to know him and his work. The course requested was "The Theology of Harvey Potthoff." As a departing gift to these members of the faculty—and to all of the equally interested students, faculty, and staff at the time—Harvey finally acceded to their repeated requests and offered the course. This allowed him to utilize, in good conscience, many of his own published materials as textbooks, as well as sharing his most recent thoughts, reflections, and views on a variety of theological issues. Eric Ford, NWU Class of 1992 and now a United Methodist clergyman currently serving the R.O.P.E. parish—which includes congregations in Orchard, Page, and Ewing, Nebraska—was Harvey's student in this class and in "Aging, Dying and Death in Religious Perspective."

Selected NWU Alumni on their Encounters with Harvey Potthoff

Ronda (Armold) Swanson, NWU Class of 1987, earned her RN at Bryan-LGH Hospital in Lincoln and is currently a practicing nurse.

> Harvey was sincerely a gentleman. I appreciate that more now, sincerely and truly. He lived a "Christ-like" life.

Bet Hannon, NWU Class of 1985, is currently the CEO of Bet Hannon Marketing, which helps nonprofit organizations with digital communications in Fresno, California (1997–present). Bet is a former pastor in several other locations.

I took Harvey's class in "Aging, Dying and Death in Religious Perspective" which later helped me through a death in my family in 1988. I also took courses with Harvey which focused on "The Problem of Evil" and "Process Theology." These helped to prepare me for graduate school, including an MA in Church History from the Union Theological Seminary in New York City and my subsequent pastoral work in a variety of contexts. Harvey was a gentle and hospitable soul, who really knew how to engage his students in small groups. In one of the classes I took with him, over the course of the semester, he took all of us in small groups out to dinner. My group went the House of Hunan, and it was the first time I was introduced to Chinese food! I knew of at least 20 people in his classes who were interested in getting a seminary education after NWU and pursuing ordination. Ten or eleven of us attended Pastor's School with Harvey at the Iliff School of Theology in Denver one year and, while there, Harvey took us to the rooftop restaurant of a Denver hotel for a fine dinner and a dessert of Bananas Foster. Harvey was a generous host, and particularly wanted to show us the spectacular view of the city at night. Harvey seemed to have no "class consciousness," but treated all he met with great respect and genuine interest in who they were and what they did. He was all about bringing people together.

Sara K. (Fletcher) Harding, NWU Class of 1989, is currently Professor of Religion and Chair of the

Department of Religion and Philosophy, Florida Southern University, Lakeland, Florida, and Co-Director of the Florida Center for Science and Religion.

Believe it or not, I did not take any courses with Harvey and had limited interaction with him. However, I was fortunate to have shared one of those meals out with him during my final semester at Wesleyan. I count it as one of the most important and formative moments along my own scholarly and professional path.

In February of 1989 I was still very unclear as to what I would do after graduation (in May) regarding graduate schools and life in general. My degree was in Psychology, with a minor in Religion. I had taken the GRE and my heart wasn't in pursuing graduate work in Psych. I didn't know what I wanted to do or was going to do. As a result, I had really made no plans beyond August since I did know that I would be spending the summer in Kansas City with my sister, who graduated from Nebraska Wesleyan in 1986.

By happenstance, I ran into Lois Coleman in the Smith-Curtis building. She had been my sister's advisor in the Education Department. We chatted about my "plans" for next year and, within minutes, she insisted that I have dinner with Harvey Potthoff. She said that she would call him and that he would be expecting me to stop by his office to coordinate the details.

I was horrified at the thought of being "sent to dinner" with a professor that I simply did not know. I knew of Harvey Potthoff, but I had never spoken to him. I had friends who had taken his courses and knew that he was a gifted teacher and a respected theologian. But I didn't even know if he knew who I was. I remember traipsing to his office to set up our dinner plans, introducing myself, and then mainly discussing a huge painting in his office that was given to him by a local female artist before arranging our time and place for dinner. We met at a restaurant, table for two, ordered our meals and then he simply asked me what my interests were and I began to talk. After a while, as he thought about all that I had said, he finally offered the suggestion that I believe he had intended to all along, that I go to Iliff in the fall and that it would be a good place to mull things over. And so I did and so it was. After all these years, I remain deeply appreciative for Harvey's mentoring, generosity and insight over that one meal in which he shared with me his great gifts of time and presence.[16]

Dave Draus, NWU Class of 1989, is currently a medical equipment salesperson for Medtronic, Inc.

Harvey was "a great moderator" in Science and Religion. He introduced each person/guest speaker as "my friend" and he was also my friend. We went on walks on campus together and down to Mel's Pharmacy and its soda fountain where we had a shake or a soda. Harvey was a great listener.

Harvey was also romantic about Colorado and Denver, as am I, and we talked about places in Colorado we both enjoyed. Harvey had a sharp memory. For instance, once I had toured the Denver Museum of

Art and found some pieces particularly interesting, I would mention them to Harvey and he would know exactly which pieces I had in mind and could discuss those individual pieces in the museum with me in some detail. Harvey was at ease in conversation, but I was never intimidated by him. Harvey took extra time with those who expressed an interest in the subject of religion. Harvey told me that his own mentors had modeled this for him.

I went to Denver at least once and visited Harvey there. Harvey wrote a letter of recommendation and I was accepted into Iliff School of Theology, but I eventually decided not to go to seminary. However, prior to that decision, Harvey showed me around the campus prior to the beginning of school and pointed out to me that one can actually see Mt. Evans from the seminary. Harvey took me to his favorite restaurant in Denver. On this occasion, we had Greek food. Harvey clearly had a love for the mountains and for Denver.

One could spend an hour or two with Harvey without the topic of process theology coming up, but I knew that Alfred North Whitehead was important to him. Harvey was generous with his time and with his books. He gave me some of his library, including some books by Whitehead. "Here's my library," Harvey said to me, pointing to the shelves in his office, "take what you want." One of the books I received from Harvey was Ulysses.

As a pre-med major at NWU, I picked up on Harvey's interest in science and took his Science and Religion course which helped me to discover an appropriate interface of the two. I learned how science impacts one's worldview and who one is. The truth matters and one's world view matters very much. However, Harvey was not intent on his own intellectual legacy. He always pointed to others, such as Whitehead.

Harvey was very proud of Iliff. Since graduation, I have taken the opportunity to reread *A Whole Person in a Whole World,* another of the books I got from Harvey's library. This one, his own composition.

I now work for Medtronic and I have found that the context of my sales of medical equipment has led me to have some conversations with ill patients which blend what I learned at NWU about both science and religion, my double major. Harvey was a friend to me, as well as a mentor.

Dr. Phillip R. Romig III, NWU Class of 1986, earned both an MS and a PhD in Computer Science at the University of Nebraska, Lincoln. He now serves as a Director of Computing and Networking Infrastructure and Chief Information Security Officer within the Campus Computing, Communications & Information Technology Department at the Colorado School of Mines in Golden, Colorado.[17]

I remember Dr. Potthoff and there is no doubt that his philosophy and his classes had a significant influence on my own theology, although it is probably symbolic of something that that influence was more evolutionary than revolutionary. At the time, Dr. Potthoff would teach a large class one evening a week on one of his more popular topics as well as the occasional class in theology for those of us in the religion department. I learned a great deal from those theology classes (I never did take any of the larger classes), both about how theology should be studied/done as well as the details of specific theologians. In particular, his class on Wesleyan theology has been very valuable.

However, the largest impact Dr. Potthoff would have had on me was outside the classroom, and that impact may have even started after I graduated (I don't remember the exact dates). Through both Dr. Potthoff and Dr. Nan Graf, I was somewhat involved in Nebraskans Against the Death Penalty (NADP) while at NWU. Dr. Potthoff had been corresponding with Wili Otey, an inmate on Nebraska's death row. Somehow (again I don't remember exactly how) Dr. Potthoff introduced me to Wili and the two of us began visiting him on a regular basis. When I met Wili Otey he was just getting interested in the French philosophers, particularly Camus. In fact, I believe it was probably my own interest in existentialism and Camus that caused Dr. Potthoff to think about suggesting I try contacting Wili. By the time I met him, Wili was remarkably well read and did want to understand the nuances of the text that sometimes can only be found in the original. I, therefore, tried to send Wili a French dictionary.

At some point, Dr. Potthoff went back to Iliff for a while and I continued to visit and correspond with Wili for several years. There is no way I would ever have had the nerve to correspond with, let alone visit, an inmate at a state penitentiary without a good push from Dr. Potthoff. I really appreciate that he believed that I would have something of value to share with Wili, and vice versa. That is, I suppose, one of the things which made Dr. Potthoff unusual—in spite of being a leading scholar and theologian, is that he was willing to spend his time and effort on an undergraduate who might not always have demonstrated an overabundance of potential.

Wili thought very highly of Dr. Potthoff. While I was skimming some of the old letters I have from him in a box in my basement tonight, I noticed that Wili referred to Dr. Potthoff as one of his two closest male friends, the other being Dr. Nelson Potter from the Philosophy Department at UNL.

As Harvey's intention *really* to retire from NWU at the end of the 1991–1992 academic year began to sink in, a number of Harvey's friends, admirers, and colleagues gathered for a dinner with Harvey on February 7, 1992, in the Renaissance Room at the Cornhusker Hotel, which was arguably the finest dining establishment in Lincoln at that time, for "A Roast of Harvey Potthoff." As master of ceremonies for that event, Ken Keith, then Professor of Psychology at NWU, demonstrated the challenging nature of that occasion with these words:

Well Harvey, here we are—dinner at the Cornhusker—a setting that you have so often made so pleasant for others.[18] We weren't sure exactly what to do for you, but we did know that the people here are friends of yours, and that if we brought you here to dinner they'd treat you right.

On other occasions, it has been customary here to roast the guest of honor. So I've been trying for two weeks to write something appropriately funny or sarcastic or cynical or otherwise appropriately inappropriate for such a setting. I just can't do it. Now don't get me wrong; I'm not suggesting that you're all that wholesome—above a good joke or anything. (In fact, your own repertoire would seem to give evidence that you are clearly not above a good joke.) It's just that you're not a good target.

People who pretend to be kind and gentle are good targets; people who really *are* kind and gentle aren't. People who present to be wise and tolerant are good targets; people who really *are* wise and tolerant aren't. Folks who talk a lot about good deeds are good targets; folks who really *do* a lot of good deeds don't make good targets. Targets that fly in predictable paths are easy to hit; targets that keep showing up in new and unexpected places aren't. A lot of us spend a lifetime talking a good game; a lot fewer actually *play* a good one. So you can see my dilemma.

And yet, I feel this urge to be able to goad you just a little, Harvey. Someone said that maybe we could tease you about your teaching. But I pointed out that, even there, you're immune to criticism or teasing. After all, I said, you can't call a person's teaching into question unless he teaches. By now, everybody's familiar with the Potthoff Method. Harvey doesn't teach; he rounds up a bunch of other people, butters them up until they think they're pretty smart, brings them into his classroom, and turns them loose to talk about the things they're pretty smart about. In the process, he gets them to talk about a lot of other things that they're not so smart about, things personal enough to actually seem important to them, and then they leave feeling like they learned something, and they thank him for the opportunity to have done it. So you see there's not much to say about that, either.

It doesn't seem fair, in a way. A guy comes here in 1981 on a one-year Distinguished Visiting Professor appointment, a guy who's supposed to be *retired,* they tell us. And then he stays the rest of the decade and more, gets hold of all of us in a way that makes us better, and has the audacity to actually be distinguished. And ten years later, I can't think of something rotten to say when we gather to roast him. Maybe I'm losing my touch.

What I *can* say is this: It is a privilege to be in a community that includes someone of your quiet strength and integrity. To anyone who doubts the power of peaceful principle, you are the proof they seek. Tonight, we just wanted to give you a little dose of your own medicine: good food, good friends, and good times. Banzai!

Also in 1992, Ken Keith was granted an international sabbatical. Of the early days of that sabbatical, he relates this story.

In 1992, my wife, Connie and I set off for a sabbatical in Japan, our first visit to a place that we will come to love and to which we will eventually return many times. But now it is, for us, a strange and exotic place, and we are not certain what to expect. As we pack our belongings for an extended time there, I toss Harvey Potthoff's book *Loneliness* into a bag, thinking it might well prove helpful if we find ourselves feeling isolated in a faraway place.

Soon after arriving at our new home at Kwansei Gakuin University, we receive an invitation to a reception at the home of an expatriate American faculty member. She invites us, along with a few other visiting scholars, and, as it happens, her elderly mother, Gladys, is there too, on a visit from the States. As the evening progresses and we all become acquainted, we exchange stories about family, work, interests, and all the other personal tidbits that help us to introduce ourselves to others.

Gladys, it turns out, is known to some of the locals as a teller of jokes, and they soon began to beg her to tell us one. After the usual polite refusals, Gladys launches into a story about a legendary, albeit apocryphal, Native American Chief named Shortcake. Eventually, after a rather convoluted narrative, Shortcake dies, and arrangements must be made for his interment. The punch line, of course, comes when his wife says "Squaw bury Shortcake."

"Where," someone asks Gladys, "did you ever hear such an awful joke?" She reports having heard it at a Methodist convention when the speaker somehow wove it into his talk. At this point, I interrupt, saying

> "Yes, his name was Harvey Potthoff." Gladys nearly falls out of her chair, wondering, I guess, whether I am psychic. I explain that we know Harvey well back home, at Nebraska Wesleyan, and that his reputation for bad jokes is exceeded only by his unbounded kindness. Gladys now seems to view us as friends of a rock star; she clearly holds Harvey in high esteem.
>
> Before she leaves, we give Gladys our copy of *Loneliness*, realizing that it will have real meaning for her. I write to Harvey, telling him this story, and of course in the return mail we receive his letter. He observes, in his typical gentle way, that Gladys may need the book more than we do, but that, just in case, he's sending along a replacement copy. This is vintage Potthoff: quietly kind, thoughtful, and generous. Without raising his voice or uttering a judgmental word, he has made us all better teachers and better people.

By the time Harvey left NWU, he had not only been honored as the L. Edward Mattingly Distinguished Visiting Professor of Religion—which he held for an unprecedented and, as yet, unchallenged and unsurpassed period of eleven years—but also with the degree of Doctor of Humane Letters, which was conferred upon him during the university's Centennial Year, 1987–1988, along with a Centennial Award, which was presented to him by the NWU Board of Governors for "exemplary commitment" to the university. A few years later, a Second Century Award was also given to Professor Potthoff at the Nebraska Wesleyan University commencement ceremony in May 1992, on which occasion he "retired" for a second time from another distinguished academic institution after serving there for more than a decade. On this occasion, Harvey delivered the commencement address to the gathered community of soon-to-be 1992 graduates of Nebraska Wesleyan University, their families, friends, former professors, faculty, staff, and administration. Harvey titled the address simply and most appropriately "Integrity."

Shortly after word of Harvey's death on February 21, 2002, arrived at NWU, members of the community who knew him best gathered in the Miller Chapel for a service in his honor and memory on Thursday April 11, 2002, at 1:00 p.m., on a day and at a time of the week during which no classes or campus activities other than chapel were permitted on campus in those years. Bill Draper Finlaw, University Chaplain at NWU at that time, arranged for this service, simply called "In Memoriam: Dr. Harvey Potthoff."

Photo from Potthoff personal collection, Iliff Archives

Potthoff at lectern delivering May 1992 commencement address at NWU

There was no sermon at this memorial, but there were several brief testimonials to the significance of Harvey's time at NWU, each delivered, in turn, by ten members of the NWU community who knew him best: Roger Cognard (Professor of English), Rick Cypert (Professor of English), Dan Howell (Professor of Chemistry), Bill Kloefkorn (Professor of English), Janet Lu (Professor of Library Science), Pat Morin (Professor of Nursing), Ebb Munden (Senior Minister at the First United Methodist Church, Lincoln), David Peabody (Professor of Religion), Leon Satterfield (Professor of English), and Bill Wyman (Professor of Music), with the Reverend Dr. Bill Draper Finlaw presiding. Maxine Fawcett-Yeske (Professor of Music) played piano for the "Hymn of Promise," and texts drawn from Harvey's *Loneliness: Understanding and Dealing with It* provided the words of "Salutation" to open the service and the words of "Benediction" to close it.

However, in accord with Harvey's typical style of teaching and writing, even in the texts chosen for this service in his honor and memory, Harvey managed to point beyond himself to the words of others he admired. For the words of Salutation, we read these words from both Dr. Potthoff and the distinguished Jewish theologian Martin Buber. Here Harvey notes:

> Martin Buber wrote, "God speaks to each of us through the life God gives us again and again. Therefore, we can only answer God with the whole of life—with the way in which one lives this given life. ... There is no human share of holiness without the hallowing of the everyday." The one who approaches each day with a sense that life is a gift to be hallowed, will not be spared the experience of loneliness, but this person's loneliness will not be without meaning.

And for the Benediction, Bill Draper Finlaw read words from the great Catholic theologian Pierre Teilhard de Chardin, also as quoted in Harvey's book on Loneliness:

> Bring me to a serene acceptance of that final phase of communion with you in which I shall attain to possession of you by diminishing within you. Grant

> me, then, something even more precious than that grace for which all your faithful followers pray: to receive communion as I die is not sufficient: teach me to take a communion of death itself.

Of the several "Shared Stories and Memories" presented at this memorial service, these observations from Rick Cypert, whose memories typify those of many at NWU during Harvey's years in our community, may also help to serve as summary and closing to what we have shared above about Harvey's eleven wonderful years at NWU. For his part in this service, Rick wrote as follows:

> Anyone who spent much time around Nebraska Wesleyan University between 1981 and 1992 probably knows something about Dr. Harvey Potthoff. Perhaps you saw him chatting with Rosemary Rhodes in the Academic Affairs Office (and having a piece of candy from their ever-filled bowl). Maybe you saw him at the large table in the snack bar surrounded by faculty who were preparing themselves for one of his infamous puns. In one of his "shaggy dogs," a psychiatrist explains to a man who complained of dreaming that one night he was a tipi and the next night a wigwam: "You're too tense/tents!"
>
> Or maybe you had an older friend, cousin, or sibling who took a class from Harvey. No? Ask alums like Dan Moran or Scott Shipman what Harvey Potthoff was about. Ask David Peabody, Patricia Morin, Dan Howell, Leon Satterfield, Elaine Kruse, Bill Wehrbein, Garry Duncan, Bill Wyman, or any number of other

folks. Their conversations with Harvey, like those of so many others, often concerned questions at the core of our existence: how, for example, does one cope with change, loneliness, death, injustice?

Teaching class, visiting with students in his office, walking around campus, attending fine arts presentations and sporting events, hosting celebratory dinners for colleagues, or inviting a couple of students to dine with him, Harvey defined the meaning of community at Nebraska Wesleyan, transcending departments, administrative divisions, and student groups.

Born April 23, 1911, in Le Sueur, Minnesota, Harvey often commented (with not the hint of a smile) that not many people were fortunate enough to share a birthday with both William Shakespeare and Rin Tin Tin. Graduating from Morningside College in Iowa, Harvey then earned an MTh and a ThD from Iliff School of Theology in Denver, as well as completing postgraduate work at Harvard University. A United Methodist minister, brought up in the German Methodist tradition, Harvey served as pastor of Christ Methodist Church in Denver; actively participated in United Methodist Church conferences, playing an important role in the 1968 union of the Methodist and EUB churches; and taught at Iliff School of Theology for more than thirty years—until Nebraska Wesleyan University was fortunate enough to get him "on loan."

Explaining his presence on campus, Harvey would often say, "Back when John White called me in 1980 and asked if I would be willing to move to Nebraska to be the Distinguished Visiting Professor of Religion,

I thought that I would come for a couple of years. I ended up staying eleven."

And in those eleven years, Harvey Potthoff changed the lives of faculty, staff, administrators, and students, in important ways. In the Religion Department, he introduced such interdisciplinary courses as "Science and Religion," inviting faculty from the Natural Sciences division to teach with him. In fact, the advanced seminars that Harvey taught were well known for the array of guest "experts" he would bring in and interact with in the course of an afternoon or evening. In addition to students, any number of faculty and administrators attended individual classes or "sat in" for the semester.

In his "Aging, Dying, and Death" class, regularly enrolling more than seventy students, Harvey, focused, not surprisingly, on the art of living well. In one of the last courses he taught at Wesleyan, a seminar in "Process Theology" (a subject which he helped to articulate for a general audience), Harvey offered those taking the class, even those of no particular faith, a view of the cosmos and the individual life worth considering.

Those who knew Harvey best appreciated his caring manner, his wicked sense of humor, his deadpan delivery (especially of puns), his teaching and scholarship (he authored nine books, including *Loneliness: Understanding and Dealing with It*), and his sense of grace and style. As a dinner companion, or host of a dinner party, he was par excellence. As a writer and speaker, he was truly Quintilian's "good man speaking well." How else could he have written a letter, out of the blue, to National Public Radio's Daniel Schorr that would prompt Schorr to visit our campus and deliver the Mattingly Symposium lecture (a program that Harvey introduced)? How else could he author books, preach sermons, and teach classes that changed the lives of so many?

More importantly, perhaps, Harvey was a fine listener, who knew when to speak, what to say, and how to practice the art of silence. Lest I offend that spirit with too exuberant a eulogy, I will do the same.[19]

NOTES

[1] Before Potthoff.

[2] Duane Hutchinson, *Matt : The Story of Lewis Edward Mattingly* (1904-1985) (Lincoln, NE: Foundation Books, 1995).

[3] According to the Outler archives at SMU, Albert C. Outler spoke in classes and in public convocations at Nebraska Wesleyan and at the First United Methodist Church in Lincoln, March 1-8, 1981.

[4] Albert C. Outler, ed., *The Works of John Wesley* (Oxford: Oxford University Press; Nashville: Abingdon Press, various dates): Vol. 1 Sermons I: 1–33; Vol. 2 Sermons II: 34–70; Vol. 3 Sermons III: 71–114; and Vol. 4 Sermons IV: 115–151.

[5] Given the fact that the records of these events in the Outler Archives at Southern Methodist University do not reflect a lecture at Nebraska Wesleyan University on Tuesday, March 3, 1981, but two lectures on Thursday, March 5, could one of these actually have been delivered on March 3?

[6] This Lincoln congregation is located just across 50th Street, only a few steps away from the NWU campus and the basement of this church once served as the site where the idea of establishing a Methodist-related college on land in this area was first formulated in 1887.

[7] At the time this is being composed, Erik Bitterbaum is serving as President of the State University of New York at Cortland, where current NWU President Frederick Ohles, at one time, attended the Lab School on campus, no longer in existence, while his parents were employed at that University.

[8] Harvey H. Potthoff, "Science and Religion: Has the Conflict Been Resolved?" *Religion in Life* (Winter 1962–1963).

[9] Potthoff, *Loneliness: Understanding and Dealing with It* (Nashville: Abingdon, 1976).

[10] Potthoff, *Current Theological Thinking* (Nashville: Abingdon, 1962); *God and the Celebration of Life*.

[11] Potthoff, "The Doctrine of God in W. H. Bernhardt's *Philosophy of Religion*," *The Iliff Review* (Winter 1954), pp. 21-38; "Bultmann, Ogden, and the Search for a Post-Liberal Theology," *The Iliff Review* (Fall 1962), pp. 19-26; "The Reality of God," *The Iliff Review* (Spring 1967), pp. 3-20; "Theology and Man's Search for Integrity," *The Drew Gateway* (Winter 1958), pp. 99-108.

[12] Potthoff, *Current Theological Thinking*.

[13] Potthoff, *A Whole Person in a Whole World* (Nashville: Tidings, 1972).

[14] Others in the penitentiary at the time who also benefitted from visits from Harvey were David Rice, who eventually changed his name to Mondo we Langa, and Edward Poindexter.

[15] Copies of each of these volumes are preserved and available in the Love Library at the University of Nebraska, Lincoln.

[16] Sara not only earned her MDiv at the Iliff School of Theology, but she also won a prize for excellence in New Testament Greek, awarded by the American Bible

Society, in the process. She then went on to Marquette University for her PhD in Biblical Studies, taught part-time at Carroll College in Waukesha, Wisconsin, and elsewhere in the process, prior to accepting her current position at Florida Southern University. For further information, see http://www.flsouthern.edu/KCMS/Faculty/Sara-Harding.aspx

[17] For further information, see http://inside.mines.edu/~promig3/CSMHomePage/Contact.html

[18] Although many members of the NWU community could testify to many such occasions, I will take an author's prerogative and mention that one other similar occasion was convened on May 16, 1987, in celebration of the publication of my first book, *Mark as Composer* (Macon, GA: Mercer University Press, 1987). Harvey read a notice of its release in the local newspaper and came down to my office to invite me to choose a number of friends and colleagues to join with us in recognizing this event. The following group of people, therefore, subsequently met in one of the private dining rooms for another, typically elegant meal sponsored and hosted by Harvey at the Cornhusker Hotel in Lincoln. At that time, the following members of the NWU community and members of their family attended and signed a first published copy of the book. These persons were, of course, Harvey Potthoff; and Nicole Peabody (my adopted daughter); my wife at the time, Martha (then a paralegal at Cline, Williams law firm in Lincoln); William E. Deahl Jr. (NWU University Minister) and his wife, Diane Deahl (textile artist); Tony Epp (NWU Professor of French and German) and his wife, Dianne N. Epp (chemistry teacher at Lincoln East High School); Mary D[aehler] Smith (NWU Professor of English); Bill Pfeffer (NWU Chair and Professor of Philosophy), and his wife, Shirley Pfeffer; John Krecji (NWU Professor of Sociology) and his wife, Jean Krejci (an advocate of social justice in a variety of forms and contexts); Louis DeGrazia (NWU Professor of Religion and Chair of the Department of Religion at the time) and his wife, Betty A. DeGrazia (a private music teacher). Harvey made a point of serving Chocolate Mousse to my daughter, Nicole, for the first time, once at this event and once on the terrace at the Denver Country Club as we admired the night lights of the city. It was a dramatic view and impressive experience for Nicole who still likes to tell people that she "once got Moussed/Moosed in Colorado," in a typical Harvey Potthoff fashion.

[19] One-time members of the Nebraska Wesleyan University student body who have contributed to this article include: (1) Ronda (Armold) Swanson (NWU Class of 1987); (2) David Draus (Class of 1989); (3) Sara K. (Fletcher) Harding (Class of 1989); (4) Eric Ford (Class of 1993); (5) Bet Hannon (Class of 1985); (6) Karla Taylor-Leybold (Class of 1991); (7) Brian Maas (Class of 1986); (8) Gretchen Naugle (a special and "nontraditional" student who was preparing to apply at Gettysburg Lutheran School of Theology at the time); (9) Gregory L. Page (Class of 1989); Phillip R. Romig, III (Class of 1986); and (11) AnnaLee (Uzueta) Pauls (Class of 1992).

Contributors among NWU's former and current faculty and staff include: (1) Frederik Ohles (current NWU President); (2) Boyd Bacon (Music); (3) Erik J. Bitterbaum (former Biology/Associate Provost, Director of the Wesleyan Institute for Lifelong Learning); (4) Staci Bell (Project Coordinator); (5) William E. "Bill" Boernke (Biology, 1971–2007, Emeritus); (6) Jeri L. Brandt (Nursing); (7) Roger A. Cognard (English, 1971–2008, Emeritus); (8) Lois T. Coleman (Education, 1970–1994, Emerita); (9) Nancy B. Cookson (Assistant

Vice President for Human Resources); (10) Rick Cypert (English); (11) Loretta L. Fairchild (Economics); (12) Nanette Hope Graf (English, 1965–1993, Emerita); (13) Twyla M. Hansen (former NWU Grounds Manager, Director of the Alice Abel Arboretum on campus, freelance writer/poet); (14) Daniel B. Howell (Chemistry, 1965–2002, Emeritus); (15) Matthew T. Kadavy (Assistant Vice President and Director of Physical Plant); (16) Kenneth D. Keith (former Psychology); (17) Rita Lester (Religion); (18) Mel H. Luetchens (Assistant to the President for Church Relations); (19) Brenda McCrady (Director of Planned Giving); (20) John J. Montag (University Librarian); (21) Patsy Moore (former Adjunct in Religion); (22) Judy Muyskens (Provost); (23) Bette J. Olson (Assistant Dean for Institution Effectiveness and University Registrar); (24) Richard H. "Dick" Quinn (English, 1972), Director of the Wesleyan Institute for Lifelong Learning, Assistant to the President, Interim Provost); (25) P. J. Rabel (Administrative Assistant to the University President's Office); (26) Gary M. Reber (Archway Fund Manager); (27) Jacquelyn R. Rezac (Data Manager and Donor Research); (28) Meylonie Schatz (Chemistry Stockroom and Biology Laboratory Technician); (29) James A. Stillman (former Chaplain); (30) Mary Swinton (Administrative Assistant to the Humanities Division); (31) Becke Voight (Nursing); (32) William Wehrbein (Physics); (33) Nancy Wehrbein (Director of Sponsored Programs and Foundation Relations); and (34) William A Wyman (Music).

Other contributors included (1) Richard "Dick" Phillips, former student of Harvey H. Potthoff at Iliff School of Theology in Denver, long-time Dean of the Hendricks Chapel at Syracuse University, and editor of this volume, who provided me with multiple pages of xeroxed copies of valuable historical documents he discovered in the Potthoff archives at the Iliff School of Theology in Denver; (2) Amy Birky (Ann Marie Eisentarger), a periodic breakfast companion with Harvey Potthoff in Lincoln; (3) Marjorie Saiser, a mutual friend of Amy Birky and Twyla Hansen who passed on the information from Amy Birky via email; and (4) Katherine L. Walter, Co-Director, Center for Digital Research in the Humanities, Professor and Chair, Digital Initiatives & Special Collections, University of Nebraska-Lincoln, and Harvey Potthoff's grand-niece.

12

POTTHOFF AS DEATH ROW PASTOR: WILI OTEY

By Richard L. Phillips

Without doubt, one of the key memories and most powerful experiences Potthoff had while at Nebraska Wesleyan University was his involvement with Harold Lamont "Wili" Otey. It started in 1981 soon after Harvey arrived in Lincoln. The Wili Otey story is commented on in other chapters of this book. The purpose of this chapter is to relate the story and its importance to both Wili and Harvey. Quotations from both of them will dominate these pages.[1]

Potthoff reported that soon after his arrival, he received a call from the Nebraska State Prison in Lincoln that a prisoner on death row wanted to talk with a philosopher or theologian. Harvey related to me that he thought the call was the result of a sermon he preached in a Lincoln church when either the warden or another prison administrator was present. Potthoff agreed to see Wili and two other prisoners. He worked with two of them for some time, but eventually each of them failed to get a reprieve of sentence. Harvey saw the third man once, and he did have a reversal of sentence.

This was Potthoff's first experience as a death row pastor/mentor. It was certainly Wili's first experience meeting with someone who seemed genuinely to care about him. Harvey was concerned about him as a total person and not just his dire predicament. The relationship bore much fruit in both lives.

Wili was convicted of murder and sentenced several years before Harvey met him. He had been on death row since 1978. The two seemed to bond very quickly and for whatever set of reasons, Wili made great strides along several lines over the next decade. Harvey and Wili both report that they visited almost every week when possible, except in the summers and at least two times when Wili was put in solitary confinement.

Wili had already begun to write poems before meeting Potthoff and shared some of them with him. With Harvey's encouragement, he wrote more and more, and Harvey arranged for him to receive coaching from fellow NWU faculty members and even from Bill Kloefkorn, the Nebraska Poet Laureate. Nelson Potter, a University of Nebraska professor of philosophy, also met frequently with Wili, who had shown a deep interest in that area of study. Wili also took a course from Potter in the prison educational offerings. Wili was in search of answers to persistent questions about who he was and what meaning his life could have. These two central questions on Wili's part could not have been more in keeping with what a relationship with Potthoff had to offer. Potthoff guided such mentors as Kloefkorn and Potter and others to Wili, and all considered him capable of college-level study.

He had earned a GED degree through his own study, not in any formal program.

Other friends and colleagues of Harvey's became aware of Wili, and some of them visited him both before and after Potthoff retired from NWU. The relationship with Wili continued after Harvey returned to Denver in 1992; correspondence continued right up until the sentence was carried out with electrocution on September 2, 1994.

Wili had a sharp mind, but was basically uneducated and had lived a life in which the experience of being loved or cared for by a parent was almost totally absent. He told Harvey at one time that as far as he could remember, there had been no one who had loved him in his whole life.

Wili had converted to Islam while in prison, but there is no record of when or how that happened. He had already developed a keen and somewhat analytical interest in religion, and that, I assume, is what led to his request to see such a person as Harvey Potthoff. Wili, a black man, and Harvey started the relationship with two things in common: poetry and interest in religion. In one reflection, Wili indicated that Harvey never made him feel uncomfortable about his religious affiliation or concerns.

The first letter I want to share is one from Wili, written due to a request by Harvey's friend Nan Graf as Harvey prepared for retirement and his return to Denver. It is from the Nebraska State Prison dated April 22, 1992. Potthoff's file on Wili is as large as most of his files on theological topics! Included is an interview of Wili done by radio station KLIN 1400 in Lincoln. It was recorded earlier and played on the air on September 1, 1994.[2]

Dr. Potthoff:

Tonight I received a letter asking that I might say a few words to you on this most joyous occasion. I have been asked to describe, outline, delineate what I have learned from you, incorporated into my own repertoire, etc., means to me. And I only have a few minutes to do this as new mail regulations now state that our mail can no longer be picked up by the officer; we have to take it downstairs and place it in a mailbox in the dining area and the last opportunity to do that is when evening meal doors are opened, at 4:30 p.m., or there about (mail is passed to us around 4 p.m. each day that it is handed out). So I am reliving a lifetime in but a few seconds. Yes, a lifetime. You see I am 40.

That is in years. But until I met you, say those ten or so years ago, I was not born. Not alive. Unfeeling. Still in the embryo stage. So all of these 40 years must be "seen" now flashing through my thoughts. For the whole that I have become, the amities I never had until you, the felicities, or happinesses, I have come to know, all of this, however one peers at such, could not be, would not be, had there not have been a Dr. Harvey Potthoff. Most would proffer a simple "Thank you!" and allow that to suffice, but not me. Not for you. My friend, my brother, my inspirer, please accept this tear, from my soul. We shall miss you. We won't forget you. Promise not to stay far away, both in communicating to and the sharing of kindred spirits.

> You have taught us so much. So much. Know that this river running down my face is that of joy. A joy elevated even higher by that of sadness. I, in speaking for Wili, am quite indebted. And in speaking for the world, definitely grateful that God was so gracious in allowing our lives to intercede. I'm hugging you... Sincerely, signed. Wili (April 22, 1992)

The letter in which Wili first spoke of Harvey as "father" came much earlier than the one in the retirement tribute above. In it, Wili closes with the bold statement: "You are the father I never had!" Wili repeated the phrase frequently over the years.

Harvey attempted several times to help Wili by supporting a stay of execution and a commutation of the sentence to life in prison. His letter to Gov. Nelson of the Nebraska Board of Parole on June 14, 1991, is typical of such attempts. In that appeal Potthoff made two points early in the letter:

> *In the ten years that I have been seeing Mr. Otey and carrying on correspondence with him, I have come to two conclusions: 1) that I have not been able to find evidence that he ever had a supportive, healthy human relationship before he got in trouble with the law; 2) and that I think he has given rather impressive evidence of his capacity to respond to positive influences.*

There were many others who supported a change in the sentence, but none proved successful. Wili indicated only once to Harvey anything about the crime, saying that he was not guilty. Harvey did not take the role of detective in that regard or any of the related legal issues. He did work with Wili's legal council to try his best to be helpful.

A letter from Harvey dated August 27, 1994, was mailed only a few days before Wili died. It speaks volumes of Potthoff as person and as friend.

> I have received clippings from the Lincoln papers of the past few days, so I am aware that things have not been moving as we would wish. I am aware that you are experiencing inner feelings that only you can fully realize. I want you to know that my thoughts and prayers reach across the miles to you and for you.
>
> Since [1981] we have had so many hours together, talking about so many things. Our letters have crossed—I think I have saved them all. I have re-read so many of them. I treasure the feelings you have expressed many times.
>
> Surely you must know that you are enveloped by the thoughts, concerns, and hopes of many, many friends. Your life has touched so many lives—including mine. I do not know if I ever told you that over forty years ago some friends of mine lost their lives in an automobile accident. They left their twelve-year-old son, Tom. All through the years we have had a close relationship. He is now a doctor in Anchorage, Alaska. For some time we have planned to have several days together in Anchorage the first week of September. This means that in those days my deepest thoughts will be in two places—with you in Lincoln and with Tom in Anchorage. At this point I do not know what your situation will be—but I can tell you that even if miles

> should separate us, I shall be with you in thought and spirit.
>
> Thank you for being my friend. May peace always attend you on your way.

As far as I know, Harvey mailed this that same day, so there should have been time for it to reach Wili.

See Chapter 8 for Tom Wood's account of how Harvey felt on September 2, 1994. Several of Harvey's NWU colleagues and friends, some who had never met Wili personally, were in attendance at the prison for the electrocution. Just one more example of the tremendous impact Harvey's eleven years at that historic college had on its people as well as on Harvey himself.

On June 18, 1989, Wili wrote the letter below to Harvey and sent it along with a copy of his poem, "how come?", which is reproduced on page 349. Wili published three books of poetry while in prison, and often shared his poems with Harvey, many before they were finished.

> Dear Dr. Potthoff, a visitor told me this morning that this was Father's Day. I had not paid that much attention (remember seeing advertisements in the newspapers but I bypassed checking them in detail). I do not have a card so I hope you don't mind this short missive. I only want to say, "thank you!" for the many, many times that you have been a father to me, both in spirit and reality. I cannot begin to say how much I have learned from you, incorporated into my thought process, and shared with others as the only way to appreciate this life, make the best one can

out of it. As I look at those around me, up here on deathrow, see how their lives never took that turn, made the watershed, I am deeply indebted to you, Dr. Potthoff, for affording me wholeness, making it possible for me to love. May all your days be memorable. As always, Wili

P.S. – How's the vacation coming along?

how come?

looking out a prison window
in the distance appears
a rainbow
sneaking away from the nebraska plain
see there beyond the grove
a thatch of brown becoming green
trees dusting the seeds of the cornfield
after the long road with the glimmer of
steel reflecting the chrome of automobiles
the rainbow appears so lonely
jumping up agnostic into the sky
yet not a drop of rain has fallen
hope that/which my naked eyes can detect
as still as the grayness moves closer toward me
the rainbow disappears.

--thursday, april 27, 1989; 7:21 a.m. --

["how come" was reproduced here as Wili had typed the poem on the prison typewriter.]

The bond between the two men was more than prisoner with pastor-mentor; it became one beyond friendship and spoke deeply of a family attachment, one of value to both of them. In my visits with Harvey during the last decade of his life, it was rare that Wili did not at some point enter our conversation. Heartfelt letters from Wili about the illness and death of Harvey's sister and also at the death of his brother reinforced the family feelings that developed on Wili's part. One would have to visit with Harvey only a few minutes to know that Wili was seen in a similar light.

Harvey supported Wili in some tangible ways, including clothing and food items as well as money. Wili reported the loss of some items that never reached him and related to Harvey how this happens in the mail processing in the prison. Wili often stood up to the prison routines and even authorities. More than once, he was beaten by fellow inmates and his "being my own man and standing up for my rights" were what seemed to result in some solitary confinement days. If he was not at times, evidently, a model prisoner, he did relate that he worked hard to preserve his dignity; after all, what else did he have?

Confirmation that life in prison can be very difficult is found in a section of an undated letter to Potthoff from Wili when Carl Potthoff was ill but before he died:

> The stitches I took came about because I was scheduled for the phone at 7:50 p.m. and at 7:54 the previous character did not want to give up the phone (so he cracked me with it); then last night I was shorted two minutes because the cretins in blue claim that his watch takes precedent over the control room clock (which is what an incarcerated person is let out of his

cell by). Tomorrow it will be something else. They will continue and continue until I am thrown in the hole or executed. They do not want me out here because I won't stop studying, I won't give up and become a vegetable like the majority around here.

At a low time, January 23, 1990, Wili wrote:

Dear Dr. Potthoff, how are you faring? Your sister? Really appreciated the cards, money and thoughts which brightened the old year and set this one off on a highnote. Thank you.

sorry that this letter took this long in the making. No one seems to know
if you are back yet and that made my laziness show (itself as) gallant.

not much to comment on here. Nothing from the courts (either appeal). Mentally I am drained. Emotionally, disgusted. Spiritually, filled with doubt(s). Nevertheless, in spite of, I grasp to hold on.

am enclosing an ode which I wrote a couple of weeks ago. Hope you like it. When you speak to your sister would you please convey that I was asking about her? Thank you.

take care. Sincerely, Wili

The poem below by Wili is a good example of a more polished poet. It is undated but in material from the 1990s.

i once had a two-wheeler
i kept it in the house
out of the rain
away from the snow and the thief.
i talked to it sometimes
when i rode down streets
and across fields.
that bike was my friend
and when i grew older
i came to believe
that best friends
are bicycles dreams &
trees. they don't hurt
people. i once had a book,
i slept with it under
my pillow ...

By 1987, Wili was articulating how he felt about his Dr. Potthoff in letters to others. Here is a paragraph from a letter he sent to a Ms. Moody, who had asked for his input about Harvey.

Ms. Moody:

The metaphoric meeting of Dr. Potthoff and myself is similar to that of the man who was brought to Jesus,

> paralyzed, and told to pick up his cot, take it up, after standing, and go home. Like a blind man being given sight I have learned so much from Dr. Potthoff that, well, in all truthfulness, my response to your inquiry must be that of tears of joy, felicity in having met this man. Six, possibly seven, years ago I was a person crippled with hate and distrust of the entire world. On deathrow, sometimes wanting to die (because the anger seethed within me), sometimes wanting to grow, other times just afraid, Dr. Potthoff entered this cloister with his infinite wisdom and bestowed, in me, a weltanschauung which not only simmered my fear of death, but also taught me how, and why, to love. I love the man, pure and simple. As I have told him before, he is the father I never had in this life and I find that feeling spiritual, sacred.

[There was more to the letter; Wili shared his response to her with Potthoff.]

By 1987, Wili's appreciation of Potthoff had reached the high level reflected in the paragraph above. In sharing his response to Moody, he told Harvey in a letter of that same day some of his thoughts about Jerry Falwell as well as his feelings toward his now well-established mentor.

> If Jerry Falwell's type of religious advocation can be compared to that of the anti-christ, you, my friend, are the savior; at least, in my life. If a little bit of you could be in each and all of us then I would not be here today or the world would not be so contentious, so

> distrustful. You are the beauty of life, my friend, its essence and I truly, truly mean that.

A month later, Harvey's brother, Carl, died. Wili's letter to him, sent to his Lincoln address is yet another indication of their relationship.

> Dear Dr. Potthoff: The symmetry of life has been altered, its equilibrium imbalanced. My warmest condolences on the passing of your brother; life, its tree, has lost a branch and though the tree lives on, its beauty is forever truncated, robbed. Your grief is my grief, our grief, forever. ....right now my heart is heavy and words have no visions, just regrets. With sympathy, Wili.

In the early 1990s, when Harvey was in a Denver hospital, Wili sent a "Sorry That You Are In The Hospital" card. Inside it said "Hope you're feeling better soon." He signed it "Harold L. Otey, for all those who love you in Nebraska."

There are certainly some obvious conclusions to be reached about Wili and about his relationship with Potthoff. The first is that the relationship itself was a very unusual one and came to be a very important one for both men. The second is that Wili himself was a very unusual person, let alone an unusual prisoner. That would obviously include his ability to express himself in writing even though with some errors. Another is that Wili related to Harvey not only as his theologian and mentor but as a friend of considerable depth; Wili frequently called it love.

In 1996 Potthoff delivered a talk during which he spoke a

great deal about Wili based on almost eleven years of visits and more years of correspondence. He speaks of the agony of going through appeal after appeal, and he shared his feelings about visiting death row for the first time in 1981 and his doubts about Wili's guilt. Harvey in that talk relates: "I do not profess to know all the relevant facts in his [Wili's] case. I do know that in talking with me he professed his innocence of the crime, saying that there was data—if it had been admitted at the trial would have cleared him—but it was not submitted." Harvey also related that Wili was "a practicing Muslim."

Wili seems to have caught Harvey's teaching about dying with dignity, which I am sure they talked about over the years. Harvey reports that one of the official witnesses of the execution was "a reporter from the *Omaha World-Herald*, who wrote this. 'The electric chair isn't a very dignified way to die—but Harold Lamont Otey died with dignity.'"

Potthoff in this talk reflected back to one of the first things he heard on death row: "If I go to the chair, I must know who I am and what I am taking with me—and I need your help." I don't think any of us who knew Harvey would be surprised that he would not reject that challenge. I know of no greater pastoral tribute to Harvey in this book than his ministry to Wili in the Nebraska State Prison.

I close this chapter with two poems, the first by Wili, the second by an unknown author written in November 1995. The latter reflects Potthoff's position on capital punishment; it may even have been written by him.[3]

The first:

like the leaf which has fallen from
its root of life i sit here
metamorphosed
at thoughts
that do not move
i see the hands
that wave at the wind
groaning to feel something
i touch the lips
that chafe the prisons
which constrain my reticence
i taste the briny malaise
that withers the thought
after the "if..."
in the sphere of emptiness
comes the realization
the leaf one day shall
fertilize new beauty from its
place on this earth
and me i am
like the leaf.

The second:

Death Row
for Wili
eleven years or so
Death Row
for you and me

how many years we'll see
for Wili
people set the date
for you and me
we simply
have to wait
Wili felt
the terrible restraint
never claimed
to be a saint
i think he thought
he would survive
that there would be a time
when he would give
he did the best
with what he had
but damn it all
what makes me mad
is that we
killed a man
because he might
have killed and ran
but damn it all
we are not sure
And yet
we killed a man
that's black and poor!
Dated: 11-14-95

NOTES

[1] All quotes in this chapter can be found in Iliff Archives, box 30, file folders 6-10.

[2] The quality of the tape, due to the background noise and perhaps the recording equipment is very poor. The interview does not add any information to the other holdings we have in the archives at Iliff but might be of interest to future researchers. It is found in box 30.

[3] If anyone knows who authored this poem, please contact the publisher.

13
FACULTY AND COLLEGIAL REFLECTIONS

Over the years, Potthoff interacted with numerous faculty and community members at Iliff and at Nebraska Wesleyan University. He also developed a great number of colleagues within many areas of church work and in many career and academic disciplines. From such persons' input, we have, in alphabetical order, created this chapter.

– Richard L. Phillips, ed.

Editor's note: Edward Antonio was able to read drafts of several chapters; this is his response.

This book on the work and legacy of Harvey H. Potthoff is important in several ways. Potthoff was a man of the church, the academy, and society at large. He was unpretentious in his theological interests, learned in his understanding of the faith, and practical in his teaching and scholarship.

Richard Phillips brings all these elements of Potthoff's life together in this informative book. The book succeeds in showing us the far-reaching positive impact of Harvey Potthoff on large numbers of students and colleagues at the Iliff School of Theology where he taught for many years, as well as on congregants in the churches he served. The importance of this book is not only that it introduces us to many aspects of the theology of Harvey Potthoff, it also shows us the man behind that theology.

Potthoff comes across as a gracious and compassionate man who cared about people and their problems. He embodied a deep sense of justice and peace. He also cared about the church, about theological ideas and their application to the everyday concerns of ordinary men and women. He was a pastor and a theologian who took religious experience seriously as a source of theological reflection, a fact attesting to his Methodist roots. The breadth and depth of his learning was evident in his many essays as well as to his students and colleagues. He cared about tradition and history. He was familiar with and was a part of one of the most significant theological and philosophical movements of the twentieth century, that movement associated with process thought. Although he did not attain the fame of a Tillich or Barth, he was a powerful mind and a presence to be reckoned with. Richard Phillips has written a book that introduces us to theological liberalism at its best. Potthoff was not a stranger to the politics of theological higher education. He participated in the relevant and leading church agencies and was recognized by the church for his service.

I found reading the essays in this book a thrilling invitation to engage with the wider and ongoing legacy and memory of Harvey H. Potthoff. As the current incumbent of the Harvey H. Potthoff Chair in Christian Theology at Iliff, I believe that this book should be read by all with a serious interest in the history of theology at Iliff over the last fifty or so years. Much of that history was shaped and influenced by Harvey H. Potthoff. His commitment to doing theology in the threefold context of church, academy, and society as well as to his dogged openness to the world is his legacy. A legacy that continues to exert a powerful influence on the thinking of many current and retired faculty, on alums, and on the churches where Dr. Potthoff served. I have met men and women in the recent past who recall his memory with great affection. This book is important because it is a testament to that enduring legacy, which needs to be more widely known and recognized because it is what every theologian should be about.

– Edward P. Antonio
Harvey H. Potthoff Associate Professor of Christian Theology,
Associate Dean of Diversities, Director of Justice and Peace Program
Iliff School of Theology

It is awkward to thank someone for being an inspiration and model but I feel such gratitude to you for being just that—thank you. As I see your influence at Nebraska Wesleyan University and see the eyes of others who ordinarily might never sense the importance of faith for the work of the college focus on you for a clearer sense of direction, I know what changing the ethos of a campus can mean. I was told how you have single-handedly refocused the attention of the NWU campus. Your work has given the whole place a different atmosphere. I recognize that your success is in large part a function of your own character and personality, but it also reflects the kinds of programs you have designed. I'm grateful to you for being both an inspiration and a model.

– Dr. Fred Blumer
Retired faculty for Baldwin Wallace College
(from a letter to HHP dated May 21, 1990)

I first knew Harvey Potthoff as a teacher/pastor in the community and was aware of his authority in Christian theology. His was a highly respected name and personality. On becoming a faculty member at Iliff, I became informed of his "silent" authority in faculty meetings. He rarely spoke on issues until the very end of the discussion. Then his word was "revealed," usually very straightforward and to the point, and most often heeded.

In his writing and teaching, he had the ability to communicate in simple, understandable words, and thoughts. He was able to be a Progressive theologian yet reach traditional laity. He contributed a practical approach to theology in his focus on religious education for adults. He wrote both curricula and study guides.

Harvey had a special commitment to mentoring students. This was emphasized by his popular morning walks and breakfasts with individual students. These would become some of the most memorable experiences of seminary for many of them. Harvey was also quite friendly and supportive to new faculty and their spouses/partners.

Harvey did significant interdisciplinary work during his Iliff days. For example, he did joint teaching and writing with researchers in astronomy, drawing interest to creation and the universe. He also developed a relationship with a psychiatrist and did teaching and writing with him, integrating their fields.

He continued this model in his postretirement teaching at NWU. He piqued student interest in the relationship of theology to subjects like medicine, death and the death penalty, grief, loneliness, aging, and science and religion. Many students were drawn to religious studies through these interdisciplinary courses. He influenced other faculty to pursue interdisciplinary work.

His interdisciplinary interest led him to start a program in Aspen in 1973. Weeklong courses for both ministers and laity were given each summer. I was privileged to participate with fellow faculty member Lou Bloede in ministry supervision courses in Aspen for a number of summers.

– Don Bossart, Iliff faculty colleague (1974–1997)

Editor's note:

✦ *This symbol denotes contributions from the 1981 winter issue of* The Iliff Review *on the occasion of Harvey Potthoff's retirement.*

✦ I am proud and grateful to comment on the life and works of Harvey Potthoff. ... He is a diligent scholar, a disciplined teacher and writer, a stimulating preacher, a compassionate and wise counselor, and one of my most valued friends.

– Ann Porter Brown
Former General Secretary of the Board of Missions of the United Methodist Church, Chula Vista, California

When we think of you as a person, we always think of your warmth as expressed to searching students or in your relationship with the Rists [Iliff faculty family] through the years. We also think of your never-failing sense of humour whether while a student at Iliff, at Christ Church, or during your full-time professorial days.

We think of your influence in the church. Yours has been a voice in and beyond Methodism at the growing edge of the religious thought of our day.

Most of the time, however, I think of you and Charles and myself as students of Bernhardt. We each expressed his influence in our own way. You emphasized his commitment to the church as an institution and his continuing concern for philosophy of religion—yes, even theology. My concerns moved over to philosophies of education, developing a typology and other more "secular concerns."

– Dr. Francis Brush

Fellow Iliff student with Harvey, a DU faculty member, and a fellow Meridian resident [He and Harvey remained close, and these words were taken from a letter written to Harvey upon his retirement from Iliff. –Ed.]

✦ It was my privilege to study for eight summers at Iliff. While I am ever grateful to several professors, I confess that I first of all took all of the courses I could from Harvey Potthoff and built the rest of the schedule around that. I cannot remember a single hour of his teaching that failed to guide me further in a meaningful understanding of the faith.

It has been my fortune to be able to maintain some contacts with him, largely through the general connection of the United Methodist Church. I have found him through a number of sessions of the General Conference, to be wise, caring, and committed in his understanding of our Wesleyan tradition and of our mission and ministry in our own time.

What a rich person, what a warm friend he is. I thank God for the pleasant and helpful touch of Harvey Potthoff's life upon mine. ...

– Monk Bryan

Bishop of the Nebraska Area of the United Methodist Church

✦ Harvey Potthoff lived by inner standards of excellence. What he said was well said, whether in private conversation or public address. A student at the school, when Harvey was on the faculty and at the same time minister of Christ Methodist Church, decided to attend some Sunday morning services. Later he said: "His sermons are like class lectures but his class lectures are like sermons." He wanted an informed congregation and also wanted students to know that theology was not unrelated to life.

His theology is a theology of hope. Recognizing the pain of being human, he also declared the wonder of being human. Thereby human beings can share in the continuing work of creation in an unfinished universe and the unfolding order of life. In *God and the Celebration of Life* he wrote: "Human nature is neither inherently evil nor inherently good. It is potential. In that potentiality lies hope." God for him is a "Divine-Real-Other," "sustaining presence, transforming power, life-giving purpose, redeeming love." Here is a basis of hope from the "ground" of all being.

He made a tremendous contribution to the United Methodist Church in Denver, the Rocky Mountain region, and from coast to coast. I was a member of the California-Nevada Conference when he spoke each evening. At the close of his last address the delegates rose in a body to applaud. This would be an unusual event in any Annual Conference which, apart from sporadic and emotional debates, can sometimes be dull.

He has possessed both strength and gentleness, an unusual combination, for the strong are not always gentle and the gentle are not always strong. Many an individual entered a door to meet with the Conference Board of Ministerial Training, which he directed for many years. If they came with trepidation they left knowing that Dr. Potthoff had a sympathetic understanding and a real interest in their future. He spoke with a calm that brought confidence.

His unusually large circle of friends witnessed to a warm and human relationship with others. For countless numbers he was and is an unforgettable person. They give thanks for the lines of life met, crossed and re-crossed so many times. Those of us who had the opportunity of knowing him count this a high privilege. ... He has enjoyed life with its rich, varied, and sometimes surprising experiences, and also has enjoyed contemporary parables. I am glad to pay this tribute to a good friend and co-worker. My life was enriched and my ministry more effective because we shared the years.

—Alexander C. Bryans (Iliff '39)
Minister Emeritus of several churches

✦ In the course of a lifetime, most of us do not know many people who show a spirit of sustained gentility and reasonableness. I counted Harvey Potthoff as a friend from the time of his first appearance to become a student at Iliff. In all those years, Harvey has manifested the qualities I have come to admire more and more, the capacity to be courteous and reasonable. Actually he has made this into an art, for it is not easy to be both courteous and reasonable in the normal routines of living.

There is so much in life that reveals people to be irrational. Not only in matters of religion but also in politics, bridge parties, church meetings, and faculty conversations. All of us remember times when our reflections upon our part in a social exchange painfully tell us that we have acted the fool. Harvey didn't often act the fool, or at least I don't remember that he ever did. But more important than not acting the fool is to be courteous to the foolish.

Back in the good old days, it so happened that fate had brought certain rascals together in the student body, and it was our daily devotion to ridicule each other, trap the faculty in any way we could, and generally bludgeon the innocents with overweening hubris we had been given in overabundance. Harvey puzzled those of us who lacked gentility and reasonableness, but he also won our affections because he didn't especially approve of our antics, but neither did he try to save us from our degraded behaviors. Toward us he turned with friendship and into the mix he generously poured gentility and reasonableness. It had its beneficial values. He was a soda bicarbonate to an acidity in the student body, and we needed the daily dosage he provided.

Through the years, I have watched this become the underlying force in his theology. If the real worth of a theology is in its underneath qualities, in its unspoken but implied meanings, there's the secret of Harvey Potthoff's attraction for me. For the highest reaches of the human spirit, or so it seems to me, are in gentility and reasonableness. He has consistently given these spiritual values to all of us for close to half a century in the Iliff halls. Thanks, Harvey.

– J. Edward Carothers (Iliff '36)
Former Chief Executive of National Ministries
in the United Methodist Board of Global Ministries

HARVEY H. POTTHOFF

In Gratitude for the Life and Thought of Harvey H. Potthoff

Harvey H. Potthoff was both an intellectual mentor and a source of welcome and inclusion for me in my early years at Iliff School of Theology. As an intellectual and as a friend to so many, Harvey embodied Iliff's history and its unique spirit. He stood for what Iliff had been but also opened the way for the Iliff of the future.

Harvey played many roles at Iliff, including faculty member, occasional administrator, and what might be termed the social director of the school. I benefitted from all of these. Harvey Potthoff was my earliest personal contact at Iliff School of Theology. I began the search for my first academic appointment in the fall of 1979. John Cobb and David Griffin, mentors and friends from a year I spent at Claremont Graduate School, pointed me toward a new position at Iliff. In all honesty, as an East Coast person, I had never heard of Iliff and my only experience of Denver was a late night train stop as a child on my way to California. But, at the urging of my Claremont friends, I applied to Iliff. Then, at the American Academy of Religion annual meeting, held that year in New York City, I received a phone call from Harvey. We were unable to meet in person, but Harvey and I talked for a long time on the phone. I think his agenda was really twofold—to inform me about Iliff and its rich history, and make sure I was a liberal. After all, my dissertation was on process philosopher Charles Hartshorne, but also on Karl Barth. Harvey really wanted to make sure I was not a Barthian.

When I came to Iliff to interview, Harvey took the lead in playing host. He, Jean and Steve Schmidt, and Charles and

Nancy Milligan took me downtown to Larimer Square to hear Harvey's beloved Queen City Jazz Band. It was a wonderful evening in which I was first introduced to Iliff's great tradition of hospitality and welcome. Once I accepted the position of Assistant Professor of Theology and moved to Denver, Harvey continued to look out for me and make sure that I was included in the social life of the faculty. At faculty retreat that first year, Harvey was my guide to Rocky Mountain National Park. Over the years, he included me in dinner and lunches, and when Larry Graham and I became engaged, he took us both to a wonderful evening at the Brown Palace. After Harvey retired and moved to Nebraska, he put me in touch with the Women's Institute for Theology in Lincoln, for which I became the resident theologian. That role led to regular Nebraska trips, and Harvey always attended programs and continued to host meals and conversations.

Legions of others also knew Harvey's generosity. Harvey Potthoff believed in the importance of relationships. Whether in Colorado or Nebraska, there are generations of colleagues, students, and friends who experienced Harvey as always welcoming and as the catalyst for real encounters of depth and significance.

Harvey and I also shared a deep appreciation for liberal theology and especially for the traditions stemming from Whitehead, Hartshorne, and the empirical schools of theological thought that developed at the University of Chicago. These were the traditions that had shaped theology at Iliff as it stood against more conservative trends in theology and that ran through the thought of persons such as Harvey, William Bernhardt, Charles Milligan, Alton Templin, and, later, Del Brown and William Dean. I was proud to be part of that line of thinkers. Iliff has always stood out as a bastion of liberal theological and social thought, and has insisted that reason, science, and critical reflection were no enemies to religious faith but key elements in a mature and relevant faith and resources for religious service in the contemporary world. Harvey Potthoff was the embodiment of Iliff's deepest intellectual commitments, and these commitments to intellectual rigor and openness to new developments paved the way for Iliff to emerge as an important center for theological education and academic excellence on the national and international scene.

Harvey also mentored me in others ways. Iliff is a theological school associated with the Methodist Church. The Iliff faculty, during Harvey's time and since, was very diverse, representing multiple religious traditions and sometimes being nonaffiliated with any tradition. I was part of the non-Methodist contingent. But as one of Iliff's theologians, I was often a resource for churches, annual clergy conferences, and even the United Methodist Bicentennial. Harvey was once more my mentor and guide. It was through him that I immersed myself in the Methodist tradition and learned about the Methodist Quadrilateral, the tradition's non-creedal character, its vision of divine and human cooperation, and its commitments to a more just society. It became increasingly clear to me why Iliff as a Methodist-related institution also embraced liberal theology, academic excellence, and a commitment to social justice.

In 2005, I was named the Harvey H. Potthoff Professor of Christian Theology at Iliff. My appointment to the Potthoff chair was, for me, a tangible connection to the Harvey who had urged me to come to Iliff and had welcomed me so fully, but equally significantly it also embodied Harvey's openness to the new, creative, and unexpected. This orientation ever toward the future, to new possibilities to be embraced, not feared, characterized Harvey H. Potthoff's life and work. This openness was Harvey's gift to Iliff, his friends, colleagues, students, and me. It is with great gratitude, both personally and professionally, that we remember Harvey H. Potthoff and seek to continue his legacy.

– Sheila Greeve Davaney
Iliff faculty 1980–2010
Harvey H. Potthoff Professor of Christian Theology 2005–2010, Emeritus; Visiting Senior Fellow, Center for American Progress

Harvey and I were colleagues at Iliff from 1967 (when I first came to Iliff) until his death in 2002. We shared many experiences and values in common and had respect for one another.

I remember Harvey as an engaging storyteller, with a wonderful sense of humor. I was enthralled by his stories of the Iliff family, especially Louise Iliff. He told of her visiting Iliff with a basket in which she carried some stock papers. When she asked Iliff's president how the school was doing and was told it was short of cash, she would clip some of the stock coupons to help the school defray its expenses.

I learned to appreciate an "Iliff tradition" embodied in Harvey, for a progressive approach to theology and theological education. Harvey did theology by drawing upon what he considered to be central biblical themes. I clearly learned to appreciate and draw upon his thinking about *God and the Celebration of Life*. Harvey helped me and many others to celebrate life. He indeed was a gracious human being and host.

I picture Harvey in a reflective posture, listening and

questioning. His approach was one of calmness and quiet engagement. He often was quiet during discussions, but he did not hesitate to share his insights and opinions at the appropriate time. Harvey had a wonderful supply of incisive questions he regularly tossed at me and others: "What do you think about...?" "What's exciting in your life these days?" He was genuinely interested in my values and my human experience.

Harvey and I team taught a course dealing with religious education and theology, and in this course I experienced one of his trademarks for teaching. He used resource persons to provide lived experience to the topic being considered. He would invite persons of all ages to share their stories. Then, he would facilitate theological reflection on those human experiences.

I remember Harvey as a pastoral theologian. He was deeply concerned with how theological reflection shaped pastoral ministry and how pastoral ministry shaped theological reflection. Both serve to enrich and educate each other. His approach is both practical and academic, experiential and philosophical, reflective and lived, thinking and feeling. Harvey embodied that dialectic.

– Dr. H. Edward Everding Jr.
Iliff Professor Emeritus, Religious Education and New Testament
1967–2002

✦ Harvey Potthoff and I were friends for over a quarter of a century. This, in spite of the fact that we are really very different in character, in ethnic origin, in religious orientation, in education, and many other things. But what have we not shared? We have been together in the presence of birth and death, of pain and pleasure. We have learned and taught together. We have been awed together by heroic people, by books and ideas and mountains. Friendship with Harvey Potthoff has been one of the blessings of the lives of my family.

– James Galvin, MD
Former adjunct faculty and periodic visiting lecturer at Iliff; Former Chief of the Department of Institutions of the State of Colorado

Remembering Harvey Potthoff

I met Harvey for the first time in April of 1977. I was a candidate for a new position in pastoral care and counseling established by Iliff when Dr. John Spangler became the director of the Master of Divinity Program. Harvey was the host at a luncheon as a part of the interview process. He had just written a book on loneliness. I was impressed that a man with such strong intellectual credentials could speak so knowingly to a painful human experience. His book meant a lot to a member of my family who had read it before I met Harvey. He was pleased to learn this and gracious in receiving the news.

At this luncheon, he asked me some astute questions about process theology (which I had studied and embraced), my Lutheranism (which was precarious at best by this time), and how I thought pastoral care and theology might help one another (I can never separate them). It was clear from this luncheon that Harvey was (1) down to earth, (2) intellectually astute, (3) tuned in to the real lives of real people, (4) a gracious host, and (5) funny. He told several anecdotes that all of us found both entertaining while having a theological, spiritual, or moral point. Harvey was always a teacher and a pastor. He was unfailingly interested in the little joys and amusements woven into the fabric of our everyday lives. (He asked Iliff's president Smith Jameson Jones once, "Did you know that no one named Jones ever won the Boston Marathon?")

I was hired by Iliff for a three-year terminal position. The position became tenure track. As I write these reflections, I have just entered my thirty-sixth year of teaching at Iliff. And while many, many people have influenced me over the years at Iliff, I can say that the tone set by Harvey at this job interview luncheon is what makes Iliff resonate so positively in my personal and professional life. The affirming welcome, enjoyment of life, intellectual seriousness, and a human pastoral touch to make life better is what has characterized Iliff for me throughout these years. And Harvey is the one who most memorably embodied these values from the very beginning and throughout his long relationship to the school.

There are two brief vignettes that speak to Harvey's contribution to my life as an academic colleague and as a person trying to figure out his life. As a colleague, Harvey was well grounded in disciplines outside of theology, and drew on them to rethink and to reformulate religious and theological meanings. Psychology was one such discipline. He taught a course on death and dying in relation to the life cycle. He invited John Spangler and me to share our insights from pastoral care and the psychology of religion, and to have a conversation with him and the class about how we were experiencing our own developmental journey at the time. He asked us to reflect psychologically and theologically on our own life cycle journeys and to open ourselves to the class. (Somewhere I have a picture of the three of us together taken after one of these class sessions.)

His personal affirmation and his desire to link theology, pastoral care, psychology, and ministry in this very astute yet human way was symbolic of the easy and natural way that Harvey could bring things together and let something new flow out of the event. He repeatedly affirmed the process theological mantra that reality is "dynamic, relational, and processional." Asking Spangler and me (and others as well) to participate in this interdisciplinary conversation was as good an example as I can remember of how his theological convictions were lived out in the details in the classroom and on the ground. It made me feel like we were partners in theological education, each bringing something to the table that the other really needed.

On a more personal note, Harvey was a source of strength and wisdom to me when I went through a personal crisis a few years after coming to Iliff. When I told him what was going on, he replied, "You will find a lot of strength and acceptance in this community. You should let yourself be nurtured by it. And as you go through this difficult time, let yourself be prepared to be surprised." Not long after that, when "two roads diverged in a wood and being one traveler could not take both," Harvey's speech at the Opening Convocation of that school year provided what I needed to make the right choice for me. Here is what I heard him say that day (and I am definitely paraphrasing!): "God is the integrity of the universe. That means authenticity in living is expressed in integrity: the integrity of acting in the directions of what you know to be most true for yourself. The universe has integrity because God is the integrity of the universe. As part of the universe, we have integrity and we can and must build lives of meaning in relation to the integrity of the universe and God."

Those wonderfully astute words spoke directly to my heart and my mind and to the situation I was addressing. When he put it that way, I knew immediately what choice to make, what path to go down. And as "way leads on to way," I have seldom looked back. And when I do look back, I feel confirmed that the direction my life has taken has been one of integrity and of deeply significant meaning for me and for those who have come into my life since.

It is an honor to remember Harvey and to write these brief reflections. But the real privilege was to meet him in the first place and to have those many years of his influence and goodness in my life and Iliff's. I remember him with pleasure and gratitude.

– Larry Kent Graham, PhD,
Professor of Pastoral Theology and Care,
Iliff School of Theology (1977–current)

The Rev. Dr. Harvey Potthoff hardly raised his eyes as we young men nervously walked into the second floor classroom in Iliff Hall. He was impeccably dressed, in what I came to recognize as his common attire, a dark blue suit, a white shirt, and a brightly colored tie. We quickly found chairs around the long oak table. Then he stood up and greeted us warmly but with formality, a sense of reserve. The year was 1943. We were first-year seminary students, mostly Methodist, mostly from the Midwest.

Dr. Potthoff introduced us to theological scholars, and we explored theological themes dealing with the nature of God, the human condition, the Bible as a source of knowledge, and how to understand the traditional creeds of the church. I began to realize that this dignified young professor was going to have a profound influence upon me, an influence that I have increasingly appreciated.

Dr. Potthoff was the senior minister who sponsored me for ordination as an Elder in the Methodist Church. In September 1956, Harvey and I became colleagues. I was appointed Chairman of the Department of Religion at the University of Denver, the institution that shares the campus with Iliff. In this new relationship, we exchanged ideas as we sat together over coffee or as we attended educational meetings together. When he was away I taught his classes, and he lectured in my classes.

After his retirement from Nebraska Wesleyan University and my retirement from Syracuse University, our friendship continued in Denver. At a celebration of our fiftieth anniversary, he delivered a short essay in praise of friendships, illustrating how we humans who form supportive groups are similar to small streams that contribute to the power and beauty of a broad river.

Harvey invited some of his friends and colleagues to join him in the dining room of his retirement home for informal discussions on current theological issues. During the first years of the discussion group, he was the central facilitator, suggesting readings and topics to explore together. His insights on the continuing importance of Progressive Theology were profound. In later years, Harvey increasingly became a listener, occasionally offering a fresh insight or one of his many humorous quips, and others became the facilitators.

– Rev. Dr. William Hall (Iliff '46)

Retired Chairman of the Department of Religion at Denver University, Stephens College, and Syracuse University

✦ Harvey Potthoff was the finest example of a pastor-educator that I have known. As a pastor of Christ United Methodist

Church in Denver his ministry was a model of excellence in the educating of a congregation. He provided effective, creative opportunities for learning and for using what was learned at every age level and in every available setting. At the same time, he was an admirable pastor, an impressive preacher, and an influential community leader.

As Professor of Theology at Iliff, he was a sensitive, caring pastor to each of his students and to numbers of young persons in the variety of groupings where his leadership was experienced. At the same time, he was a challenging and inspiring teacher, a scholar of considerable renown, and an examiner of scholarship who could not be deceived. In each of the situations where I observed him at work, he brought understanding, enlightenment, and fresh perspectives to the persons present.

As a faculty colleague, I encountered in him a sharp, penetrating mind concerned with issues and questions that were of utmost importance, an awesome integrity of thought and action, scholarship that is both profound and impressive in its vision and wisdom, and a persistent demand for relevance to the processes of human living.

In the curriculum processes of Methodism, Harvey has contributed significantly to the improvement of educational opportunities for persons in many local churches. He has patiently taught the editors, the program developers, the leadership trainers, and the bureaucratic administrators what Christian education can be and what their obligations are in relation to this possibility. Many of the finest theoretical formulations, the most responsible curriculum content, and the most relevant series of studies have come into being as a result of his influence. And much of this was without personal recognition.

Harvey Potthoff is a person whose existence has enriched my life and the lives of unnumbered others. From him I learned the meaning of education, as he not only allowed but encouraged me to pursue the quest for truth to the limits of my abilities, no matter where the quest led and regardless of what those findings did to the accumulated "knowledge" of the human race. He opened opportunities for me to learn, to grow, and to share what I could not have had without his help. He was and continues to be my teacher.

As a faculty colleague, he taught me by his example and by his encouragement to be open to other scholars and to other fields of scholarship in trying to be a responsible scholar in my own area of specialization. But beyond all of that, was Harvey's ability to be a friend. He was both supportive and growth-inducing. I felt accepted and respected in his presence, yet he continuously enabled me to see possibilities that I had not known were present.

I am profoundly thankful for the existence of Harvey Potthoff. I value his influence, respect his scholarship, and cherish his friendship. The world I know and have experienced is significantly benefited by his life.

– Howard M. Ham (Iliff '46, ThD '47)
Former Iliff Professor of Religious Education and Psychology (1951–1960),
Former Associate General Secretary of the Board of Discipleship,
Division of Education, the United Methodist Church

Dr. Potthoff was a very much liked and respected figure at the Englewood Meridian where he spent his last years. My mother, who called herself an "inmate" of the "institution," spent her last years on the third floor, the nursing home division. Her days were considerably brightened as she could look forward to Dr. Potthoff's talks to the Meridian community and later, as table companion while he was recovering on the third floor from various medical setbacks. This may have been a trial for him, but it was a positive experience for my mother and most likely for the other residents on the floor. Dr. Potthoff had the ability to make you feel that you were the most important person in the world. This, plus his erudition and polite courtly ways, charmed my mother. When I teased her with having a crush on Dr. Potthoff, she would blush like a young girl. It was heartwarming to see her reaction—another soul orbiting around this charming learned man.

– Alexandra L. Happer
Former Iliff librarian and compiler
of the bibliography in Appendix B

✦ The Impact of Harvey H. Potthoff upon The Iliff School of Theology cannot be overestimated. In his student days, he achieved such excellence that he was chosen by the faculty to receive the Elizabeth Iliff Warren Fellowship. His reputation as a pastor of Christ Methodist Church brought honor to the School. As an adjunct member of the faculty from 1941 until 1951, and as a full-time member of the faculty from 1952 to the present, he has brought scholarship, great teaching skills, wisdom, and personal warmth into the classroom. Through those years, he probably has been the chief pastor at Iliff, not only with current students but with many generations of alumni. For years, he was the person who most represented Iliff to the Church-at-large.

In many circles, his name is synonymous with that of the School. Extremely rare is the student who has gone through Iliff in these decades without being significantly affected by

Harvey Potthoff. He also has had significant impact upon his colleagues on the faculty, and upon the program and growth of the School. Within faculty and administrative circles, he has been a statesman, a wise planner, a man of insight and sound judgment. The history of this institution for almost half a century has been shaped by the life and spirit of Harvey Potthoff, and for this contribution, past, present, and future generations are and will be deeply grateful.

– Jameson Jones
President of Iliff (1969–1981)

Memo to Dr. Harvey Potthoff: "I want to express deep appreciation to you for the speeches on two recent occasions. What you did at the banquet for the Penningtons was extremely appropriate and constructive and helpful. I felt we had an excellent evening, and I was very pleased with the mood and spirit of it all. You contributed greatly to this. I thank you for the investment of your time and energy to make that possible.

I also feel that what you did at the services for Martin Rist was extremely appropriate. I commend you for always saying the right thing at the right time and in a very fine way. Your words were very moving to the whole congregation, and to me. I do thank you."

– Jameson Jones

✦ I have known Harvey Potthoff since we were classmates together at Iliff in the 1930's. I don't know how much I taught him about religion, but I do claim to have taught him something about playing handball. He and two other United Methodist ministers and I used to have a foursome playing every Monday morning at the YMCA before the three of them went on to their weekly Monday meeting.

Through the years, I have watched with great delight his development as an outstanding scholar and professor. I have read his books and listened to his addresses on various occasions, and always came away inspired and impressed, and delighted that I could call him a friend.

– Manuel Laderman (Iliff '37)
Rabbi Emeritus, Hebrew Educational Alliance, Denver, Colorado

I joined the Iliff faculty in 1995, well after Harvey Potthoff's retirement. But his legacy continued to be quite tangible.

First, he was still physically and intellectually present. He lived nearby and was fairly often on campus. Not long after my arrival at Iliff, Dr. Potthoff came looking for me. He was a charming, welcoming older colleague. Even in retirement, Harvey continued to feel proprietary about the school, and he wanted the chance to interpret Iliff's liberal intellectual legacy. He was gracious and discreet in exploring what I brought to the faculty mix and how the school might be changing as he and some of his colleagues retired.

I came to see and appreciate the ways that Iliff continued to bear the Potthoff stamp. His name was a kind of shorthand for the liberal modernist theology that has marked and identified Iliff through its history, and for the conviction that such a theology could undergird compassionate and socially concerned Christian ministry. Numbers of alums would speak of Dr. Potthoff's influence and his compassionate presence in their lives. More than once, alums have described the way they came to doubt the premodern theological assumptions of their youth, and spoke with gratitude of Dr. Potthoff's role in helping them build the intellectually viable and sustaining faith that undergirds their ministries.

The history which Harvey embodied continues to give Iliff a unique flavor and to shape our mission. It is appropriate that his picture hangs in what we call "the Potthoff Room," a seminar room that looks out through a large round window into the lobby through which students, staff, and faculty come and go. For it was deep conversation about how his students would carry theology out into the world that was at the center of Harvey's work and legacy.

– Professor Jeffrey H. Mahan
Ralph E. and Norma E. Peck Chair in Religion and Public Communication, Director of Professional Formation, Iliff School of Theology (1995–current)

"Treat every person you meet today kindly, for they are having a hard day" was a message I learned from Harvey H. Potthoff, a pastoral theologian and church leader par excellence. This approach to people I always considered Harvey's great gift in relating to others and sharing the Christian message of love.

I first met Harvey when I was a student at Dakota Wesleyan University in 1960. He was our choice for the "religious life week" speaker, and I was involved in the publicity. Later, when I became a pastor in South Dakota, I invited Harvey as the weekend speaker for an all-church retreat. Always popular with lay groups, he effectively communicated a theology of life that appealed to people and helped them grapple with their daily lives.

In 1981 Harvey welcomed me as the new president of Iliff. Harvey had been serving as the interim president for a few months after the departure of Dr. Jameson Jones. We never served on the faculty at the same time, as Harvey had just retired from the faculty. He accepted a position at Nebraska Wesleyan

University, and we kept in close contact and visited when he returned to campus.

No one outside of the Iliff family per se has ever more symbolized the values and mission of the Iliff School of Theology than Harvey Potthoff. He truly was "Mr. Iliff" in the minds of most alumni and friends of the school. He had great influence throughout the denomination with both clergy and laity.

His books and articles impacted people far beyond the classrooms of Iliff. He wrote with a clarity that escapes most academic theologians, who confuse obscurity with profundity. Bishops and clergy often cited Potthoff in their sermons and writings. Laity found in his sermons and books insight and truth in the Christian message.

As president, it was my joy to raise the money to establish the Harvey Potthoff Chair in Christian Theology and to dedicate a room in Skaggs Hall in his honor. In both cases, I was hoping to not only preserve his memory, but also honor a unique pastor, professor, and friend who had indeed tried to "treat every person" kindly, because they were "having a hard day."

– Dr. Donald E. Messer, President Emeritus
and Henry White Warren Professor Emeritus of Practical Theology,
Iliff School of Theology (1981–2006)

After earning my master of divinity degree from the Iliff School of Theology, I had the good fortune to work in the Ira J. Taylor Library from 1985 through 1998, and it was during this time, in 1992–1993 specifically, that I processed for the school's archives collection the personal papers of Dr. Potthoff. The passage of twenty years has done nothing but confirm that this undertaking was the highlight of my tenure as a staff member in the library. Our frequent meetings in his apartment in the Meridian were informative times, where Dr. Potthoff would explain and discuss in detail the papers that he had left to Iliff. These were also convivial times. Always the perfect host, he would insist that each meeting be followed by lunch in the dining room.

My most vivid recollection is working with Harvey's papers that deal with capital punishment. There is in his archives a most remarkable gathering of materials—sermons, lectures, and correspondence, much of which is deeply personal—that addresses this topic. Reading these items greatly influenced my thinking, perhaps none more so than the exchange of correspondence between Harvey and a death row inmate whose sentence Dr. Potthoff (and others) tried unsuccessfully to commute from death to life in prison. From this exchange and from his other writings about capital punishment, I learned more about hope, grace, and redemption than was possible from any textbook.

From as long as he lived, I always called and referred to Dr. Potthoff as Dr. Potthoff; awestruck as I was. It has only been in the years ensuing since his death that I came to comfortably refer to him as Harvey, appreciate him as the friend that he was, and realize that not only did he teach me to think about hope, grace, and redemption, he assisted me in experiencing such in my own life. For many of us in the Iliff community, Harvey will forever be our professor, minister, and friend.

– Paul Millett (MDiv, Iliff '87)

I was associated with Harvey for three years as a student and eight years as an Iliff faculty member. I was always impressed that Harvey kept his cool whenever any difficult issue came before the faculty.

He was always quietly measured and wise in his participation in the Rocky Mountain Conference, especially as a member of the Board of Ordained Ministry. I very much appreciate his contribution to the section on "Our Theological Task" in the Discipline. For that and many other contributions, I, with many others, am grateful for his rich and measured addition to the heritage of the United Methodist Church.

– Dr. Kenneth Neal (Iliff '60)
Iliff Professor of Homiletics (1962–1971)

✦ It was my good fortune as a young professor to have been a colleague with Harvey Potthoff on the Iliff faculty. To me, he is many things all wrapped in one, as he is to many others. He is able to be all things to all people, yet distinctively and decisively himself in every instance. There is much that could be said about the many-splendored dimensions of his life, but I want to speak of him as a colleague and a friend.

When my family came to Denver we were searching for a community in which to locate our home. College, graduate school, and the first two years of teaching were clearly transitional years. Harvey's spirit and kindness, and that of many others, soon made us feel at home.

I remember introductions by Harvey to trustees of the school, alumni, and persons in the community that were so warm and generous that I began to feel privileged to know myself. Wherever possible, Harvey seemed to enable one to broaden one's roots and involvements in the community. His contacts and personal web of relationships was incredible. In the faculty, he and the other members had established a spirit and tone that insure instant peerage. It was an environment conducive to intellectual and religious growth, for which I am deeply grateful.

Harvey helped bless our home with his curious capacity to enjoy our joy as much as we did. He introduced us to fine restaurants and funky places with sawdust on the floor. The children remember a trip to watch the Yule log hunt, and Harvey's special enjoyment of the down home aspects of the ritual. And who could forget all those jokes and puns? Or the characteristic twinkle in his eye when I asked him to take Peggy to a concert while I was out of town?

Harvey Potthoff is the embodiment of the celebration of life. There is a congruence between his life and thought, an integrity to his person. That, in itself, is deserving of a hymn of praise. But Harvey would undoubtedly consider that a little pompous. He is so human, filled with such a lighthearted, full-bodied love and enjoyment of life, that a folk song seems just as appropriate. Only in such a person, who combines austerity with enjoyment, and sensitivity with distance, does the profound become simple, and the simple profound.

– Dr. Dan D. Rhodes

Former Iliff Professor of Christian Ethics (1964–1968)

I have thought of Harvey many times since our last face-to-face meeting. I ran into him last week while straightening up the library in a church I am serving in southeastern Connecticut, after over forty years in the academy. Were Harvey to know this small fact, I think he would be very gratified, since he thought many of us who had never served in pastoral ministry prior to guiding people in theological education might be better teachers had we taken his route to teaching and research.

Harvey wasn't in my church library in person. That was a shame, since I am sure he would have had something to say to my immediate observation when I saw the book I found, *Acts: Then and Now, 1965*: "I did not know you wrote anything on the Bible!"

Harvey would have continued the exchange on the Acts book. His retort, had our chance meeting been face to face, would have even been better to hear because of my implied challenge about his writing something on a biblical book.

I read this book for the first time when I was straightening up the church library. It is the real Harvey. He, as the title indicates, brought home the idea that what worked for the early church has a way of speaking to the contemporary church.

He had perused the strongest works on Acts. The bibliography for each section of the book names many well-known biblical scholars. I am confident he would have engaged all of them with his critical questions. That was Harvey's quiet strength.

The Iliff Review published in Winter 1981 contained a group of essays honoring Harvey. Toward the end of these alphabetically ordered tributes is one by Ruth M. Underhill, a respected, well-known, and published anthropologist. At nearly one hundred years old when she wrote the tribute, she uses two phrases in her brief tribute that for me poignantly and simply express who Harvey H. Potthoff was and is. She says, "...Harvey Potthoff has been an island of peace in a very busy life. His quiet acceptance of events brings to mind the calm steady flow of the Hudson River (near where she grew up). ... The Hudson is broad, deep, and straight. ... I think of its quiet depth when I think of Harvey." Harvey continues to flow with that deep, abiding strength in all of us whom he touched.

May we pass that on to others. Thanks, Harvey, for encouraging our questioning spirits.

– Dr. Kent Richards
Iliff Proffessor of Old Testament (1972–2004)

✦ All of us leave prints in the sands of time. Some foot-prints are very dim and those who follow have difficulty seeing them. Others leave imprints so deep they can never be forgotten. Harvey Potthoff left footprints that are deep and abiding. The lives of those students whom he touched will never be the same because of the kind of teaching he did, the kind of counseling he gave, his thoughtful deed when a student was in need.

But the lives of those who were not privileged to sit in his classes also have felt his influence through his friendship and through the books which he has written. His influence was felt not only by the students at Iliff, but by his fellow-members of the Rocky Mountain Annual Conference. He was an active member of many committees of the Conference. And his foot-prints have been seen by the entire United Methodist Church because he was a member on national boards and committees, was a delegate to General Conference for a number of years, not as an on-looker, but as an active participant. ... You will be remembered down through the years as a leader, a teacher, a friend.

– Margaret E. Scheve (Iliff '34)
Former President of the Iliff Alumni Association

✦ One of the facets of Harvey Potthoff which may not be widely known but deserves to be acknowledged and celebrated is his generosity toward younger colleagues, particularly newcomers to the Iliff faculty. As the first woman to become part of the full-time faculty at Iliff (1975), I have been especially appreciative of the gracious openness of the senior member of the faculty toward this new person whose very presence at Iliff symbolized a new day in the school's history. Harvey went out of his way to welcome our family to Denver (very appropriately taking us to an evening of Western melodrama) and was careful to let me know in countless ways that first year that he was interested in what I was teaching and thinking and glad that I was at Iliff. Since then, I witnessed that same generous spirit toward others who have joined the faculty.

Dr. Harvey Potthoff is a man who carries his stature with ease, grace, and humor, and I am grateful to have been his colleague these six years.

– Jean Miller Schmidt

Professor of Modern Church History, Iliff School of Theology (1975–2008)

Colleague Harvey Potthoff was a multifaceted human being. At once, he was a brilliant scholar, devoted and loyal friend, whimsical punster, faculty leader, theologian who appreciated cognate disciplines, committed churchman.

After finishing his Iliff degree, he used his Elizabeth Iliff Warren Fellowship to immerse himself in the thought of Alfred North Whitehead at Harvard. As a scholar and teacher, he became perhaps the foremost scholar in applying Whitehead's philosophical thought to the task of theology.

Throughout his tenure at Iliff, there was a magnificent community spirit unmatched—in this writer's experience—in any other school of theology. This recherché spirit was due, in large part, to his kindness and hospitality. But perhaps more important than his hospitality was his concern to right wrongs. He was impelled to stand with and for anyone being mistreated—student, faculty member, trustee, administrator. Harvey's being named Iliff's interim president on several occasions is evidence of his respected leadership of the faculty.

To this writer, the preeminent facet of Harvey's character was his deep-seated commitment to the church, in particular the United Methodist Church. At Iliff he saw the primary task to be that of preparing students to be effective clergypersons. The overriding concern in his teaching was that students understand theology, not as a copy-book exercise, but as a tool to help parishioners find meaning and value in their lives.

For nearly three-quarters of a century, Harvey Potthoff's life was intimately entwined with the Iliff School of Theology, to the benefit of the school, the church, and society.

– Dr. John D. Spangler
Iliff Professor of Psychology of Religion, Counseling (1971–1993)

My lingering memories of Harvey Potthoff are of a fine theologian—although I always disappointed him in my failure to take Whitehead seriously—a marvelous intellect, and a deeply caring and generous human being. Harvey was a wonderful introduction to Iliff for this young neophyte back nearly three decades ago.

– Tink Tinker
Iliff School of Theology Faculty (1985–current)

✦ My friendship with Harvey Potthoff has been an island of peace in a very busy life. His quiet acceptance of events brings to my mind the calm, steady flow of the Hudson River—the typical item of my home landscape. The Hudson is broad, deep and straight. It flows without deviation at least from Albany to the sea, and I think of its quiet depth when I think of Harvey.

– *Ruth M. Underhill*
Professor Emeritus of Anthropology, University of Denver

Harvey Potthoff ended his sixteen year pastorate at Christ United Methodist Church, Denver, in 1952 to become full-time Professor of Christian Theology at the Iliff School of Theology. Having lived in the Christ Church parsonage, he moved his residence to an apartment at 2125 South Josephine Street, a block from the Iliff campus and just several doors down from the University Park Church.

His colleague and friend, Alexander Bryans, was in the ninth year of a twenty-two year pastorate at University Park Church, so it was natural that Harvey would name that congregation as his Charge Conference in his "Special Appointment."[1] Thus began a fifty-year love affair between the laity of University Park Church and Harvey.

Having developed a reputation for his emphasis on religious education for adults, it was natural that Harvey would become a "regular" instructor in the Adult Christian Education courses offered at the church. However, it must be observed that whether the course was on process theology or on some aspect of pastoral care (loneliness, forgiveness, etc.) persons were drawn to participate, not so much because of the intellectual content of the course, as for the personal exposure to the personage of Harvey Potthoff.

One of Harvey's greatest gifts to that church was his non-anxious presence and calming words at times of pastoral transition, change, and, often, turmoil. As far as it is known, Harvey was always publicly supportive of the appointed senior pastor and ordained staff of the church.

When Harvey retired from the Iliff faculty in 1981, the concern was where he was to locate his office. Because of the number of retirements of senior faculty members in ensuing years, the administration at Iliff did not feel that Harvey should remain in his office on campus in emeritus status. At this point the offer was made by the pastor and trustees of University Park Church to house Harvey's office in a prominent and easily accessible room at the church facility. It was a space he occupied until he left University Park Church to become a resident at the Meridian Senior Living complex in Englewood.

It was fortuitous that Harvey should be on premises, for the time came when Harvey was to head a pastoral transition team composed of retired clergy associated with University Park Church in one of those periods of pastoral trauma and turmoil.

– Richard A. Vickery, Jr.
Clergy colleague

✦ *The Iliff Review* is a distinguished publication read by a scholarly constituency. Therefore I would not want in any way to demean it or Harvey Potthoff by choosing to dwell briefly on his faults. However, the thought occurred to me that the high esteem in which Harvey has so long been held by so many persons just might lead to his being tempted to think too highly of himself when he reads the collected accolades.

There has never been the slightest indication that he has ever done so, or is likely to, but page after page should perhaps include a balancing aspect. Now one thing on which there would probably be consensus is that he is generous to a fault. It is difficult to determine when or how that point is reached, but since I do not know anyone who has done more for a greater number of persons over a long period of time, let's assume it must be to a fault!

Then there is the matter of life being serious business. Harvey seems at times to forget that. He always has an appropriate joke or witticism to make one laugh and feel lighthearted, and better about problems and anxieties.

That covers the faults as I've experienced them—and really, I sort of hope he keeps them. It did seem that they should get into the mix of tributes to this wonderful whole person as we honor ourselves by honoring him.

– Lucile Wheatley
Church and community activist, Denver, Colorado

✦ I am deeply indebted to Harvey Potthoff for two distinctive contributions to my life: his theological descriptions of the Ultimate and his personal attention to the intimate. His published works in this journal in 1959 were my introduction to his writings. What "good news" his positive, dynamic word on "The Reality of God," "The Doctrine of Man," and "'The Vision of Greatness" was for me at that particular time, when there was so much depressing commentary coming from so many sources.

Not until I arrived in Denver in 1972, however, was I privileged to begin to experience Harvey's incredibly extensive range of very personal and very gracious dealings with other individuals. Now, one of my cherished sources of daily inspiration is my awareness of Harvey going about doing good to, with, and for so many long-time friends and newly-met acquaintances—of all ages and occupations, of all states of failure and success, in all degrees of sorrow and of joy.

It is this combination of gifts received from him that causes me gratefully to perceive Harvey Potthoff as living out both the law and the prophets in keeping with the Master's mind and mood.

– Melvin E. Wheatley Jr.
Former Bishop of the Denver Area, United Methodist Church

✦ Many who heard Harvey Potthoff speak on numerous occasions have probably heard him, with characteristic humor, refer to the Egyptian mummy who was pressed for time. Instead, as I seek to write about him in a few words I feel exceedingly pressed for space! I would like to comment on Harvey Potthoff as theologian and colleague.

I believe Harvey Potthoff is above all a pastoral theologian. He brings to his vocation as theologian a wealth of pastoral experience and a deep commitment to the church and its ministries. In his thought he insists, first, that theology take human experience seriously. Consequently, the joys and pains of persons' struggles for humanness, as a pastor comes to know them, are consistently at the center of his theological reflections. Yet, second, he also insists that human experience in its wholeness and at its deepest levels must be understood theologically. In this endeavor he draws on process philosophy to develop a creative and distinctive style of Christian theology. His capacity to appropriate a highly complex and frequently abstract philosophy for the development of a functional pastoral theology represents to me his most significant theological contribution. This contribution is manifest not only in the students, pastors and laity he has influenced, but also in the theological self-understanding of the United Methodist Church in which he has exercised significant leadership, and in his impact on many persons outside churches who were skeptical about the credibility of theology in a scientific age.

For us who know him Harvey Potthoff's theology is communicated not only in his lectures and writings but also in the kind of person he is. As a faculty colleague, he is our friend, on many occasions our pastor, and consistently our leader in the life of the Iliff community. I cannot say enough about the warmth of his welcome to me when I arrived at Iliff as a "green" beginner in teaching and faculty matters. His generosity and support for me and my family continues unabated, and I know my experience is characteristic of his relation with each faculty member. He humanizes relationships at Iliff through his deep and manifest care for each person and the whole Iliff environment in which we work. In his leadership at Iliff he encourages and challenges us all to heightened academic quality and to enriched patterns of relationship. In the coherence of theology and life, Harvey Potthoff models a style of integrity and grace which ministers profoundly to all who know him.

– Dana W. Wilbanks
Iliff Professor of Christian Ethics (1968–2005)

Additional Reflections

Editor's note: The following Potthoff reflections are from people in Lincoln and at NWU. The first item is by President White. The second is by Patsy Moore who claims Potthoff as both a mentor and faculty colleague. Her brief article speaks for itself and I am sure for many other women and men at NWU who were touched by Harvey both as a person and a scholar.

Office of the President, April 25, 1992

Dear Harvey,

All of us are blessed from time to time through life in many different ways. Occasionally, we are fortunate enough to be blessed by the friendship of a very special person. Marty and I have had that experience [and] come to be friends of yours, and we treasure this friendship as highly as any we know.

Not only have you come into our lives, but you came into the life of Nebraska Wesleyan University and more specifically of numerous students, faculty, and staff, as one who enriches all he touches.

We are grateful to you, Harvey, beyond expression for the gift of yourself which you have given to Nebraska Wesleyan students, faculty, and staff over these eleven years. That is a gift beyond value.

May the years ahead be as enriching for you as you have made the years past for us.

–John White Jr.
Former President of Nebraska Wesleyan University

Harvey Potthoff. Supportive Friend. Mentor and Colleague.

In 1982, my husband Scott and I returned to Lincoln from Kansas City, where I had just graduated from St. Paul School of Theology and Scott had finished a three-year residency program. I soon heard that the Mattingly Chair had recently been filled by a professor from the Iliff School of Theology in Denver, Colorado.

The Mattingly Chair was almost sacred to me because it represented my memory of the many years I had attended classes taught by L. Edward Mattingly, affectionately known simply as Matt. I first matriculated at NWU as a freshman in 1949 and, being a wife and mother and involved in the church and community, I subsequently held the "distinct" record for being a senior on the Wesleyan campus for more than twenty years. Finally I graduated in 1973 with a religion major and made the big decision to go to seminary and to seek ordination.

A seminary friend visited me during the summer of 1982, and I took her to see the NWU campus. Entering the west door of Old Main, we saw this cheery-looking older man visiting with some of my friends from the English Department. They introduced me to Harvey and I introduced my friend to them. Harvey immediately wanted to hear my story and invited us up to his office on the third floor for a cup of coffee. The conversation centered on why and how I had decided to go to seminary at the age of fifty. This was a taste of Harvey's wonderful ability to listen to others' stories and immediately bond with them.

When we arrived back in Lincoln, Matt was still alive and doing well, and I visited him often at NWU. A few years later, Matt became quite ill and was hospitalized. Since Matt was single and didn't have family to visit him, Harvey and I took turns being with Matt. When Matt had to have surgery, I stayed with him during the day and Harvey at night. It was our gift to Matt.

At the same time, I was determined to do something to promote theology from a woman's perspective at NWU. I was fascinated with feminist theology and process theology. I surveyed the city of Lincoln and found there were only two women actively serving churches. I believed we needed more women clergy in Lincoln. I talked with Harvey and told him about my dream of teaching a course on feminist thought. I also talked with the Department of Religion faculty and President White. President White suggested I meet with Dick Quinn, then Director of the Wesleyan Institute for Lifelong Learning, an evening program then primarily aimed at nontraditional students. Dick was receptive but said there must be at least six students and money to pay for my teaching as at that time NWU could not pay me. I talked with my husband, and he said he would financially back the class. I handpicked six women to attend my class and ended up teaching on Tuesday nights.

The first night, I discovered my class was next door to Harvey's class on Aging, Dying and Death in Religious Perspective. I had six students, and Harvey had eighty. During a break one evening, Harvey came into my classroom and asked, "What's going on in here?" We answered, "Big Things!" He laughed and wished us luck.

Harvey's office was across the hall from mine in Old Main, and his door was always open and inviting. It was like having my own personal mentor and, during our visits, short or long, I always learned something.

I kept drilling on the idea of women's theology on campus and that ended in the creation of an ecumenical group of women called The Women's Institute for Theology. We sponsored a couple of major symposia on the NWU campus, bringing in famous female theologians as speakers and many other feminist spiritual leaders. Harvey, the master of the symposium, was always helpful. His best suggestion was that I should ask the distinguished theologian Dr. Sheila Devaney, then teaching at Iliff, to be our national advisor. Harvey thought

I was a genius because I could get a video player to work. What would he think of the electronic aids for teaching that we have to deal with today?

Harvey once invited me to speak to his classes about feminist thought, and the year that I attended one of his weeklong sessions of the Iliff-at-Aspen program, he asked me to lead the worship services and to speak the last day on feminist thought. I was flattered that he thought that much of my ability.

When Harvey left Lincoln and NWU in 1992, there was a giant hole in many lives. His influence through his NWU Symposium on Native American culture and spirituality, and the speakers whom he brought to the campus for this and other Mattingly Symposia, were educational and spiritual highlights for faculty, staff, students, and the whole Lincoln and southeastern Nebraska communities. Daniel Long Soldier, a Lincoln-area Native American artist, certainly missed him. Harvey was one of his best customers.

Wili Otey, an African American inmate at the Nebraska State Penitentiary, also lost his best friend; in fact, Harvey had become like a father to Wili Otey. The night of Wili Otey's execution I, my husband, and many NWU professors went to stand with the crowd of anti-death penalty friends. Harvey was there in spirit, of course, and that kind of influence on your peers says it all.

Everyone loved Harvey, and Matt would have been proud of Harvey's long tenure at Nebraska Wesleyan. By the way, five of the six women I taught in my first class at NWU went on to seminary. Harvey knew that and felt proud that the small group of women in that class were subsequently doing "big things." I'm sure Harvey's continued support for me helped to establish my continued presence on campus as a visiting professor in the Religion Department for several more years, but it was never the same without Harvey. His eleven years on campus served as a very bright light for all of us. Thank you, Harvey!

– Patsy Moore,
Former Adjunct
Professor of Religion,
Nebraska Wesleyan University

Photo provided by David Peabody used with permission

Colleague Patsy Moore and Harvey at NWU in front of the tree planted in his honor

Editor's note: The following are letters to Potthoff at the time of his retirement from NWU. They are contained in a scrapbook presented to Harvey at a special fare-ye-well party.[2]

April 1992

I have learned through my father's recent retirement that wishing one well in their "leisure years" is not only insensitive but inaccurate as well. So, I wish you well in the next active and fulfilling chapter of your life! I am about to complete my master's of museum studies at the University of Nebraska Lincoln.

Good luck and take care.

– Rebecca Copple

April 23, 1992

… .thanks for being at Nebraska Wesleyan University these past eleven years. What a joy it has been for us that your life's journey and ours have come together these past few years. Our lives have been spiritually blessed, our world map changed, our knowledge grown, our friendships enriched, and we have grown much fatter.

It has been a privilege to have been a part of the Science and Religion course where we wrestled with the crux of bringing our religious understandings into line with our modern scientific understandings. And of course the Mattingly Symposium that dealt with the same topic was so exciting.

You have made such major changes on this campus!!! The Mattingly Symposiums are the most obvious. But your presence and relationships with people have made the most profound change. Faculty members who once "ate by departments" now sit together and enjoy one another's company. Faculty members who were feeling excluded now feel a part of the whole. Faculty members are talking about significant religious convictions in dialogue with one another over the lunch table. You have been the catalyst for change in so many ways.

For us personally, what joy you have brought as we attended the symphony, the Nebraska Chamber Orchestra, and other musical events together. And, of course, along with the musical events we frequently shared a meal, ranging from an elegant repast at the University Club to a "good food" dinner at the Pantry.

Our rich experiences with you there amongst the mountains as we searched for meaning, laughed, hiked, listened to music, and enjoyed one another's company is one of the jewels along life's journey. It is a time we treasure with special reverence.

Thanks, Harvey, for sharing a part of your life with us. Thanks for your very being.

– *George and Lois Coleman*

-April 1992

Thank you for being such a great teacher, leader, and friend at Nebraska Wesleyan for so many of us.

I personally feel fortunate to know you. You helped me with my Senior Thesis as no one else could have, working on the Theology of Paul Tillich. Your evening classes nurtured a vocabulary and wonder that really opened up new doors for me.

But mostly I see you as a mentor. Someone with sensitivity and a gracious understanding of what you have to share.

Thank you for that, and best wishes to you.

– *Dave Draus*

April 4, 1992

Thinking of your name fills my heart with love and Joy.

You were one of the key sparks that reignited my enthusiasm for life, especially my spiritual life, followed by reassessment of my professional life. I faced my own imperfections, even my own death through involvement as a student then teacher in your course.

Nebraska Wesleyan will miss you, Lincoln will miss you, all your friends will miss you; last we will never forget you.

– *Dr. Alan Forker*

April 4, 1992

Several months ago, while driving from Kansas City to Wichita for my mother's funeral, I remember saying to myself, "Thank God I have Harvey Potthoff under my belt!" A lot of my growth process about Life and Death and issues in between has been greatly accelerated by my relationship with Harvey Potthoff ... teacher, mentor, and friend. It seems to me that Harvey's wonderful wisdom has to do with his beautiful acceptance of the other individual, which of course makes him a listener with true empathy. And no one can throw great dinner parties better than Harvey; knowing Harvey Potthoff is a heck of a lot of FUN!

Remember, Dear Friend, you once said to me, "Have FUN ... It's your duty! It's your Christian Duty!

– *Susie Forker*

April 27, 1992

Although I was unable to attend the gathering held in your honor on Saturday, I want to add my heartfelt gratitude for all you have contributed to Nebraska Wesleyan University. I especially appreciate the many ways you have touched the lives and consciousness of returning adult students. You have had an extraordinary impact on students of all ages, which has been an indescribable gift to them and to this college.

You will always be loved and respected here. Thank you so very much.

– *Ruth Harper*

April 7, 1992

We want to add our thanks for your presence in our lives to the thanks of all the others you have influenced these last eleven years. The good music, good food, and good conversation we have enjoyed with you would be enough to guarantee you a permanent place in our hearts. Even more, the depth and beauty of the religious and philosophical perspectives you have brought to Wesleyan will be a continuing influence on us both. With affection and gratitude.

– Dan and Mary Howell

April 23, 1992

You are a very special person, and I am privileged to have known you. Your presence on campus gave so much life to all the people around you, although I didn't get to see you everyday like the people did in Old Main and Smith/Curtis Hall. I felt I have been touched by your kindness and warm friendship just the same. I want to let you know how much I enjoyed sitting at the same lunch table with you and other wonderful people in the student snack bar and listening to your inspiring and humorous conversation for the past 11 years. It was great fun laughing together and enjoying the most relaxing moment of our days together.

The Chinese often wish others to have a "colorful life" besides a prosperous one. I often wondered how colorful could a life be! But your kindness, open-mindedness, loving and caring personality as well as your willingness to share your knowledge and wisdom with everyone made me realize that your life is truly a very colorful one indeed.

Best Wishes. Your friend,

– Janet Lu, Library

April 1992

You have changed my life! Not only have you had a great impact on the person I have become but also on the person I hope to be. I know I speak for many whose lives you have touched. Thank you for nurturing my mind and soul over the last eleven years.

Your student and your friend. All my love,

– Kim Mickels

April 1992

You have made such a positive impact on my life. I am so glad that we were at Wesleyan at the same time. I consider myself fortunate to have had you as a teacher. I feel honored to call you my friend.

You have celebrated my successes and watched my growth as I embarked on different adventures. Through your words you have taught me that every person has a story and a potential. Through your actions you have shown me that each individual must be treated with gentleness, respect and dignity. I have much to thank you for Harvey.

Now that I am a professor, I have tried to apply lessons I have learned from you as I interact with all of my students whether they are adults or "little people." You are such a special person, my friend. I wish you the best as you embark on your next adventure.

Fondly,

– *Sue Morin*

April 1992

Shortly after Harvey came to Wesleyan in 1981, someone from the student newspaper asked me to identify the most important thing that had happened at Wesleyan that year. "The most important thing that's happened here in the last year," I think I said, "was Harvey Potthoff."

Now, ten years later, I don't regret that judgment. I would only expand on it: Harvey Potthoff is the best thing that's happened to Wesleyan in the last decade. He's taught us how to celebrate, how to sing songs of ourselves, how to transcend the everlasting nay without getting sappy and sentimental. And I'm going to stop before that happens. Thanks Harvey,

– *Leon Satterfield*

April 6, 1992

You have been an inspiration to our lives. We have turned to you as a mentor, a pastor, a friend, and as a "grandpa." It has been with tremendous joy that we have shared the journey of life and faith, moving toward greater meaning and wholeness.

Lee is thankful for your influence in developing a cognitive map of meaning and understanding the importance of transitions in the changing seasons and chapter of life; Diane treasures the evenings and the Cornhusker, and the emotional support; Benjamin remembers a certain night at the Cornhusker (decked in a suit and bow tie) when the meal was prepared table-side, flaming; Nathan holds near and dear your participation in his baptism, and the many precious gifts; and Ashley's eyes sparkle and face glows when we talk about Harvey Potthoff.

All of us feel gifted and privileged that you have referred to us as family and friends.

Harvey, thank you for the memories!! May your re-retirement be filled with "the gifts of treasured memories, precious relationships, and renewal of faith, hope and love."

Peace and Love,

– *The Wigerts: Lee, Diane, Benjamin, Nathan, Ashley*

NOTES

[1] *Colorado Conference Journal*, 1952, 495.

[2] NWU scrapbook, Iliff Archives, box 41.

14

STUDENT REFLECTIONS

AFFIRMATIONS OF HARVEY POTTHOFF FROM OUR MEMORIES, REFLECTIONS, AND RECOLLECTIONS

Edited by Howard R. Bailey, Iliff Class of '60, '63

Passion and compassion, grace and generosity, humor and humility, pastor and professor, friend and mentor—these characterize the memories, reflections, and recollections of Dr. Harvey H. Potthoff, which are disclosed in the following personal affirmations. This collection represents the responses returned from a special appeal in conjunction with this tribute to Harvey Potthoff. The contributors have selected their own style and format. Some of the statements have been edited slightly, but they appear substantially as submitted, and with a few exceptions arranged alphabetically.

– Howard Bailey

"Tell me something I don't know instead of everything I do know," were the words I heard in a song Mary Chapin

Carpenter sang with the Boston Pops Orchestra. [Dr. Potthoff] this is what you did for me in Seminary: the freshness of your language, the newness of your ideas, the sparkle of your humor. You told me to be myself, to create my own language, and to find my own theology beyond all teachers. In fact, what you did was to lead me to my own wisdom, a creation of past and present, a mixture of many ideas and many experiences that I alone interpreted and made my own. This is what you did for me. Now you are the truest of friends, someone I can share deep places with and enjoy those deep places of yours. As you said, we must continue this "playfulness" and let our springs of meaning and joy come together.

– Bill Satterfield (Iliff '62)

* * *

When I have been asked from time to time who was my greatest teacher, Harvey Potthoff always comes first to mind. Wisdom and wit and a lightheartedness permeated not only his classes, but also his personhood. I believe we became quite close, and I was privileged to have quite a bit of time with him. Because of Harvey and others of positive influence, I became a Methodist minister and an Iliff graduate twice.

For some reason, I remember a moment at lunch with Harvey at the Harvest Restaurant in Denver. I was running a little late and I felt terrible being late for a lunch with Dr. Potthoff. When I arrived and apologized, Harvey said, "No problem, Gregg, when you get to be my age, you learn what is important and what is not." I guess I remember this slice of life because not only did Harvey teach me much about theology, but more so, about life and what is ultimately most important.

There is another simple message I will always remember from Harvey and have repeated it a hundred times: "A church is as effective as it meets the needs of the people. Needs can change, and the church must always be assessing and reassessing the needs of the people within its neighborhood." This has been a motto for me and others at the Aspen Chapel as we continue to meet the unique needs of the people and visitors of Aspen. We are most grateful for all the foundations of faith Dr. Potthoff has ingrained within the stoned walls and wooden beams of the Aspen Chapel and the people within, especially me. Thank you, Harvey Potthoff.

– Gregg Anderson (Ililff '78)
[Anderson was very involved in the Iliff-at-Aspen program; see Chapter 7]

* * *

During my time at Iliff, the subtlety of Harvey Potthoff's knowledge and wisdom were underappreciated by me, and Process Theology was an unfathomable mystery; however, [Harvey] was a significant presence inside and outside the classroom. I won't parse the meaning of these statements, but they stuck with me for more than thirty years.

"God is not a being, God is Being." For me, the sum total of process theology, and I still cite it (much to my wife's consternation).

"Be kind to everyone, for they are suffering." A hallway conversation when Potthoff was discussing his experiences as a pastor.

In class he told how one day he was walking the back alleyway in his neighborhood and passed by a garbage truck.

He heard the radio playing classical music as the men dumped trash into the truck bin. "Now that is spirituality," he declared.

– Mike Burdick (MDiv Iliff '79)

* * *

As a student at Iliff, I was honored to take several courses under Harvey Potthoff. Most of them must have been during my third year. In addition, I became his student office assistant. My main task was to proofread all of the articles to be published in *The Iliff Review*. Potthoff at that time was editor. Many of the articles were about Dr. William Bernhardt's analysis of religion or articles by Bernhardt himself. That is where I really began to appreciate Bernhardt's philosophy of religion. This was in addition to taking several of Bernhardt's classes.

This made me feel that Potthoff basically was reinterpreting traditional Christian religion from the Bernhardtian analysis of religion, to make it more meaningful and significant in our contemporary scientific society. Actually, to me, Harvey Potthoff's material is a very fine way of giving Christian theology a more realistic and significant meaning.

– Bill Cascini (Iliff '55)
Retired Professor of Sociology, Anthropology, and Social Work
Nebraska Wesleyan University

* * *

I was surprised and pleased when Dr. Potthoff invited me to be his student assistant in 1962–63. Then I was further surprised when he promptly went on sabbatical! But as the year unfolded, he returned after a quarter break and asked me to research an obscure author. It turned out he was reviewing what the author had written in advance of interviews to be considered for the Iliff faculty. I enjoyed that bit of detective work and wondered how the follow-up went. I think the subject had a brief tenure and certainly his bibliography would suggest such an outcome.

– Jim Christopher (Iliff '63)

* * *

Editor's note:

✦ *This symbol denotes contributions from the 1981 winter issue of* The Iliff Review *on the occasion of Harvey Potthoff's retirement.*

✦ Of all the human beings I have known, Harvey Potthoff is without doubt the most remarkable. It is not that one may point to one or two remarkable characteristics. It is his life itself in its wholeness: his mind, his manners, his speaking, his friendships, his artistic and culinary tastes, his sense of humor, his vocation, his kindness, his discipline—in short, all the things that are Harvey Potthoff—are integrated with such coherence, and yet with such complexity, that as a person he cannot help but have a profound impact upon those who have known him. The strength of Dr. Potthoff's consistency is in the amazing regularity with which his own inner integrity enables him to transcend himself to the point of having an enlivening and redeeming influence upon those around him. His inimitability derives finally from his way of meaningfully combining personal qualities so diverse that in most others the same traits would simply be internally divisive. He is at once a scholar and a punster; a teacher and yet a student of his pupils; quiet-spoken and yet commanding by his very quietness; genuinely intimate, yet intensely private; a slender gourmet; a convivial disciplinarian; an irreligious clergyman; a skeptical pietist.

A quality that stands out is that his intellectual life—his philosophy, his theology, and so on—makes a genuine difference in what he does not only professionally, but socially, privately, personally, and in all that he is. No one who has been his student can escape the conclusion that he believes that the life of the mind ought to be both great fun and yet deadly serious. This belief finds overt expression in Potthoff's "functional-empirical theology," which emphasizes the application and exemplification of scholarly concerns to the daily life of faith and practice. One of his primary concepts has been that of "wholeness." In *God and the Celebration of Life*, he explores the religious significance of the fact that organic wholes and relationships tend to emerge from the patterns of existence. And beyond the level of content, wholeness is a primary methodological consideration, since it is the whole of experience (and not merely isolated phenomena or certain revealed doctrines) which serves as the legitimate source of theological data. It was just such an integration of theory and experience that one sees in Harvey Potthoff himself.

I speak for a very large contingent when I say that he has been not only the best of all teachers, but the brightest of all friends. The final expression of our gratitude is to be derived from the way he has contributed to our own ability to minister and from his unfading enhancement of our own celebration of life.

— David E. Conner
Minister of the Americus United Methodist Charge, Lucedale, Mississippi, former student assistant to Dr. Potthoff and current ThD candidate.

* * *

It's hard to know which memories are the strongest, his marvelous stories or his lasting influence upon the fundamentals of my ministry. Regarding the first is the story of a man who moved from eastern Colorado, to Kansas, then to Oklahoma and on to Texas where he died and went to hell. But he never noticed the difference because the change had been so gradual.

My first class with Potthoff was in homiletics, while he was still pastoring a local Methodist Church. The course title was something like "Planning a Year's Preaching Program." He structured it around the three categories William Bernhardt identified in his philosophy of religion—function, reinterpretation, and technique. In developing one's sermon themes in equal number around these three themes, one would be assured of offering a comprehensive preaching program. Whether good or not, my subject matter was at least comprehensive.

Potthoff's theological teachings became one of the cornerstones of my ministry. For me, he connected Bernhardt's philosophy to everyday experience in a way that I could sense it functioning in routine life experiences. While he certainly was not the only Iliff professor I admired, I cannot imagine what my ministry would have been like without him.

– Cy Eberhart (Iliff '54)

* * *

Concerning Dr. Harvey Potthoff—what can I say? I am overwhelmed by the honesty, the integrity, the humanness of this man. He will never really know how much he, and his "Harveyness," means to me. He remains the model for my ministry. He fused critical thinking and compassion with the elegance of simplicity. Perhaps someday I can do the same. Perhaps the most important thing that I learned at Iliff was that while our faith shows us that at the heart of things we are all one, this "one," the light of God, is only set ablaze with color and made visible when refracted through the prism of our own particularity.

– Charles N. Fasanaro (Iliff '83)
First student to receive the Iliff University of Denver PhD

* * *

✦ Among theologians Harvey Potthoff speaks and writes with a clarity that is rare and refreshing. His ability to bridge the language of older faiths with newer concepts and discoveries of a modern world enabled some of us to continue to seek and love the Lord of faith with all our mind. His capacity for critique of idols and vague nonsense parading as piety has been the furnace for removing the dross from the durable substance of truth.

His genius for conveying reasons for hope, renewal, regeneration, and redemption found in the providential conditions of human life, but not raising unrealistic expectations, reveals him as a gospel preacher of extraordinary power and appeal. He shared faith from a deep wellspring that nourishes his own soul.

Of all of his capacities, that which endears him is his ability to focus the powers of his mind and spirit in personal response to the person with whom he enters into conversation. For many of us he has been not only a teacher whose ideas had decisive impact, he has been counselor and friend whose influence has enlarged us and opened greater opportunities of usefulness.

It is late in this statement to be pointing up how humor ripples through the man like a stream tumbling and jumping over rocks for sheer fun. His surprise punch lines from a face of mock seriousness, and his inveterate impulse to poke fun, reveals a companionable nature in a world that is best taken with a grain of salt and a dash of spice. He is truly a man for all seasons, whose company enlivens and warms and cheers. While no one, I think, would call Harvey a charismatic, he has charisma. His gifts of insight, and grace flowing through him, have surely blessed a lot of us.

– Allen K. Jackson (Iliff '58)
Former President of Huntingdon College, Montgomery, Alabama

* * *

It was my privilege to know Dr. Harvey H. Potthoff for half a century. Like many, many others, I considered him to be a friend. He was not only a great theologian, but he was a genuine friend to so many of his students and colleagues.

My fondest memory of Harvey Potthoff is during the moon landing in July 1969. During those years, the Iliff School of Theology sponsored a weeklong event known as "Youth at Iliff." Senior high youth from across the mountain and midwestern regions would come together and share a week of informal discussions and studies of theology. Among the leaders were Dr. Ed Everding, Dr. Dana Wilbanks, and Dr. Harvey Potthoff. While on the staff at Arvada UMC with Dr. Earl Hanna, I served as registrar and administrator for this Iliff event. On the evening of July 20, 1969, the youth gathered with Dr. Potthoff in the fellowship hall of Christ UMC in Denver. The occasion was to observe the historic moon landing by our astronauts. It was fun and meaningful watching Harvey and the youth in a significant interchange of theological ideas.

The whole experience made such an impression on me that I decided later that year to write "A Space Age Paraphrasing of Psalm 19." I first used this as an administrative board devotional; then it was used with youth, and finally in teacher training at Arvada.

What matters to me is that Dr. Potthoff was the individual who most profoundly influenced my theological growth. My only regret is that somehow I overlooked sending him a copy of my paraphrase. He was always interested in the workings of the annual conference and, indeed, was a leader at General Conference on behalf of all of us. Most of all, he loved to dialogue with his students and peers. He always had their interests at heart. His funny stories (many puns) simply underlined his love of persons.

As a Minister of Education, on the evening of November 8, 1965, along with others in our conference, I attended the first national meeting of Christian educators in Cincinnati, Ohio. Along with Dr. Potthoff, Dr. Carl Michalson, theologian from Drew Theological School, was to be a key speaker on the opening night. Carl's life was cut short when American Airlines Flight #383, in a heavy rainstorm, hit the Kentucky hillside across the Ohio River. Sixty-one persons were killed. Drew and the church at large had lost a great theologian in Carl Michalson. These two men may have differed with each other in certain aspects of theology, but they were genuine friends. Dr. Potthoff carefully and caringly used some of his time to help us all deal with the trauma of that unforgettable evening.

– Lonnie B. Johnson (Iliff '58)

* * *

When I got to Iliff, I was surprised to discover that, because my father was a fine pastor, I knew more about actually being a pastor than most of the Iliff faculty! Except for Dr. Potthoff. He understood what I was talking about, nodded, and told me that he had been pastor, for several years, of a rather large church in Denver. He fully articulated my concern and told me that my job was to integrate my new learning with what I had learned from my father.

The best advice he gave me, I think, was that people in our congregations really like to think. They have big questions which they cannot always articulate. The average lay person, especially if well educated, can comprehend and think through the largest theological problems and ideas—if those ideas are presented in nontechnical language they understand. Theological language is technical jargon and saves a lot of time for theologians, but it is not useful for people in the pews or study classes. But people really like to think, if given the great ideas in their language.

I found that to be eminently true. My sermons have always been crafted around the Biblical Story and the powerful theological issues that are involved. Process theology is best suited to the narrative of the Biblical Story. Over the weeks, I listened carefully to people and engaged them in depth about their lives and understandings of the world so that I would know how to direct the sermons. It worked. People were surprised and elated by the big ideas, and often told me how they had been thinking about something in a sermon for weeks.

One of the most surprising and delightful ideas is that God is actually changing, becoming, and creating the universe and that we have a part in that. Process theology is exciting to people who are struggling to make schools and communities better and to do justice. The world is a work of progress, and "God needs us to help make it come out right." That expression came from a confirmand!

It was amusing to me one time, when John Cobb came to Evanston to preach for us. He was amazed at how the people there not only understood everything he said but were enthused about it and were full of wonderful questions. What was most amusing was that one of the professors at Garrett was amazed at how much his fellow parishioners were thinking theologically—though not academically!

My years at Iliff were wonderful and exciting. I learned a great deal from each of my professors. But Harvey Potthoff helped me put it all to use in the context of pastoral ministry.

Professor Harvey Potthoff was the seminary teacher who knew most about being a pastor. With his pastor's heart, he understood the dynamics and processes of pastoral leadership from the inside. It was a great blessing to those of us in student appointments and to all of us preparing for parish ministry.

He was "pastor" to us as much as he was "professor." I shall always be grateful for the discussions he had where he guided us in our own struggles and suggested how to minister in hard situations.

– Emery Percell (Iliff '61)

* * *

Dr. Potthoff told the story of a dog that wandered into a country church. He came down to the front of the church and lay down in front of the first row of chairs. A problem arose during the singing of the hymns. The dog stood up and began to howl. The same thing happened in the middle of the sermon.

Finally the student pastor got someone to come and take the dog out. When the student got back to the seminary, he asked his professors if they could start a short course on dogmatics.

– Al Scarffe (Iliff '49)

* * *

I'm sorry that it has been impossible for me to participate fully. Perhaps the following anecdote will say something about Harvey's sensibilities.

At his invitation, a small group of us gathered at his apartment on a winter night in 1954. He had prepared to play two recordings of Bach organ music—one was played by Albert Schweitzer, and the other (the same composition) by E. Power Biggs. Not only did we enjoy the music, the technical comparison of interpreters, and the conversation of erudite friends, but he expanded our appreciation of theology as well.

– Jim Kirk (Iliff '59)

Photo by R. L. Phillips

The South Josephine Street apartment (lower left) where HHP lived during his teaching at Iliff so many years. Many students and faculty shared Jim Kirk's experience of music there.

I arrived at Iliff to begin graduate studies in the fall of 1953. The first year at Iliff was probably one of the most stimulating and challenging years of my life. At that time the school was small, with one professor teaching courses in each area of study. The beginning course in theology was taught by Dr. Potthoff, and immediately I was introduced to a new way of understanding our Christian faith as it relates to all of life. How refreshing this happened to be.

From the day I arrived on campus, I felt a special connection to this man of many special qualities because of his personal interest in each student. This was my perception and experience. I was able to experience this connecting in a special way after my first year. I decided to take a break from studies and became a short-term missionary in Angola, Africa, with the Methodist Church. While serving in Angola, I kept up a regular correspondence with Dr. Potthoff. He wrote often, in response to my letters with news of life in Angola. His letters were filled with news, encouragement, and affirmation. I was encouraged by many to continue my education at other seminaries after serving in Angola. Dr. Potthoff was the main reason I returned to Iliff to complete my last two years of higher education for ministry.

Dr. Potthoff was always available and took personal interest in students by inviting them to his home or to travel with him to speaking engagements and accepting invitations to dinner with families of his students. I will always remember the Thanksgiving dinner Dr. Potthoff shared with us at the home of my wife, Kathy, and her parents. His interest in our family continued through the years, and he always asked about our children. Going out in the evening after a few hours of study to have a piece of black bottom pie with Dr. Potthoff was something to remember. Dr. Harvey H. Potthoff was without a doubt one of the most influential persons in my life.

– Burl Kreps (Iliff '60)

* * *

Dr. Potthoff was a loved and trusted teacher of theology to our class, but even more he was a model of Christian grace for us in our lives and developing ministries. A few years into my pastoral ministry, I left the ordained professional ministry of the United Methodist Church over a disagreement about the place of my developmentally handicapped son in a local church, which could not be resolved to my satisfaction. I moved into a very fulfilling career in services to citizens with developmental handicaps, which proved to be a twenty-five-year ministry in itself. Harvey Potthoff's spirit was a guiding force through all this ministry in both forms. I can only thank the Holy Spirit for him and his presence and inspiration in my life. I have also used his book, *God and the Celebration of Life*, as the focus of study groups at least five times since leaving Iliff, the most recent in 2010.

Thank you for this opportunity to reflect on a well-loved teacher.

– Thomas J. LeClerc (Iliff '78)

* * *

Our favorite memory of Dr. Potthoff was October 4, 1960—we had just become engaged to be married and were in his Freewill vs. Determinism class. He had heard the news and, before beginning his lecture, he paused to ask (no less than three times) if anyone had exercised their freewill lately. The others in the class were encouraging Sheridan to stand up and confess, but I kept saying, "Keep your seat." Finally, with one of his knowing, engaging grins, he began his lecture.

Dr. Potthoff was always one of our favorite professors—kind, understanding, helpful—and had wonderful motivational skills. We will never forget him.

– Charlotte (Iliff '68) and Sheridan Mallott (Iliff '61)

* * *

✦ How does one capture the essence of God's spirit as reflected in the life of Harvey Potthoff? The fruits of the spirit such as love, acceptance, understanding, enlightenment, joy, enthusiasm, resoluteness, wisdom, hope, and justice are manifest in Dr. Potthoff's personal witness and professional activities. His own raison d'etre is radiated through his prolific writings and lectures. Whether Harvey is addressing a university graduating class, moderating a seminar, participating in polemics, attending a concert, or encouraging the countless lonely individuals, he lifts the sights and dignity of all who are within his company. In Harvey Potthoff one senses the eagerness of Peter, the erudition of Paul, the freshness of Mark, the healing of Luke, the reconciliation of John, and the steadfastness of Stephen. We are all recipients of his compassion and contribution.

– John A. Marvel
President of the Consortium of State Colleges in Colorado
Denver, Colorado

* * *

I was Dr. Potthoff's TA during 1971–1972. ... A favorite story about Harvey I always enjoyed was the one about his drinking a mixed drink in a famous bar in Cripple Creek, Colorado. Harvey liked to take drives into the mountains. And, on this occasion, he stopped at a famous and historic bar. He was sitting at the bar when two of his former parishioners from Christ UMC in Denver approached him from behind. They were surprised to see the great Methodist churchman drinking at the bar and said in disbelief: "Dr. Potthoff, what a surprise to see you here. We didn't know you drink." Harvey responded in all seriousness, "I don't. But, I must say, this water tastes awfully strange to me." Harvey loved telling this story, and he'd always break into the faintest smile with a bit of a twinkle in his eye.

Another remembrance is that of his first and so far as I know only love. He told me once that he had fallen in love with a girl when he was young. She was killed in an auto accident, I believe. Harvey said that he was shattered by her sudden death, and he told me that he never wanted to date after her death. He held her in his heart throughout his life and honored their love always.

Finally, I was a top student at Iliff, but during my second year, I went through a divorce and was not in class as often as I should have been. That said, I still took his tests and did A quality work. One day, however, after missing several days of classes, Dr. Potthoff sent me a beautiful card through student mail. I thought it was an invitation to a special party. The card stock was heavy and very formal, a cotton paper mix. Eagerly, I opened the letter and read his simple and beautifully handwritten note. It read: "Dear Bill, Please see the Iliff Student Handbook, page 4, paragraph 2. Wishing you all the best, Harvey." I thought the note odd, but pulled out the student handbook and read the paragraph and laughed. Even though I had an A- in the class, the handbook said that any student missing a set number of classes would automatically receive a failing grade and be dropped from the course. Needless to say, that was the only "F" I ever received in my life —and the following year, I retook the class, got an A, and was awarded the Elizabeth Iliff Warren Fellowship. Several faculty members were friends of mine, and one later told me that there were two students being considered for the award, but that Harvey lobbied hard for me to receive it based on my academic strengths. Later that spring, Harvey helped me get into the University of Chicago Divinity School, where I began my PhD in Process Theology.

I always treasured his special note, his lasting friendship, and the only F that marred my academic record.

– William McCreary (Iliff '72)
Associate Dean of Finance & Human Resources,
College of Pharmacy, University of Utah

* * *

On the encouragement of Dr. Harvey Potthoff, I came to Iliff in 1962 (after two masters' degrees from Drew and Boston) and soon found Iliff's ThD program to be the most insightful and effective of my academic endeavors. He was very much a part of my Iliff experience during residency, along with W. H. Bernhardt. My thanks in large measure go to Dr. Potthoff, who chaired the dissertation committee with care and guidance over the years to the completion of the graduate program. I found him to be an efficient and well-prepared teacher in the zenith of his career.

Potthoff's book *God and the Celebration of Life* was in process during my residency. This theology combines the sensitivity of a parish minister with the clarity of academic scholarship involving Bernhardt's functional philosophy as well as

Whitehead's process theology. In his brief volume on loneliness he includes his most insightful, personal, and meaningful life experiences.

The last time my wife and I spoke with Dr. Potthoff was at the Iliff Week of Lectures after his retirement from Nebraska Wesleyan University. He talked about seldom having anything to do during the week or the like. He spoke of his former church, across from the Iliff campus, named a room in the church after him, but no meetings were being held there. At first I thought he was speaking with tongue in cheek, but on second thought I think he was mainly expressing his deep sense of vocation to the church which, to him, was "of God and will be preserved to the end of time." His life was totally focused on all students and congregations who would hear, or read, a message of enduring hope. It was fitting that years before, he ended his own Iliff thesis with this couplet:

Change and decay in all round I see;
O Thou who changest not, abide with me.

– P. Dale Neufer (ThD Iliff '72)

* * *

I happily share three memories of Dr. Potthoff during my years at Iliff. I was a student at Iliff from 1951 to 1954.

First memory: I was taking a class from Dr. Potthoff the summer of 1954 just before graduating. For one of the sessions, he invited the class to meet in his apartment. His mother was visiting him at the time, and I remember he introduced his mother to us. She stayed in the background most of the period. I remember how kind and polite he was to his mother, as might be expected.

Another memory that comes to mind: A discussion was going on in the class and Dr. Potthoff was asked a question. I don't remember what it was now and apparently he didn't know the answer. So he simply replied, "To be perfectly frank, I really don't know." His honesty impressed us, for he usually had an answer to every question.

A third memory I might share about Dr. Potthoff was that in the fall of 1954, after I had graduated from Iliff that August, I was serving my first full-time parish in South Dakota. I received a letter from Dr. Potthoff. It was a letter of encouragement and a letter to let me know I wasn't forgotten by Iliff now that I was "out in the world."

– Russell Peirce (Iliff '54)

* * *

In 1978, I was an international marketing executive with General Motors Corporation, an American living in Scotland. That September the time came for a response to a longtime calling I had ignored for nearly twenty years. In my days of wandering and wondering, I had visited several United Methodist seminaries in the United States, but never the Iliff School of Theology.

On one of my library shelves was *God and the Celebration of Life* by Dr. Harvey Potthoff, Professor of Theology at Iliff. His book prompted my inquiry and ultimately my three years of study there. I may have shared that story with him; whether I did or not, I know that his response would have been modest and gracious.

– Rev. Sam Ritchey (MDiv Iliff '80)
Las Cruces, New Mexico

* * *

I am always proud to recount that I was Dr. Potthoff's last student assistant prior to his retirement from Iliff. For me, as I am sure is true for many of his students, Harvey was the heart of Iliff. That means more than just saying he was the core of our learning experience. It means Harvey brought his heart to teaching, mentoring, guiding, counseling, leading the school as president when called upon, and just simply relating to people as whole persons. Harvey brought out the heart of every subject he taught because he did not just teach subject matter but taught students AS the subject matter. Harvey brought heart to high-minded, complex, abstract, and often abstruse topics and concepts. Without compromising the tough, challenging, or conflicted issues, Dr. Potthoff was always intent on making theology accessible to common understanding. His homey metaphors and analogies gave life to theological perspectives that might seem merely academic or out of reach. Dr. Potthoff helped us reach higher because there was so much heart in the way he presented himself and his teachings. In fact, it is not cliché to say that who he was, at heart, was his teaching and his teaching was who he was.

Great athletes are often said to have a slow heartbeat. This typically means that the game or competition slows down more for them than the rapid pace it appears to be moving for others. A great baseball hitter sees the spin on the ball and recognizes what kind of pitch is coming, increasing the possibility of getting a hit. Great basketball, tennis, soccer, or hockey players are said to see the angles, dimensions, and interactions of all elements of the game in a sort of slow-motion fashion that allows them to anticipate things in ways other players do not. Dr. Potthoff was a spiritual athlete in just this sense. I recall the months working with him as he served as interim president of Iliff when the weight of all his administrative, teaching, and pastoral duties could have and should have increased his stress levels and heart rate. Yet, what remains a vivid image in my mind is how Harvey would palpably, physically SLOW DOWN amidst the crushing burdens of responsibility. Dr. Potthoff had a slow spiritual heartbeat.

That slow spiritual heartbeat is what I personally aspire to. That slow spiritual heartbeat is what I am sure was sensed by all those who came under his influence. Dr. Potthoff's slow spiritual heartbeat is what came through every class, every lesson, every encounter with him. The slow spiritual heartbeat of Dr. Harvey H. Potthoff is what Iliff is to me.

– Daniel Sage (Iliff '80)

* * *

✦ It has been a privilege and pleasure to know Dr. Potthoff through the years as an outstanding pastor and member of the faculty of Iliff, as well as a good friend of my aunt, Miss Louise Iliff. She was devoted to him and depended upon him to keep her informed about the school. She valued his appraisal of the teaching and curriculum. Also, she was delighted to attend the weddings conducted by Dr. Potthoff whenever the Iliff family kneeling bench was used in the ceremony. (It was first used at the wedding of her mother, Elizabeth Sarah Iliff, to Bishop Henry White Warren on December 17, 1883.) I also have great admiration for him and his many abilities.

– Alberta Iliff Shattuck
Member of the Board of Trustees of the Iliff School of Theology
Littleton, Colorado

* * *

There will be more stories than you can possibly put in one book. Here are three:

Harvey came to the church where I was appointed to speak on the subject "Aging, Death, and Dying." He got to the church early and I was setting up chairs, shoveling the snow off the walk, and making coffee. He took me aside and said: "Charles, you look tired. You need to be kind to the old person you will one day become."

One day he called me up and asked if I would drive him to First United Methodist Church in Greeley. He was to make a presentation on process theology, and he didn't like to drive at night. He had taught a couple of classes that day, and I anticipated he might be a bit fatigued and that he might rest a bit on the way. He talked the whole time. His class was riveting. The people hung on every word. On the way home, I commented to Harvey I was surprised that he got through that whole day and didn't seem to be any less energized. If anything, he seemed to be more animated than he had been. He said to me: "Sometimes, when you are doing what you really love to do in ministry, it gives you energy rather than depletes your energy."

At that time, I was taking a class with Dr. Potthoff and Dr. Chester Pennington on Theology of Ministry. It was a doctoral level class, and my first paper received an F. Dr. Pennington was a Barthian expert, and he didn't appreciate the natural theology which was the foundation to my paper. I rewrote the paper and hadn't received the result. When we arrived at Iliff Harvey asked me to come to his office. He put the paper in front of me and, again, it had a letter grade of F. Doctoral students aren't supposed to receive those kind[s] of grades. He looked at me and said: "Dr. Pennington and I have agreed to treat this course as if it never happened. This will be a disappointment for you but, in the long run, you may see it as an important learning experience."

I don't know what got into me to say this, but I looked at Harvey and I said: "Do I get my tuition money back?"

I still recall the expression of disappointment and incredulity on his face as he looked at me and said: "Let's just be happy this chapter is closed."

Dr. Potthoff was a friend, a mentor, a driving force, and an inspirational influence. I think of him often and miss him still.

– Charles Schuster (Iliff '74, '78)

* * *

Harvey H. Potthoff: An Appreciation for Being in the Presence of Greatness

Name-dropper that I can be, I have been "in the presence of greatness" many times during a denominational, ecumenical, and interreligious career that now spans three decades plus. Harvey H. Potthoff would regale me, without any obvious note of pretense or the slightest hint of affection, with tales of his many brushes of being "in the presence of greatness" and one could readily conjure the "who's who" type of names he had in mind. Foremost among those he might mention would be Alfred North Whitehead, with whom he studied at Harvard. It got a grip on me, I suppose. That is why I can feel free to pay tribute to him with the theme of "being in the presence of greatness." He was aware that the potential for greatness was available to those in all callings, including those entering the ministry.

Subsequently, I have been enriched by being "in the presence of greatness" with luminaries of the ecclesiastical firmament, numerous general secretaries of ecumenical bodies across the country and around the world, and uncounted theologians from any number of schools of thought. ... Harvey H. Potthoff taught me to be comfortable "in the presence of greatness."

The very first time in my life I realized I was "in the presence of greatness" was when I first met Dr. Potthoff in January 1972 as I matriculated in the MDiv program at The Iliff School of Theology. In the following academic year, at his gracious invitation, I became Dr. Potthoff's student assistant and soon understood the honor he had bestowed upon me and quickly wondered if I could ever be worthy of it. He saw things in me that I did not see in myself. That was part of his greatness. He had developed a capacity to discern in individuals what they might not otherwise be able to perceive in themselves. He called out the very best in everyone he encountered—and then some.

There will be no end to testimonies of those who are yet alive for what Dr. Potthoff meant to them and what he did for them. Ample affirmation of Dr. Potthoff's deep commitment to be there for others in the way he was for me will be found in these pages. My relationship to him was an abundant and abiding blessing and a sure source of enduring inspiration. Indeed, without his ongoing encouragement, steadfast support, and unrelenting challenge, I would have failed to live up to what he thought was ahead for me. It was a life-changing experience. Without Harvey Potthoff believing in me, I could have hardly believed in myself.

It is my distinct privilege to drop his name.

Dr. Potthoff was the embodiment of what today we know as "generous hospitality." Generously, he offered hospitality in myriad ways—classroom lecturing, seminar presiding, academic advising, career guiding, pastoral counseling, interpersonal sharing, humorous exchanging, and fine dining. On the latter, whenever I offered to pick up my part of the tab, he would invariably say, "No thanks, Steve, just pass it on." It is a principle that I have since tried to put into practice—giving of myself to others the way Dr. Potthoff gave of himself to me. Granted, I usually had the benefit of an expense account to tap into whereas he undoubtedly paid out of his own pocket!

After so many years have passed, I can still see the sweet smile on his face and the endearing twinkle in his eye. Perhaps my beloved photos of him or the two of us together in various venues that decorate my study make this possible. They provide great reminders of what it was like to be in his *presence*. It was always a wonderfully heartwarming experience merely to be with him, and my heart was always strangely warmed when we were together. It was in precious one-on-ones in his presence where it eventually dawned on me that his *greatness* was not only humbly expressed in his scholarly erudition and aesthetic sophistication. His gentleness and solicitude while in his *presence* were equally attributable to his *greatness*.

He taught me to be concerned with the quality of relationships I entered into and the importance of them. Dr. Potthoff understood the significance of all sorts of relationships and the imperative to cultivate them carefully and sustain them intentionally. This lesson served me well in the local church I pastored in the Rocky Mountain Annual Conference, the state councils of churches (Colorado and Connecticut) I led, and the position I now hold as General Secretary of the General Commission on Christian Unity and Interreligious Concerns of the United Methodist Church. He was prescient in his vision of relational realities and their everlasting relevance, especially in conciliar circles. He anticipated, long before the concept became popular, that the kind of ecumenism required of the churches and their leaders was "relational ecumenism."

Dr. Potthoff once said to me that "to live is to outlive." As he made this unassuming observation, the stinging pain of its clear, poignant implications were immediately palpable. I miss him so much. He remains close to me in ways he might scarcely imagine. Why? Although he would never make the claim for himself, it is because he also said there is a certain solace in "a sense of companionship with the .... great of all times."

The theory of the "great man" lives on in the dear memory of those who know and loved Dr. Potthoff—and those who were, in turn, known and loved by him.

There, I dropped his name again. Did I say enough about how much I miss him, down to this day? In his absence, I still remember his *greatness.*

– Reverend Dr. Stephen J. Sidorak Jr. (Iliff student 1972, 1973)
General Secretary, General Commission on Christian Unity
and Interreligious Concerns,
The United Methodist Church

* * *

I was a young seminarian, and it was he who made the Christian faith real. He incarnated the faith, alive. His life was a teaching. His openness, his humanity, his sharing the faith with simplicity made it possible for me to genuinely want that kind of expression in my life. While I came, later, to know he was a superb theologian, it was the life he lived that was my greatest teacher, greatest affirmation of the Christian faith. He is a spiritual mentor to this day.

– Don Sperber (Iliff '62)

I took courses from Dr. Potthoff as a student. I am 86½ years old. I attended the funeral of Dr. Potthoff. Many of us were asked to come up and make a choir. No women were in the liturgy or service.

Dr. Potthoff said many things we remember. One summer we were in a class with him in the basement of Old Main. A rather large dog wandered in, walked around—Dr. Potthoff said quickly: "I don't believe he understands, this is not on dogmatic theology."

Around the time he was doing some of his last teaching, the words *for whom the bell tolls* and the words *no man is an island* were being used a lot in sermons and funerals. Dr. Potthoff said to many of us: "Be kind to all you meet, they too are having a hard time."

I knew him first as a layperson and attended a class on Theology of God as an "audit." We were a good size class, and he was gracious to me. Later I declared for the ministry. I was at Iliff twelve years, including under appointment and parenting.

– Rev. Jean H Steiner (Iliff '82)

* * *

✦ My association with Dr. Harvey H. Potthoff began while I was in college, and he made campus visits. In talking with him about the issues on campus (in which he was always interested), he showed respect for the views of the students: "At Iliff we treat students as adults." As my association with Dr. Potthoff grew at Iliff, I came to know this man of quiet and gracious manner. His smile, signs of friendship, his sense of humor, the twinkle in his eye when he told a joke or pun, the obvious concern for students as people—these qualities are ones which have made a great impression. Just as he can talk about people who greatly affected his life, so also I can talk about the effect he had on mine.

Apart from the influence upon my own thinking and the nurturing of that thinking, an emphasis upon the discipline of learning is crystal clear. After a presentation in class by some student, a frequent response would be to remove his glasses and say: "What is your judgment about ...?" I anticipated those moments because I knew the discussion to follow would be very worthwhile. Yet I waited for such moments with some fear (when I was the reporter) because I was not sure that I was as well versed as I should be in order to respond to his inquiry. I never felt intimidated. I frequently felt affirmed and respected because someone was willing to ask for my judgment and to discuss its implications.

Dr. Harvey H. Potthoff is a whole person. His integrity as a scholar and as a sensitive human being comes through loud and clear. The effects of this man upon my life are substantial. I thank him for being the man who he is.

– Rodney J. Stemme (Iliff '77)
Minnesota United Methodist Church

* * *

Dr. Potthoff was my theology professor at Iliff. In addition to helping me immensely in a difficult task of formulating and justifying my own personal theology, Dr. Potthoff had a warm and personal side. I once arranged a luncheon with Dr. Potthoff and Dr. John Spangler (Iliff Psychology of Religion professor) with myself and another Iliff student. I arranged for the four of us to have lunch at the then trendy restaurant, Rick's Café, just southeast of the Cherry Creek Mall. I was dating one of Rick's waitresses and had recently attended a Rick's Café employee Fourth of July party at the restaurant. At the party I had become acquainted with many of the other employees at the restaurant. Dr. Spangler and Dr. Potthoff arrived in their de riguer suits and John and I were fashionably clad in our de riguer T-shirts and jeans.

After the four of us were seated, several of the minimally clad waitresses would pass our table and greet me by name. Dr. Potthoff took note of this, and after several waitresses had greeted me, he commented that I seemed to know all the ladies. I told him I just knew the pretty ones. Both Dr. Potthoff and Dr. Spangler thought that was quite funny. But I could tell that Dr. Potthoff was just a bit envious of my social milieu in contrast to the comparatively conservative milieu at Iliff. The incident lightened the mood, and we went on to have quite an enjoyable and synchronistic luncheon, as disparate as our lives seemed to be.

Dr. Potthoff was a warm and wonderful man who will always occupy a special place in my heart.

– Duane Stjernhold (Iliff '79)

* * *

I remember Dr. Potthoff's warmth and affection for the congregation and students. Every New Year's Day, he would pray through a list of the congregation. I believe he did it at regular intervals throughout the year.

I was never fond of academic theology, so I only took the minimum courses required. My wife audited the Introduction to Theology course to get a taste of what I was studying in seminary. At the common meal, Dr. Potthoff mentioned her participation to me saying: "We're giving her a good dose of theology." Being a wiseass, I said: "Does a good dose of it make you immune to it?" He replied, looking me in the eye, "It seems to work that way with some persons."

– Neil "Sandy" Sweet Jr. (Iliff '73)

* * *

I came to hear of and eventually personally know Harvey Potthoff by way of a seventy to seventy-five-year family history my family had with him. He performed my parent's marriage ceremony. My father while at Iliff also served as an assistant under Harvey. My father went on to get his doctorate from Iliff, become a philosophy professor at Emporia State Teachers College, and a full professor at Kansas State University. He founded and headed the Department of Religious Studies at the University of South Florida for twenty-six years and published half a dozen books on religion [also several articles over the years in *The Iliff Review*–Ed.].

Maybe because of my family tradition, upon graduation from Kansas State University, I attended Iliff from 1969 to roughly 1972.

In my last quarter, I was enrolled in a theology class taught by Harvey Potthoff. At the time, he was held in high esteem as the "theologian" for an important United Methodist seminary. Much of his class was based upon his recent book at the time *God and the Celebration of Life*. Around Iliff it was regarded as quality theology, but for me it fell short of what I had studied as an undergraduate.

Late in my tenure at Iliff, I had a part-time job delivering pap smears and blood samples between doctor's offices and a local hospital. Sometimes I could not finish work and get back to school by Harvey's class time. Close to the end of that quarter, Harvey called me into his office. He said I was "cutting" too many classes. I asked him to document how many classes I had missed. He said he did not actually take attendance, but I had missed too many. I asked him what my grade was up to that point; he said it was an A-. Then I said, what does attendance matter if I am making an A- if I attend at all? Oops, that was not the right answer. He said that to get a passing grade, I would need to read and report on additional books. I refused. He chose to give me the only F I have ever received in my whole life.

As for the failing grade, in Harvey's defense, if I had not missed any classes, I might have improved upon the A- grade. As it has turned out, my life has been very good. For all I know, that failing grade may have been a small part of the catalyst that compelled me to move on in other directions. So, no harm, no foul.

– *Michael Tremmel*

[Compiled from two separate submissions. – Ed.]

* * *

✦ As I have thought about your influence in the field of theology from the time I first studied in your classes in the early 1950s, I have concluded that there are at least three aspects I wish to emphasize in appreciation. These three emphases have resulted in an approach which I have found meaningful, which I have used, and which I have taught in many settings.

First, you humanized theology. By this I mean you have made it a human science (insofar as it is a science); you have related it to very human concerns and illuminated the human condition.

This I contrast to the more usual or "systematic" approach which sees theology as a catalog of ultimate or universal interpretations far removed from daily human strivings. Rather than developing a "system" from a logical or a philosophical framework, you have begun with the experiences of people and their real needs and aspirations. You have shown us how theology can truly be inductive rather than deductive, and developed it from an understanding of real people rather than "ideal" people. You have advocated a theology in functional relation to life as it is actually lived, and thereby have raised it to the level of a truly integrative and meaning-providing tool. You have shown how theology can inform and interpret all of our experiences, rather than be merely a set of propositions to be believed or affirmed. This human experience has been very helpful to me.

Second, you have placed theology in the context of many other disciplines in the modern intellectual scene. You have shown, for example, how our world-view must be consonant with contemporary astronomical knowledge, our view of life must be informed by contemporary biological developments, and our view of the human person must be paralleled with contemporary understandings in psychology. In this way theology could be based on the best knowledge we have, and can remain intellectually respectable. Your resulting theology is anything but static, and this flexibility makes it relevant especially in the midst of changing viewpoints.

Third, your approach has led to interpretations which are relevant and meaningful in the contemporary scene. Thinking people today need an organizing framework of interpretation which provides for meaning, wholeness, and vision. Your interpretation has not been satisfied with reformulating the status quo, but you have abandoned the static when a better interpretation presented itself. This integration of theology into the broad spectrum of contemporary intellectual developments remains the only way that theology can have a valid and determinative place in our society as a whole. You are to be commended in your attempt to give new life, new vision and new concepts to the contemporary theological task.

– J. Atlon Templin (Iliff '53–'56)
Professor of Historical Theology and Church History, Iliff

* * *

An Encomium for Dr. Harvey Potthoff

In the first place, Dr. Potthoff was born in Le Sueur, Minnesota, a son of the soil and its labors. In the second place, he was a graduate of Morningside College in Iowa, where those inspired Methodists under Wilson Seeley Lewis had "held aloft the ideals of learning and character. ...And in the third place, he chose The Iliff School of Theology in Denver to pursue his master's and doctoral studies.

Of course, my only academic relationship with Dr. Potthoff was his course, "God in Contemporary Theology," in the winter term of 1946 at Iliff. Now, at the time, Dr. Potthoff was the full-time pastor of Christ Church, Denver, and taught one course at Iliff. Interestingly enough, the course was filled with current theologians such as Brightman, Wieman, Hartshorne, and especially Whitehead.

I must say, however, that my relationship with Dr. Potthoff was never limited to the classroom, for he was, hands down, the favorite speaker and teacher, at every Methodist Youth meeting that I would concoct at the Conference Office, as Director of Youth Work (1946–1950).

But, back to the classroom. Why Whitehead? Well, the simple reason was that Mr. Potthoff, at his graduation, was named to receive the prestigious Iliff scholarship for additional graduate study, in the name of Elizabeth Iliff Warren, and chose to use it to study at Harvard. And, there was Whitehead, who wrote *Process and Reality*, the Gifford lectures of 1929. Of course, nearby, at Yale, there was Hartshorne, who wrote *The Divine Relativity* in 1948. The many writings of these two thinkers ought to be brought back and critically assessed again, don't you think?

Soon, Dr. Potthoff was recognized and appointed a full-time professor of theology at Iliff. And, soon also, he and Iliff became the foremost of places for "process theologians" in the nation. I suppose Claremont might dispute this reputation, but I think that Iliff can hold its own, historically and actually by remembering the life and accomplishments of Dr. Potthoff.

– Joseph N. Uemura, 1949, 1951 PhD
Professor of Philosophy Emeritus, Hamline University,
St. Paul, Minnesota

* * *

Harvey and I became good friends, although we were not close theologically. Because of this, Harvey and I got together once a week for breakfast. He then would proceed to point out where he thought I was wrong. He was always cordial and kind. His differences with me were never reflected in my grades.

I believe Dr. Potthoff was an outstanding Christian and theologian.

– Dr. Richard Ward (Iliff '67)

* * *

Dr. Potthoff made a very strong impression on me during my days at Iliff, and that has affected my work ever since. First of all, I experienced him as a kind, compassionate man who cared about us students. As a professor, he was very knowledgeable, very organized, and a clear speaker, so I enjoyed my classes with him.

Most importantly for me, Dr. Potthoff's theological understandings and presentations about process theology changed my thinking about God, and I carry those changes in my faith development to this day. He held a strong interest in the connections between religion and medicine, which inspired me during my seminary days and continues to do so.

One crowning achievement of my life as a teacher was to co-lead a class at Iliff entitled Theology, Ethics, and Medicine with Dr. Potthoff and Dr. Dana Wilbanks. Dr. Potthoff expressed interest in my thoughts and treated me as a co-equal in this teaching project.

I have read a number of his books. I have retained in my files a wonderful outline of a presentation he made in January 1978, entitled "A Theology of Aging: Religious Faith and the Experience of Growing Older."

– Thomas C. Washburn, MD, MAR with focus in Bioethics (Iliff '81)

* * *

My memories of Harvey are of him doing many, many large things for students that most people knew nothing of. He met me when I was finishing my bachelor's degree and not knowing what to do or how to do it with a degree in psychology. He not only encouraged me to apply to Iliff, but made sure that I was accepted into the MDiv program and also that I had the funds necessary for the full three years of my journey there. As far as I know, he and I are the only ones who knew of this incredible contribution not only to my life's journey, but also to the lives and journeys of others with whom I have come in contact during my forty-five years of ordained ministry.

Not only did he give the gift of education to me and others, but his teaching ability was stellar. I was one of many students who learned of his conceptualization of process theology, which has been the theological cornerstone of my life and ministry. Many years later, I had a chance to thank him, shortly before he died. Our conversation was one of deep and abiding friendship—not as a professor to a student, but as an equal, a colleague, and a friend.

– Roger W. Weeks, MDiv, DMin (Iliff '56)

* * *

The Pain and Splendor of Grace Moments

Harvey told the story of a father and daughter walking together along a lakeshore. They came upon an old dead tree that had fallen into the shallow water. Stopping, the eight-year-old daughter stared at the log, then walked out on it, but after several feet she fell from the log. She was scared, wet, and disappointed. Her father helped her back to the shore, dried her off as much as possible, and comforted her with a hug. They continued their walk. Sometime later they came back again to the dead log. Again the young daughter stares at the log and again walks out and back. This time she makes it, returning to a joyful father's hug.

Harvey says, "This is a grace moment! Pay very close attention to the grace moments of life, and you will experience reality and learn more theology than all the theologians can teach you."

"Grace Moments" became a profound, in-depth influence in the pain and splendor of my life experiences. Grace Moments happen in our suffering, loss, conflict, loneliness, and joy, and can be as simple as humor, as captivating as birth or death, or in the solitude of a sunset. In Grace Moments, one experiences the essence and the interrelated, interdependent meaning of life. From Grace Moments come unbounded learning experiences—some from pain in your heart and others from unrestrained joy. You stand before these moments in awe, and they become indelible in who we are and in what we become. These Grace Moments operate in human experience to transform, inspire, and give home to the encounter of the reality and the splendid manifestations of *God and the Celebration of Life*.

– Fletch Wideman (Iliff '66)

* * *

A group of us were discussing the problems we were having in the churches we were serving while at Iliff. Some of the stories were the basis for much frustration and even anger.

For some reason, Dr. Potthoff was present during our discussion. After some time had passed, he said, as best as I can remember, "Gentlemen, let me give you an old saying: *Illetitimus non-carborundum*, translated "Don't let the bastards grind you down!"

With the laughter that followed, the spirits of the group improved a great deal.

– Herbert Wingard (Iliff '56)

* * *

✦ Dr. Potthoff and I have had many interesting experiences, the kinds that are very rich and memorable. The Aspen experience with him (in the land that God made) was memorable in that it not only provided outstanding leadership but an opportunity for dialogue and encounter with beautiful people from differing religious persuasions and geographical locations.

The Chaplains of the military services have so many times in so many ways expressed their appreciation for Dr. Potthoff's leadership and warm friendship. I personally have traveled over the far east, assisting him in conducting Chaplain Career Development Institutes. The times we shared together in Japan, the Philippines, and other countries in the far east will long be remembered.

His mind was ever alert, his knowledge valuable, his humor entertaining, and his friendship always valued.

– Ransom B. (Bud) Woods (Iliff '81)
Chaplain, Colonel, USAF (Retired), Honolulu, Hawaii

* * *

Theologians come in a wide variety of stripes, foci, and flavors. Some are analytical and apologetic, others are biblical, comparative, critical, denominational, or dogmatic; still others are evangelical, feminist, historical, liberation, or orthodox; and yet others are philosophical, pastoral, process, reformation, systematic, or traditional. The following affirmations support the recognition of Harvey Potthoff as a Pastoral Process theologian.
– Ed.

I felt particularly privileged to have had Dr. Harvey Potthoff as a professor during my time at Iliff, as did my students when he came to speak to my World Religions classes at Arapahoe

High School in Littleton, Colorado. Many of them had been wounded by various organized religious denominations as young children, subject to gory images of hellfire, brimstone, sin, and damnation, but they were curious about the subject and beginning to explore the possibility that it might yet speak to them.

I will never forget their delighted responses to Dr. Potthoff, especially when he shared with them the ancient derivation of the word salvation as health and healing.

He said that religion, at its best, should teach you that life, human beings, are blessings, that we are meant to live wholesome lives. If you feel healthy and uplifted when you are in a church, synagogue, mosque, or temple, that would be a sign that you just might be on the right path. But if you feel sick or unhealthy in one of those places, afraid, sinful, then you should leave. Immediately! Because that is sick religion. Not only was it your right to leave, he said: "It was your duty!" For your health, for your healing, for your wholeness.

I saw so many young people transformed as a result of meeting Dr. Potthoff, and as I reflect back on them and him—and on the world today, where, sadly, there are still too many institutions, religious and otherwise, who continue to stoke the fires of fear and guilt—I see the wisdom of Dr. Potthoff as more relevant than ever and providing inspiration to all of us whose lives he so graciously touched.

– Sandra Gordon Pettijon, MAR (Iliff '92)

* * *

Dr. Harvey Potthoff: A Methodist Mentor

In your faith-journey, who has helped you become your

adult self? Who are your Confucian "true parents"?

For thousands of United Methodists in the Denver area, Iliff School of Theology alumni, and scholars throughout the nation, theologian Dr. Harvey Potthoff has been pastor, mentor, friend, and "true parent."

I first met Dr. Potthoff in October 1978. My life had fallen apart, and I desperately needed encouragement. After listening to my tearful laments and offering a comforting hug, he passed along advice he'd received in the 1920s: "Be kind to the old person you'll be someday." Much later, when eighty-eight years young, Dr. Potthoff gave tribute to the mentors who nourished his intellectual and spiritual growth: "I have drunk from wells I did not dig."

In 1935, Dr. Potthoff studied at Harvard with the famous English philosopher Alfred North Whitehead. Whitehead wanted Potthoff to stay there, but Potthoff had made a commitment to return to his church in Denver. He honored that promise.

While pastor at Christ Church, Dr. Potthoff helped the CU medical community integrate mature religious faith with medical practice and ethics. He also played handball regularly with an Orthodox Jewish rabbi, who boldly suggested that Dr. Potthoff preach to his congregation. He did, about Jesus the Jew. They were delighted.

Along with Dr. Albert Outler and others, Dr. Potthoff shaped the Wesleyan Quadrilateral, the model of United Methodist spirituality embracing Scripture, Tradition, Reason, and Experience as vital components of a holistic Christian faith.

After serving the Iliff School of Theology and Denver-area churches for forty-four years, Dr. Potthoff "retired" to Nebraska

Wesleyan University for one year to teach undergraduates. The year became eleven years, as he mentored hundreds of struggling undergraduates. A confused freshman once asked Dr. Potthoff, "Were you ever my age?" "Yes, I was," he replied, "and I made it. And you will make it too."

Two death-row inmates in the Lincoln Penitentiary had heard that a philosopher was teaching at the college and asked if he would visit them. He did, monthly, for eleven years. One wrote in a Father's Day card: "Thank you for being the father I never had." In spite of Dr. Potthoff's appeals to the governor, Wili Otey was executed. Through Dr. Potthoff's mentoring, Otey left a legacy of poetry.

Dr. Potthoff invited Native American elders and scholars to "tell us who you are," to share their traditions in a conference at Nebraska Wesleyan. Because of that gathering, there is now a scholarship program for Native American students. Potthoff was also invited to teach a Sunday school class by former Big Red coach Tom Osborne. An anthropologist provided a fitting metaphor for Potthoff's impact in Lincoln: "Harvey is a bridge."

As we at Cameron United Methodist church build bridges to serve our neighborhood and world, we have much to learn from "true parents" in the faith like Dr. Harvey Potthoff. From his books *God and the Celebration of Life* and *A Whole Person in a Whole World*, and especially from the witness of Dr. Potthoff's life of faith, hope, and love, we have refreshing spiritual water to drink, from "wells we did not dig."

– John Anduri [student but not a graduate]

* * *

My father and I both studied theology under Dr. Potthoff's tutelage at Iliff. Knowing that Dr. Potthoff was retiring from Iliff was a motivating factor in my completing my undergraduate work a year early. In my father's case, it was more propitious than desirable.

In the late 1940s and early 1950s, the academic and theological challenges that faced seminarians at Iliff were monumental, especially to young men who, for the most part, gained their faith on the plains of rural America. While many professors were great at challenging the faith of the pastors-to-be, it was the pastoral heart of a younger Dr. Potthoff who had compassion on a young seminarian and helped my father to rebuild his faith in the midst of those theological challenges. My father once said that if it had not been for Dr. Potthoff, he would have very easily lost his faith altogether, and potentially his life. Instead, my father pastored churches for several years and served as a teacher and head counselor at the Oregon State Boys Correctional facility for over twenty-five years—touching the hearts and minds of those whom society had given up on, much like Dr. Potthoff touched his.

– Frank B. Drew, MDiv (Iliff '50) and K. Keith Drew, MDiv (Iliff '83)

* * *

I grew up in Arkansas where the majority of persons I knew believed they had the absolute truth about God, Jesus, and the gospel. When I graduated from college, I had so many doubts and questions that I decided I could not be a minister. The ministers I knew seemed to have answers and no doubts or questions.

When I came to Iliff, I was contemplating giving up, not only the ministry, but also the Christian faith. Dr. Potthoff's holistic view of life expanded my life and opened me to the wonder of being human in all its dimensions. I was challenged and inspired to a lifetime of being and becoming.

A concept I learned from him that has guided me over the years is that one can "live wholeheartedly without absolute certainty."

Dr. Potthoff and the Iliff community saved my life and moved me forward on my journey toward "a whole person in a whole world," a world that is "dynamic, interrelated, and emerging."

Years ago, I was walking along a street in Vail. I heard someone ask, "Are you saved?" I turned to see Dr. Potthoff seated at a table. I asked, "From what, by what, to what?" This was how Dr. Potthoff said we were to respond if someone asked if we were saved.

In the late '60s, when I was a pastor in Boulder, my kindergarten daughter Michelle seriously injured her eye. Dr. Potthoff learned of this, came to Boulder, and spent time with her. He gave her a ride around the neighborhood. She, to this day, speaks warmly of that experience with Dr. Potthoff.

– Tom English (Iliff '65)

* * *

I remember how gentle and wise he was—so understanding of first-year seminarians and generous in sharing his wisdom throughout our seminary career and afterwards, if you were ever lucky enough to spend time with him again! Dr. Potthoff was and is and always will be a "classic."

– Rev. Mary K. Green, (MDiv, Iliff '61)

* * *

Dr. Potthoff was a source of enrichment in my journey of life. He was my professor, my counselor, and my friend.

Harvey had a special gift of interpreting "theology" in

language that could be expressed in the local church. During my long pastorate at Arvada United Methodist Church, he preached many times, and members of the congregation could relate to his interpretations of our heritage. Advance announcement of some guest preachers tended to diminish attendance at worship. When Dr. Potthoff preached, everyone wanted to be present.

In my personal journey, Harvey was a valuable source as a "counselor." After approximately twenty years as pastor of Arvada United Methodist Church, I was seriously considering the need to move to another appointment. Harvey reviewed with me the significant value of a long pastorate and suggested that instead of moving I consider returning to Iliff for the Doctor of Ministry Program. This proved to be a most meaningful endeavor. Dr. Potthoff was my faculty advisor. This was an enriching experience for me and therefore enriching to the congregation I was serving.

A few years later, Bishop Melvin E. Wheatley requested that I consider an appointment to First United Methodist Church in Colorado Springs. Again, I conferred with Harvey. He deemed it would be great to have a "liberal voice" in that church. Following an interview with the SPR Committee and the church staff, it was determined that my "theology" would not be acceptable in that church. Harvey, with a warm smile, assured me that being rejected was probably a "blessing."

Dr. Potthoff was inspiring as a professor and consultant, but also as a friend. Many wonderful memories included Rhonda and I and the Naylors, being Harvey's guest at the Burnsley Hotel for dinner and conversation. Harvey was a great host. The best wine and "warmest fellowship" were enjoyed. Harvey's presence generated warmth, humor, and meaningful conversation.

My life, like multitudes of others, would have been incomplete without Harvey Potthoff. Thank God for memories.

– Rev. Earl K. Hanna (Iliff '52, '78)

* * *

From the time I was a student at Iliff throughout most of my ministry, I felt that I could talk with Dr. Potthoff about any problem that might come up. Just the knowledge that he was there was a source of strength and comfort.

At one point in my ministry, I was invited to come on the Cabinet. I wanted to accept the invitation, but it was not a good time for our two children who were in high school. I asked Dr. Potthoff if he could have lunch with me. I shared my struggle with him. I don't remember what he said, but it enabled me to see clearly what I should do.

After my father retired from a successful business career, he and my mother decided to move from suburban Philadelphia to Denver, where they could be close to my family and me. My mother went into a deep depression over giving up her beautiful home and many dear friends. I asked her if she would talk with Dr. Potthoff. She agreed. After her session with Dr. Potthoff, she began to slowly pull out of her depression. One of the things we remembered him saying was: "You can still smile, Mrs. Keesey. You're going to be alright."

From time to time, I would have dinner with Dr. Potthoff and other members of the Conference. Almost without exception, Dr. Potthoff would come up with a joke that helped us all to relax and enjoy our dinner.

– James C. Keesey (Iliff '53)

* * *

My first contact with Harvey Potthoff was many years ago when we were fellow students at Iliff. The student body was very small, and we became well acquainted with almost everybody. Potthoff was often among small groups who used to stand around the halls at Iliff discussing the new ideas we were getting, especially from Dr. Longacre and Dr. Bernhardt. It has been my privilege since then to see and hear Harvey and to audit a few of his classes in recent years.

Every quarter except the winter one we had an Iliff picnic. We always went to the mountains. At the picnic, the faculty always challenged the students to a ball game. I had to be umpire. There were many other activities as well. We scrambled to the top of Mount Evans, climbed the fire tower at Devil's Head, paddled a raft on Echo Lake, and slid on St. Mary's Glacier.

Potthoff performed his first wedding while we were still students. The groom was an Iliff student. The bride's parents weren't sure they wanted a minister for a son-in-law, so the couple decided to have a quiet wedding. One evening, two carloads of us went up to the Red Rocks, where we found a beautiful spot, and there they were married at twilight. It was an impressive ceremony.

Some of the male students formed the Bull Club. Later on, they invited me to become a member, but I had to be initiated as a daughter of the Pharaoh—in the bulrushes. Potthoff initiated me. He sat at one end of the table and I at the other. I had been informed that I needed to bring an initiation fee of eleven cents. Potthoff said, very solemnly, something like, "A great change will take place. Now pay your initiation fee." I put down a dime and a penny. I was told to ask, "Where is this great change?" The very solemn reply was, "There is no change."

Along with the pranks and fun, we were learning to see new visions and were cultivating a deep appreciation and love for Iliff and all she stands for. Through the years, I have had contacts with Harvey Potthoff, and I think I can count him among my most kindly and loyal friends.

– Josephine Leamer, Iliff student,
Formerly on the Staff of the Board of Education
of the United Methodist Church
and former faculty member of Rust College

* * *

I'm not the intellectual type, but I know that Harvey helped shape my thoughts about death/dying/immortality and helped me across the years as I met with families at times of death.

My best remembrances about Harvey Potthoff come more from the "feeling" level. I always felt like I was a person who counted in his classroom, not just another student. I also remember his kindness to Jeannie and me at the time of the death of our daughter, Merrikay, while we lived in Aspen, even though I had been out of Iliff eight years at the time. I also remember sitting in the ante-room at the back of the Iliff Chapel. About a dozen members of the Board of Ordained Ministry sat in a circle around the room, and I was ushered in. Needless to say, it was an intimidating group—Alex Bryans, Rufus Baker, Ben Christner, and others, including Harvey. It was Harvey's reassuring smile that got me through the session. My impression was that he was a "gentle giant."

– Keith Merriman (Iliff '57)

* * *

I have a personal note from my mother who knew Dr. Potthoff very well. She felt that no one could marry him because he was the perfect gentlemen. This was humor, but true. We remember how he served Christ Methodist Church in Denver for so many years. He was always very delightful at all times.

– Genny Newton [not an Iliff graduate – Ed.]

* * *

Dr. Harvey Potthoff was a sweet, thoughtful, and warm-hearted man. My first introduction to Dr. Potthoff came on Labor Day weekend, September 1953. He and Dr. Williams had arranged a trip to Mt. Evans for new students coming to The Iliff School of Theology. I was not one of the best students and a questionable candidate for pastoral ministry. Harvey seemed to be attracted to those of us outside the correct avenue of vocation.

His approach was always one of quiet respect for a question, for every thought expressed or idea presented. He was a great teacher, who moved my goals forward, always challenging, and with a firm hand requiring more than I was able to deliver, but with a smile and encouragement.

He attended my wedding in 1954 and invited my wife to attend class on occasion. When he saw an opportunity, he included all spouses to participate. He showed up for my EdD graduation at the University of Denver. Years later, he attended my inaugural at Southwestern College. He lectured at Columbia College when I became president there.

During the time he was at Nebraska Wesleyan with Dr. John White, he got me invited to participate in activities at

Lincoln, Nebraska, and Morningside, Iowa. He maintained a correspondence with me, which gave some fascinating insights into his struggles to improve every situation in which he found himself. He always inquired with probing positive logic to see what I thought. During the mid to late decade of 1980, he really held some forward-looking insights into what we were missing in United Methodist clergy preparation.

His work at Ring Lake was very satisfying to him. He kept reminding me that "Salvation is free in John Wesley's church, and radical theology should be a development of the church." He was especially proud of his representation to Jurisdictional and General Conferences of the UMC. Then he would ask, "How do you feel about that?" or "What is your thought on this?"

When he retired to the Meridian Retirement Center, I visited him there for several years. (My mother-in-law was a resident there, and she spoke of him with great affection.) We exchanged books and journal articles on several occasions until his death.

During seminary days, I had been assigned a paper to follow up on one done earlier by Dr. Howard Ham when he was a student. During the research, I discovered Harvey had written on the same subject when he was a student. He challenged conclusions on the report, but never tagged me for what was surely some plagiarism on my part.

It seems I have told you more about me than Harvey. However, that is the point. When he was interested in a student, the student was the center of the universe. What better mentor is there? A Christian gentleman who led by example. A scholar who created opportunities for students, and a friend to the future "Worker in the Vineyard."

– Donald B. Ruthenberg, ThM (Iliff '56)
President Emeritus, Columbia College

* * *

I met Dr. Potthoff at University Park United Methodist Church many years ago ... but really became a friend, socially, through Dr. Ruth Murray Underhill. I did volunteer work for Dr. Underhill. We were both members of Denver Women's Press Club. I often drove her to meetings and lectures she gave as an anthropologist at the University of Denver.

Ruth was known for her social gatherings in her unique log cabin home on South Clayton Street. She enjoyed hosting her cocktail hour. Her guest list always included professors from the university and Iliff. Frequently Harvey would attend, as would Dr. James Galvin, a psychiatrist friend, and many others.

I was always impressed with Harvey's warmth, sense of humor, and how easily he made people feel "at home" with him. In the beginning, I think I was a bit intimidated by this real gentleman. Later he was a dinner guest in our home, became a friend to our children, and one day asked me if I would like to attend one of the last classes he would be teaching at Iliff. He said he would be retiring within a year. We had spoken at a church meeting where John Anduri was talking about his journey with cancer. I had introduced him to Harvey. My son Bruce had known Anduri at CSU and asked if I knew anyone who could help John, spiritually, as he faced cancer. I immediately knew Harvey was the person.

The most significant lesson I learned from Harvey was this: "Life is filled with many gracious moments ... learn to notice that ... everyday can bring something to your life ... be aware, share from this lesson." He awakened me to seeing joy and humor in life's little moments. I can honestly say that this Harvey lesson is with me daily ... a child's smile, the kindness of others, the beauty of nature. He possessed a lilt and a life

... challenged me and supported my Iliff studies. (I graduated in 1987 with a Master of Religion degree.) An amazing man—gracious, warm, and caring. I was blessed by this friendship!

– Marliyn J. Stoddard (Iliff '87)

Former member of the Iliff School of Theology Board of Trustees

[In part from an interview on April 19, 2012, by R. L. Phillips]

* * *

✦ One of the most precious assets of a struggling young pastor is a good model for ministry. Harvey became that model for me with his first visit to our small rural charge. We were celebrating "Harvest Home," a most important event in the life of the church. We were expected to have Someone of Significance to do the sermon that Sunday. Harvey accepted the invitation to be that Someone. The great day arrived, and so did Harvey—early. Instead of withdrawing to the study to prepare for the worship service (as this green and anxious pastor would have done!), Harvey prowled the premises. He talked with the kids out in the yard. He explored the kitchen, visiting with the women preparing the meal. He got acquainted with the men setting up tables in Fellowship Hall. Nowhere did he meet a stranger; these were his sisters and brothers in Christ. Needless to say, his sermon came from all of us, not the hallowed halls of a distant seminary. Harvey taught me the value of listening in love. It is a lesson I will always treasure.

– Jan Sumner (Iliff '73)

Thornton United Methodist Church

* * *

There are many things I could contribute, but the one telling quality of his concern for his students is that for over ten years after I graduated and went on active duty, Dr. Potthoff corresponded with me once or twice a year. It was wonderful support from a caring man.

– Chaplain Robert G. Swager (Iliff '57)
US Army, Ret.

* * *

Finally, here are several Potthoff adages that have been noted above, which have resonated and have remained with some of his students through the years:

"Life is filled with many gracious moments; learn to notice that ... everyday can bring something to your life; be aware and, share from this lesson."

"Be kind to everyone, for they are having a hard time."

"Be kind to the old person you'll be someday."

"I have drunk from wells I did not dig."

* * *

And, here's a tribute to Harvey on the occasion of his birthday in 1977:

To one who chose to grow with Time...

Some fight the hours
They grasp at moments they never had,
They rush,
They hoard,
They grow weary.

Some grow with time,
They let the moments flow through them,

They pause,
They love,
They ripen.

You grow with time
Because you share the past:
    Your memories,
    Your books,
    Your writings
        are windows
            to the gossamer world.

You grow with Time
Because your heart is open.

– Shaun, Sally, Mike ... 1977

* * *

As all of these memories, reflections, and recollections indicate, Harvey's affirmation that "I have drunk from wells I did not dig" is both an accurate and appropriate affirmation for each of us. Harvey's contribution to the United Methodist Church's Book of Discipline in laying out "Our Theological Task" and the Wesleyan Quadrilateral has added to the depth and breadth of our theological well. And, for those of us who have drunk from the "Harvey H. Potthoff Well," we are aware that we have drunk from a life-nurturing well—a well that has nourished us with hope, inspiration, understanding, and adaptive meaning throughout our living and ministries within this awesome, dynamic, ever-emerging, intricately interrelated "existential matrix" within which "we live and move and have our being."

– Howard Bailey

15

THE FINAL DECADE: 1992-2002

By Richard L. Phillips

The final ten years of Potthoff's life began at the time he made the permanent move from Lincoln, Nebraska, back to Denver. They were good years for him and for many others. They were also years of significant health issues and concern about Iliff and its changing educational focus, its faculty makeup and vastly changed student demographics. His love of Iliff and his years laboring in the heart of the Iliff vineyard, especially his love of his colleagues and students in the vineyard, were at the heart of his life.

He spent much time organizing his library, making lists of such things as the courses he had taught over the years, the papers he wrote but were never published, organizing his sermons, and getting other items ready to turn over to the Iliff Archives in the Iliff Library. He also spent time deciding what of his possessions to give to whom. Some of his notes from these activities survive in current holdings.

During the years of 1992–1993, Paul Millett of the Iliff Library staff helped Harvey organize his papers for the Iliff Archives. (See Paul Millett's reflections in Chapter 13). Several pages listing all the courses Harvey taught are contained in Appendix E.

Harvey's relationships continued to be a primary focus. There were trips to Alaska to be with the Wood family, time with Peter Gay when possible (mostly in phone calls and letters), and no less important were his relationships with his colleagues at Iliff both retired and active. Former students, including myself, provided many visits at University Park United Methodist Church, his home on South Josephine Street, and starting in 1994 at the Meridian. Teaching at Iliff in occasional classes in Denver and at Aspen (including at least one at the University of Denver) was very important to Harvey. The never-ending social gatherings numbering in the hundreds and ranging from groups of two to twenty, usually a meal included, were a given in Harvey's life.

HHP photo in Iliff Archives

The University Park UMC interim pastoral team led by Potthoff. Potthoff, Spangler, Bloede, Bishop Swenson, and Templin.

It was early in those years that Harvey entered his last officially assigned pastorate in his beloved United Methodist Church. University Park UM Church, across the street from Iliff, had been his primary church affiliation over many years; his presence there was steady, and he was well known by the laity. In 1993 this church was in need of an interim pastorate starting in mid-church year. Appointed by Bishop Mary Ann Swenson, Harvey served as the lead minister of a team of retired Iliff faculty members. It was both a unique and very important assignment. I know of no other appointment like it in my knowledge of the church. Not only did it involve regular preaching and pastoral work for all four of them, but they worked closely together to develop a plan for the church's future. Leadership by committee worked well, as Harvey, Lou Bloede, John Spangler, and Alton Templin filled roles late in their ministries that could not have been predicted by any of them. That they each found fulfillment is without question.

Following their service, Paul Kottke was the next senior minister, and he remains in that position as this is being written. The next paragraphs by Paul are his "reflections" on his long association with Harvey. They capture many aspects of Potthoff's personhood that may not have come through in other chapters but which I believe are excellent insights into the depth of this complex theologian and minister. University Park Church maintained an office for Harvey some years after the team pastorate.

From the time of the interim pastorate, Paul Kottke and Potthoff remained close, with Paul serving as Harvey's pastor for the remainder of Potthoff's life.

* * *

As I reflect on my relationship with Dr. Potthoff, I have two driving images:

a) First and foremost, Harvey valued the pastoral relationship he had with people, whether or not they were members of a particular church [Christ United Methodist Church or University Park UMC]. Even as a professor of theology at Iliff, he continued to nurture the persona of being a pastor.
b) Second, he clearly steered away from engagements of emotions and personal intimacies.

In the years that I knew Dr. Potthoff—first as a student, next as a junior clergy colleague, and then as the senior pastor of his final days—he was masterful at inviting people to talk about themselves, to invite them to reflect on the meaning of life, and to engage in theological conversations. All this within the context of what can be understood as a rational, cognitive faith, or to use the phrase "a thinking man's faith." He was one who was willing to hear a person talk about his/her hopes and fears (the emotive), but he would steer the conversation in a way that would engage the cognitive, the "thinking" awareness.

There was one area that was always off-limits: that was to engage Dr. Potthoff regarding his personal intimate feelings. If one attempted to broach this area, he would redirect it, saying something like "enough of that, let's talk theology" or as was often the case with me once I became the senior pastor at University Park UMC, "let's talk about the church." If one would attempt to ask a pointed question about his feelings or about his intimate life, which a few times I did as his pastor, one would sense a strong barrier and he would likely say, "that is not something that we need to talk about."

What I marvel about regarding Dr. Potthoff is that even though he had a very private life, which I suspect only a very few ever were allowed to enter, he had a vast array of individuals—from church members, to academics, to successful leaders of the community, and even individuals who lived on the margins of society—who counted Harvey as their friend. He could be with them, listen to them, provide them a sense of dignity. They would always feel as if they had been deeply heard. To whom did he turn for emotive/relational support? One of the great pleasures that Dr. Potthoff allowed himself was to select various individuals and invite them out to a nice restaurant for dinner. Harvey did this on a number of occasions with my wife and me. Such a setting allowed for two or three hours of conversation, which he would direct. Such moments allowed him, I believe, the "pastoral' role that he found so meaningful, which probably went a long way toward providing for his personal needs.

There is one story that Harvey told me a few times, which reflects how deeply he honored the pastoral role. It was on a Sunday sometime in his early years at Christ Church. A small boy came up to him before worship and as a sign of friendship extended his clutched hand. As he opened the clutched hand extended towards the minister, in the palm were some M&M candy pieces that clearly had been in that hand for an extended period of time. Plus, by the looks of the hand, it seemed apparent that the hand had not been washed for some time. The boy was offering his prized M&Ms to his pastor. Harvey felt compelled to reach out and take the M&Ms. But of course the boy stood there to watch. So Harvey did what any pastor would do and popped the candy pieces into his mouth with a silent prayer for good health. The boy smiled and walked off.

Each time Harvey told me this story, he would chuckle and shake his head, saying the role of pastor takes many forms.

Harvey's use of language invited an openness of interpretations. Even though he felt that he communicated a certain idea, Harvey used to tell me that he was always amazed how many different ways people would hear his sermons. He never corrected them, saying, "no this is what I meant." He always allowed them the "space" to take away their own meaning.

Of his various books, it is my belief that the one published in 1976 *Understanding Loneliness*[1] gives insight into the inner workings of this man who touched the lives of thousands, particularly as he moved into the aging years of his life.

> *The purpose of this book is simple and practical. It is designed to help the reader better understand his or her own experience of loneliness. It is intended to show that while we cannot escape some experience of loneliness we need not be completely victimized by it. What loneliness does to us and in us is partly a matter of our own decisions.*[2]
>
> *To be oneself involves both satisfaction and loneliness.*[3]

Harvey once told me that he thought Dr. Viktor Frankl's book *Man's Search for Meaning* was one of the best books written. In his book on loneliness, Harvey quoted this paragraph by Dr. Frankl.

> *A human being is not one thing among others; things determine each other, but man is ultimately self-determining. What he becomes—within the limits of endowment and environment—he has made out of himself ... life ultimately*

> *means taking the responsibility to find the right answer to its problems and to fulfill the tasks which it constantly sets for each individual.*[4]

Later in the book *Understanding Loneliness*, Harvey wrote:

> *As we live through various chapters of life we quickly discover that there are some things beyond our control. To acknowledge them as part of life and to come to terms with them with some measure of serenity is essential for meaningful living. Every human being lives within limitations of some sort. On the other hand, there are many things that can be changed. Furthermore, our attitude toward what can and cannot be changed makes a crucial difference.*[5]
>
> *One of the most important of all resources in our later years is a mature philosophy of life. Central to such a philosophy is the understanding that the purpose of life is to live and the purpose of being a human being is to be human and to grow in human qualities. Since being fully human involves creative relationships, success in living involves the quality of our relationships. The later years ought to represent a culmination in the art of living rather than the termination of a life of getting, winning, using, outdoing. Fortunate are those persons who carry into the later years a philosophy of life which treasures the values of heart and mind and spirit—and not simply the values of power, position, and possession.*[6]

Dr. Potthoff understood that loneliness was that human experience which pushes us out of contentment. Seen from this perspective, loneliness is what leads to new life, as long as we do not allow ourselves to be paralyzed by its "shadows."

> *The experience of loneliness can make a positive contribution to our lives if out of it there comes the search for a richer inner life, a deeper religious faith, and a more creative lifestyle.*[7]
>
> *Prayer, worship, communion, and meditation are among the human responses to "the Beyond that is within." He who so responds—not in order to use God, but to draw closer to God and to become more Godlike—knows in the depths of his being that he is not ultimately alone.*[8]

Dr. Potthoff's life reflected this awareness. He sought to develop this awareness with those whom he touched. This was his "gospel." This was his passion both within the seminary and with the church.

I would be amiss if I did not reflect some on Harvey's love of the United Methodist Church. I am only qualified to do this from one perspective: that of being his pastor in his closing years. Yet for at least four decades, he was in the upper echelon of the United Methodist Church, of which I only had brief glimpses. He helped move the UMC in the direction of a progressive, rational church. He was instrumental in the early days of the merger with the EUB and helped to form an articulation of the progressive Social Creed and the Quadrilateral. He never took any apparent sides with the gay movement of the early '80s, though his good friend, Bishop Melvin E. Wheatley, was on the front line of this movement. He was well aware that in the last decade of his life, the UMC was taking a considerable turn towards a more conservative stance in theology, in scripture, and in social issues. He was deeply troubled that the Church which he loved was dying with him, becoming something of a throwback to another time.

When I would visit with him (By the way, pastoral visits to Harvey at the Meridian were never twenty minutes. They often involved eating lunch or at least a two-hour conversation in his room.), we would talk some theology but more often than not when I visited he wanted to hear about University Park UMC or about my thoughts of the general Church.

Harvey was an institutional man. In some ways, one can best understand him if one understood how deeply invested he was in the institutional Church. One could go so far as to say that Dr. Potthoff was "married" to the United Methodist Church. Questions surface as to why Harvey never married. We will probably never know the full reasons. But, at some risk, I would venture to suggest that the institutions of Church and academia filled every aspect of his private and public life.

Out of his own loneliness, he found purpose, meaning, and a constant engagement of new life. And in the process, he became a pastor to untold thousands of men, women, and children.

– Paul Kottke

* * *

HHP photo in Iliff Archives

The stained glass window in Harvey's office at University Park UMC

One of Potthoff's last sermons at University Park UMC, one which he found himself later preaching in other venues, was his "Reflections on 60 Years of Ministry."[9] It should be read by anyone interested in his self-understanding of his life and ministry. Indeed, Harvey did much reflecting on his teaching and his ministry during his final decade. He reflected on it in many of the speeches he was to make and in responses to honors he received at Iliff and other places. While he did not write an autobiography, he did some rather significant autobiographical reflections in notes and speeches. Harvey appreciated his own heritage both from a family and a career standpoint, and reflecting on it came easily for him. His personal reflections could best be labeled as "appreciative"!

Harvey had a talent for writing biographical material. In reflecting on his life after the Iliff retirement in 1981, I [Phillips] have often asked myself what he might have done had it not been for the eleven years at Nebraska Wesleyan University and his pastoring, preaching, and social roles during his remaining years. One answer, I am confident, is that he would have written some biographies. He wrote many mini biographies, some of which are in the archives. Some notable ones are about Lindsay Longacre, William Bernhardt, A. N. Whitehead, Charles Milligan, Martin Rist, Jameson Jones, Lowell Swan, and others for whom he was asked to do memorial services or funerals. Peter Gay asked Harvey to do the memorial service for his father; Harvey's remarks on that occasion are in the Iliff Archives.[10] I have found that what he wrote in a biographical mode had a way of getting to the very heart of the person in a few well-chosen words. Potthoff's words of deep appreciation for the person are characteristically present. It cannot be said often enough that he treasured his relationships and hated to see them fade into the past.

HHP photo in Iliff Archives

Harvey and Charles in one of thousands of animated discussions

Potthoff continued to teach, preach, and do special lectures and speeches during this final decade, only slowing down when ill or when the energy was just not there. The real slowdown years were 1996 and 1997. His content more and more regularly reflected his deepest summary thinking about his theology and often what his own meaning in life could add to what he had to offer to others. An Iliff-at-Aspen course taught at age eighty-two in the summer of 1993 carried the title "Process Theology and Life's Meaning." Here is a telling quote, with his careful organization of his thoughts in response to a class member's question.

> *My impression is that in those lives where we do discern growth in the quality of one's faithing, hoping and loving—in depth and outreach ... several things are present:*

1. *A sense of value—and what is worth seeking in life.*
2. *An intentional quest for those values.*
3. *The inner commitment to live each day well.*
4. *The endeavor to live in harmony with the fundamental ways of things ... living in and through the inexorable changes and transitions of life, not in denial or bitterness, but in openness to the raw materials life offers.*
5. *The capacity to discern the divine, the sacred, in new and untried situations instead of complaining like those of an ancient captivity, "How can we sing the Lord's song in this strange land?"*[11]

I am sure Harvey went on to illustrate and develop the above outline. His emphasis on meaning in life, the search for a mature spiritual life, and the role of the self in such pursuits was always present in his work. It reached its height in his later years.

The Meridian, a retirement complex not far from Iliff, became Potthoff's home in 1994, its staff and residents his companions right up until his death. Only a few trips and hospitalizations interrupted his residency. Harvey started a book review group at the Meridian. Among the many residents joining the group was Dr. Francis Brush. Dr. Brush was a student at Iliff with Harvey and was retired from the University of Denver. They had a long history as close colleagues and friends. Of some note is that Harvey, together with a few former Iliff students and retired faculty, started a different monthly luncheon discussion group that focused on process thought and current theological issues. The Meridian staff arranged tables for the group and sometimes a special room for our lunch and discussions. It has grown over the years and still meets monthly, now on the Iliff campus, during nine months of each year. We now fondly refer to it as The Potthoff Discussion Group. Usually we read and discuss articles and papers germane to Harvey's theological interests. Former Potthoff students and retired faculty make up the bulk of the participants.

During the Meridian years, many former students visited Potthoff, some with great regularity, and most of us found helpful duties, like a shopping trip, easily incorporated into a visit. Always theology was the chief focus of our conversations. As Kottke has indicated above, Potthoff guided conversation away from himself, even about how he was feeling! Harvey's fellow Iliff retiree and close colleague Charles Milligan provided the most regular and dependable companionship and help during these years. Charles was, right up until his death, a key member of the discussion group; infrequently our readings for discussion were Milligan's articles. From student days forward, Harvey and Charles were a theological team worthy of very special note. The Milligan family and Harvey were together both professionally and socially more than often.

During the final decade, Harvey did much preaching as a guest in many different area churches. For the first seven years, he continued to travel, but slowly and sadly, he began to say no to many invitations to lecture, preach, and travel. An example was my own retirement reception at Syracuse University in December 1998; his response was that he just did not have the energy to do such travel as he once had. His attendance at musical, cultural, and athletic events was less and less frequent, and even conversation about Broncos football, Nuggets basketball, and Rockies baseball was less and less frequent. Athletics was never high in his conversational ranks, but he had always shown interest and often attended games. His own past as a good athlete, while he never bragged about it, was certainly a source of some pride for him.

The contrast between this reduced schedule and his former habitual schedule is stark. That is well documented in this letter he wrote to me in 1985 while teaching at Nebraska Wesleyan University. I had asked and he accepted an invitation to come to Syracuse University to be involved in a full weekend of events. The letter is dated August 7, 1985.

Thank you for your letter of July 23 with news of the various forms of deviltry you have cooking for the weekend of October 19 and 20. … I have been doing a variety of things in California, Minnesota, Alaska, Breckenridge, Aspen and Denver. I just finished a two-week course here on campus [Iliff] on Theology of Ministry.

You might be interested in what I will be up to in [the October] block of time:

> *10/2-4: Theological respondent to the report of the Faith Development In The Adult Life Cycle Project—Evergreen, later they meet in Stony Point, NY.*
>
> *10/6 – Preach, Christ Church, Denver.*
>
> *10/8-10 – Classes at NWU.*
>
> *10/10 – Dialog with Bishop Hearn at Nebr. Conference –Futures Convo.*
>
> *10/11-12 – Meet with Rocky Mountain Conference Council on Ministry.*
>
> *10/13 – Preach University Park Church, Denver.*
>
> *P.S. Tomorrow I zip down to Texas to give a couple of lectures*
>
> *Warmly, Harvey* [12]

Diminishment with dignity was more than an intellectual and pastoral focus for Harvey; he lived it, usually with ease, in these declining years. There were times when it had to have been a struggle. Several hospitalizations, frequent pneumonia, and probably a stroke, and once, while in the hospital, a heart attack left him weak and with a long recovery, once necessitating a rehab center. My own visits with him during such times were difficult and sometimes he had no energy to discuss theology. What indicator for serious illness could be more obvious! On at least one occasion, I did not expect to see him alive again. His spark and passion for life won, on several occasions, the battle for survival. His surrogate son Dr. Tom Wood, by phone, often shared with Denver physicians in Harvey's medical care. Until the very last weeks, the real Harvey Potthoff was always present. Peter Gay's memorial service reflections tell the endgame with love and compassion.

Richard Vickery, now retired, while not an Iliff graduate, was a clergy colleague of Potthoff's for many years. One of the roles he still plays in the Rocky Mountain Conference is the writing and delivery of the tributes at the conference sessions for all the clergy who have died during the year. The following are the remarks made by Vickery at the 2002 conference session, printed in that year's journal.

Harvey H. Potthoff

Harvey H. Potthoff was born on April 23, 1911, in Le Sueur, Minnesota. He graduated from Jeffers High School in Jeffers, Minnesota, as Valedictorian in 1928, from Morningside College, Sioux City, Iowa, with a Bachelor of Arts in English in 1932, and from Iliff School of Theology, Denver, with a Masters in Theology and Doctor of Theology in 1935 and 1941 respectively. As part of the doctoral program he was Elizabeth Warren Iliff Fellow at Harvard University,

Cambridge, Massachusetts, studying with the esteemed Alfred North Whitehead.

Having been admitted on Trial to the Colorado Conference in 1934, he was ordained an Elder and received into full membership in 1936. For sixteen years, 1936–1952, he was Pastor of Christ Church, Denver, and part-time faculty member at Iliff School of Theology. In the pastorate Dr. Potthoff's gifts included weekly sermons and an emphasis on religious education of adults.

Dr. Potthoff served on the Iliff Faculty as full-time Professor of Christian Theology from 1952 until 1981. Upon his retirement he was named Professor Emeritus to that institution and became Distinguished Visiting Professor of Religion at Nebraska Wesleyan University, Lincoln, Nebraska from 1981 through 1992. The 1982 establishment of the Harvey H. Potthoff Chair of Christian Theology became the first endowed chair in the history of the Iliff School. Over the years Dr. Potthoff received many distinguished awards for his service to church and academia, including the Distinguished Service Award (1975) from his undergraduate alma mater and the Distinguished Alumnus Award (1986) from Iliff.

In addition to being involved in the local church and seminary Dr. Potthoff had been involved at both the Annual and General Conference of the United Methodist Church. Between 1952 and 1980, he was elected as a delegate to eight sessions of the General and Jurisdictional Conferences, including being named one of the framers of the Doctrine and Doctrinal

Standards for the uniting denomination between the Methodist and Evangelical United Brethren Churches. He was a delegate to the Fourth Assembly of the World Council of Churches in Uppsala, Sweden, in 1968 and twice delegate to the World Methodist Conference.

Harvey is the author of eight books and more than one hundred articles in Methodist and scholarly journals.

He is survived by one foster son, Tom Wood, including Tom's family of three children, three grandchildren, and one great-grandchild.

Harvey died on February 21, 2002, in Englewood, Colorado, at ninety years of age. The benediction which he often pronounced at the close of worship speaks of him and brings closure to all who knew him: "And the peace of God which passes all human understanding, keep your hearts and minds in Christ Jesus and dwell in your hearts from this day and ever more." (Philippians 4:7)

We made every effort to contact Dr. Peter Gay during the research and writing of this book. The Emeritus Office at Yale was helpful with an email address but could not give us other information. We sincerely hope Peter is doing well in his retirement. He also, when young, experienced Dr. Potthoff's support and concern, and the content below is taken from his remarks at the Memorial Service on February 27, 2002.[13]

I have so many memories of Harvey, such important ones, that I have decided I will be brief. Harvey Potthoff lived most of his life in this part of the world, this part of the country, but his mind, I believe, was open to all of the world. We met for the first time in 1943, introduced by some fellow students, freshmen, sophomores at the University of Denver. It was a group that met with Harvey regularly, weekly. I was a newcomer not only to Denver but to the United States, I had been here only for three years. I was not, am not, a Methodist, not a Christian, not even a good Jew. But, as a matter of fact, in principal an unbeliever, something that didn't disturb Harvey in the least, even though there were no prospects for my spiritual regeneration. He accepted me at once—without reserve, without hesitation. And just as other members of that group, we became friends, he and I.

I asked myself, I have in the last few days, what if anything I had to teach him—it's not clear to me anything. But what he had to teach me was what I want to call—without grandiosity—the promise that America held for me endless realistic possibilities. After having spent six years as a growing boy in Nazi Germany, this was very wonderful, unforgettable news. He did his teaching, such as it was and it was in every area I can think of generously and kindly, without a touch of arrogance or condescension, but quietly. And one particular example will have to stand for others. I had told him one Sunday when we were sitting in his living room that my parents had, in early life, a good collection of classical music, and that it consisted almost entirely of opera arias—Caruso and others like him, whereupon he asked me whether I had any interest in chamber music. When I told him that I did not, that I knew little of it, and what I had heard of it seemed boring to me. Thereupon, he said "Listen to this," and he put on the record player a recording of Beethoven's last spring quartet, the Opus 135, the shortest and in many ways the most accessible of Beethoven's last five quartets. I must say that if I ever had a conversion experience, it was that evening. In part perhaps because Harvey exerted no pressure, just simply letting me know that he enjoyed something enormously that would also be open to me as it has been since. And whenever I hear good recitals or hear recordings of chamber music, I think of that evening.

I saw a great deal of him and we had become I think close friends, until I left Denver in 1946 to go to Columbia to graduate school. But on the other hand, I stayed in touch with him. And whether I came to Denver or occasionally when he came to New York, and also of course we had mail, even though email had not yet been born – we talked. We talked I think without reserve and without venom about philosophy, even about theology, for that matter. He introduced me in a time of great need at the University of Denver to Iliff, right across the way, where he told me they taught very interesting philosophy, and thus I became a student of Bill Bernhardt's, and still remember that as well.

And of course we kept in touch. He showed me what he was writing, I sent him what I was writing, we had visits, and we had many conversations indeed. He followed my career in the nicest possible way. He never said, although I always knew, that he had done a great deal to foster it. And it was not just kindness, although there was much of that, but it was also that there was this greatness — intellectual greatness. He was not only very well read, he had absorbed what he read, and had made important decisions.

So now I must say in retrospect, I am sorry I did not see him in his last days. We talked about everything, and one thing we talked about particularly, and he had a real interest, a professional one, I might say even a wicked one, in right wing charismatic religious figures, with their clouded theology, their vast buildings and their uncertain political views. We would listen to them sometimes on Sunday mornings, and talk about it afterwards.

We shared other interests as well. I have mentioned music, I have mentioned politics, but I would like to end with one final memory. A memory that I cherish, and I will continue to cherish. The last time I spoke to him, and he was failing and I knew that, it was a week ago Thursday by telephone. He could no longer speak. But Joanne [a Meridian staff member] put the receiver next to his ear and asked me to talk to him. So I talked to him, what I was doing, what I was writing, and while he didn't answer and he couldn't answer, he showed me that he was listening, as always. His labored breathing calmed down and sounded normal by the time I had hung up. He seemed to be saying to me I thought, in the only way he then could, that he was still there for me, still listening, and still approving.

Now, you will note of course that in talking about Harvey I have talked a great deal about myself as well. I think he would understand, and would approve of this as well, because as a friend he was a kind friend that was ideal and indeed unforgettable. I shall miss him very much and I will not forget him.

– Peter Gay

University Park United Methodist Church was packed on February 27, 2002, for the memorial service. Harvey's hand in the music and the shared reflections was evident throughout. As he did for life, he planned well for death, his teaching and writing on the subject were from deep inside! He not only blazed pathways for us, he taught of the joys along the way. All involved were most grateful that both Tom Wood and Peter Gay were among those offering reflections and tributes. Charles Milligan was to live ten more years, and both on that day and many times after added greatly to the Potthoff legacy.

Harvey's cremated remains are located in the memorial section of the sanctuary of the University Park United Methodist Church, Box 61. The photo of the plaque was taken by UPUMC photographer Cindy Smith and used with permission. Debby Lawrence, a UM clergywoman and one of the pastors at the church, was most helpful in making arrangements for the photo.

In my own remarks at the memorial service, I read a portion of Potthoff's reflections on being a student in A. N. Whitehead's classes in 1935–1936 (see Chapter 1).

I am confident that Harvey used Whitehead as a model for his own life, commitment, and even personal demeanor. Maybe seeing everything in creation as interesting was a trait they both shared as the basis of who they were. In Harvey's reflection on his study with Whitehead, he says, "I hope that I shall always be able to preserve some of the glow coming from his personality."

My closing memorial service remark was "Harvey, you did it!"

A Celebration of the Life of
Dr. Harvey H. Potthoff

February 27, 2002
2:00pm

University Park United Methodist Church
2180 S. University Blvd.
Denver CO 80210

Prelude		*JoAnn Gudvangen-Brown*
**Processional Hymn #711*	*For All the Saints*	*SINE NOMINE*
Gathering and Prayer		*The Rev. Paul J. Kottke*
Scriptures	*Psalm 121 and Micah 6:6-8*	*Edward Naylor*
**Hymn*	*God of Our Life through All the Circling Years* *From the 1964 The Methodist Hymnal*	*SANDON*
Scripture	*Matthew 22:34-40*	*Dr. David Maldonado*
Reading of Alfred North Whitehead		*Dr. Richard Phillips*
Words of Remembrance		*Dr. Tom Wood* *Dr. Peter Gay*
Words of Faith		*Dr. Charles S. Milligan*
Lord's Prayer		
**Recessional Hymn #117*	*O God, Our Help in Ages Past*	*ST. ANNE*
**Benediction*		*The Rev. Paul J. Kottke*
Postlude		*JoAnn Gudvangen-Brown*

**please stand*

Photo in Iliff Archives, box 32, file folder 2

The Memorial Service bulletin

Photo by UPUMC used with permission

Plate on the columbarium box containing HHP's ashes, west transept of University Park UMC

NOTES

[1] Harvey H. Potthoff, *Understanding Loneliness* (New York: Harper & Row Publishers, 1977; also published under the title *Loneliness: Understanding and Dealing with It* by Abingdon in 1976); also in Iliff Archives, box 2, file folder 7.

[2] Ibid., 12.

[3] Ibid., 51.

[4] Ibid., 28.

[5] Ibid., 48, 49.

[6] Ibid., 95.

[7] Ibid., 109.

[8] Ibid., 117.

[9] Iliff Archives, box 18, file folder 26.

[10] Iliff Archives, box 19, file folder 27.

[11] Notes from a 1993 Aspen course, "Process Theology and Life's Meaning," Iliff Archives, box 12, file folder 43.

[12] Phillips letter August 7, 1985, Harvey H. Potthoff Papers, Iliff Archives, box 43, file folder 3.

[13] The archives has a video, a voice recording, and a transcript of Gay's remarks. Iliff Archives, box 33A.

16

POTTHOFF'S LEGACY FOR THE CHRISTIAN

By Richard L. Phillips

In his personal life and in his theology, Harvey Potthoff exhibited a way of being Christian that provides a real legacy for anyone inclined to explore his neo-liberal, process thought, empirical, naturalistic theology. He labored very hard in the various theological vineyards to put it all together so a whole picture of a whole person as Christian could be meaningful and rewarding. While he was not the first, nor will he be the last, Christian theologian with essentially this basic orientation, he did a great deal of pioneering work to bring it to a full and mature expression. At the same time, he never once doubted that for many the denial of belief in absolute certainty and supernaturalistic eternal rewards was not going to win the day in regard to religious belief and practice. He had no animosity toward those who chose to stay the course in one or another of the more traditional theological and institutional expressions of the Christian faith. In fact, he saw clearly the meaning these systems held for many such practitioners.

His appeal was directed to those who now hold a world view derived from the physical sciences, social science, and psychology, and from literary, biblical, and other forms of modern scholarship. He did not think it necessary that religion be based upon a form of knowledge (often referred to as divine revelation from a super- or extra-natural realm) not available to human reason and experience. Supernatural revelation as the basis of our knowledge of God is, in fact, only a few centuries old. It is important to note that the world view of the biblical writers did not assume a natural and supernatural separation. They saw God as present in and participating in the natural flow of things, even if in some ways transcendent or not fully transparent to them.

Potthoff certainly saw God as transcendent in a naturalistic way of understanding transcendence. He believed a naturalistic rather than supernaturalistic locus of the divine to be fully compatible with the Bible and with early Christian history and theology. At the same time, within our current world view, there is need for some reinterpretation of ancient texts and practices to yield a clearer understanding and practice of the Christian faith. Here, as in any case, great care must be taken in any practice of reinterpretation. It can never be a whimsical effort.

While Potthoff was guided by a current world view, he did not think of science as something that replaces religion. In fact, he believed that *scientism* was a wrong approach to our understanding of both knowledge in general and knowledge of the real world. He firmly believed that religion has deep concerns as well as truth and help for the human family, which are not possible to know and understand and appropriate directly from the world of science. A key example would be the inability of science to tell us just what love, grief, and human commitments are all about. Along with aesthetic appreciation and other such things, there is much we experience that we know other than through science.

What, then, does the Potthoff legacy offer us regarding the understanding and practice of the Christian faith? The purpose of this chapter is to briefly summarize how Potthoff's theology can be meaningful and practical for those religious people holding a contemporary world view and who do not believe religious concerns to be in conflict with that world view. Frequently within this book, I have emphasized that Potthoff has many peers in the naturalistically oriented theological world but perhaps none have tried to give so much emphasis to issues related to the everyday practice of the Christian faith as his work and writing has provided.

The belief that God is to be found in the natural (cosmic) world and that God is totally contained within the cosmos had for Potthoff—and can have for us, he believed—several very specific and very important meanings. He was fond of many other theologies about God but needed to add something he found missing. Tillich's "ground of being," for example, was on target for Harvey but did not say enough about the "making for wholeness" characteristic he saw as a necessary aspect of divinity. He liked his mentor A. N. Whitehead's term *principle of concretion* but found it lacking a valuing component. God as the source and agent of ongoing creation that keeps bringing specific and ever new and more complex aspects of reality into being was for Harvey only part of the picture. Reality is more than the sum of its parts, just as the human is more than the sum of the chemical and physical interactions taking place in the human body. For Potthoff, both the cosmos and an individual human life have a *transcendent* quality. So he came to envision God as the creating agent for *wholeness*. If God is to be worthy of divine status, God must be the creative, all inclusive, and living depth of what it is to be a mature, whole person having a share in creation. For Harvey, this was/is the key to the sanctity of life.

This view of God gives all of existence a sacred quality. We all participate in this sacred aspect of the world in which we "live and move and have our being." God is right here, all the time! To understand ourselves in such a context is to elevate life far beyond the more mundane existence of rocks and other parts of creation that have not developed reflective wonder and awareness as has some of the animal world, especially the Homo sapiens.

This concept of God as immanent makes awareness of God accessible to our powers of reason and experience, even if the immediacy of our awareness waxes and wanes within our experience.

We need, as did Potthoff himself, mediating agents to help us become aware of and appreciative of God. For Brother Lawrence many centuries ago, a mediating agent was no less or no more than a common tree. Upon contemplation of the tree, he said to himself something like: if God can do, season in and season out, such wondrous things as God does with this tree, then what can God do in my life! From that insight, Brother Lawrence wrote one of the great spiritual classics of all time.

For Potthoff, there were many mediating agents. Important ones in his life were the standard practices of the Christian faith. For him, worship, the hymns, the Bible, the celebration of Easter, Christmas, and the communion table all resonated with the experience of God. He found the most important mediating reality to be in Jesus the Christ. He acknowledged that in other faiths, there would be other mediators. In both the Bible and in church tradition, we see in Jesus the Christ the most complete and accessible revealing of the caring, forgiving, creating, and relating understanding of God available to the Christian. For Potthoff, grasping the central figure in Christianity as *my mystery* present in *my universe* is very biblical and modern. That is not to say that the biblical writers and historic church fathers have always rendered the essence of the Christ understandable. We must, after all, each do that for ourselves.

In mediating the human/God relationship, esthetic endeavors like music, poetry and other of the arts, the wonders of nature, the mystery of life itself—in all of these—there is a potential for at least partial awareness of God. Potthoff believed that those less inclined to find God in church practices and traditions can and do experience God in a great variety of ways including, as he did himself, in the sharing of life with other persons. The experience of mystery (the unknown and perhaps unknowable) can itself be an avenue to experiencing God. We are, in other words, surrounded constantly with endless possibilities for sensing our oneness with God. It is not that such mediating experiences are not available in supernaturalism; they are. But a God out there is much less spiritually appealing to someone with a world view such as Potthoff's than is a God who or which is imbedded in the world, that is, with us constantly.

There is much that we give up of traditional thinking about God when we view God as part of a natural world view interpretation of divinity. *God is within, not an intervention into the ongoing natural world.* For many believers, the very idea of giving up seeing God as a being existing somewhere as a discrete being and, in addition, functioning as a personal (as in, to me) God is too much to either ask or expect. Potthoff understood well that many cannot make that change in their assumptions about God.

Miracles are not extra-natural events; they are nevertheless happening all the time. Potthoff would say, like the poet Walt Whitman: "As to me, I know of nothing else but miracles." This immanent God is not a personal being available for granting something for personal gain or corrective intervention into the natural world. God does not answer the prayer of one family to save a child and ignore the prayers of others resulting in the death of another child. By the same token, natural events like earthquake, fire, and storm cannot be seen as punishment handed out to either persons or nations. Creation with its powers may deal anyone an earthquake; it is not something handed out with any immediate human value or dis-value.

Prayer is not a matter for personal gain but more in line with an expression of appreciation and thanksgiving, the gaining of personal insight and self-alignment with divinity. Ironically, at the same time prayers do indeed have a quality of personal gain, we may be enriched when we expand our horizons! Certainly Potthoff believed we are enriched when one comes to see self as personal being—more closely allied with our understandings of God.

Churchship in a theology spoken of within a current world view perspective can allow for enjoyment and meaning often not thought possible. For Potthoff and many other theologians, the hymns, the biblical passages, the church traditions and holy days, the great creeds and prayers of the church—*without* taking them in their literal meanings—can provide, a refreshing look into Christian life and thinking. Such understanding of the church and its traditions make way for our use, in a new way, rewarding interpretation, appreciation, and joy. In itself, this is a legacy with wonderful potential in the church's future.

In Potthoff's thought, there is no philosophical problem of evil as there is in traditional theology. We humans are called upon to take a cosmic or global view of natural events, some of which enhance our lives and some of which threaten and can take human life. Humankind is not created good and then becomes at least separated from God, if not evil. Creatures are characterized by potential, capable of becoming either good or bad. We have the capacity within circumstances often beyond our making or our control, and within the limits of our inherited and developed skills and insights, to make of ourselves what we can. We are not pawns in a cosmic game of chance; we are creative partners with God. We do not die because of some centuries-old sin; we die because we are a dynamic part of the natural world and must live our lives in that context and awareness. Both the natural world around us and our individual unique makeup bestow upon us great potential, including for good or ill, for wholeness and maturity, or, to be sure, sustained immaturity—and in that given reality we also have thrust upon us tremendous responsibility for who and what we will become.

There is no escape from the dangers of life beyond our own genetic makeup, skills, and wits and those of our fellow humans. What we do have is a wonderfully forgiving "mother" nature that also manifests, from the human perspective, great destructive powers with which we must learn to deal as best we can. Earthquakes, while creative as a part of the natural world, can be a real negative from an immediate human perspective—but maybe a great human value in a broader, long-range view. Many times, Potthoff has reminded us that our world view, our understanding of reality, is what determines how we relate to and react to the world in which we find ourselves. He is not naive, there is much about nature that does not have our human values as the guiding principle. We must come to grips with that. Our view of the divine can be a terribly significant part of just how we do that. The bottom line — for Potthoff — is that life is sacred, that we share in and participate in creation. Even though we did not ask for it we bear as living beings great responsibility for just how we do that.

For better or for worse we must adjust to our circumstances and share ourselves in the quest for whole and mature expressions of humanity, for ourselves and our fellow human beings. In doing so, there is much joy as well as pain and uncertainty. In the fellowship of a Christian community, we can come together as a saving (healing) community to enhance our existence in many ways. In the absence of such a religious community, we must work even harder to adjust to our pilgrimage with any sense of meaning or purpose. *Hope*, for Potthoff, is a key, perhaps *the* key, to how we engage life and find meaning, purpose, joy, and at-one-ness with God. Without hope, we cannot begin to realize our human potential; indeed, we do just the opposite: we shrink into ourselves and often die.

Reinterpretation is foundational to the human animal, and we cannot escape its importance in making sense of our lives. In medicine, we constantly have to reinterpret (understand in new and different ways) the history of discovery about illness and injury, healing, and nature's capacity to forgive.

Poets are professionals at asking us to reinterpret, to gain new and different insights about our selves and our world. Reinterpretation in these two areas of life seem simple and easy when compared with finding it necessary to reinterpret long-entrenched theological beliefs. Reinterpretation of divinity requires a change of viewpoint about the nature of scripture. On the other hand, a change in how we understand the nature of scripture demands changes in our theology.

Theology does not disappear with reinterpretation. Like medicine, it becomes more in tune with the world as it really is and within which we humans must interact in the most helpful and fulfilling ways possible. Theology, perhaps more than any other academic endeavor, can point us in directions that add wholeness and a spiritual quality to our collective and individual struggles in this pilgrimage called life.

The age-old theological concept of grace was a favorite and productive concept for Potthoff. The literal meanings of grace are many, but central to all is grace as gift. Within life, we all can point to what he called "moments of grace." It might be as simple as helping someone across the street who cannot move fast enough to otherwise be safe. It is often found in parenting when a child is gently helped through a childish mistake. We give others moments of grace when we see some good where others may see only weakness or failure. We stand on the rim of the Grand Canyon and see centuries of God as creator and as also centuries of grace, both indeed spiritually rewarding. Moments of grace usually do not need much reinterpretation but may come to us through the very process of reinterpretation. What more foundational in human life can be a better moment of grace than to hear the words or experience an act that says "I love you."

Harvey charged us to be on the lookout for moments of grace. They come at unexpected times and places and in forms we cannot imagine. We must be alert to the possibility of experiencing grace at any time. In my own education, there came a moment of grace when I first read the works of Rudolf Bultmann and realized that the virgin birth can be reinterpreted as the divine reality infused within the human reality, a valuable metaphor, not a literal event.

Something once happened to and for me when I went into the men's room in a chapel to see why the "worker" sign was up. Our custodian, Effie, a wonderful and very powerful woman, was cleaning the urinals. I asked Effie why she worked so hard to make them shiny clean. "Because," she said, "people use them." That was a moment of grace! Effie's powerful personality was demonstrated in another way when she then told me that her supervisor had told her she must wear gloves when cleaning toilets rather than doing so with bare hands. She told me her response at the time was, "I have been cleaning toilets for 35 years, and I do not need a supervisor to tell me how to do it!" Even if that might have not been a wise practice, it gave Effie a part of her independent identity. It was genuine grace just knowing Effie, let alone having the good luck to work with her. Her work was grace to me, for it underlined the sanctity of all work.

Harvey Potthoff left a legacy for being a Christian while being a whole person in the whole world (as he liked to put it)—in the world as it is understood today by the totality of our knowledge, even as we recognize that our knowledge is always incomplete and always subject to change.

In every aspect of Potthoff's work, we see how he lifts up the importance of relationships. Too often, we take our relationships in every area of life far too lightly, even casually. It is not just our human-to-human relationships, but our relationships to the rest of the animal world, the plant world, the natural world, the practice of stewardship of what we own or have responsibility for. It ranges from how we treat one another to how we make and keep personal budgets, take care of our vehicles, prepare for our times of illness, and even prepare for our own departure from the human parade. In my own experience, it is hard to find a better example than Harvey as a guide for the passion and the responsibility that goes with the gift (grace) of living.

Potthoff's life was marked by his belief in people, especially young people, which he viewed as a necessary passion for the work and the future of the church and society. One result was his ultra-serious approach to the importance of education and lifelong learning. He viewed participation in the aesthetic dimensions of life—like great music, the graphic arts, poetry, and certainly participation in worship—as keys to a meaningful and productive life. He liked his mentor A.N. Whitehead's comment that nothing was more religiously rewarding than a life fully lived! How he treasured his student days with Whitehead and the measure of the man himself. Harvey did not use terms casually, and his favorite parting word after being with an individual or group was "Enjoy!" Persons were always a divine encounter for him, even with someone on death row.

Even when feeling negative about something, Potthoff expressed it with a positive twist. One day, I came for a visit at his apartment when he was, late in life, recovering from serious illness. The front door was always open when he knew I was coming. In the previous visit, he had looked tired and ill, but on this occasion he looked much better. I made, as a result, a pastoral move never appropriate, knowing so even as the words came out of my mouth. I said with some glee, "How are you feeling?" Without hesitation, Harvey said, "Well, how do you want me to feel?" I responded, "I want you to feel better. You look better!" The immediate response, "Okay, I feel better, now let's talk theology!" It was as if he said something like, "Now that you have done something stupid, let's get to something far more important than how I feel."

In his work as a churchman, which was indeed his passion, Potthoff leaves a legacy of commitment and involvement worthy of our careful consideration. Harvey often said that his theology was really a church based rather than a philosophically based theology, and his work validates that self-understanding. He came to believe the Christian church, including the United Methodist Church, had in so many places become a social club type of organization, rather than being on a mission to follow both the teachings and life of Jesus and to pursue a Christlike mission within the church itself and within the whole world. When a church becomes another social club, the biblical issues of justice and peace can easily get lost.

In his declining years, Harvey struggled to find a way to bring the needed correctives to the church, to help it overcome an often narrow focus and shallow depth when it concerned itself with a petty rather than divine-like view of itself and its potential. Yet even in his questioning that the church was losing its self-identity, its awareness of purpose, and its healing (saving) power, Potthoff still believed passionately that the church was the great hope to bring the human family to a new level of awareness of us as co-creators with God, as mediators of an awareness of Christ as the heart of Christianity—a Christianity fully at home in and a leaven in today's world.

This, of course, while he was fully aware that Christianity grew from an ancient and very different time with a much different view of reality. Potthoff's passion for the church remained along with his passionate hope for its continual resurrection. The church Harvey treasured must see itself as a "saving fellowship" rather than a "fellowship of the saved." That is as a healing fellowship rather than as a fellowship of the healed. All of us stand in need of one kind or another of healing or, if you will, salvation.

Shining brighter than any other legacy is that of Potthoff as pastor. That is saying something very special in light of how superb is his multi-faceted legacy in theology, as a member of the Iliff faculty and then the Nebraska Wesleyan University faculty, as a member of the Rocky Mountain Conference and the United Methodist Church in general, as institutional change agent, as a community citizen, and as a model of Christian living and passion for the faith. Harvey H. Potthoff will abide forever in so very many lives for his pastoral touch with peers, students, and colleagues of many faiths or no professed faith, and as a person with a genuine depth of concern even for those with short, even one-time contact. What is not true about this legacy is that it is exaggerated! Of course, there are many lives, including those of former students, he did not touch so deeply as others. Here I would remember Albert Schweitzer's line, "A man can do only what a man can do." Not ever an excuse, just a reality. Harvey made no excuses for that limitation.

In teaching his own theology in a special 1981 class at Iliff, Potthoff delved deeply into his view that his theology was not only nurtured by but indeed developed by being a part of the church and his being a theologian in residence. Here is how he put it in one of the class sessions.

I've read a great deal of Tillich, and when I read what he has to say about the method of correlation, correlating message with situation, correlating gospel and the problems rising out of the human situation, I really don't think first of all of highly abstract philosophical questions. My whole temperament and my experience leads me to think of persons who are struggling with pain and loneliness, seeking meaning in their lives. I'm inclined to think of some people wishing to be at church and not being quite sure how to go about it. In the midst of major financial problems in a depression, in the midst of theological diversities, in a world at war ... how does one respond to all that theologically? ... [Y]ou don't respond to this sort of thing abstractly. I have found philosophical theology to be a major resource—it is indeed foundational. But I think it must be related to very real experienced living situations.[1]

Little mention is made in these pages of Potthoff's engagement as a community member. The archival record of his community involvement is extensive. Over the years, he served on boards, committees, task forces, some that emphasized fitness, youth, childhood and social responsibility in the Denver area. As a panelist for area discussions of issues like the death penalty, women's rights, poverty, and many

HHP photo in Iliff Archives

HHP in downtown Denver across the street from Trinity UMC, 1980s, where he preached many times.

religiously related concerns, he was very popular and usually ended up being interviewed by the local press. Harvey believed in wide community social involvement and in being an informed voter, and he did not shy away from making his perspective or position on matters known. At the same time, he was a strong believer in the separation of church and state. During the movement known as the "Death of God," Harvey was called upon frequently to help both the religious and the secular citizenship make sense of the issues at stake. Being helpful could be what the second *H* in his initials (HHP) stood for. When challenged by representatives of the right about social matters, he would often muse for a second and then say, "Don't I remember that Jesus was involved in this sort of thing?"

No account of Potthoff's legacy would be complete without a word about humor. He found humor everywhere, including in the Bible. I am sure Elton Trueblood's 1964 book *The Humor of Christ* (Harper and Row) only touched the surface of Harvey's appreciation for biblical humor. So many people approach the Bible with a filter that does not allow humor to be present in their understanding. Harvey not only saw humor in all phases of life and theology, he used humor regularly in dealing with the most serious of matters. He was known for using humor to bring faculty meetings to successful results when others might not have thought a solution could be reached. He could tell a story in almost any context and not only get a laugh but bring serious points to the awareness of all present.

Harvey liked complex humor, double and even triple puns. He made fun of people who were punsters: "Psychiatrists tell us, you know, that people who tell puns are very immature." I have heard him say this, sometimes ending with the word *insecure* or *hostile*. Then, within minutes, he would repeat the pun to others and end with a good laugh of his own.

One of his favorite story-jokes with a theological twist is worth relating. It seems that Jesus was with a crowd and while kneeling where the woman had been caught in adultery (see John 8:1–11) was asked what he would do. He stopped writing on the ground and said, "Let the one among you who is without sin be the first to throw a stone at her." For a brief time, nothing happened. Then a stone came over the crowd, hit the woman, and killed her. Jesus slowly turned to look over the crowd and said, "Oh mother, sometimes you make me so mad!" Sometimes Harvey had to wait for the theological part to rise to awareness and thus to share in the humor of the story.

Perhaps the humor crown was placed on Harvey's head at one of the many parties held for him near the time of his retirement from Nebraska Wesleyan University. His humor was obviously a very popular part of the Potthoff identity at NWU. On October 31, 1991, a tribute to Potthoff's humor was celebrated at a mock College Lecture Series with the title "Potthoff Puns and Perplexities in Today's World."[2] A printed flyer noted that the purpose of the event "is to educate and entertain those who encounter the renowned Dr. Harvey Potthoff and are subject to his verbal twisting of language and imagery. This one-day seminar provides practical clues about the mental gymnastics utilized by Dr. Potthoff in his magical, mysterious cerebral play and the art of self defense for fending off fits of uncontrollable laughter (or groaning) in the face of his formidable verbal fencing." Several academic departments at NWU joined in putting on the program. One of the six objectives was: "To demonstrate the verbal tenacity required to repeat any of the aforementioned jokes with humor equal to that elicited by Dr. Potthoff."

As a manifestation of Harvey's personhood, humor was omnipresent. It is hard for me to remember a class session, a lecture, or a sermon that did not contain an example of his joy in sharing a humorous story or joke. Usually a visit with him produced several examples. I think he would have us find something of humor in all we experience, in all we do.

One of Harvey's favorite story-jokes is one he often told during his class sessions. It seemed that a very old cemetery in Europe was being moved to make way for modern urban development. As the workmen uncovered a grave, the lid to a coffin was pulled off. Inside was a man erasing sheets of music. "What," exclaimed the workman, "are you doing?" The response came, "I am Beethoven, and I am decomposing."

Harvey loved scholarship. He loved his work as a scholar, and he appreciated, indeed relished, the fine scholarship of others. Biblical scholarship was special, as was scholarship in the physical sciences, social sciences, the world of human psychology, literature, and so on. He wanted the theologian to be two things: first a scholar and then equally adept at putting scholarships' results into action in life and thought. In this arena, his constant hope and plea was that the pastor would always be a theologian/scholar in residence in his or her church.

Potthoff quoted many scholarly persons regarding thoughts on theology and religion in general. Here are some examples.

> The essential philosophical quest in the world is for integration—which is to say, the need to bring together rational philosophy, spiritual belief,

> scientific knowledge, personal experience, and direct observation into an organic whole. – *Norman Cousins* [3]

Margaret Mead was quoted from her book *Twentieth Century Faith*:

> If theology be illuminated by a greater knowledge of the world in which we live, theology will be given new life in our time. We will not be losing a large proportion of our young people because they feel lonely in an atmosphere that does not take into account what they know. It is absolutely urgent that Christians should take as a first responsibility to know what is known. Theologians must work with scientists to build this new faith, because without faith and love we may destroy the world. With faith and love and no knowledge the world may also be destroyed.[4]

One more quote, this time from fellow theologian John Cobb from an address:

> The question is whether the church can understand its faith in a way that enters into the current state of the culture and intellectual life of the west. Can it, sustained by its faith, enter into and advance the frontier of western thinking? To those questions, the answer that has sounded more and more often among the theologically educated persons in recent years is No. If we are to think, we must separate ourselves from the church. The tradition and images of the church—are an impediment to thinking.[5]

Potthoff was a collector of such statements from the scholars of his time and earlier times as well. What is remarkable is how closely he followed the advice contained in the writings and remarks of such persons. His theology can be viewed as an attempt to fulfill the advice and council of such scholarship.

At the same time, being alert to and incorporating advancements in scholarship, but not necessarily agreeing with someone's conclusion, was one of Potthoff's most important legacies. His personal doubter was in full bloom.

It is one of my hopes that Harvey had lived long enough to fully read and incorporate the work known as the Jesus Seminar. Marcus J. Borg, one of the leaders, has written extensively on the New Testament studies emanating from the seminar. As results were coming out in many publications in the mid-1990s, Harvey was no longer able to continue with such rigorous reading as is required to process the literature. He knew of the seminar work and told me he held great hope for the results.

Recently I attended a program featuring Borg here in Denver. I came away even more aware that Borg and Potthoff traveled a common theological and biblical highway.

Borg's subsequent publications would, I am sure, be seen by Harvey as confirming of many of his own conclusions in both biblical insights and theological implications. I have already referred the readers of this biography to Borg's writings. Let me add a suggestion of two of his other books. One is a 1997 volume he edited entitled *Jesus at 2000* (Westview Press). It contains chapters by many of Harvey's personal acquaintances. In addition to Borg, the authors are John Dominic Crossan, Alan F. Segal, Karen Jo Torjesen, Harvey Cox, and Huston Smith. I refer readers to this volume because it contains scholarly reflections on the very kinds of scholarship Potthoff deeply appreciated. It moves in directions of church-related scholarship for which Harvey yearned and for which he held out much hope for the future. The second book, *Reading the Bible for the First Time*, Borg thinks might be his most important publication.

In the mid- and late 1990s, Harvey shared with me his greatest disappointment. He did not see a resurgence of a neo-liberal theology taking hold as he had hoped for in his lifetime. Borg's work seems to me to be a great step in this direction, and he is not the only person doing so.

Potthoff seemed to have time for the pastoral touch almost endlessly. In the 1950s, he regularly visited Otto Domer, a retired Methodist minister in his nineties who had lost his wife and was no longer able to get out much on his own. During one of the visits, Harvey related to me that he asked Otto, "What do you do with your time that gives your life meaning?" Harvey asked that question of many people, even at times when it might be a bit jarring, if not embarrassing. Otto replied: "Every day I sit down and write a letter or a note to someone I think would like to hear from me." Harvey relished that response.

Potthoff's pastoral touch often involved monetary help. When some Iliff students were arrested in civil rights marches and sit-downs in the South, Harvey sent personal contributions to bail them out of jail or get them back to Denver. He was not the only Iliff faculty member to do so. Such pastoral support was never made a public news item; the only way anyone knew the facts was when a recipient told friends.

Harvey's legacy is that every Christian can be a pastor to persons needing an ear or a helping hand. In fact, his very presence had something of a pastoral touch to it. In the *Rocky Mountain News* obituaries, we find this quote from an interview by Jean Torkelson after Potthoff's death: "You had a sense of being noble when you were around [Potthoff]," said the Rev. Paul Kottke, "He gave you that sense there was something within you that was sacred and had profound meaning."[6]

Self-promotion was not on Harvey's internal screen. When the various elections were being held for the office of bishop in the United Methodist Church, he was several times a favorite son candidate put forward by his colleagues in the Rocky Mountain Conference. His position was not to do anything to harm or help the candidacy. When it appeared the Jurisdictional Conference was hung up on reaching a decision, Harvey withdrew in favor of the candidate in the best position to be elected. He saw such things as the episcopal office as a calling of the Church and not something to be sought. At the same time, he related to me that he would not have declined the election because it was the highest office that the church could offer for anyone's service.

When Iliff needed someone to fill a vacant or new role, Harvey responded to the need, but never, in our discussions, did he seek a role, such as acting president. Harvey was without doubt a very popular guest preacher during his career. He did not seek such roles but made it a point to respond with a yes whenever possible. Those of us fellow clergy, in churches, on campuses, or in other special appointments knew when Harvey said yes, we were lined up for a great event. Being available but not self-promoting is a wonderful heritage, a healthy example to leave for his successors.

Potthoff's skill as a speaker and preacher were equal in importance to his skill as a listener. We often lamented together that for many clergy serving churches today neither skill seems to be of great importance.

Harvey's parting word to colleagues and friends in a great variety of contexts was most often his enthusiastically spoken "Enjoy!" Harvey was a joyful person and wanted others to be open to that important and sacred approach to life, and did what he could to assure some success in passing on the beauty and warmth of relationships. One did not have to agree with any theological orientation to be so encouraged. To me, this may be one of the most important elements in Harvey's amazing popularity. Some good food always helps!

There is no question but that the Potthoff theological thinking was dominant at Iliff during his long tenure on the faculty. That legacy has not been challenged, but there have been attempts to downplay that reality. Even so, Potthoff's was never the only theological position at the school or represented in the curriculum. Potthoff, well beyond any theological orientation, was for most of his Iliff faculty service known as "Mr. Iliff" and treated that reality with reserve and dignity, never with a hint of arrogance. Both the variety of roles he played and his winsome personality did mean that everyone knew and had some experience with Dr. Potthoff! That is still true of the faculty and most of the staff in 2013. His name still rings a bell for a few of the current students with whom I have visited. Most do not really know why.

Given his rather comprehensive roles at Iliff, one might expect little Potthoffs to have come off some sort of theological production line. There is no doubt that some of that took place. However, there were many students and fellow faculty members who did not emerge from the Iliff experience as theological images of Potthoff. Some in fact, for a variety of reasons, were never attracted to his theology or his dominant role in the academy. Some of the input from former students contained in Chapter 13 will verify this. In almost all cases with which I am familiar, even those who did not follow Potthoff theologically experienced his pastoral touch and his great love and concern for Iliff and her students with warmth and often deep appreciation. His legacy is indeed multifaceted. He made a call when our first child, a son, was born. He made a call on death row, and that one lasted eleven years! (See Chapter 12.)

I know from conversations with Potthoff that his remarks upon the establishment of the Potthoff faculty chair can be viewed as a part of what he wanted his legacy to Iliff to be:

> *I believe that if Iliff is to be faithful to its professed mission it must have on its faculty at least one theologian who gives full time to the interpretation and nature of Christian faith (in a world of many faiths)—demonstrating in practice a knowledge of the church and commitment to the church—affirming that the church could and should be a major instrument of religious vision and values in contemporary society.*
>
> *A well-educated minister needs to be prepared to function as a theologian-in-residence.*
>
> *I am grateful for the experience of working with many faculty members who thought of the seminary as "the intellectual center of the church's life."*

Poetry has often been mentioned as one of the arts that best expresses Harvey's thoughts and indeed his passion about life. The single poem he cited with regularity should be read by anyone interested in more of his personhood and his legacy. It is "Character of the Happy Warrior" by William Wordsworth.

Who is the happy Warrior? Who is he
That every man in arms should wish to be?
—It is the generous Spirit, who, when brought
Among the tasks of real life, hath wrought
Upon the plan that pleased his boyish thought:
Whose high endeavours are an inward light
That makes the path before him always bright;
Who, with a natural instinct to discern
What knowledge can perform, is diligent to learn;
Abides by this resolve, and stops not there,
But makes his moral being his prime care;
Who, doomed to go in company with Pain,
And Fear, and Bloodshed, miserable train!
Turns his necessity to glorious gain;
In face of these doth exercise a power
Which is our human nature's highest dower:
Controls them and subdues, transmutes, bereaves
Of their bad influence, and their good receives:
By objects, which might force the soul to abate
Her feeling, rendered more compassionate;
Is placable—because occasions rise
So often that demand such sacrifice;
More skilful in self-knowledge, even more pure,
As tempted more; more able to endure,
As more exposed to suffering and distress;
Thence, also, more alive to tenderness.
—'Tis he whose law is reason; who depends
Upon that law as on the best of friends;
Whence, in a state where men are tempted still
To evil for a guard against worse ill,
And what in quality or act is best

Doth seldom on a right foundation rest,
He labours good on good to fix, and owes
To virtue every triumph that he knows:
—Who, if he rise to station of command,
Rises by open means; and there will stand
On honourable terms, or else retire,
And in himself possess his own desire;
Who comprehends his trust, and to the same
Keeps faithful with a singleness of aim;
And therefore does not stoop, nor lie in wait
For wealth, or honours, or for worldly state;
Whom they must follow; on whose head must fall,
Like showers of manna, if they come at all:
Whose powers shed round him in the common strife,
Or mild concerns of ordinary life,
A constant influence, a peculiar grace;
But who, if he be called upon to face
Some awful moment to which Heaven has joined
Great issues, good or bad for human kind,
Is happy as a Lover; and attired
With sudden brightness, like a Man inspired;
And, through the heat of conflict, keeps the law
In calmness made, and sees what he foresaw;
Or if an unexpected call succeed,
Come when it will, is equal to the need:
—He who, though thus endued as with a sense
And faculty for storm and turbulence,
Is yet a Soul whose master-bias leans
To homefelt pleasures and to gentle scenes;
Sweet images! which, wheresoe'er he be,
Are at his heart; and such fidelity

It is his darling passion to approve;
More brave for this, that he hath much to love:—
'Tis, finally, the Man, who, lifted high,
Conspicuous object in a Nation's eye,
Or left unthought-of in obscurity,—
Who, with a toward or untoward lot,
Prosperous or adverse, to his wish or not—
Plays, in the many games of life, that one
Where what he most doth value must be won:
Whom neither shape or danger can dismay,
Nor thought of tender happiness betray;
Who, not content that former worth stand fast,
Looks forward, persevering to the last,
From well to better, daily self-surpast:
Who, whether praise of him must walk the earth
For ever, and to noble deeds give birth,
Or he must fall, to sleep without his fame,
And leave a dead unprofitable name—
Finds comfort in himself and in his cause;
And, while the mortal mist is gathering, draws
His breath in confidence of Heaven's applause:
This is the happy Warrior; this is he
That every man in arms should wish to be.

Before closing, a quotation from Potthoff written while at NWU. It appeared in the *Quarterly Review*, in an article titled "The Sermon as Theological Event." The quotation is on the understanding of God and the transforming power of the Christian vision. It does not come, he wrote, "by way of legalistic demands or threats." The paragraph is an excellent summary of Potthoff's legacy in thinking about God.

> *We have come to a point in history when it is given to us to know that God is not a God of magic or occasional intervening rewards and punishments, or a God who guarantees that everything is going to come out all right. Rather, God is the integrity which underlies reality, the creative power making for wholeness in nature and in human relations, the luring and transforming power expressed in the creative ideas, beliefs, and ideals calling forth the best in human beings. God is undergirding presence through all life brings, the redemptive power which in love transmutes some of loss and suffering into gain. To know this God, to relate to this God, to seek to organize life and relationships around this God is to know the hope of a new order of things. It is to find inspiration for carrying on.*[7]

It is difficult to pick out one or two points and say that they were the most important parts of his legacy for the church and those who embrace her. Hard work, appreciation, curiosity, and intentionality are key ones that must be put at the top, but any such list is lengthy.

His teaching on aging, dying, and death were popular; he was not sure they would be but they were, even with undergraduate students at NWU. Perhaps his central advocacy in teaching that course was his phrase *diminishment with dignity*. Harvey in his last decades demonstrated very well that he knew how to do that!

Photo from Iliff Archives used with permission

Iliff Hall, north entrance. During most of HHP's career at Iliff, this was the main entrance to his beloved theology academy.

HARVEY H. POTTHOFF

NOTES

[1] Harvey Potthoff, "One Person's Religious/Theological Journey," transcription of Tape 2, pages 4, 5, Iliff Library CST 800. Iliff Archives, box 44, file folder 7.

[2] Nebraska Wesleyan Scrapbook, Iliff Archives, box 41.

[3] Norman Cousins quoted in Potthoff, *God and the Celebration of Life*, 2.

[4] From HHP's "The Theological Assumptions We Bring to Campus Ministry," circa 1980s, pages 7, 8, Iliff Archives, box 6, file folder 9.

[5] Ibid., 15, 16.

[6] *Rocky Mountain News* Obituaries, February 26, 2002.

[7] "The Sermon as Theological Event," *Quarterly Review* 4, no. 2 (1984) 97.

Appendix A
Sermons of Harvey Potthoff

The listings of sermons, speeches, writings, and classes by Harvey Potthoff in this and following Appendixes are available on-line at The Iliff School of Theology web site. The material may be accessed via the following URL: http://archon.iliff.edu/index.php?p=collections/controlcard&id=42

These Appendixes do not list all of the extant Potthoff speaking and writing; much had to remain filed in the archives. Notably absent are the many funeral and memorial services that he conducted. They can be found in the Iliff Archives in box 19, file folder 27.

Date	Title	Location	Box, Folder
10/07/32	Give Me This Stranger!	Not Available - N/A	14, 1
03/12/33	Trails	Epworth Church. Denver, CO	14, 2
04/01/33	The Eternal Jesus— an Easter Sermon	Argo Methodist Church. 44th Ave. and Jason St. Denver, CO	14, 2
04/09/33	Trails	Lafayette M.E. Church	14, 2
04/09/33	The Triumphant Jesus (Palm Sunday)	Argo Methodist Church. Denver, CO.	14, 2
04/16/33	The Eternal Jesus— an Easter Sermon	State Industrial School for Girls. Morrison, CO	14, 2
04/16/33	The Eternal Jesus— an Easter Sermon	Argo Methodist Church. Denver, CO	14, 2
04/23/33	The Runner and the Race	Argo Methodist Church. Denver, CO	14, 2
04/23/33	Trails	Swedish M.E. Denver, CO	14, 2
04/30/33	The Narrow Cover	Argo Methodist Church. Denver, CO	14, 2
05/07/33	At the Foot of the Rainbow	N/A	14, 2
06/06/33	At the Foot of the Rainbow	Iliff	14, 2
06/11/33	Early Seekers	Argo Methodist Church. Denver, CO.	14, 2
06/18/33	Up to Manhood: Four Steps to Character	Argo Methodist Church. Denver, CO	14, 2

Date	Title	Location	Box, Folder
06/25/33	Trails	Argo Methodist Church. Denver, CO	14, 2
07/02/33	A New Declaration of Independence	Argo Methodist Church. Denver, CO	14, 2
07/09/33	Who Is My Neighbor?	N/A	14, 2
07/16/33	When Jesus Prayed	Argo Methodist Church. Denver, CO	14, 2
07/30/33	The Sin of Indifference	Argo Methodist Church. Denver, CO	14, 2
08/13/33	The Rich Young Ruler	Argo Methodist Church. Denver, CO	14, 2
08/16/33	A Century of Progress	Argo Methodist Church. Denver, CO	14, 2
08/20/33	The Quest of the Ages	Argo Methodist Church. Denver, CO	14, 2
08/27/33	Moving Mountains	Argo Methodist Church. Denver, CO	14, 2
09/24/33	The Prodigal Son	Argo Methodist Church. Denver, CO	14, 2
10/01/33	The Fountain of Living Water	Argo Methodist Church. Denver, CO	14, 2
10/08/33	A New Song	Argo Methodist Church. Denver, CO	14, 2
10/22/33	Paul's Letter to Philemon	Argo Methodist Church. Denver, CO	14, 2
11/05/33	What Shall It Profit a Man if He Gain the Whole World and Lose His Own Soul?	Argo Methodist Church. Denver, CO	14, 2
11/12/33	Our Friend, the Enemy	Argo Methodist Church. Denver, CO	14, 2
02/11/34	The Drama of Life	Christ Methodist Church. Denver, CO	14, 3
04/01/34	The Courageous Christ—Holy Week 1934	Berkeley Church. Denver, CO	14, 3
06/10/34	The Christ of Youth	Christ Methodist Church. Denver, CO	14, 3
07/01/34	An Adequate Defense	Christ Methodist Church. Denver, CO	14, 3

APPENDIX A: SERMONS OF HARVEY POTTHOFF

Date	Title	Location	Box, Folder
07/08/34	High and Low Religion	Christ Methodist Church. Denver, CO	14, 3
07/15/34	The Vanishing Sinner	Christ Methodist Church. Denver, CO	14, 3
07/22/34	The Man Within	Christ Methodist Church. Denver, CO	14, 3
07/29/34	Seeing the Unseen	Christ Methodist Church. Denver, CO	14, 3
11/18/34	Mountains and Molehills	Christ Methodist Church. Denver, CO	14, 3
12/02/34	No Room in the Inn	Christ Methodist Church. Denver, CO	14, 3
01/27/35	Communion with God	Christ Methodist Church. Denver, CO	14, 4
03/17/35	Jesus Awoke	Christ Methodist Church. Denver, CO	14, 4
03/20/35	I Believe in the Holy Spirit	Christ Methodist Church. Denver, CO	14, 4
03/24/35	"Where Dwellest Thou?"	Cameron Church. Denver, CO	14, 4
03/31/35	Jesus Was a Teacher	Christ Methodist Church. Denver, CO	14, 4
04/03/35	I Believe in the Bible (Lenten Dinner)	Christ Methodist Church. Denver, CO	14, 4
04/07/35	Why I Believe in God	Trinity Methodist Church College League. Denver, CO	14, 4
04/14/35	The Triumphant Jesus (Palm Sunday)	Christ Methodist Church. Denver, CO	14, 4
04/15/35	A Virile Jesus	Christ Methodist Church. Denver, CO	14, 4
04/18/35	Submission	Christ Methodist Church. Denver, CO	14, 4
04/21/35	The Song of Triumph	Christ Methodist Church. Denver, CO	14, 4
05/05/35	Religion without God	Christ Methodist Church. Denver, CO	14, 4
06/02/35	"Where Dwellest Thou?"	Lakewood Methodist Church. Denver, CO	14, 4

Date	Title	Location	Box, Folder
06/16/35	By Bread Alone	Christ Methodist Church. Denver, CO	14, 4
06/23/35	Windows of the Soul: Religion as a Way of Seeing Things	Christ Methodist Church.Denver, CO	14, 4
08/04/35	A Christian's Creed	Christ Methodist Church. Denver, CO	14, 4
09/01/35	Windows of the Soul: Religion as a Way of Seeing Things	Morgan Methodist Church. Morgan, MN	14, 4
09/15/35	Windows of the Soul: Religion as a Way of Seeing Things	N/A. Sioux Rapids, IA	14, 4
10/22/35	Building a Life	N/A	14, 4
10/29/35	The Quest for Life	Argo Methodist Church Denver, CO	14, 4
01/10/36	Controlling Life from Within	Christ Methodist Church. Denver, CO	14, 5
01/26/36	God in Modern Thought	Young People's Group Cambridge, MA	14, 5
06/08/36	The Perspective of God (First Sermon as Pastor)	Christ Methodist Church. Denver, CO	14, 5
06/12/36	Our Unconscious Influence	Christ Methodist Church. Denver, CO	14, 5
06/14/36	Sermonette	Salem Church. Newport, KY	14, 5
07/19/36	A Religion of One's Own	Christ Methodist Church. Denver, CO	14, 5
07/26/36	Giving Ourselves to the World	Christ Methodist Church. Denver, CO	14, 5
08/02/36	Dealing with Discouragement	Christ Methodist Church. Denver, CO	14, 5
08/09/36	When God Seems Far Away	Christ Methodist Church. Denver, CO	14, 5
08/10/36	Giving Ourselves to the World	Goodwill Industries. Denver, CO	14, 5
08/23/36	Giving Ourselves to the World	Eden Church. MN	14, 5
08/30/36	To God Through Service	Christ Methodist Church. Denver, CO	14, 5
09/06/36	God Is Still at Work! (Labor Day Sunday)	Christ Methodist Church. Denver, CO	14, 5
09/13/36	Our God Goes Marching On!	Christ Methodist Church. Denver, CO	14, 5

APPENDIX A: SERMONS OF HARVEY POTTHOFF

Date	Title	Location	Box, Folder
09/20/36	Being Worthy of One's Tradition	Christ Methodist Church. Denver, CO	14, 5
09/27/36	The Fellowship of Faith	Christ Methodist Church. Denver, CO	14, 5
10/04/36	The Church in Modern Life	Christ Methodist Church. Denver, CO	14, 5
10/11/36	The Faith to Live By	Christ Methodist Church. Denver, CO	14, 5
10/18/36	Climbing on Top of Our Troubles	Christ Methodist Church. Denver, CO	14, 5
10/25/36	Rethinking Prayer	Christ Methodist	14, 5
11/01/36	How Shall We Go About Praying?	Christ Methodist Church. Denver, CO Church. Denver, CO	14, 5
11/15/36	Something to Live For	Christ Methodist Church. Denver, CO	14, 5
11/22/36	The Meaning of Thanksgiving	Christ Methodist Church. Denver, CO	19, 29
11/29/36	Being Religious in Our Own Way	Christ Methodist Church. Denver, CO	14, 5
12/06/36	Rethinking the Bible	Christ Methodist Church. Denver, CO	14, 5
12/27/36	Resolved: To Live!	Christ Methodist Church. Denver, CO	14, 5
12/31/36	New Year's Eve Meditation	Christ Methodist Church. Denver, CO	14, 5
01/03/37	What Are You Standing For? (Communion Meditation)	Christ Methodist Church. Denver, CO	14, 6
01/10/37	Controlling Life from Within	Christ Methodist Church. Denver, CO	14, 6
01/17/37	The Return to Religion	Christ Methodist Church. Denver, CO	14, 6
01/24/37	Why Not Be Good Without Religion?	Christ Methodist Church. Denver, CO	14, 6
01/31/37	Religion in the Home	Christ Methodist Church. Denver, CO	14, 6
02/07/37	What Is Our Duty to God? (National Boy Scout Sunday)	Christ Methodist Church. Denver, CO	14, 6
02/14/37	What Is the Religious Approach to Life?	Christ Methodist Church. Denver, CO	14, 6

Date	Title	Location	Box, Folder
02/14/37	The Creed of a Religious Person	University Park Methodist Church. Denver, CO	14, 6
02/14/37	What Is the Religious Approach to Life?	Christ Methodist Church. Denver, CO	14, 6
02/21/37	What and Where Is God?	Christ Methodist Church. Denver, CO	14, 6
03/07/37	How Can We Cooperate with God?	Christ Methodist Church. Denver, CO	14, 6
03/17/37	Jesus: The Man	Christ Methodist Church. Denver, CO	14, 6
03/21/37	King for a Day (Palm Sunday)	Christ Methodist Church. Denver, CO	14, 6
03/25/37	Gethsemane	Christ Methodist Church. Denver, CO	14, 6
03/26/37	The Meaning of the Cross (Good Friday)	Christ Methodist Church. Denver, CO	14, 6
03/28/37	The Meaning of Easter	Christ Methodist Church. Denver, CO	14, 6
04/04/37	Some Lost Horizons	Christ Methodist Church. Denver, CO	14, 6
04/11/37	Glimpses of God	Christ Methodist Church. Denver, CO	14, 6
04/18/37	A Sensible Way of Life	Christ Methodist Church. Denver, CO	14, 6
04/25/37	Let Religion Set the Stage	Christ Methodist Church. Denver, CO	14, 6
05/09/37	Three Mothers (Mothers' Day)	Christ Methodist Church. Denver, CO	14, 6
05/12/37	Glimpses of God	Epworth Church. Denver, CO	14, 6
05/16/37	When Religion Takes Hold (Pentecost)	Christ Methodist Church. Denver, CO	14, 6
05/23/37	Ways by Which God Speaks to Us	Grant Avenue Church, Geneva Glen	14, 6
05/23/37	Communion Meditation	Christ Methodist. Church. Denver, CO	14, 6
06/06/37	Thoughts on Growing a Soul (Children's Day)	Christ Methodist Church. Denver, CO	14, 6
06/27/37	The Divine Side of Life	Christ Methodist Church. Denver, CO	14, 6
07/04/37	A Declaration of Independence	Christ Methodist Church. Denver, CO	14, 6

APPENDIX A: SERMONS OF HARVEY POTTHOFF

Date	Title	Location	Box, Folder
07/11/37	Growing Up Religiously	Christ Methodist Church. Denver, CO	14, 6
07/18/37	A Great Man in Spite of Himself	Christ Methodist Church. Denver, CO	14, 6
07/25/37	The Disciplines of God	Christ Methodist Church. Denver, CO	14, 6
08/01/37	The Uncommon Commonplace	Christ Methodist Church. Denver, CO	14, 6
08/08/37	Communion Service	Pinecrest Methodist Camp. Palmer Lake, CO	14, 6
08/08/37	The Parable of the Talents	Pinecrest Methodist Camp. Palmer Lake, CO	14, 6
08/15/37	Religion Gives Lift to Life	Christ Methodist Church. Denver, CO	14, 6
08/22/37	Ways in Which God Reveals Himself	Morgan Methodist Church. Morgan, MN	14, 6
08/29/37	A Sensible Way of Life	Morgan Methodist Church. Morgan, MN	14, 6
09/05/37	The Disciplines of God	Morgan Methodist Church. Morgan, MN	14, 6
09/12/37	What Shall We Do with Life?	Christ Methodist Church. Denver, CO	14, 6
09/19/37	The Victory of the Christian Life	Christ Methodist Church. Denver, CO	14, 6
09/26/37	The Conquest of Fear	Christ Methodist Church. Denver, CO	14, 6
10/03/37	The Place of Religion in Life	Christ Methodist Church. Denver, CO	14, 6
10/10/37	God: And Our Times	Christ Methodist Church. Denver, CO	14, 6
10/17/37	The Bible: Then and Now	Christ Methodist Church. Denver, CO	14, 6
10/24/37	Jesus in the Life of Today	Christ Methodist Church. Denver, CO	14, 6
10/31/37	The Church in Modern Life	Christ Methodist Church. Denver, CO	14, 6
11/07/37	Discovering the Spiritual Presence	Christ Methodist Church. Denver, CO	14, 6
11/14/37	Adjusting Our Lives to the Spiritual Presence	Christ Methodist Church. Denver, CO	14, 6
11/21/37	Thoughts on Being Thankful (Thanksgiving)	Christ Methodist Church. Denver, CO	14, 6

Date	Title	Location	Box, Folder
11/28/37	The Ladder of Our Loyalties	Christ Methodist Church. Denver, CO	14, 6
12/05/37	The Career That Enabled Life	Christ Methodist Church. Denver, CO	14, 6
12/12/37	The Message That Magnifies Life	Christ Methodist Church. Denver, CO	14, 6
12/31/37	New Year's Eve Meditation	Christ Methodist Church. Denver, CO	14, 6
01/02/38	The Open Door	Christ Methodist Church. Denver, CO	14, 7
01/09/38	Taking Pride in Our Religion	Christ Methodist Church. Denver, CO	14, 7
01/16/38	Conditions by Which Religion Becomes Vital	Christ Methodist Church. Denver, CO	14, 7
01/23/38	Judging Right from Wrong	Christ Methodist Church. Denver, CO	14, 7
01/30/38	The Transient and the Permanent in Christianity	Christ Methodist Church. Denver, CO	14, 7
02/06/38	"On My Honor—" (Boy Scout Sunday)	Christ Methodist Church. Denver, CO	14, 7
02/20/38	The Art of Appreciation	Christ Methodist Church. Denver, CO	14, 7
02/27/38	Religion and the Quest for Happiness	Christ Methodist Church. Denver, CO	14, 7
03/04/38	World Day of Prayer Observance	Christ Methodist Church. Denver, CO	14, 7
03/13/38	Answering the Call of Life	Christ Methodist Church. Denver, CO	14, 7
03/20/38	The Highway of a Living Faith	Christ Methodist Church. Denver, CO	14, 7
03/27/38	The Highway of Broadened Sympathies	Christ Methodist Church. Denver, CO	14, 7
04/03/38	The Highway of Great Companionships	Christ Methodist Church. Denver, CO	14, 7
04/10/38	The Untried Highway	Christ Methodist Church. Denver, CO	14, 7
04/17/38	The Eternal Highway (Easter Sunday)	Christ Methodist Church. Denver, CO	14, 7
04/24/38	Conditions of Successful Religious Living	Christ Methodist Church. Denver, CO	14, 7
05/01/38	The Simplicity of Vital Religion	Christ Methodist Church. Denver, CO	14, 7

APPENDIX A: SERMONS OF HARVEY POTTHOFF

Date	Title	Location	Box, Folder
05/04/38	Iliff Chapel Talk	Iliff Chapel. Denver, CO	14, 7
05/08/38	Mothers Day Sermon	Christ Methodist Church. Denver, CO	14, 7
05/15/38	The Other Side of Trouble	Christ Methodist Church. Denver, CO	14, 7
05/22/38	The Fellowship of Believers	Christ Methodist Church. Denver, CO	14, 7
05/29/38	This Believing World	Christ Methodist Church. Denver, CO	14, 7
06/05/38	God Is Spirit (Pentecost)	Christ Methodist Church. Denver, CO	14, 7
06/12/38	Facing Some Enemies of Wholesome Living: Fear	Christ Methodist Church. Denver, CO	14, 7
06/19/38	Facing Some Enemies of Wholesome Living: Cynicism	Christ Methodist Church. Denver, CO	14, 7
06/26/38	Facing Some Enemies of Wholesome Living: Unrelieved Hurry	Christ Methodist Church. Denver, CO	14, 7
07/03/38	Facing Some Enemies of Wholesome Living: The Sense of Inferiority	Christ Methodist Church. Denver, CO	14, 7
07/24/38	Help from The Hills	Christ Methodist Church. Denver, CO	14, 7
07/31/38	The Gods in Whom We Trust	Christ Methodist Church. Denver, CO	14, 7
08/07/38	Three Heroes of the Way	Christ Methodist Church. Denver, CO	14, 7
08/14/38	Various Conceptions of the Ideal Christian	Christ Methodist Church. Denver, CO	14, 7
08/28/38	The Paradox of Finding Life	Christ Methodist Church. Denver, CO	14, 7
09/04/38	Tests of Character: Honesty	Christ Methodist Church. Denver, CO	14, 7
09/11/38	Tests of Character: Courage	Christ Methodist Church. Denver, CO	14, 7
09/18/38	Tests of Character: Kindness	Christ Methodist Church. Denver, CO	14, 7
09/25/38	What Does It Mean to Be Religious?	Christ Methodist Church. Denver, CO	14, 7
10/02/38	Fundamental Religious Beliefs: I Believe in God	Christ Methodist Church. Denver, CO	14, 7

Date	Title	Location	Box, Folder
10/09/38	Fundamental Religious Beliefs: I Believe in the Sanctity of Human Life	Christ Methodist Church. Denver, CO	14, 7
10/16/38	Fundamental Religious Beliefs: I Believe in the Church	Christ Methodist Church. Denver, CO	14, 7
10/30/38	What Is Man?	Washington Park Methodist Church. Denver, CO	14, 7
11/06/38	Fundamental Religious Practices: Prayer	Christ Methodist Church. Denver, CO	14, 7
11/13/38	Fundamental Religious Practices: Sharing	Christ Methodist Church. Denver, CO	14, 7
11/20/38	Thanksgiving	Christ Methodist Church. Denver, CO	14, 7
12/04/38	Living in Terms of Our Second Choices	Christ Methodist Church. Denver, CO	14, 7
12/11/38	Some Things That Money Cannot Buy	Christ Methodist Church. Denver, CO	14, 7
01/01/39	Each Day Is Made for Living	Christ Methodist Church. Denver, CO	15, 8
01/08/39	What People Are Looking for in Religion Today	Christ Methodist Church. Denver, CO	15, 8
01/08/39	Putting Our Lives to the Test of God's Approval	Christ Methodist Church. Denver, CO	15, 8
01/15/39	God Is at Work in Our World	Christ Methodist Church. Denver, CO	15, 8
01/22/39	The Unknown Purposes of God	Christ Methodist Church. Denver, CO	15, 8
01/29/39	An Experiment in Finding Freedom	Christ Methodist Church. Denver, CO	15, 8
02/05/39	The Power of Our Influence	Christ Methodist Church. Denver, CO	15, 8
02/19/39	To Own Is to Owe	Christ Methodist Church. Denver, CO	15, 8
02/26/39	Keeping Lent: Coming Face to Face with Ourselves	Christ Methodist Church. Denver, CO	15, 8
03/05/39	Keeping Lent: Thinking Through on Our Temptations	Christ Methodist Church. Denver, CO	15, 8
03/12/39	Keeping Lent: Seeking the Sources of Morale	Christ Methodist Church. Denver, CO	15, 8
03/19/39	Keeping Lent: Thinking Through on Life's Highest Goods	Christ Methodist Church. Denver, CO	15, 8

Date	Title	Location	Box, Folder
03/26/39	Keeping Lent: Rethinking the Significance of Jesus for Our Modern Lives	Christ Methodist Church. Denver, CO	15, 8
04/02/39	The Sources of Courage—Palm Sunday	Christ Methodist Church. Denver, CO	15, 8
04/07/39	Communion Meditation—Good Friday	Christ Methodist Church. Denver, CO	15, 8
04/07/39	It Is Finished	Montview Presbyterian Church. Denver, CO	15, 8
04/09/39	A Faith That Restores Life	Christ Methodist Church. Denver, CO	15, 8
04/16/39	Growing Religiously	Christ Methodist Church. Denver, CO	15, 8
04/20/39	Morning Devotions	KOA Radio. Denver, CO	15, 8
04/23/39	The Power of Encouragement	Christ Methodist Church. Denver, CO	15, 8
04/30/39	The Importance of Right Thinking	Christ Methodist Church. Denver, CO	15, 8
05/02/39	Ambassadors of God	Christ Methodist Church. Denver, CO	15, 8
05/07/39	The Place of Faith in Religious Living	Christ Methodist Church. Denver, CO	15, 8
05/09/39	Marks of Religious Growth	Iliff Chapel. Denver, CO	15, 8
05/11/39	Iliff Chapel Talk: Mark 12:28–39	Iliff Chapel. Denver, CO	15, 8
05/14/39	Talk on Uniting Conference	Christ Methodist Church. Denver, CO	15, 8
05/14/39	Homemade Religion (Mother's Day)	Christ Methodist Church. Denver, CO	15, 8
05/21/39	What Is Religious Conversion?	Christ Methodist Church. Denver, CO	15, 8
06/18/39	Great Personalities in Christian History: Martin Luther	Christ Methodist Church. Denver, CO	15, 8
06/25/39	Great Personalities in Christian History: The Unknown Christian	Christ Methodist Church. Denver, CO	15, 8
07/09/39	Great Works in the Bible Library: The Account of Isaiah's Vision	Christ Methodist Church. Denver, CO	15, 8
07/23/39	Great Works in the Bible Library: Paul's Letters to the Church at Corinth	Christ Methodist Church. Denver, CO	15, 8
07/30/39	Great Works in the Bible Library: The Gospels	Christ Methodist Church. Denver, CO	15, 9

Date	Title	Location	Box, Folder
08/06/39	Living One Day at a Time	Christ Methodist Church. Denver, CO	15, 8
08/27/39	The Nearness of God	Morgan Methodist Church. Morgan, MN	15, 8
09/03/39	We Can Be Creators	Christ Methodist Church. Denver, CO	15, 8
09/10/39	Three Rules for Becoming a Real Person	Christ Methodist Church. Denver, CO	15, 8
09/17/39	Life Is Full of New Beginnings	Christ Methodist Church. Denver, CO	15, 8
09/24/39	Mankind's Persistent Quest for God	Christ Methodist Church. Denver, CO	15, 8
10/01/39	The Kind of God in Whom We Can Believe	Christ Methodist Church. Denver, CO	15, 8
10/01/39	Religion Gives Life New Meanings	Simpson Church. N/A	15, 8
10/08/39	Why Double the Load?	N/A	15, 9
10/22/39	A Formula for Religious Living	N/A	15, 9
10/29/39	Progressing in Our Thought of Prayer	N/A	15, 9
11/05/39	Life Can Be Rich Despite Our Limitations	N/A	15, 9
11/12/39	The Importance of the Church in Days Like These	N/A	15, 9
11/19/39	University of Life	St. John's Cathedral. Denver, CO	15, 9
11/22/39	When Gratitude Is Genuine—Thanksgiving Eve Service	Christ Methodist Church. Denver, CO	15, 9
11/26/39	The Religion of Tomorrow	Christ Methodist Church. Denver, CO	15, 9
11/28/39	Worship	Christ Methodist Church. Denver, CO	15, 9
12/03/39	The Use of Power: A Fundamental Test of Character	Christ Methodist Church. Denver, CO	15, 9
12/10/39	The Need for Optimism in a Pessimistic World	Christ Methodist Church. Denver, CO	15, 9
12/17/39	Communion Meditation	Christ Methodist Church. Denver, CO	15, 9
12/24/39	We Celebrate the Birth of Jesus	Christ Methodist Church. Denver, CO	15, 9
01/02/40	The Passing Years and the Growing Sense of God	Christ Methodist Church. Denver, CO	15, 10

APPENDIX A: SERMONS OF HARVEY POTTHOFF

Date	Title	Location	Box, Folder
01/12/40	Welcoming Life's New Experiences	Christ Methodist Church. Denver, CO	15, 10
01/14/40	Can We Be Realistic and Religious at the Same Time?	Christ Methodist Church. Denver, CO	15, 10
01/21/40	Of What Are You Afraid?	Christ Methodist Church. Denver, CO	15, 10
01/28/40	Applying the Golden Rule	Christ Methodist Church. Denver, CO	15, 10
02/04/40	Ought We Really Turn the Other Cheek?	Christ Methodist Church. Denver, CO	15, 10
02/06/40	Iliff Chapel	N/A	15, 10
02/11/40	The Need of Reverence in Our Modern World	Christ Methodist Church. Denver, CO	15, 10
02/18/40	The Privilege of Religious Freedom	Christ Methodist Church. Denver, CO	15, 10
02/25/40	The Religious Significance of Giving	Christ Methodist Church. Denver, CO	15, 10
03/06/40	How Christian Is Our Christianity? (Lenten Dinner)	Christ Methodist Church. Denver, CO	15, 10
03/17/40	He Went to Jerusalem (Palm Sunday)	Christ Methodist Church. Denver, CO	15, 10
03/19/40	Jesus in Conflict with the Religious Authorities of His Day	Christ Methodist Church. Denver, CO	15, 10
03/22/40	Father Forgive Them for They Know Not What They Do	Sixth Avenue Community Church. Denver, CO	15, 10
03/22/40	It Is Finished	University Park Methodist Church. Denver, CO	15,10
03/22/40	Good Friday Meditation	Christ Methodist Church. Denver, CO	15, 10
03/24/40	The Religious Significance of Easter	Christ Methodist Church. Denver, CO	15, 10
03/31/40	It Makes a Difference What We Do with Life	Christ Methodist Church. Denver, CO	15, 10
04/07/40	The Ever-Present God We Sometimes Fail to See	Christ Methodist Church. Denver, CO	15, 10
04/14/40	Possessing One's Own Soul	Christ Methodist Church. Denver, CO	15, 10
04/21/40	The Problem of Handling Our Virtues	Christ Methodist Church. Denver, CO	15, 10

Date	Title	Location	Box, Folder
04/25/40	Possessing One's Own Soul	Iliff Chapel. Denver, CO	15, 10
04/28/40	Human Nature Being What It Is	Christ Methodist Church. Denver, CO	15, 10
05/12/40	Mother's Day and Pentecost Sermon	Christ Methodist Church. Denver, CO	15, 10
05/26/40	Communion Meditation: Jeremiah	Christ Methodist Church. Denver, CO	15, 10
06/02/40	The Far-Reaching Influence of Our Thoughts	Christ Methodist Church. Denver, CO	15, 10
06/09/40	Types of Security	Christ Methodist Church. Denver, CO	15, 10
06/16/40	What We Have and What We Are	Christ Methodist Church. Denver, CO	15, 10
07/14/40	We Turned Their Thoughts to God	Christ Methodist Church. Denver, CO	15, 10
07/21/40	The Courage to Try Again	Christ Methodist Church. Denver, CO	15, 10
07/28/40	Letting Our Faith Shine Out	Christ Methodist Church. Denver, CO	15, 10
08/04/40	Finding Life	Leadville Methodist Church. Denver, CO	15, 10
8/11/40	Fundamentals for a Modern Religion	Christ Methodist Church. Denver, CO	15, 10
08/18/40	Lay Up Not for Yourselves Treasures...	Christ Methodist Church. Denver, CO	15, 10
08/25/40	A Religion That Makes Us Strong	Christ Methodist Church. Denver, CO	15, 10
09/01/40	If God Really Is at Work	Christ Methodist Church. Denver, CO	15, 10
09/08/40	The Church in a Democratic Society	Christ Methodist Church. Denver, CO	15, 10
09/15/40	Is Religion Really Necessary?	Christ Methodist Church. Denver, CO	15, 10
09/22/40	What Is God Like?	Christ Methodist Church. Denver, CO	15, 10
09/29/40	What Is God Doing?	Christ Methodist Church. Denver, CO	15, 10
10/13/40	Religion Can Help You	Christ Methodist Church. Denver, CO	15, 10
10/13/40	How Can We Get Help from God?	Christ Methodist Church. Denver, CO	15, 10
10/20/40	The Meaning of Repentance	Christ Methodist Church. Denver, CO	15, 10

APPENDIX A: SERMONS OF HARVEY POTTHOFF

Date	Title	Location	Box, Folder
10/27/40	Looking at Life Through the Eyes of Someone Else	Christ Methodist Church. Denver, CO	15, 10
11/10/40	Look Up and Live!	Christ Methodist Church. Denver, CO	15, 10
12/08/40	The Greatest Library in the World	Station KLZ. Denver, CO	15, 10
12/15/40	Preparing for Christmas	Christ Methodist Church. Denver, CO	15, 10
12/31/40	New Year's Eve Meditation	Christ Methodist Church. Denver, CO	15, 11
01/04/41	Communion Meditation	Christ Methodist Church. Denver, CO	15, 11
01/05/41	Statement of FinancialVictory—Christ Church Refinancing Program	Christ Methodist Church. Denver, CO	15, 11
01/11/41	Inner Freedom in a World of Outward Compulsion	Christ Methodist Church. Denver, CO	15, 11
01/26/41	Communion Meditation	Christ Methodist Church. Denver, CO	15, 11
02/16/41	Being Christian in a Time Like This	Christ Methodist hurch. Denver, CO	15, 11
03/02/41	What Is Religious Living?	Christ Methodist Church. Denver, CO	15, 11
03/09/41	Obstacles to Religious Living	Christ Methodist Church. Denver, CO	15, 11
03/16/41	Prayer: The Heart of Personal Religious Living	Christ Methodist Church. Denver, CO	15, 11
03/23/41	Jesus: Guide and Example in Religious Living	Christ Methodist Church. Denver, CO	15, 11
04/06/41	Between Two Journeys to Jerusalem (Palm Sunday)	Christ Methodist Church. Denver, CO	15, 11
04/06/41	Looking at Life Through the Eyes of Someone Else	Trinity Methodist Church. Denver, CO	15, 11
04/09/41	An Interpretation of the Meaning of Easter	KVOD. Denver, CO	15, 11
04/11/41	Good Friday Meditation	Christ Methodist Church. Denver, CO	15, 11
04/11/41	Woman Behold Thy Son	Park Hill Methodist Church. Denver, CO	15, 11
04/20/41	Life's Lost and Found Column	Christ Methodist Church. Denver, CO	15, 11
04/27/41	Diamonds at Your Doorstep	Christ Methodist Church. Denver, CO	15, 11

Date	Title	Location	Box, Folder
05/04/41	Distinguishing Between the Essentials and Non-Essentials in Religion	Christ Methodist Church. Denver, CO	15, 11
05/11/41	A Home in Nazareth (Mother's Day)	Christ Methodist Church. Denver, CO	15, 11
05/25/41	Great Convictions Which Undergird Life	Christ Methodist Church. Denver, CO	15, 11
06/01/41	That Something Which Finally Gets the Best of Us	Christ Methodist Church. Denver, CO	15, 11
06/01/41	Memories Which Hallow Life	Christ Methodist Church. Denver, CO	15, 11
06/08/41	The Lure of the Second Mile	Christ Methodist Church. Denver, CO	16, 13
06/15/41	When Life Seems Overburdened	Christ Methodist Church. Denver, CO	15, 11
07/06/41	Old Truths for a New Day	St. James Methodist Church. Central City, CO	15, 11
08/10/41	The Man Who Came at Night	Christ Methodist Church. Denver, CO	15, 12
08/24/41	Finding God Where You Are	Christ Methodist Church. Denver, CO	15, 12
08/31/41	The Man Who Carried On	Christ Methodist Church. Denver, CO	15, 12
09/07/41	The Ten Commandments	Christ Methodist Church. Denver, CO	15, 12
09/14/41	A Natural Religion	Christ Methodist Church. Denver, CO	15, 12
09/21/41	When Life Puts You on the Defensive	Christ Methodist Church. Denver, CO	15, 12
10/05/41	The Heart of the Sermon on the Mount	Christ Methodist Church. Denver, CO	15, 12
10/12/41	Sin: An Old Word with a Modern Meaning	Christ Methodist Church. Denver, CO	15, 12
10/19/41	Religion and the Feeling of Inferiority	Christ Methodist Church. Denver, CO	15, 12
11/02/41	Religion and a Healthy Mind	Christ Methodist Church. Denver, CO	15, 12
11/09/41	Where Is God in a Warring World?	Christ Methodist Church. Denver, CO	15, 12
11/23/41	Finding Our Way through Changing Circumstances	Christ Methodist Church. Denver, CO	15, 12
12/07/41	Reflections on the 53rd Chapter of the Book of Isaiah	Christ Methodist Church. Denver, CO	15, 12

APPENDIX A: SERMONS OF HARVEY POTTHOFF

Date	Title	Location	Box, Folder
12/21/41	The God of Christmas	Christ Methodist Church. Denver, CO	15, 12
12/28/41	The Church across the Centuries	Christ Methodist Church. Denver, CO	15, 12
01/18/42	An Experiment with Human Nature	Christ Methodist Church. Denver, CO	16, 13
01/25/42	The Story of Man's Enlarging Thought of God	Christ Methodist Church. Denver, CO	16, 13
02/01/42	The Building of a Soul	Christ Methodist Church. Denver, CO	16, 13
02/08/42	Facing Our Fears	Christ Methodist Church. Denver, CO	16, 13
02/15/42	A Sermon on Investments	Christ Methodist Church. Denver, CO	16, 13
02/25/42	Maintaining the Sense of God's Presence and Reality	Iliff Preaching Conference Denver, CO	16, 13
03/01/42	Observing Lent: Coming to Terms with Ourselves	Christ Methodist Church. Denver, CO	16, 13
03/08/42	Observing Lent: Facing Our Self-Centeredness	Christ Methodist Church. Denver, CO	16, 13
03/15/42	Opening Our Lives to God's Transforming Power	Christ Methodist Church. Denver, CO	16, 13
03/29/42	Victories That Lie Within (Palm Sunday)	Christ Methodist Church. Denver, CO	16, 13
03/29/42	Finding the Resources for Triumphant Living	KVOD. Denver, CO	16, 13
04/05/42	Good Friday	Christ Methodist Church. Denver, CO	16, 13
04/05/42	Relating Easter to Life	Christ Methodist Church. Denver, CO	16, 13
04/19/42	The Quest for Certainty in an Uncertain World	Christ Methodist Church. Denver, CO	16, 13
04/26/42	What Is the Peace of God?	Christ Methodist Church. Denver, CO	16, 13
05/24/42	Living Meaningfully within Our Limitations	Christ Methodist Church. Denver, CO	16, 13
05/31/42	The Enduring Influence of a Life	Christ Methodist Church. Denver, CO	16, 13
06/14/42	Keeping Alive the Sense of Wonder	Christ Methodist Church. Denver, CO	16, 13
06/28/42	Inner Standards of Excellence	Christ Methodist Church. Denver, CO	16, 13

Date	Title	Location	Box, Folder
07/05/42	The Lure of the Second Mile	Morgan Methodist Church. Morgan, MN	16, 13
07/19/42	What Is God Like?	Christ Methodist Church. Denver, CO	16, 13
07/26/42	Life Is Today	Christ Methodist Church. Denver, CO	16, 13
08/23/42	What We May Expect from Life	Christ Methodist Church. Denver, CO	16, 13
08/30/42	Words Have Wings	Christ Methodist Church. Denver, CO	16, 13
09/13/42	Religion in Life	Christ Methodist Church. Denver, CO	16, 13
09/20/42	Religious Movements in America: An Analysis and Prophecy	Christ Methodist Church. Denver, CO	16, 13
09/27/42	Worship as a Resource for Living.	Christ Methodist Church. Denver, CO	16, 13
10/04/42	Values We Need to Keep in Days Like This	Christ Methodist Church. Denver, CO	16, 13
10/11/42	God and Order	Christ Methodist Church. Denver, CO	16, 13
11/08/42	Four Antidotes to Fear	Christ Methodist Church. Denver, CO	16, 13
11/15/42	Obedience to the Unenforceable	Christ Methodist Church. Denver, CO	16, 13
11/22/42	The Lifting Power of Gratitude	Christ Methodist Church. Denver, CO	16, 13
11/29/42	Life's Law of Alternation	Christ Methodist Church. Denver, CO	16, 13
12/13/42	The Return to the Real Jesus	Christ Methodist Church. Denver, CO	16, 13
12/20/42	How the Great Guest Comes	Christ Methodist Church. Denver, CO	16, 13
12/27/42	The Measure of a Life	Christ Methodist Church. Denver, CO	16, 13
01/03/43	A Faith with which to Face the Future	Christ Methodist Church. Denver, CO	16, 14
01/10/43	Imagination: A Requirement for Christian Living	Christ Methodist Church. Denver, CO	16, 14
01/17/43	A Meditation on the 24th Psalm	Christ Methodist Church. Denver, CO	16, 14
01/24/43	Mountains and Molehills	Christ Methodist Church. Denver, CO	16, 14

APPENDIX A: SERMONS OF HARVEY POTTHOFF

Date	Title	Location	Box, Folder
01/31/43	The Healing Power of God	Christ Methodist Church. Denver, CO	16, 14
02/07/43	Educating for Religion	Christ Methodist Church. Denver, CO	16, 14
02/14/43	The Peril of Prejudice	Christ Methodist Church. Denver, CO	16, 14
02/28/43	God and Human Suffering	Christ Methodist Church. Denver, CO	16, 14
03/07/43	The Things for Which We Live	Christ Methodist Church. Denver, CO	16, 14
04/04/43	A Living Creed: I Believe in God as a Source of Help	Christ Methodist Church. Denver, CO	16, 14
04/11/43	I Believe in the Living Ministry of Christ	Christ Methodist Church. Denver, CO	16, 14
04/15/43	Good Friday and Easter	Iliff Chapel. Denver, CO	16, 14
04/18/43	A Living Creed: I Believe in the Church (Palm Sunday)	Christ Methodist Church. Denver, CO	16, 14
04/23/43	With His Stripes We Are Healed (Good Friday)	Christ Methodist Church. Denver, CO	16, 14
04/25/43	When Easter Comes True (Easter Service)	Christ Methodist Church. Denver, CO	16, 14
05/16/43	The Meaning of Forgiveness	Christ Methodist Church. Denver, CO	16, 14
06/06/43	"He That Ruleth His Own Spirit"	Christ Methodist Church. Denver, CO	16, 14
06/13/43	The Meaning of Pentecost	Christ Methodist Church. Denver, CO	16, 14
06/27/43	Transforming Evil into Good	Christ Methodist Church. Denver, CO	16, 14
07/04/43	The Second Freedom	Christ Methodist Church. Denver, CO	16, 14
07/11/43	The Anniversary of Emerson's Divinity School Address	Christ Methodist Church. Denver, CO	16, 14
07/25/43	A Living Creed: I Believe in God as a Source of Help	N/A. Paonia, CO	16, 14
07/27/43	Putting God at the Center of Life	Grand Mesa Institute. Grand Mesa, CO	16, 14
07/30/43	Appreciating Our Heritage of Religious Freedom	Grand Mesa Institute. Grand Mesa, CO	16, 14
07/31/43	Being a World Citizen	Grand Mesa Institute. Grand Mesa, CO	16, 14
08/08/43	The Language of Nature	Christ Methodist Church. Denver, CO	16, 14

Date	Title	Location	Box, Folder
08/08/43	Why We Worship and How to Make Our Worship More Meaningful	Christ Methodist Church. Denver, CO	16, 14
09/11/43	Putting God at the Center of Life	Christ Methodist Church. Denver, CO	16, 14
09/19/43	To God through Worship	Christ Methodist Church. Denver, CO	16, 14
09/26/43	Helping to Create a Friendly World	Christ Methodist Church. Denver, CO	16, 14
10/03/43	The Bread and the Cup	Christ Methodist Church. Denver, CO	16, 14
10/17/43	You Can Take It with You	Christ Methodist Church. Denver, CO	16, 14
10/24/43	Gaining a Clearer Sense of Right and Wrong	Christ Methodist Church. Denver, CO	16, 14
10/31/43	Making the Most of the Rest of Life	Christ Methodist Church. Denver, CO	16, 14
11/07/43	That These Sacrifices Shall Not Have Been Made in Vain	Christ Methodist Church. Denver, CO	16, 14
11/14/43	Private Devotions which Enrich Our Lives	Christ Methodist Church. Denver, CO	16, 14
11/21/43	Seeing the Good in These Times	Christ Methodist Church. Denver, CO	16, 14
11/28/43	The Things We Look Back Upon with Satisfaction	Christ Methodist Church. Denver, CO	16, 14
12/19/43	Christmas: An Interlude or an Insight?	Christ Methodist Church. Denver, CO	16, 14
12/26/43	These Truths Endure	Christ Methodist Church. Denver, CO	16, 14
01/23/44	The Quest which Makes Us One	Christ Methodist Church. Denver, CO	16, 15
01/30/44	Churchmen and the Problems of Peace	Christ Methodist Church. Denver, CO	16, 15
02/06/44	Three Authors and their Views of Life	Christ Methodist Church. Denver, CO	16, 15
02/13/44	Judging the Worth of a Person	Christ Methodist Church. Denver, CO	16, 15
02/27/44	Wholesome Attitudes in the Midst of Trying Circumstances	Christ Methodist Church. Denver, CO	16, 15
03/05/44	Placing Ourselves in the Presence of Life's Saving Influences	Christ Methodist Church. Denver, CO	16, 15

Date	Title	Location	Box, Folder
03/19/44	This Above All	Christ Methodist Church. Denver, CO	16, 15
03/26/44	Giving Others a Chance to Be Their Best	Christ Methodist Church. Denver, CO	16, 15
04/02/44	The Highest Loyalty	Christ Methodist Church. Denver, CO	16, 15
04/02/44	Significance of the Lenten Season for Our Own Religious Life	Christ Methodist Church. Denver, CO	16, 15
04/04/44	Jesus as Teacher	Trinity Methodist Church. Denver, CO	16, 15
04/07/44	Good Friday Meditation	Park Hill Methodist Church. Denver, CO	16, 15
04/07/44	Good Friday Meditation	Christ Methodist Church. Denver, CO	16, 15
04/09/44	Easter Means Faith in Life	Christ Methodist Church. Denver, CO	16, 15
04/16/44	Breaking the Grip of Fear	Christ Methodist Church. Denver, CO	16, 15
04/23/44	When Religion is Real	Christ Methodist Church. Denver, CO	16, 15
04/30/44	Life's Law of Compensation	Christ Methodist Church. Denver, CO	16, 15
05/07/44	On Believing in Oneself	Christ Methodist Church. Denver, CO	16, 15
05/14/44	Means and Ends	Christ Methodist Church. Denver, CO	16, 15
05/21/44	On Being Still	Christ Methodist Church. Denver, CO	16, 15
05/22/44	The Immortality We Cannot Escape	Christ Methodist Church. Denver, CO	16, 15
06/04/44	The Glory of God	Christ Methodist Church. Denver, CO	16, 15
06/11/44	Levels of Prayer	Christ Methodist Church. Denver, CO	16, 15
06/25/44	The Language of Nature	Christ Methodist Church. Denver, CO	16, 14
06/25/44	Glorifying the Daily Task	Christ Methodist Church. Denver, CO	16, 15
07/02/44	Qualifying for Freedom	Christ Methodist Church. Denver, CO	16, 15
07/09/44	From Cynicism to a more Realistic Faith	Christ Methodist Church. Denver, CO	16, 15

Date	Title	Location	Box, Folder
07/16/44	The Wisdom of Wanting the Right Things	Christ Methodist Church. Denver, CO	16, 15
07/23/44	A Religion One Can Carry With Him	Christ Methodist Church. Denver, CO	16, 15
08/06/44	Wholesome Attitudes in the Midst of Trying Circumstances	N/A. Paonia, CO	16, 15
08/13/44	Finding New Meaning in Old and Familiar Things	Christ Methodist Church. Denver, CO	16, 15
08/27/44	Philemon	Morgan Methodist Church. Morgan, MN	16, 15
09/10/44	When Something Deep Within Responds to Something Great Beyond	Christ Methodist Church. Denver, CO	16, 15
09/17/44	Marks of Christian Character: Hope	Christ Methodist Church. Denver, CO	16, 15
09/24/44	Marks of Christian Character: Integrity	Christ Methodist Church. Denver, CO	16, 15
10/01/44	Marks of Christian Character: A Recognition of Need	Christ Methodist Church. Denver, CO	16, 15
10/08/44	Marks of Christian Character: Courage	Christ Methodist Church. Denver, CO	16, 15
10/22/44	On Growing Older	Christ Methodist Church. Denver, CO	16, 15
11/05/44	As We Remember a Peace which Did Not Last	Christ Methodist Church. Denver, CO	16, 15
11/12/44	The Courage to Carry On	Christ Methodist Church. Denver, CO	16, 15
11/19/44	Through Difficulty to Gratitude (Thanksgiving)	Christ Methodist Church. Denver, CO	16, 15
12/02/44	Achieve a Meaningful Life Out of the Raw Materials	Highlands Methodist Church. Ft. Thomas, KY	16, 15
12/03/44	Toward Serenity of Spirit	Christ Methodist Church. Denver, CO	16, 15
12/10/44	Seeing Advantage in Disadvantage	Christ Methodist Church. Denver, CO	16, 15
12/17/44	The Place of Ideals in Life	Christ Methodist Church. Denver, CO	16, 15
12/31/44	In All Generations	Christ Methodist Church. Denver, CO	16, 15
01/06/45	Follow Thou Me	Christ Methodist Church. Denver, CO	17, 16
01/07/45	When We Miss the Mark	Christ Methodist Church. Denver, CO	17, 16

Date	Title	Location	Box, Folder
01/13/45	Relating Our Lives to the Enduring	Christ Methodist Church. Denver, CO	17, 16
02/04/45	Making Our Habits Our Allies	Christ Methodist Church. Denver, CO	17, 16
02/18/45	A Living Church in a Growing World	Christ Methodist Church. Denver, CO	17, 16
03/04/45	The Silences of Life	Christ Methodist Church. Denver, CO	17, 16
03/18/45	When Life Becomes Divine in Quality	Christ Methodist Church. Denver, CO	17, 16
03/25/45	The Balance of Praise and Practice	Christ Methodist Church. Denver, CO	17, 16
03/30/45	Towering O'er the Wrecks of Time	Christ Methodist Church. Denver, CO	17, 16
04/01/45	When Sacrifice is Crowned with Meaning	Christ Methodist Church. Denver, CO	17, 16
04/15/45	When Limitations Release the Best	Christ Methodist Church. Denver, CO	17, 16
04/22/45	The Heart of Prayer	Christ Methodist Church. Denver, CO	17, 16
04/29/45	The Larger Victory	Christ Methodist Church. Denver, CO	17, 16
05/13/45	A Prayer for Breadth of Vision (End of WWII in Europe)	Christ Methodist Church. Denver, CO	17, 16
06/03/45	God is in Our Midst (Children's Day)	Christ Methodist Church. Denver, CO	17, 16
06/10/45	Something to Fall Back On	Christ Methodist Church. Denver, CO	17, 16
07/01/45	Religion and Mankind's Agelong Quest for Freedom	Christ Methodist Church. Denver, CO	17, 16
07/08/45	On Knowing What the Future Holds	Christ Methodist Church. Denver, CO	17, 16
07/29/45	On Knowing What the Future Holds	N/A. Grand Junction, CO	17, 16
08/12/45	Enriching Our Relationship with God	Christ Methodist Church. Denver, CO	17, 16
08/19/45	Still Stands Thine Ancient Sacrifice (Japan Surrenders)	Christ Methodist Church. Denver, CO	17, 16
09/09/45	Religion and the Inquiring Mind	Christ Methodist Church. Denver, CO	17, 16
09/16/45	Religion and the Humane Spirit	Christ Methodist Church. Denver, CO	17, 16

Date	Title	Location	Box, Folder
09/30/45	Religion and the Finding of God	Christ Methodist Church. Denver, CO	17, 16
10/07/45	The Table, the Bread, and the Cup	Christ Methodist Church. Denver, CO	17, 16
10/14/45	The Human Side of Reconversion	Christ Methodist Church. Denver, CO	17, 16
10/21/45	The Self-Respect Religion Brings	Christ Methodist Church. Denver, CO	17, 16
10/28/45	Our Protestant Heritage	Christ Methodist Church. Denver, CO	17, 16
11/11/45	Keeping a Balance Between the Actual and the Ideal	Christ Methodist Church. Denver, CO	17, 16
11/18/45	The Gift of Gratitude	Christ Methodist Church. Denver, CO	17, 16
12/02/45	The Ethical Emphasis in the Ministry of Jesus	Christ Methodist Church. Denver, CO	17, 16
12/09/45	The Emphasis on God in the Ministry of Jesus	Christ Methodist Church. Denver, CO	17, 16
12/16/45	The Emphasis on a New Day in the Ministry of Jesus	Christ Methodist Church. Denver, CO	17, 16
12/23/45	What Do You Find in Christmas?	Christ Methodist Church. Denver, CO	17, 16
01/05/46	The Enduring Values of Life	Christ Methodist Church. Denver, CO	17, 17
01/20/46	Forgiving and Being Forgiven	Christ Methodist Church. Denver, CO	17, 17
01/27/46	Using What Comes	Christ Methodist Church. Denver, CO	17, 17
02/03/46	A Religious Heritage	Christ Methodist Church. Denver, CO	17, 17
02/10/46	Seeking Grounds of Understanding	Christ Methodist Church. Denver, CO	17, 17
02/21/46	No title - Quotes Wordsworth Poem	Iliff Chapel. Denver, CO	17, 17
02/24/46	When Our Plans Are Interrupted	Christ Methodist Church. Denver, CO	17, 17
03/03/46	He Went Apart	Christ Methodist Church. Denver, CO	17, 17
03/10/46	He Considered His Purposes	Christ Methodist Church. Denver, CO	17, 17
03/17/46	He Disciplined Himself	Christ Methodist Church. Denver, CO	17, 17

APPENDIX A: SERMONS OF HARVEY POTTHOFF

Date	Title	Location	Box, Folder
03/24/46	He Cared	Christ Methodist Church. Denver, CO	17, 17
03/31/46	He Found Strength in God	Christ Methodist Church. Denver, CO	17, 17
04/14/46	Palm Sunday and Holy Week	KVOD. Denver, CO	17, 17
04/19/46	The Meaning of the Cross (Good Friday)	Christ Methodist Church. Denver, CO	17, 17
04/21/46	Easter: Christian Festival of Hope	Christ Methodist Church. Denver, CO	17, 17
05/26/46	Winning the Wars Within Oneself	Christ Methodist Church. Denver, CO	17, 17
06/16/46	What it Means to Believe in God	Christ Methodist Church. Denver, CO	17, 17
07/07/46	The Right To Be Free	Christ Methodist Church. Denver, CO	17, 17
07/28/46	The Seeming Indifference of God	Christ Methodist Church. Denver, CO	17, 17
08/11/46	The Christian Quality of Life	Christ Methodist Church. Denver, CO	17, 17
09/01/46	The Christian Quality of Life	Morgan Methodist Church. Morgan, MN	17, 17
09/01/46	Finding God in the World around Us	Morgan Methodist Church. Morgan, MN	17, 17
09/08/46	Our Inescapable Need for God	Christ Methodist Church. Denver, CO	17, 17
09/15/46	A Reasonable Belief in God	Christ Methodist Church. Denver, CO	17, 17
09/22/46	God and Our Daily Living	Christ Methodist Church. Denver, CO	17, 17
10/06/46	The Journey of Life	Christ Methodist Church. Denver, CO	17, 17
10/13/46	Stewardship as a Way of Life	Christ Methodist Church. Denver, CO	17, 17
11/10/46	What is Happening to Our Moral Standards?	Christ Methodist Church. Denver, CO	17, 17
11/28/46	Thanksgiving	Christ Methodist Church. Denver, CO	17, 17
12/29/46	Our Tradition and Our Trust	Christ Methodist Church. Denver, CO8	19, 2
02/02/47	Religion is Caught and Taught	Christ Methodist Church. Denver, CO	17, 18
03/02/47	Forgiveness—One of Life's Profoundest Facts	Christ Methodist Church. Denver, CO	17, 18

Date	Title	Location	Box, Folder
04/04/47	The Cross and the Christian's Concern (Good Friday)	Christ Methodist Church. Denver, CO	17, 18
04/06/47	This Is Our Father's World (Easter)	Christ Methodist Church. Denver, CO	17, 18
04/20/47	Living in Harmony with the Time Process	Christ Methodist Church. Denver, CO	17, 18
04/27/47	The Preventive Work of Religion	Christ Methodist Church. Denver, CO	17, 18
05/04/47	The Outreach of a Life	Christ Methodist Church. Denver, CO	17, 18
06/01/47	Let Your Light Shine	Christ Methodist Church. Denver, CO	17, 18
06/08/47	When Patience is a Virtue	Christ Methodist Church. Denver, CO	17, 18
06/29/47	Keeping Alive the Spirit of Expectancy	Christ Methodist Church. Denver, CO	17, 18
09/07/47	The Difference God Makes	Christ Methodist Church. Denver, CO	17, 18
09/14/47	The Farness and Nearness of God	Christ Methodist Church. Denver, CO	17, 18
09/21/47	Maintaining Assurance of God	Christ Methodist Church. Denver, CO	17, 18
09/28/47	Placing Our Lives in the Hands of a Higher Power	Christ Methodist Church. Denver, CO	17, 18
10/05/47	Religion and Human Relationships	Christ Methodist Church. Denver, CO	17, 18
10/12/47	Is the Christian Teaching of Goodwill Practical?	Christ Methodist Church. Denver, CO	17, 18
10/19/47	The Forward Looking Church	Christ Methodist Church. Denver, CO	17, 18
10/26/47	The Search for Self-Confidence	Christ Methodist Church. Denver, CO	17, 18
11/02/47	The Search for Significance	Christ Methodist Church. Denver, CO	17, 18
11/09/47	The Search for Maturity	Christ Methodist Church. Denver, CO	17, 18
11/23/47	Our Seen and Unseen Blessings	Christ Methodist Church. Denver, CO	17, 18
12/07/47	Our Inner Preparation for Christmas	Christ Methodist Church. Denver, CO	17, 18
12/14/47	Enduring Elements in the Message of Jesus	Christ Methodist Church. Denver, CO	17, 18

APPENDIX A: SERMONS OF HARVEY POTTHOFF

Date	Title	Location	Box, Folder
12/28/47	The Harvest of the Years	Christ Methodist Church. Denver, CO	17, 18
01/04/48	At the Beginning of a New Year	Christ Methodist Church. Denver, CO	17, 19
01/18/48	The Bible in the Life of Today	Christ Methodist Church. Denver, CO	17, 19
01/25/48	The Justice and Mercy of God	Christ Methodist Church. Denver, CO	17, 19
02/01/48	These are Days for Significant Living	Christ Methodist Church. Denver, CO	17, 19
02/08/48	When Fear is Matched with Faith	Christ Methodist Church. Denver, CO	17, 19
02/15/48	When Lent Really Ministers to Our Spiritual Need	Christ Methodist Church. Denver, CO	17, 19
02/22/48	On Being Followers of Christ	Christ Methodist Church. Denver, CO	17, 19
02/29/48	The Human Side of Christianity	Christ Methodist Church. Denver, CO	17, 19
03/07/48	When Obstacles are Turned to Opportunities	Christ Methodist Church. Denver, CO	17, 19
03/14/48	The Satisfying Life	Christ Methodist Church. Denver, CO	17, 19
03/26/48	Where the Cross Touches Life (Good Friday)	Christ Methodist Church. Denver, CO	17, 19
04/04/48	Religion for Ordinary Days	Christ Methodist Church. Denver, CO	17, 19
04/11/48	Seeking and Finding	Christ Methodist Church. Denver, CO	17, 19
04/25/48	Foundations for a Stable Life	Christ Methodist Church. Denver, CO	17, 19
05/16/48	Life's Finer Hours	Christ Methodist Church. Denver, CO	17, 19
05/23/48	The Inexhaustible Resources of God	Christ Methodist Church. Denver, CO	17, 19
05/30/48	The Building of Fine Memories	Christ Methodist Church. Denver, CO	17, 19
06/06/48	The Three R's of	Christ Methodist Church. Denver, CO	17, 19
06/20/48	Taking Thought for the Morrow	Christ Methodist Church. Denver, CO	17, 19
06/27/48	How are the Righteous Rewarded?	Christ Methodist Church. Denver, CO	17, 19

Date	Title	Location	Box, Folder
07/25/48	Even There Shall Thy Hand Lead Me	Christ Methodist Church. Denver, CO	17, 19
08/01/48	The Reality of Spiritual Laws	KFEL FM. Denver, CO	17, 19
08/08/48	The God of Creation and Re-Creation	Christ Methodist Church. Denver, CO	17, 19
08/26/48	The Church in Our Lives	Christ Methodist Church. Denver, CO	17, 19
10/10/48	Life Demands a Living Faith	Christ Methodist Church. Denver, CO	17, 19
10/17/48	God is the Supreme Fact	Christ Methodist Church. Denver, CO	17, 19
10/24/48	God is At Work in Our World	Christ Methodist Church. Denver, CO	17, 19
10/31/48	Your Life is Important	Christ Methodist Church. Denver, CO	17, 19
11/07/48	We Can Build on Human Nature	Christ Methodist Church. Denver, CO	17, 19
11/21/48	The Christian Approach to Life's Blessings	Christ Methodist Church. Denver, CO	17, 19
12/05/48	Love is the Great Redeeming Power	Christ Methodist Church. Denver, CO	17, 19
12/12/48	The Ministry of Christ to the Sorrowing	Christ Methodist Church. Denver, CO	17, 19
12/26/48	Translating the Vision into Life	Christ Methodist Church. Denver, CO	17, 19
01/09/49	Christian Attitudes in the Midst of Shifting Moral Standards	Christ Methodist Church. Denver, CO	17, 20
01/23/49	What Religion Adds to Ethics	Christ Methodist Church. Denver, CO	17, 20
01/30/49	Can We Be Realistic and Optimistic at the Same Time?	Christ Methodist Church. Denver, CO	17, 20
02/06/49	A Religious Approach to Our Handicaps	Christ Methodist Church. Denver, CO	17, 20
02/13/49	A New Birth of Freedom	Christ Methodist Church. Denver, CO	17, 20
02/27/49	Catching the Goodness in Each Day	Christ Methodist Church. Denver, CO	17, 20
03/13/49	The Way of Self-Searching	Christ Methodist Church. Denver, CO	17, 20
03/20/49	The Way of New Beginnings	Christ Methodist Church. Denver, CO	17, 20

Date	Title	Location	Box, Folder
03/27/49	The Way of Appreciation	Christ Methodist Church. Denver, CO	17, 20
04/03/49	The Way of Communion with God	Christ Methodist Church. Denver, CO	17, 20
04/15/49	The Way of a Cross	Christ Methodist Church. Denver, CO	17, 20
05/22/49	Religion and the Art of Growing Older Gracefully	Christ Methodist Church. Denver, CO	17, 20
05/29/49	Finding the Help Religion has to Offer	Christ Methodist Church. Denver, CO	17, 20
06/05/49	Religion and Personal Integrity	Christ Methodist Church. Denver, CO	17, 20
06/19/49	Appealing to the Best in Others	Christ Methodist Church. Denver, CO	17, 20
09/04/49	Seeing Our Work Through the Eyes of Religion	Christ Methodist Church. Denver, CO	17, 20
09/11/49	Can We Find a Pattern for Living?	Christ Methodist Church. Denver, CO	17, 20
09/18/49	A Religion of Encouragement	Christ Methodist Church. Denver, CO	17, 20
09/25/49	Religious Resources for Dealing with Fear	Christ Methodist Church. Denver, CO	17, 20
10/02/49	Togetherness in Christ	Christ Methodist Church. Denver, CO	17, 20
10/09/49	Releasing the Religious Impulse	Christ Methodist Church. Denver, CO	17, 20
10/18/49	How Can Religion Contribute to Better Personal Living?	Wheat Ridge Methodist Church. Wheat Ridge, CO	17, 20
10/23/49	Keeping Faith Through the Dark Hours	Christ Methodist Church. Denver, CO	17, 20
11/13/49	Religion and the Tensions of Life	Christ Methodist Church. Denver, CO	17, 20
11/20/49	Thanksgiving Means Reinvestment	Christ Methodist Church. Denver, CO	17, 20
11/27/49	The Place of Faith in Creative Living	Christ Methodist Church. Denver, CO	17, 20
12/04/49	How Realistic is the Christian Doctrine of Loving Our Fellow Men?	Christ Methodist Church. Denver, CO	17, 20
01/01/50	The Treasures of Our Years	Christ Methodist Church. Denver, CO	18, 21

Date	Title	Location	Box, Folder
01/15/50	A Living Bible	Christ Methodist Church. Denver, CO	18, 21
01/22/50	The Bible and Our Growing Understanding of Life	Christ Methodist Church. Denver, CO	18, 21
01/29/50	The Life of God in the Soul of Man	Christ Methodist Church. Denver, CO	18, 21
02/05/50	The Law and the Spirit	Christ Methodist Church. Denver, CO	18, 21
02/12/50	The Spiritual Basis of Democracy	Christ Methodist Church. Denver, CO	18, 21
03/05/50	Major Themes of the Religious Life: Praise	Christ Methodist Church. Denver, CO	18, 21
03/12/50	Major Themes of the Religious Life: Confession	Christ Methodist Church. Denver, CO	18, 21
03/19/50	Great Themes of the Religious Life: Reassurance	Christ Methodist Church. Denver, CO	18, 21
03/26/50	Great Themes of the Religious Life: Dedication	Christ Methodist Church. Denver, CO	18, 21
04/02/50	Standing in the Presence of Greatness (Palm Sunday)	Christ Methodist Church. Denver, CO	18,21
04/05/50	Wednesday of Holy Week	Christ Methodist Church. Denver, CO	18, 21
04/07/50	His Cross and Ours (Good Friday)	Christ Methodist Church. Denver, CO	18, 21
04/07/50	Father Into Thy Hands I Commend My Spirit	City Park Baptist Church. Denver, CO	18, 21
05/14/50	The Touch of Life on Life (Mothers Day)	Christ Methodist Church. Denver, CO	18, 21
05/21/50	Living Within Limitations	Christ Methodist Church. Denver, CO	18, 21
06/11/50	Some Unseen Realities	Christ Methodist Church. Denver, CO	18, 21
06/18/50	The Naturalness of Prayer	Christ Methodist Church. Denver, CO	18, 21
06/25/50	The Satisfactions of the Christian Life	Christ Methodist Church. Denver, CO	18, 21
07/09/50	The Elder Brother	Christ Methodist Church. Denver, CO	18, 21
07/30/50	The Kingdom, the Power, and the Glory	Christ Methodist Church. Denver, CO	18, 21
09/10/50	The Salvation We All Are Seeking	Christ Methodist Church. Denver, CO	18, 21

APPENDIX A: SERMONS OF HARVEY POTTHOFF

Date	Title	Location	Box, Folder
09/24/50	Finding Help Through Our Religion	Christ Methodist Church. Denver, CO	18, 21
10/15/50	Religion and Happiness	Christ Methodist Church. Denver, CO	18, 21
10/22/50	Signs of Hope	Christ Methodist Church. Denver, CO	18, 21
10/29/50	Releasing the Power of Protestantism	Christ Methodist Church. Denver, CO	18, 21
11/05/50	Christian Citizenship	Christ Methodist Church. Denver, CO	18, 21
11/19/50	The Highest Gratitude	Christ Methodist Church. Denver, CO	18, 21
12/17/50	The Recovery of Confidence in Ourselves	Christ Methodist Church. Denver, CO	18, 21
12/31/50	The God of Our Passing Years	Christ Methodist Church. Denver, CO	18, 21
01/28/51	Life is a Journey over a Winding Road	Christ Methodist Church. Denver, CO	18, 22
04/08/51	Staying on in Ephesus	Christ Methodist Church. Denver, CO	18, 22
05/13/51	Influences Which Live (Mothers Day)	Christ Methodist Church. Denver, CO	18, 22
06/17/51	How Prayer Helps	Christ Methodist Church. Denver, CO	18, 22
06/24/51	The Wisdom of the Long View	Christ Methodist Church. Denver, CO	18, 22
07/29/51	What is Happening to the Art of Reflection?	Christ Methodist Church. Denver, CO	18, 22
09/25/51	How Prayer Helps	Laramie Methodist Church. Laramie, WY	18, 22
01/20/52	Making Prayer a Part of Life	Christ Methodist Church. Denver, CO	18, 22
02/24/52	The Glory of Each Day Well Lived	Christ Methodist Church. Denver, CO	18, 22
03/23/52	Grief's Slow Wisdom	Christ Methodist Church. Denver, CO	18, 22
03/30/52	Finding Joy in Living	Christ Methodist Church. Denver, CO	18, 22
05/31/53	The Immortality We Cannot Escape	Warren Memorial Church. Denver, CO	16, 15
08/30/53	Life is a Journey over a Winding Road	Carbondale Methodist Church. Carbondale, CO	18, 22

Date	Title	Location	Box, Folder
08/30/53	Life is a Journey over a Winding Road	Glenwood Springs Methodist Church. Glenwood Springs, CO	18, 22
09/06/53	Life is a Journey over a Winding Road	Highlands Methodist Church. Denver, CO	18, 22
02/21/54	The Glory of Each Day Well Lived	Girls Industrial School. Denver, CO	18, 22
08/08/54	Life is a Journey over a Winding Road	Emmanuel Methodist Church. Denver, CO	18, 22
08/29/54	God and the Meaning of Life	Englewood Methodist Church. Englewood, CO	18, 22
09/23/54	No title - Quotes Wordsworth Poem	Iliff Chapel. Denver, CO. University	17, 17
11/14/54	Life is a Journey over a Winding Road	Park. Methodist Church. Denver, CO	18, 22
02/21/55	How Prayer Helps	Ft. Warren. Casper, WY	18, 22
06/05/55	Life is a Journey over a Winding Road	Cheyenne Methodist Church. Cheyenne, WY	18, 22
06/26/55	Life is a Journey over a Winding Road	Boulder Methodist Church. Boulder, CO	18, 22
08/07/55	A Religion of the Spirit	Washington Park Community Church. Casper, WY	18, 22
11/06/55	Life is a Journey over a Winding Road	Longmont Congregational Church. Longmont, CO	18, 22
11/27/55	The Good Samaritan	Longmont Congregational Church. Longmont, CO	18, 22
12/11/55	The Glory of Each Day Well Lived	Longmont Congregational Church. Longmont, CO	18, 22
03/08/56	How Prayer Helps	D.U.M.S.M. Denver, CO	18, 22
03/26/56	The Glory of Each Day Well Lived	Delta Methodist Church. Delta, CO	18, 22
05/19/56	The Harvest of Our Years	Troy Conference. N/A	18, 22
05/27/56	The Harvest of Our Years	Sixth Avenue Community Church. Denver, CO	18, 22
06/17/56	The Harvest of Our Years	University Park Methodist Church. Denver, CO	18, 22
07/22/56	The Immortality We Cannot Escape	Sixth Avenue Congregational Church. Denver, CO	18, 22

APPENDIX A: SERMONS OF HARVEY POTTHOFF

Date	Title	Location	Box, Folder
08/12/56	The Harvest of Our Years	Laramie Methodist Church. Laramie, WY	18, 22
08/19/56	The Immortality We Cannot Escape	Asbury Methodist Church. Denver, CO	18, 22
10/07/56	The Set of the Soul	Mental Science Church. N/A	18, 22
10/09/56	The Reverence of Laughter	Iliff Chapel. Denver, CO	18, 22
10/14/56	The Experience of Growing Older	Mental Science Group. Denver, CO	18, 22
11/28/56	Religion and Mental Health	D.U. Chapel. Denver, CO	18, 22
11/29/56	Thoughts on Prayer	Taylor Hall. Denver, CO	18, 22
12/30/56	The Harvest of Our Years	Boulder Methodist Church. Boulder, CO	18, 22
01/13/57	The Set of the Soul	Mesita Methodist Church. Mesita, CO	18, 22
02/03/57	The Set of the Soul	East Methodist Church. Colorado Springs, CO	18, 22
02/17/57	The Set of the Soul	Haxtun Methodist Church. Haxtun, CO	18, 22
02/18/57	The Experience of Growing Older	Haxtun Methodist Church. Haxtun, CO	18, 22
04/01/57	The Minister Looks at his own Spiritual Life	Denver Ministerial Alliance. Denver, CO	18, 22
04/07/57	The Set of the Soul	Eagle and Gypsum Camber. Eagle, CO	18, 22
07/07/57	The Reverence of Laughter	First Congregational Church. Colorado Springs, CO	18, 22
07/14/57	The Reverence of Laughter	Warren Memorial Church. Denver, CO	18, 22
07/28/57	The Reverence of Laughter	Washington Park Community Church. Denver, CO	18, 22
10/13/57	The Set of the Soul	Black Forest Congregational Church. Black Forest, CO	18, 22
01/26/58	The Reverence of Laughter	Longmont Congregational Church. Longmont, CO	18, 22
02/09/58	The Reverence of Laughter	University Park Methodist Church. Denver, CO	18, 22
03/05/58	Faith and Humor	D.U. Chapel. Denver, CO	18, 22

Date	Title	Location	Box, Folder
03/23/58	Your Own Experience of God (Finding God Where We Are)	Limon Methodist Church. Limon, CO	18, 22
04/27/58	Your Own Experience of God (Finding God Where We Are)	Mountain View Methodist Church. Boulder, CO	18, 22
05/18/58	Your Own Experience of God (Finding God Where We Are)	Berkeley Methodist Church. Denver, CO	18, 22
06/19/58	The Other Side of Aldersgate	Iliff Chapel. Denver, CO	18, 22
07/13/58	What Does the Past Have to Say?	St. James Methodist Church. Central City, CO	19, 28
08/10/58	Life's Sacramental Experiences	First Congregational Church. Colorado Springs, CO	18, 22
11/12/58	What is The Meaning of Life?	McMurry College. Abilene, TX	18, 22
02/15/59	The Set of the Soul	Westminster Methodist Church. Westminster, CO	18, 22
03/13/59	The Power of Personal Influence	Beth-El Synagogue. Colorado Springs, CO	18, 22
03/23/59	The Set of the Soul	Thornton Methodist Church. Thornton, CO	18, 22
04/05/59	What Does the Past Have to Say?	Brentwood Methodist Church. Denver, CO	19, 28
04/11/59	What Does the Past Have to Say?	Park Hill Methodist Church. Denver, CO	19, 28
04/12/59	What Does the Past Have to Say?	Florence Methodist Church. Florence, CO	19, 28
05/03/59	What Does the Past Have to Say?	Sub-District Youth Rally. Ft. Lupton, CO	19, 28
05/31/59	What Does the Past Have to Say?	St. Paul Methodist Church. Denver, CO	19, 28
06/09/59	The Good Samaritan	N/A. Central City, CO	18, 22
06/21/59	What Does the Past Have to Say?	Akron Methodist Church. Akron, CO	19, 28
07/12/59	What Does the Past Have to Say?	Westcliffe Methodist Church. Westcliffe, CO	19, 28
07/14/59	Sanctity in Existence	Iliff Chapel. Denver, CO	18, 22
07/19/59	The Set of the Soul	First Methodist Church. Cheyenne, WY	18, 22
07/26/59	The Experience of Growing Older	Wheat Ridge Congregational Church. Wheat Ridge, CO	18, 22

APPENDIX A: SERMONS OF HARVEY POTTHOFF

Date	Title	Location	Box, Folder
08/02/59	The Experience of Growing Older	Highlands Methodist Church. Denver, CO	18, 22
10/25/59	The Healing Power of God	Christ Methodist Church. Denver, CO	18, 22
11/11/59	What is The Meaning of Life?	Ohio Northern. Ohio	18, 22
01/24/60	What is The Meaning of Life?	Trinity Methodist Church. Denver, CO	18, 22
02/14/60	What is The Meaning of Life?	Windsor Methodist Church. Windsor, CO	18, 22
03/27/60	What is The Meaning of Life?	Wesley Memorial Methodist Church. Boulder, CO	18, 22
07/10/60	Discovering Who We Are (Based on "Who Am I?")	Central City Homecoming. Central City, CO	18, 23
07/31/60	Discovering Who We Are (Based on "Who Am I?")	COP. Stockton, CA	18, 23
10/30/60	Discovering Who We Are (Based on "Who Am I?")	St. Paul Methodist Church. Omaha, NE	18, 23
01/12/61	Discovering Who We Are (Based on "Who Am I?")	Dakota Wesleyan. N/A	18, 23
02/12/61	Discovering Who We Are (Based on "Who Am I?")	N/A. Steamboat Springs, CO	18, 23
02/19/61	Thoughts on Prayer	Englewood Methodist Church. Englewood, CO	18, 22
03/12/61	Discovering Who We Are (Based on "Who Am I?")	Methodist Church. Moscow, ID	18, 23
04/23/61	Discovering Who We Are (Based on "Who Am I?")	First Church. Boulder, CO	18, 23
06/25/61	Discovering Who We Are (Based on "Who Am I?")	Rockwood Methodist Church. Portland, OR	18, 23
07/07/63	Each Day is a Life in Miniature	Central City Church. Central City, CO	18, 23
07/05/64	Finding God in Unlikely Places	University Park Methodist Church. Denver, CO	18, 23
10/01/64	Treasure in Earthen Vessels	Iliff Chapel. Denver, CO	18, 23
10/05/64	Religion and Mental Health	Liberal Kansas Lions Club. Liberal, KS	18, 22
02/07/65	Faith in a Space Age	Denver Council of Churches. Denver, CO	18, 23

Date	Title	Location	Box, Folder
02/21/65	Life as Summons and Commitment	Christ Methodist Church. Denver, CO	18, 23
03/02/65	Faith in a Space Age	Kansas Wesleyan Chapel. Salina, KS	18, 23
03/14/65	Faith in a Space Age	Broomfield Methodist Church. Broomfield, CO	18, 23
04/07/65	Faith in a Space Age	Lakewood Methodist Church. Lakewood, CO	18, 23
04/11/65	Faith in a Space Age	N/A. Aberdeen, SD	18, 23
04/25/65	Life as Summons and Commitment	Mountain View Methodist Church. Boulder, CO	18, 23
05/16/65	The Glory of Each Day Well Lived	Frasier Meadows Manor. Boulder, CO	18, 22
06/04/65	The Living Ministry	Kansas Conference Ordination Service. KS	18, 23
08/08/65	Each Day is A Life In Miniature	Asbury Methodist Church. Denver, CO	18, 23
12/02/65	The Wonder Of It All	Frasier Meadows Manor. Boulder, CO	18, 23
12/29/65	Faith in a Space Age	Pueblo Sr. High Conference Black Forest, CO	18, 23
03/13/66	Human Nature Being What It Is	University Park Methodist Church. Denver, CO	18, 23
03/15/66	Faith in a Space Age	Air Force Academy. Colorado Springs, CO	18, 23
03/27/66	Human Nature Being What It Is	Christ Methodist Church. Denver, CO	18, 23
03/31/66	Faith in a Space Age	Air Force Academy. Colorado Springs, CO	18, 23
05/01/66	Human Nature Being What It Is	Mason Street Methodist Church. Tacoma, WA	18, 23
05/15/66	Human Nature Being What It Is	St. Paul Methodist Church. Boulder, CO	18, 23
05/18/66	Faith in a Space Age	Ellsworth Air Force Base. N/A	18, 23
05/22/66	Faith in a Space Age	Pocatella Methodist Church. Pocatella, ID	18, 23
05/27/66	Faith in a Space Age	Jefferson H.S. Commencement. Jefferson, MN	18, 23

APPENDIX A: SERMONS OF HARVEY POTTHOFF

Date	Title	Location	Box, Folder
05/29/66	Faith in a Space Age	Jefferson County H.S. Baccalaureate. Jefferson, MN	18, 23
05/29/66	The Wonder of it All	University Park Methodist Church. Denver, CO	18, 23
06/26/66	The Wonder of it All	Broomfield Methodist Church. Broomfield, CO	18, 23
07/07/66	The Lord's Song in a Strange Land	Iliff Chapel. Denver, CO	18, 23
07/10/66	The Wonder of it All	Englewood Methodist Church. Englewood, CO	18, 23
07/24/66	The Wonder of it All	South Broadway Christian Church. Denver, CO	18, 23
10/25/66	The Hallowing of the Everyday	Iliff Chapel. Denver, CO	18, 23
11/06/66	The Past Is Prologue	Christ Methodist Church. Denver, CO	18, 23
03/15/67	Can The Church Be Christian?	Greeley Methodist Church. Greeley, CO	18, 23
03/18/67	Each Day Is a Life in Miniature	Ellsworth Avenue. Denver, CO	18, 23
05/20/67	The Living Ministry	North Dakota Annual Conference. Fargo, ND	18, 23
05/10/68	Faith in a Space Age	Iliff Lounge. Denver, CO	18, 23
05/19/68	Can The Church Be Christian?	Palisade United Methodist Church. Palisade, CO	18,23
09/14/68	Can The Church Be Christian?	St. Paul United Methodist Church. Boulder, CO	18, 23
11/17/68	The Wonder of it All	Estes Park Community Church. Estes Park, CO	18, 23
06/29/69	Each Day is a Life in Miniature	Airstream Trailer National Convention. Laramie, WY	18, 23
07/20/69	Each Day is a Life in Miniature	Broomfield United Methodist Church. Broomfield, CO	18, 23
05/17/70	Can The Church Be Christian?	Thornton United Methodist Church. Thornton, CO	18, 23

Date	Title	Location	Box, Folder
05/24/70	The Religious Vision and the Hopes of Mankind	Morningside College Baccalaureate. Sioux City, Iowa	18, 24
05/31/70	Each Day is a Life in Miniature	N/A. Erie, CO	18, 23
07/02/70	Each Day is a Life in Miniature	Iliff Chapel. Denver, CO	18, 23
07/19/70	Can The Church Be Christian?	Family Camp. Grand Mesa, CO	18, 23
09/13/70	Can The Church Be Christian?	First Church. Sioux Falls, SD	18, 23
10/11/70	Can The Church Be Christian?	First UMC. Riverside, CA	18, 23
11/22/70	Can The Church Be Christian?	Nichols Hills UMC. Oklahoma City, OK	18, 23
11/25/70	Moments of Grace	Iliff Chapel. Denver, CO	18, 24
12/27/70	Moments of Grace	Frasier Meadows Manor. Boulder, CO	18, 24
08/01/71	Each Day is a Life in Miniature	Louisville UMC. Louisville, CO	18, 23
11/01/71	Can The Church Be Christian?	Alamosa UMC. Alamosa, CO	18, 23
11/07/71	Each Day is a Life in Miniature	Christ UMC. Ft. Collins, CO	18, 23
12/12/71	Can The Church Be Christian?	St. Paul UMC. Colorado Springs, CO	18, 23
01/09/72	Each Day is a Life in Miniature	University Park UMC. Denver, CO	18, 23
03/08/72	Thoughts on Prayer	Theology and Devotional Life. Denver, CO	18, 22
03/05/72	Each Day is a Life in Miniature	Pleasant Valley, CO and Wages, CO	18, 23
03/19/72	Can The Church Be Christian?	Brentwood UMC. Denver, CO	18, 23
03/24/72	Can The Church Be Christian?	Bishop Convocation. Lincoln, NE	18, 23
11/26/72	The Wonder of it All	Christ UMC. Ft. Collins, CO	18, 24
03/25/73	Each Day is a Life in Miniature	Highlands UMC. Denver, CO	18, 23
04/07/73	Each Day is a Life in Miniature	Greeley UMC. Greeley, CO	18, 23
04/13/73	Thoughts on Prayer	University Park UMC. Denver, CO	18, 22
04/29/73	Each Day is a Life in Miniature	Laramie UMC. Laramie, WY	18, 23

APPENDIX A: SERMONS OF HARVEY POTTHOFF

Date	Title	Location	Box, Folder
07/08/73	As I Reflect	St. James UMC. Central City, CO	19, 28
08/12/73	Each Day is a Life in Miniature	Aspen Community Church. Aspen, CO	18, 23
10/28/73	Each Day is a Life in Miniature	Longmont UMC. Longmont, CO	18, 23
02/24/74	Can The Church Be Christian?	Aspen UMC. Aspen, CO	18, 23
03/19/74	Each Day is a Life in Miniature	Northglenn UMC. Northglenn, CO	18, 23
04/13/75	Each Day is a Life in Miniature	Applewood Valley UMC. Wheat Ridge, CO	18, 23
04/29/75	Each Day is a Life in Miniature	Grand Junction UMC. Grand Junction, CO	18, 23
07/06/75	Each Day is a Life in Miniature	Edgewater UMC. Denver, CO	18, 23
09/14/75	What Does the Past Have to Say?	Lafayette UMC. Lafayette, CO	19, 28
11/30/75	Humor and Religious Faith	First Church of Divine Science. Denver, CO	18, 24
01/18/76	Humor and Religious Faith	Arvada UMC. Arvada, CO	18, 24
01/29/76	The Iliff Community at Worship	Iliff Chapel. Denver, CO	18, 24
02/01/76	Humor and Religious Faith	Highlands UMC. Denver, CO	18, 24
02/22/76	Humor and Religious Faith	N/A. Wenatchee, WA	18, 24
03/07/76	Humor and Religious Faith	Northglenn UMC. Northglenn, CO	18, 24
03/14/76	Humor and Religious Faith	Montclair UMC. Denver, CO	18, 24
07/11/76	Humor and Religious Faith	First Church. Salt Lake City, UT	18, 24
09/19/76	What Life Comes to Mean or Finding Meaning in Life	Sterling UMC. Sterling, CO	18, 24
12/04/76	What Life Comes to Mean or Finding Meaning in Life	Father Dyer UMC. Breckenridge, CO	18, 24
01/16/77	What Life Comes to Mean or Finding Meaning in Life	Highlands UMC. Denver, CO	18, 24
01/30/77	What Life Comes to Mean or Finding Meaning in Life	Alameda Heights UMC. Denver, CO	18, 24
02/20/77	What Life Comes to Mean or Finding Meaning in Life	Arvada UMC. Arvada, CO	18, 24
02/27/77	What Life Comes to Mean or Finding Meaning in Life	College Hill UMC. Wichita, KS	18, 24

Date	Title	Location	Box, Folder
02/28/77	Humor and Religious Faith	College Hill UMC. Wichita, KS	18, 24
03/20/77	What Life Comes to Mean or Finding Meaning in Life	LaJunta UMC. LaJunta, CO	18, 24
03/26/77	What Life Comes to Mean or Finding Meaning in Life	Muskogee First UMC. Muskogee, OK	18, 24
05/15/77	What Life Comes to Mean or Finding Meaning in Life	Long's Peak UMC. Longmont, CO	18, 24
05/19/77	Humor and Religious Faith	Lowry Air Force Base. Denver, CO	18, 24
05/22/77	What Life Comes to Mean or Finding Meaning in Life	Fleming UMC. Fleming, CO	18, 24
07/17/77	Humor and Religious Faith	First UMC. Boulder, CO	18, 24
07/24/77	Humor and Religious Faith	Aspen Community Church. Aspen, CO	18, 24
08/21/77	A Good Aging	Arvada UMC. Arvada, CO	18, 24
09/26/77	Humor and Religious Faith	Pueblo Ministries Retreat. Pueblo, CO	18, 24
11/26/77	Thoughts on Prayer	Christ UMC. Denver, CO	18, 22
04/18/78	Simple Faith and Struggling Faith	Iliff Chapel. Denver, CO	18, 24
07/02/78	What Life Comes to Mean or Finding Meaning in Life	Christ UMC. Denver, CO	18, 24
07/23/78	Spirituality: What Is It?	Aspen, UMC. Aspen, CO	18, 24
07/26/78	Humor and Religious Faith	Iliff-at-Aspen. Aspen, CO	18, 24
07/30/78	The Wonder of it All	Aspen Chapel of the Prince of Peace. Aspen, CO	18, 23
08/16/78	Simple Faith and Struggling Faith	Camp Minnewonka. Shelby, MI	18, 24
09/17/78	Spirituality: What Is It?	Air Force Community Chapel. Colorado Springs, CO	18, 24
10/04/78	Simple Faith and Struggling Faith	Iowa Area Cabinet and Staff. Geneva Lake, WI	18, 24
10/07/78	Simple Faith and Struggling Faith	School of Missional Strategy. Estes Park, CO	18, 24
10/22/78	Thoughts on Prayer	Trinity UMC. Denver, CO	18, 22
01/06/79	Simple Faith and Struggling Faith	Rocky Mountain Conference. Estes Park, CO	18, 24
01/25/79	Each Day is A Life in Miniature	Sunny Acres. Northglenn, CO	18, 23
02/05/79	Simple Faith and Struggling Faith	Tacoma District. Tacoma, WA	18, 24

APPENDIX A: SERMONS OF HARVEY POTTHOFF

Date	Title	Location	Box, Folder
03/21/79	Spirituality: What Is It?	Keenesburg UMC. Keenesburg, CO	18,24
05/13/79	The Power of Personal Influence	Park Hill UMC. Denver, CO	18, 24
05/27/79	The Power of Personal Influence	South Broadway Christian Church. Denver, CO	18, 24
07/22/79	The Power of Personal Influence	Bassett and Thomasville. N/A	18, 24
07/29/79	What Does the Past Have to Say?	Trinity UMC. Denver, CO	19, 28
07/29/79	What Shall We Do with our Memories?	Trinity UMC. Denver, CO	19, 28
08/05/79	Humor and Religious Faith	Carbondale UMC. Carbondale, CO	18, 24
11/11/79	What Shall We Do with our Memories?	First UMC. Boulder, CO	19, 28
02/15/80	Simple Faith and Struggling Faith	First UMC. Salt Lake City, UT	18, 24
05/16/80	Humor and Religious Faith	Las Animas UMC. Las Animas, CO	18, 24
06/18/80	The Association of Theological Schools in the U.S. and Canada	Iliff. Denver, CO	18, 25
06/19/80	Humor and Religious Faith	American Theological Library Association. Denver, CO	18, 24
08/03/80	The Wonder of it All	Aspen Community Church. Aspen, CO	18, 23
08/10/80	The Power of Personal Influence	Aspen Chapel of the Prince of Peace. Aspen, CO	18, 24
03/21/79	Spirituality: What Is It?	Keenesburg UMC. Keenesburg, CO	18,24
08/17/80	The Wonder of it All	Evergreen UMC. Evergreen, CO	18, 23
08/24/80	What Shall We Do with Our Memories?	Father Dyer UMC. Breckenridge, CO	19, 28
09/11/80	The Church as a Ministering Fellowship	Ogden First UMC. Ogden, UT	18, 25
09/18/80	The Church as a Ministering Fellowship	Greeley UMC. Greeley, CO	18, 25
09/19/80	When Experience is Lifted to the Level of Devotion	Iliff Chapel. Denver, CO	18, 25

Date	Title	Location	Box, Folder
09/28/80	The Wonder of it All	Holyoke Harvest Festival. Holyoke, CO	18, 23
11/22/80	The Meaning of Thanksgiving	Aurora Kiwanis Club. Denver, CO	19, 29
04/09/81	Humor and Religious Faith	Syracuse University—Theta Chi Beta. Syracuse, NY	18, 24
05/21/81	Humor and Religious Faith	Boulder First UMC. Boulder, CO	18, 24
06/10/81	Pain and Joy in Ministry	Rocky Mountain Conference. Ft. Collins, CO	18, 25
11/22/81	The Wonder of it All	Lakeview UMC. Lincoln, NE	18, 25
02/21/82	The Power of Personal Influence	First UMC. Omaha, NE	18, 24
10/30/83	The Power of Personal Influence	Alliance UMC. Alliance, NE	18, 24
01/29/84	Inventory of the Spiritual Life	University Park UMC. Denver, CO	18, 25
02/19/84	The Power of Personal Influence	Wesley House. Lincoln, NE	18, 24
03/02/84	Living Water from Christ Our Hope	St. Andrew Lutheran Church. Lincoln, NE	18, 25
04/25/84	When Life Comes Out of Death—Easter	St. Andrew Lutheran Church. Lincoln, NE	18, 25
05/20/84	Serene and Struggling Faith	Arvada UMC. Arvada, CO	18, 25
06/24/84	Serene and Struggling Faith	University Park UMC. Denver, CO	18, 25
07/22/84	The Experience of Wholeness	University Park UMC. Denver, CO	18, 25
08/12/84	The Experience of Being a Worldly Christian	University Park UMC. Denver, CO	18, 25
09/07/85	Inventory of the Spiritual Life	East District UMC. Fremont, NE	18, 25
09/08/85	The Power of Personal Influence	Faith UMC. Lincoln, NE	18, 24
10/13/85	What Shall We Do with our Memories?	University Park UMC. Denver, CO	18, 25
01/21/86	You Shall Be My Witnesses	First Lutheran Church. Lincoln, NE	18, 25
02/26/86	Loving God with our Minds	First UMC. Huntsville, AL	18, 25
05/11/86	The Power of Personal Influence	Christ UMC. Lincoln, NE	18, 24
08/03/86	The Power of Personal Influence	Centenary UMC. Beatrice, NE	18, 24

APPENDIX A: SERMONS OF HARVEY POTTHOFF

Date	Title	Location	Box, Folder
11/02/86	What Shall We Do with our Memories?	Faith UMC. Lincoln, NE	19, 28
12/28/86	Loving God with our Minds	University Park UMC. Denver, CO	18, 25
03/01/87	The Power of Personal Influence	Emmanuel UMC. Denver, CO	18, 24
03/29/87	The Power of Personal Influence	Aldersgate UMC. Montgomery, AL	18, 24
04/01/87	Inventory of the Spiritual Life	Fourth Presbyterian Church. Lincoln, NE	18, 25
05/08/88	The Power of Personal Influence	First UMC. Lincoln, NE	18, 24
11/20/88	Finding God in Unlikely Places	Christ UMC. Denver, CO	18, 23
04/22/90	A Modern Theology of Earth	First UMC. Lincoln, NE	19, 26
07/01/90	In Praise of Humor	Iliff Chapel. Denver, CO	19, 26
07/15/90	A Modern Theology of Earth	Aspen Community Church. Aspen, CO	19, 26
10/20/90	A Modern Theology of Earth	Arvada UMC. Arvada, CO	19, 26
01/06/91	Reflections on the First Sunday of a New Year	University Park UMC. Denver, CO	19, 26
07/01/91	Church as a Community of Memory and Hope	Christ UMC. Denver, CO	31A, 26
11/02/91	Humor and Religious Faith	Chino UMC. Chino, CA	18, 24
06/28/92	The Experience of Grace	University Park UMC. Denver, CO	19, 26
10/11/92	The Experience of Grace	Alameda Heights UMC. Denver, CO	19, 26
08/01/93	A Question on the Streets of Aspen: "What's the Meaning of Life for You?"	Aspen Community Church. Aspen, CO	19, 26
07/17/94	A Discernment of the Holy in the Ordinary	University Park UMC. Denver, CO	19, 26
08/07/94	The Glory of a Single Day Well-Lived	University Park UMC Denver, CO	19, 26
08/07/94	Education and the Worship of God	Morningside College Centennial Reunion. Grace Church. Sioux City, IA	19, 26
09/11/94	Education and the Worship of God	University Park UMC. Denver, CO	19, 26
09/25/94	The Message of the Aspen September	University Park UMC. Denver, CO	19, 26
11/20/94	From Thanksgiving to Stewardship	University Park UMC. Denver, CO	19, 29

Date	Title	Location	Box, Folder
01/01/95	The God of All Generations	University Park UMC. Denver, CO	19, 26
07/02/95	From Declaring Independence to Living Interdependence	University Park UMC. Denver, CO	19, 26
06/16/96	Reflections of Sixty Years in Ministry	University Park UMC. Denver, CO	19, 26
06/01/97	What Gives Meaning to a Day and to a Life?	Christ UMC. Denver, CO	19, 26
06/15/97	What Gives Meaning to a Day and to a Life?	University Park UMC. Denver, CO	19, 26
N/A	Seeing the Unseen	N/A	14, 2
N/A	Beauty in Religion	N/A	14, 2
N/A	Growing Up	N/A	14, 2
N/A	Monuments of Love (Memorial Day)	N/A	14, 2
N/A	The Greatest of These is Love	N/A	14, 2
N/A	The Meaning of Lent	N/A	14, 3
N/A	The Meaning of the Cross (Good Friday)	Lakewood UMC. Denver, CO	14, 3
N/A	A Tribute to Motherhood	N/A	14, 3
N/A	God and the Depression	N/A	14, 3
N/A	Religion and Poise	Iliff Chapel. Denver, CO	14, 3
N/A	Religion and Poise	Christ UMC. Denver, CO	14, 3
N/A	Three Tributes: A Mother's Day Sermon	N/A	14, 4
N/A	What the Church Means to Me	Christ UMC. Denver, CO	15, 9
N/A	The Older Brother	Christ UMC. Denver, CO	15, 9
N/A	Adjusting our Lives to Changing Conditions.	Christ UMC. Denver, CO	15, 9
N/A	Great Personalities in Christian History: Paul	Christ UMC. Denver, CO	15, 9
N/A	Remedies for Worry	N/A	15, 10
N/A	Obedience to the Unenforceable	Iliff Chapel. Denver, CO	16, 13
N/A	Your Own Experience of God (Finding God Where We Are)	University Park UMC. Denver, CO	18, 22
N/A	The Higher Gratitude (Thanksgiving)	Cotner Center. N/A	19, 29
N/A	Artistry in Living	N/A. Denver, CO	19, 29
N/A	Living and Dying with Grace	N/A	19, 29
N/A	Maintaining Assurance of God	N/A	19, 29

Appendix B
Bibliography of the Writings of Harvey H. Potthoff

Part 1. Books, Articles, and Other Writings
Compiled by Alexandra L. Happer

The works are listed in chronological order, with an initial section for books and a subsequent section for all other materials. Book reviews are limited to those published in *The Iliff Review*.

BOOKS

Current Theological Thinking: An Elective Unit for Adults. Leader's Guide by Howard M. Ham. New York: Abingdon Press, 1962. Reprint of "Current Theological Thinking," *Adult Student* 21 (March 1962): 24–43; (April 1962): 14–38.

A Theology for Christian Witnessing. Nashville, TN: Tidings, 1964.

Acts: Then and Now. New York: Joint Commission on Education and Cultivation, Board of Missions of the Methodist Church, 1965.

The Christian in Today's World. Foundation Studies in Christian Faith, pt. 8. Nashville, TN: Graded Press, 1969.

God and the Celebration of Life. Chicago: Rand McNally & Co., 1969. [Second Edition, 1981. Iliff Archives, box 1, file folder 2.]

The Inner Life. Foundation Studies in Christian Faith, pt. 7. Nashville, TN: Graded Press, 1969.

A Whole Person in a Whole World. Nashville, TN: Tidings, 1972.

Loneliness: Understanding and Dealing with It. Nashville: Abingdon, 1976.

ARTICLES AND OTHER WRITINGS

Dissertation: The Doctrine of Immortality in the Philosophies of Edgar Sheffield Brightman and Alfred North Whitehead. Th.D. Dissertation, The Iliff School of Theology, 1941. [Iliff Archives, box 1, file folder 1.]

"Some Comments on the Doctrine of Forgiveness." *The Iliff Review* 1 (Winter 1944): 22–30.

Review: *The Nature and Destiny of Man: A Christian Interpretation*. Vol. 2: *Human Destiny*, by Reinhold Niebuhr. *The Iliff Review* 1 (Spring 1944): 94–96.

ALEXANDRA L. HAPPER is an Assistant Librarian for Technical Services, Taylor Library, Iliff School of Theology. The assistance of Paul T. Wilson and Professor Andrew D. Scrimgeour, Librarian, in this project is gratefully acknowledged.

Review: *Protestantism: A Symposium*, edited by W. K. Anderson. *The Iliff Review* 1 (Fall 1944): 137.

"Theological Preaching in the Liberal Pulpit." *The Iliff Review* 2 (Spring 1945): 207–217.

Review: *God and Evil*, by C. E. M. Joad. *The Iliff Review* 2 (Winter 1945): 189–190.

"Some Comments on the Doctrine of Sin." *The Iliff Review* 3 (Spring 1946): 56–61.

Review: *Nature and Values*, by Edgar S. Brightman. *The Iliff Review* 3 (Fall 1946): 143–144.

Review: *The Great Prisoners*, by Isidore Abramowitz. *The Iliff Review* 4 (Winter 1947): 47.

Review: *His Word Through Preaching*, by Gerald Kennedy. *The Iliff Review* 4 (Fall 1947): 140–141.

Review: *Seeds of Redemption*, by Bernard E. Meland. *The Iliff Review* 5 (Winter 1948): 47–48.

Review: *What Is a Man*, by Robert Russell Wicks. *The Iliff Review* 5 (Winter 1948): 48.

"God in Nature." *Adult Student 8* (June 1949): 23–34.

"What Is Mature Religion?" *Motive* 12 (Orientation Issue 1951): 19. Reprinted in *Motive* 13 (Orientation Issue 1952): 13. [Iliff Archives, box 3, file folder 12.]

"Will College Change My Religion?" *Motive* 12 (Orientation Issue 1951): 16–19. Reprinted in *Motive* 20 (Orientation Issue 1959): 22–25. [Iliff Archives, box 3, file folder 12.]

Editor of *The Iliff Review* from the Fall issue 1952 (IX, 3) to Spring 1958 (XV, 2).

"Education Principles in the Curriculum. A Report to the Curriculum Committee of The Methodist Church." N.p., 1952.

"New Lives for Old." *Learning for Life* 2 (April–June 1952): 2–19.

Review: *A Theology of the Living Church*, by Harold L. DeWolf. *The Iliff Review* 10 (Fall 1953): 143–145.

Review: *What Present-Day Theologians Are Thinking*, by Daniel D. Williams. *The Iliff Review* 10 (Spring 1953): 98–100.

"The Churches Speak of Hope." *The Iliff Review* 11 (Fall 1954): 37–49.

"The Doctrine of God in W. H. Bernhardt's Philosophy of Religion." *The Iliff Review* 11 (Winter 1954): 21–38.

"The Free Spirit and the Church's Theological Task." *The Iliff Review* 12 (Spring 1955): 3–12.

Understanding Loneliness. Denver: Christ Methodist Church, 1955. Paper read 20 October 1955 at Christ Methodist Church, Denver, on the occasion of the ninth annual series of seminar discussions sponsored by the Adult Education Division of Christ Church.

APPENDIX B: WRITINGS OF HARVEY H. POTTHOFF

"Floyd Luman Sampson: A Tribute." *The Iliff Review* 13 (Fall 1956): 43–45.

"Living Our Faith in Immortality." *Christian Advocate* 29 (March 1956): 8–9, 30, 33–34. [Iliff Archives, box 3, file folder 10.]

Review: *A Compend of Wesley's Theology*, edited by Robert Burtner and Robert Chiles. *The Iliff Review* 12 (Fall 1956): 52–53.

Review: *A Layman's Guide to Protestant Theology*, edited by William Horndern. *The Iliff Review* 13 (Fall 1956): 52.

"Dr. Fosdick Speaks of Fundamentalism, Neo-Orthodoxy and the Liberal Spirit." *The Iliff Review* 14 (Fall 1957): 41–48.

Review: *The Purpose of the Church and Its Ministry*, by H. Richard Neibuhr in collaboration with Daniel D. Williams and James M. Gustafson. *The Iliff Review* 14 (Winter 1957): 48.

Review: *The Saving Person*, by Angus Dun. *The Iliff Review* 14 (Winter 1957): 48.

Review: *Theology You Can Understand*, by Rachel H. King. *The Iliff Review* 14 (Fall 1957): 51–52.

"The Christian's Vocation." *Adult Teacher* 10 (April 1957): 3–5. [Iliff Archives, box 3, file folder 12.]

"The Different Understandings of the Church and Its Ministry Which Are Found in the Major Confessional Streams of the Christian Church." In *Papers on the Theology of Mission*, 3–12. N.p.: Division of World Mission of the Board of Missions of The Methodist Church, 1958.

"Theology and Man's Search for Integrity." *The Drew Gateway* 28 (Winter 1958): 99–108. [Iliff Archives, box 3, file folder 9.]

Review: *The Christian Tradition and the Unity We Seek*, by Albert C. Outler. *The Iliff Review* 15 (Winter 1958): 49–50.

"Theology and the Vision of Greatness." Part 1 of "Theology in a Space Age." *The Iliff Review* 16 (Winter 1959): 1–13.

"Rethinking the Doctrine of Man." Part 2 of "Theology in a Space Age." *The Iliff Review* 16 (Winter 1959): 13–23.

"God and the Newer View of the Universe." Part 3 of "Theology in a Space Age." *The Iliff Review* 16 (Winter 1959): 41–52.

"No Time for Scared Theology!" [Originally "No Time for Sacred Theology!"] *Christian Advocate*, October 1, 1959, 5-6. [Iliff Archives, box 3, file folder 10.]

"Every Man a Priest." *Adult Student* 18 (October 1959): 9–11.

"Life's Eternal Values." *Adult Student* 18 (August 1959): 39–53.

"Contemporary Theology and the Christian Mission." In *The Christian Mission Today*, pp. 13–22. Edited by the Joint Section of Education and Cultivation of the Board of Missions of The Methodist Church. New York: Abingdon Press, 1960.

"The Doctrine of God." *The Church School* 13 (April 1960): 9–10.

"Of Stars and Men [by] Harlow Shapley: Reader's Guide." *Adult Student* 19 (July 1960): 12–13; (August 1960): 22–23; (September 1960): 22–23, cover III.

"Our Armenian Tradition and Trust." *Christian Advocate*, 22 June, 1961, pp. 7–8. [Iliff Archives, box 3, file folder 10.]

"Faith and Honest Doubt." *Adult Teacher* 14 (July 1961): 3–5.

"The Significance of the Work of Christ." *Adult Student* 20 (January 1961): 39–63; (February 1961): 44–63.

"Bultmann, Ogden, and the Search for a 'Post-Liberal' Theology: A Review Article." *The Iliff Review* 19 (Fall 1962): 19–26.

"Science and Religion: Has the Conflict Been Resolved?" *Religion in Life* 32 (Winter 1962-63): 19–28.

"Bible Study in the Church School." *The Church School* 15 (July 1962): 3–4.

"Good News for Strenuous Times." *Bible Teacher for Adults* 17 (October–December 1962): 5–7.

"Symbols in the Christian Life." *Adult Student* 21 (February 1962): 12–15.

"Theology: The Layman's Concern." *Adult Teacher* 15 (March 1962): 8–10.

"The Vision of Mission in the Local Church." *The Methodist Woman* 23 (June 1963): 20–21. [Iliff Archives, box 3, file folder 10.]

"[Statement on the Progress of the Subcommittee of the Committee on Curriculum for Adults of the Methodist Church.]" In "Do We Need New Materials?" *Adult Student* 22 (March 1963): 1, 59.

"The Denver Heritage." *The Pulpit* 36 (April 1965): 10–12. [Iliff Archives, box 3, file folder 10.]

"Faith for the New Year." *The Christian Home* 24 (January 1965): 2–4, 64.

"Kerygma and Myth by Rudolf Bultmann: Leader's Suggestions," *Adult Teacher* 19 (October 1965): 11–13, 38.

"The Objective of the Church's Educational Ministry." *The Methodist Teacher IV–VI* 2 (Fall 1965): 2–3. Reprinted in *The Methodist Teacher V-VI* 2 (Spring 1966): 8–9.

"Concern for Renewal." *Together Area News Edition (Denver)* 10 (January 1966): A2.

"Life as Summons and Commitment: A New Year's Meditation." *The Methodist Woman* 26 (January 1966): 4–5, 42. [Iliff Archives, box 3, file folder 10.]

"The Seminary and the New Day." *Christian Advocate*, December 1, 1966, 9–10. [Iliff Archives, box 3, file folder 10.]

Lecture: "The Iliff Tradition." Unpublished presentation at the Fall Convocation of The Iliff School of Theology, Denver, 28 September 1966, (reel-to-reel tape).

"For the Superintendent of the Adult Division." *The Church School* 19 (March 1966): 32.

"The New Adult Curriculum: An Analysis of Its Presuppositions." *Bible Teacher for Adults* 21 (March–May 1966): 8–10.

APPENDIX B: WRITINGS OF HARVEY H. POTTHOFF

"The New Adult Curriculum: Some Assumptions." *Wesley Quarterly* 25 (March–May 1966): 6–8. Also published in *Adult Student* 25 (March 1966): 10–11; and *Bible Lessons for Adults* 21 (March–May 1966): 10–12.

"The Reality of God." *The Iliff Review* 24 (Spring 1967): 3–20. Revision of his paper "The Reality of God: The Meaning and Experience of God's Continuing Revelation" read to the Methodist Conference on Christian Education, Cincinnati, November 10, 1965 (reel-to-reel tape).

"Foundation Studies: A Look Behind the Scenes." *Bible Teacher for Adults* 22 (March–May 1967): 36–39.

"Newer Developments in Theology." *The Church School* 20 (February 1967): 1–2.

"The Mission of the Church." In *Theological Perspectives of Stewardship*, pp. 115-126, edited by E. A. Briggs. Evanston, IL: General Board of the Laity, Divisions of Stewardship and Finance, The United Methodist Church, 1969.

Review: *The Pusher and Puller*, by J. Edward Carothers. *The Iliff Review* 26 (Winter 1969): 43.

"The Freedom to Be Human." *The Christian Home* 2 (July 1970): 2–3, 60–61.

"Life Styles in Theological Perspective." *The Iliff Review* 30 (Fall 1973): 5–22. Revision of his first lecture "Changing Life Styles from a Theological Perspective," presented during The Iliff Week of Lectures, February 1972 (reel-to-reel tape).

"What and How United Methodists Believe." *Adult Leader* 5 (March–May 1973): 4–6.

"Styles in Churchmanship." *The Iliff Review* 31 (Fall 1974): 3–20. Revision of his second lecture "The Church in Relation to Changing Life Styles," presented during The Iliff Week of Lectures, February 1972 (reel-to-reel tape).

"When Preaching Comes Alive." In *You and Communication in the Church: Skills and Techniques*, pp. 57–66. Edited by B.F. Jackson, Jr. Waco, TX: World Books, 1974.

"Theologies of Liberation." *Cross Talk* 3, no. 1 (March–May 1974): pt. 7.

"United Methodists: A Faith Affirming People." Co edited with Wayne K. Clynmer, Ira Gallaway and Frank B. Stanger. In *God's Action: Our Affirmation*, pp. 59–116. Nashville, TN: Graded Press, 1975.

"How Is the Church's Good News Communicated?" *The New Pulpit Digest* 55 (March–April 1975): pp. 27–29.

"Making the Most of the Middle and Later Years." *Mature Years* 11 (June–August 1977): 24–29. [Iliff Archives, box 3, file folder 11.]

Lecture: "Time, Transitions, and the Search for Meanings." Unpublished presentation at the seminar "Toward a Theology of Aging," Denver, 1 May 1978. (Cassette tape.)

"William Henry Bernhardt, 1893–1979." *The Iliff Review* 36 (Fall 1979): 3–4.

"Martin Rist, 1896–1979." *The Iliff Review* 37 (Winter 1980): 3–6.

Part 2. Additional Writings Compiled by Amy Phillips

Review: *Counseling and Theology* by William E. Hulms. *The New Christian Advocate*, January 1957. Iliff Archives, box 3, file folder 9.

Review: *Personality and Religion* by Paul E. Johnson. *The New Christian Advocate*, December 1957. Iliff Archives, box 3, file folder 9.

"Theology And Man's Search For Integrity." *The Drew Gateway* 28 no. 2 (Winter 1958): 99–109. Publication of Drew Theological Seminary. Iliff Archives, box 3, file folder 9.

"Foundation of Christian Teachings in Methodist Churches." Curriculum Committee of the General Board of Education, Methodist Church (1960). Iliff Archives, box 25, file folder 4.

"The Church as a Saving Fellowship." Part 4 of "Theology and the Space Age." *The Iliff Review* 17, no. 1 (1960): 35–46. Iliff Archives, box 3, file folder 10.

Review: *Protestant Thought and Natural Science* by John Dillenberger. *Christian Advocate*, February 16, 1961.

Review: *World Cultures and World Religions—The Coming Dialogue* by Hendrick Kraemer. *Faculty Forum*, Division of Higher Education of the Methodist Church and Board of Education of the Presbyterian Church, (December 1961): no. 19, 3. Iliff Archives, box 3, file folder 10.

Review: *The Epic of Revelation* by Mack B. Stoke. *Christian Advocate, 6 no. 6* (March 15, 1962):15. Iliff Archives, box 3, file folder 10.

Review: *The Christian Message in a Scientific Age* by Albert N. Wells. *Christian Advocate*, April 1963.

Review: *Science and Religion* by Harold K. Schilling. *Christian Advocate*, April 1963.

"A Good Aging: A Christian Perspective."Reflect—A Series of Faculty Reflections on Contemporary Issues,1966. Iliff Archives, box 2, file folder 4.

"The Theology of Evangelism." *Mississippi Methodist Advocate*, February 1967.

"Ministering to the Dying Patient." *The Ministry Journal* (April 1972): 34–36. Iliff Archives, box 4, file folder 14.

"The Theological Orientations to Change and the Functions of the Church." *American Baptist Chaplain* (November 1972): 21–24. Iliff Archives, box 13, file folder 50.

"Loneliness." (excerpted from *Loneliness: Understanding and Dealing with It) SIGN National Catholic Magazine* 56, no. 4 (December 1976/January 1977): 34–37. Iliff Archives, box 3, file folder 11.

"How Shall We Speak of God?" *The Iliff Forum* (last issue) (1977): p. 3.

Understanding Loneliness (retitled version of *Loneliness: Understanding and Dealing with It*). New York: Harper & Row, 1977. Iliff Archives, box 1, file folder 4.

"When Experience Is Lifted to the Level of Devotion." *The Iliff Review* 38, no. 3 (Fall 1981): 5–7. Iliff Archives, box 3, file folder 11.

Selected Papers of Harvey H. Potthoff. Denver, CO: Criterion Press, 1981. Iliff Archives, box 2, file folder 7.

"Homiletical Resources: The Sermon as Theological Event: Interpretations of Parables." *Quarterly Review* 4, no. 2 (Summer 1984). Iliff Archives, box 3, file folder 11.

"A Letter from Harvey Potthoff." *The Wesleyan*, Point-Counterpoint section, 1986–87. Iliff Archives, box 3, file folder 11.

"Dying Said Not Isolated Event: Views of Death Differ." *Lincoln Star-Journal*, April 12, 1987.

"The Languages of a Renaissance Man," *The Iliff Review* (Spring 1988): 7–24.

"Lindsay B. Longacre (1910–1942)." In *An Intellectual History of the Iliff School of Theology: A Centennial Tribute, 1892–1992*, edited by Alton Templin. Denver, CO: Iliff School of Theology, 1992.

"Loren Eiseley's Religious Pilgrimage," Published by Friends of Loren Esiely with the cooperation of the Nebraska Humanistic Council (1992). Iliff Archives, box 2, file folder 4.

Appendix C
Unpublished Papers

Title	Box, Folder
A Christian Spirituality of the Whole Person	31A, 24
A Classification of Christologies	4, 14
A Response to Leo Uzyck's Article on "Euthanasia, Assisted Suicide and Medical Ethics"	31, 15
A Statement of Religious Purpose	31A, 22
A Theological, Life-Cycle Approach to Christian Education in the Local Church	4, 14
A Theology of Aging (Religious Faith and the Experience of Growing Older)	4, 14
Chapter One: The Biblical Jesus	4, 15
Chapter Two: The Historic Jesus	4, 15
Empirical Theology and the Experience of Meaning	6, 7
Empirical Theology and Basis of Hope (Reflections On a Personal Journey)	6, 9
Hope in a World Where Death is a Fact	6, 9
Life/World Orientations: With and Without God	4, 14
Lindsay B. Longacre	2, 7
Religious Faith (With Special Reference to the Judaic-Christian Tradition)	4, 14
Some Introductory Comments on Process Theology	11, 34
Suicide—Should it Always Be Discouraged?	31, 15
The Church's Helping-Healing Ministries in Theological Perspective	4, 14
The Future - Is Hope Possible?	31A, 26
The Theological Assumptions We Bring to Campus Ministry	6, 9
Theological Uses of Process Philosophy	13, 48
What is a Theology of Ministry? (or The Quest For an Authentic Theological Framework for the Practice of Ministry)	9, 22
What is a Theology of Ministry?	4, 14
William Henry Bernhardt's Contribution to the Iliff Tradition	4, 14

Appendix D
Speeches and Addresses

Date	Title	Delivered	Box, Folder
05/29/28	Today Decides Tomorrow—Valedictory	Jeffers, MN	5, 1
02/09/35	Adventuring on the Highway of High Ideals	Denver District Winter Institute. Denver, CO	5, 1
12/14/35	The Influence of Cosmology Upon Theological Concepts	Alfred North Whitehead Class—Philosophy 3b. Cambridge, MA	31, 19
03/07/37	Religion as Friendship With God	Sub-District League Rally. Limon, CO	5, 1
05/16/37	Religion as Friendship With God	Denver District Epworth League. Campfire Service. Evergreen, CO	5, 1
06/03/37	Untitled	Women's Club Devotional and Installation Service. Denver, CO	5, 1
08/07/37	Developing a Program of Personal Religious Living	College Group Pinecrest Institute. Pinecrest Methodist Camp. Palmer Lake, CO	5, 1
10/10/37	The Life of Francis Asbury	Christ Methodist Church and Asbury Leagues. Denver, CO	5, 1
1938	Some of the Problems of an Iliff Graduate in the Pastorate	Iliff School of Theology (to faculty). Denver, CO	6, 9
03/04/38	After All, Why History?	Colorado Conference Historical Society Dinner. Denver, CO	5, 1
03/06/38	The Plan of Church Unification for the Three Branches of Methodism	Combined Meeting of Adult Classes. Christ Methodist Church. Denver, CO	5, 1
03/23/38	The Singing Religion that Swept through England	Christ Methodist Church Lenten Dinner. Denver, CO	5, 1
04/07/38	Skinner Junior High Easter Week Talk	Skinner Junior High. Denver, CO	5, 1

Date	Title	Delivered	Box, Folder
04/07/38	Some Unexpected Revelations of God	Topeka Branch W.F.M.S. Grant Avenue Church. Denver, CO	5, 1
12/01/38	The Starting Point of Christian Missions	District Officers of W.F.M.S. Trinity Methodist Church. Denver, CO	5, 1
08/39	Course in Personality Development	College Group. Grand Mesa Institute	13, 44
03/12/39	The Christian Philosophy of Life	Wesley Foundation. Ft. Collins, CO	5, 1
04/03/39	Religion as a Resource for Living	KOA Radio-University of Denver Hour. Denver, CO	5, 1
04/04/39	Pre-Easter Talk	Advertising Club-Albany Hotel. Denver, CO	5, 1
12/19/39	Tillicum Club	YMCA Dinner. Denver, CO	5, 1
03/04/40	Deepening the Spiritual Life through the Bible and Other Devotional Literature	Denver Ministerial Alliance. Denver, CO	5, 1
03/08/40	The Privilege of Religious Liberty	Hebrew Educational Alliance. Denver, CO	5, 1
04/07/40	The Privilege of Religious Liberty	Grant Avenue League. Denver, CO	5, 1
06/17/40	To Drink or Not To Drink	KPOF Radio. Denver, CO	5, 1
11/30/40	What is This Thing Called Christianity?	Keynote Address. State Older Boys YMCA Conference. Denver, CO	
1941	The Pastor and Public Worship	Rocky Mountain Assembly. Pinecrest Methodist Camp. Palmer Lake, CO	6, 9
Fall 1941	God and the War	Iliff – Inter-seminary Conference (Charles Milligan's Group). Denver, CO	6, 9
02/26/41	Trends in Current Religious Thinking	Park Hill Methodist Church. Denver, CO	5, 1
09/11/41	Religion as a Resource for Living	University Park Methodist Church W.S.C.S Group. Denver, CO	5, 1
10/42	Anatomy of Humor	Round Table. Denver, CO	5, 1
02/43	Anatomy of Humor	D. Crabb's Home – Students for Discussion Denver, CO	5, 1

APPENDIX D: SPEECHES AND ADDRESSES

Date	Title	Delivered	Box, Folder
01/03/44	Anatomy of Humor	English 221. Denver, CO	5, 1
07/24 -29/44	Course on Worship	Pinecrest Institute. Pinecrest Methodist Camp. Palmer Lake, CO	13, 44
05/07/47	Laws of the Spiritual Life – Schofield	W.S.C.S. Study Group. Christ Methodist Church. Denver, CO	5, 1
04/06/48	Principles of Worship	Institute Workers of Colorado Methodism. Trinity Methodist Church. Denver, CO	5, 1
05/10/49	Iliff Founders' Day Service	Iliff Chapel. Denver, CO	31, 16
05/21/49	The Techniques of Prayer	CFO D&F Tearoom. Denver, CO	5, 1
03/15/53	Religion as Friendship With God	Senior High Fellowship. Bethel Church. Pueblo, CO	5, 1
10/09/54	An Experimental Approach to Prayer and Worship	MSM Retreat, Pinecrest Methodist Camp. Palmer Lake, CO	13, 50
02/22/55	Have You Ever Been Ashamed of Yourself?	Ft. Warren	5, 1
07/26/55	A Holy Curiosity	Iliff Chapel. Denver, CO	5, 1
10/02/55	Understanding Loneliness	Christ Methodist Church. Adult Seminar. Denver, CO	2, 4
02/24/57	Religion and Mental Health Education	University of Colorado Religious Emphasis Week. Boulder, CO	5, 1
1960	Theological Foundations of Evangelism	Rocky Mountain General Conference	13, 46
06/30/61	The Church as a Redemptive Fellowship: A Resource in Suffering	Western Jurisdiction School of Missions. Forest Grove, OR	13, 44
09/07/61	The Saving Fellowship: The Doctrine of the Church	Southern California-Nevada Pastor's School. San Diego, CA	5, 1
09/13/61	The Saving Fellowship: The Doctrine of the Church	Greeley District Ministers Retreat. Meeker Lodge. Estes Park, CO	5, 1
02/01/62	The Saving Fellowship: The Doctrine of the Church	Iowa Area Pastors School	5, 1

Date	Title	Delivered	Box, Folder
02/27/62	The Blake Proposal	Iliff Lounge. Denver, CO	5, 1
03/05/62	The Blake Proposal	Denver Ministerial Alliance. Denver, CO	5, 1
08/27-31/62	The Saving Fellowship: The Doctrine of the Church	The Minister's School. Minnesota Annual Conference. Carleton College. Northfield, MN	5. 1
08/31/62	The Saving Fellowship: The Doctrine of the Church	Wisconsin Area Pastor's School. Appleton, WI	5, 1
10/24/62	Alfred North Whitehead: A Man in Touch	D.U. Chapel. Denver, CO	31, 18
02/05/63	The Faith That Compels Us	Our Mission Today Regional Study Conference. St. Louis, MO	5, 1
02/24/63	Alfred North Whitehead: A Man in Touch	MSM University Park Methodist Church. Denver, CO	31, 18
09/06/63	The Church's Ministry of Education: The Church as a Learning Fellowship	District Workers Conference. University of Oklahoma City. Oklahoma City, OK	5,1
10/01/63	The Church's Ministry of Education: The Church as a Teaching Fellowship	Golden Council of Churches Leadership TrainingSchool. Golden Methodist Church. Golden, CO	5, 1
10/07/63	The Church's Ministry of Education: The Church as a Learning Fellowship	Church School Workers Recognition Dinner. St. Luke's Methodist Church. Houston, TX	5, 1
04/12/64	The Idea of Creation	Adult Class. Broomfield Broomfield, CO	5, 1
07/23/64	The Saving Fellowship: The Doctrine of the Church	Wilson Lecture III. Mt. Sequoyah, AK	5, 1
09/29/64	The Church's Ministry of Education	St Paul's Methodist Church Staff Recognition Dinner. Pueblo, CO	5, 1

APPENDIX D: SPEECHES AND ADDRESSES

Date	Title	Delivered	Box, Folder
05/26/65	The Fun and Frustration of Being a Senior	Federation of Organizations of Older People. Trinity Methodist Church. Denver, CO	5, 2
06/08/65	The Church's Ministry of Education	Virginia Annual Conference. Virginia Beach, VA	5, 1
06/09/65	The Church's Ministry of Education	Rocky Mountain Conference. Denver, CO	5, 1
09/25/65	The Church's Ministry of Education	Board of Education Report. St. Luke's Staff. Oklahoma City, OK	5, 1
11/10/65	The Reality of God: The Meaning and Experience of God's Continuing Revelation	Methodist Conference on Christian Education. Cincinnati, OH	5, 1
01/14/66	A Look at the God Is Dead Theology	United Churchmen. Grampy's Pancake House	3, 12
02/25/66	A Look at the God Is Dead Theology	University of Denver Conference on Religion. Dodge Ranch Evergreen, CO	5, 1
03/23/66	A Look at the God Is Dead Theology	Park Hill Methodist Church Dinner. Denver, CO	5, 1
04/20/66	The Church's Ministry of Education	Atlanta, GA.	5, 1
05/19/66	What is Iliff?	All Iliff Day. Iliff Chapel. Denver, CO	5, 2
09/18/66	The Church's Ministry of Education	Ft. Lupton Methodist Church. Ft. Lupton, CO	5, 1
09/27/66	The Church's Ministry of Education	Lovers Lane Club. Dallas, TX	5, 1
09/28/66	The Iliff Tradition	75th Anniversary Convocation. Iliff Chapel. Denver, CO	5, 2
01/09/67	The Church's Ministry of Education	Staffs of Galloway Memorial and St. Luke's Methodist Church. Jackson, MS	5, 1
11/19/67	The Church's Ministry of Education	First Methodist Church. Colby, KS	5, 1
01/11/70	The Church's Ministry of Education	Mountain View United Methodist Church. Boulder, CO	5, 1

Date	Title	Delivered	Box, Folder
06/16/73	Margaret Sheve (On Her Retirement)	Rocky Mountain Conference. Denver, CO	5, 2
10/29/73	Values in a Changing World	Adult Education Luncheon honoring Rabbi Laderman. Brown Palace Hotel. Denver, CO	5, 2
01/22/77	Father Damien	Arvada United Methodist Church Men's Breakfast. Arvada, CO	5, 2
03/08/77	Father Damien	Iliff Chapel. Denver, CO	5, 2
04/05/77	Father Damien	Redlands United Methodist Church. Grand Junction, CO	5, 2
04/21/77	Father Damien	University Park United Methodist Church. Denver, CO	5,2
04/21/77	Inter-Play: Theology and the Practice of Religion	Iliff Interns Colloquiums of Religion Supervisors. Denver, CO	5, 2
06/19/77	Inter-Play: Theology and the Practice of Religion	South Denver Ministries Denver, CO.	5, 2
09/77	Inter-Play: Theology and the Practice of Religion	Pueblo Ministers Retreat	5, 2
10/23/77	Father Damien	Bethany United Methodist Church. Denver, CO	5, 2
03/23/79	The Search for a Contemporary Faith	Huntington College. Montgomery, AL	5, 2
08/09/79	Iliff-at-Aspen	Aspen Rotary Club. Aspen, CO	5, 2
08/28/79	Iliff-at-Aspen	Hope United Methodist Church. Denver, CO	5, 2
06/08/80	We Have This Treasure	Iowa Annual Conference. Des Moines, IA	5, 5
04/09/81	Humor and Religious Faith	Theta Chi Beta, Syracuse University. Syracuse, NY	5, 3
04/10/81	Integrity in Work and Worship: Toward a Vision of Wholeness	Syracuse University Hendricks Chapel. Installation of Dean Richrad Phillips. Syracuse, NY	5, 3

APPENDIX D: SPEECHES AND ADDRESSES

Date	Title	Delivered	Box, Folder
08/23/81	Celebration of New Beginnings	First Year Class of Faculty at Nebraska Wesleyan University. First United Methodist Church, Lincoln, NE	5, 3
02/28/82	Growth in Grace: An Old Doctrine in a New Day	United Methodist Church Waverly, NE	5, 3
03/11/82	Bishop Henry White Warren: A Man for All Seasons	Iliff Chapel Denver, CO	5,3
05/18/82	Portraits of the World	NWU Commencement Address. Lincoln, NE	5, 3
06/24/82	Where the Artist and the Theologian Come Together	Rocky Ridge Music School. Estes Park, CO	5, 3
09/16/82	Growth in Grace: An Old Doctrine in a New Day	Lincoln District UMW Warren United Methodist Church. Lincoln, NE	5, 5
09/17/82	Where the Artist and the Theologian Come Together	Discussion Group at the Kays. Lincoln, NE	5, 3
01/22/83	Bishop Henry White Warren: A Man for All Seasons	Arvada UMC. Arvada, CO	31, 16
04/27/83	The Vision of the Peacemaker	Nan Graf's Class on Peace. Nebraska Wesleyan University. Lincoln, NE	5, 3
12/04/83	Growth in Grace: An Old Doctrine in a New Day	Questioners Class Trinity United Methodist Church, Lincoln, NE	5, 5
06/01/84	Tribute: 50th Anniversary Dinner	Green Cheese Club Club at The Golden Ox. Denver, CO	5, 3
Fall 1985	Loneliness and Grief	Alzheimer's Support Group. Lincoln, NE	5, 5
09/07/85	Growth in Grace: An Old Doctrine in a New Day	East District UMW. Fremont, NE	5, 3
03/29-31/87	Symposium: Hope and Responsibility in a Nuclear Age	Huntington College. Montgomery, AL	5, 3
05/02/87	Food for the Spiritual Journey	Iliff Student Retreat. Snow Mountain Ranch. Estes Park Area	13, 50
04/05/88	The Future: Is Hope Possible?	Dakota Area Pastors School. Bismarck, ND	5, 4

Date	Title	Delivered	Box, Folder
05/19/88	Tribute: Honoring Charles Milligan on His Retirement	Iliff Faculty Dinner. Phipps House. Denver, CO	5, 5
06/26/88	The Noble Character of Noble Kime (Retirement)	Washington Park United Methodist Church. Denver, CO	5, 5
08/13/88	Obstacles to Spiritual Growth	Methodist Church Retreat. Salt Lake City, UT	5, 5
09/12/88	Coping with Adversity	Lincoln General Hospital. Lincoln, NE	5, 5
01/22/89	Living with Our Limitations	University Park United Methodist Church. Denver, CO	5, 5
02/02/89	A Holy Curiosity	Huntington College. Montgomery, AL	5, 1
04/18/89	The Quest for the Historical Iliff: Iliff History 1932 – 1981	All Iliff Day. Iliff School of Theology. Denver, CO	5, 5
04/19/89	Spirituality: Boon or Bane of the Church	All Iliff Day. Iliff School of Theology. Denver, CO	5, 5
06/09/89	Medical and Religious Contribution to a Good Aging	Alaska Medical Society. Sitka, AK	5, 5
06/27/89	My Appreciation of Iliff	Iliff Trustees and John Wesley Iliff Society. Denver, CO	5, 5
07/09/89	Living with Our Limitations	Washington Park UMC. Denver, CO	5, 5
09/14/89	Speech to Hospital Volunteers	Nebraska Methodist Hospital. Omaha, NE	5, 5
03/25/90	Tribute: Marvin Essing - 25th Anniversary of Being Ordained Elder	Berthoud UMC Berthoud, CO	5, 5
04/02/90	Science and Religion (Part 1): Has the Conflict Been Resolved?	Baldwin Wallace College Moll Lectures. Berea, OH	6, 6
04/02/90	Science and Religion (Part 2): Speaking of God in a Scientific and Technological Age	Baldwin Wallace College Moll Lectures. Berea, OH	6, 6
04/03/90	Science and Religion (Part 3): Resources in the Quest for Quality of Life	Baldwin Wallace College Moll Lectures. Berea, OH	6, 6

APPENDIX D: SPEECHES AND ADDRESSES

Date	Title	Delivered	Box, Folder
04/19/90	Environmentalism as a Religious Way of Life	Nebraska Wesleyan University Mattingly Symposium. Lincoln, NE	12, 37
06/24/90	The Wonderful Gift of Humor	Rocky Ridge Music School. Estes Park, CO	31, 14
05/10/91	Medical and Religious Contributions to a Good Aging	University of Missouri Medical School. Kansas City, MO	5, 5
06/18/91	Empirical Theology and the Vision of Hope (Reflections on a Personal Journey)	Highlands Institute. Highlands, NC	6, 7
03/92	Life/World Orientation With and Without God	Nebraska Wesleyan University Mattingly Symposium. Lincoln, NE	12, 37
04/04/92	What's In A Name?	Iliff Family Reunion. Denver University Club. Denver, CO	6, 7
05/16/92	Integrity	Nebraska Wesleyan University Commencement (100th Anniversary). Lincoln, NE	6, 7
05/29/92	Progress in Doctrine and Experience	Iliff Commencement. Denver, CO	6, 7
06/28/92	A Tribute to the Boigegrains	Wheat Ridge UMC. Wheat Ridge, CO	6, 7
10/09/92	Assumptions in Decision Making	Rose Hospital. Denver, CO	6, 7
11/21/92	Religion in the Experience of Suicide	Denver Hemlock Society. Denver, CO	31, 15
01/16/93	Getting Better Acquainted with the United Methodist Church	University Park UMC Men's Breakfast. Denver, CO	6, 8
08/28/93	A Theological, Life-Cycle Approach to Christian Education in the Local Church	University Park UMC Chapel. Denver, CO	4, 14
12/16/93	Religions of the World	Arapahoe High School. Littleton, CO	13, 47
01/24/94	Theology, Spirituality and a Good Aging	Iliff Week of Lecturers and Rocky Mountain Pastors' School. Denver, CO	6, 8

Date	Title	Delivered	Box, Folder
08/18/94	The Difference a Teacher Can Make	Heritage High School. Littleton, CO	6, 8
12/15/94	Religions of the World	Arapahoe High School. Littleton, CO	13, 47
05/96	A Class on World Religions	Arapahoe High School. Littleton, CO	13, 47
12/04/96	A Class on World Religions	Arapahoe High School Littleton, CO	13, 47
12/16/96	The Experience of Contributing	Honor Society Induction. Arapahoe High School. Littleton, CO	13, 47
4/20, 4/27, 5/11	Process Theology: A Three-Part Series	Mountain View United Methodist Church Boulder, CO	13, 48
05/20/97	A Class on World Religions	Arapahoe High School. Littleton, CO	13, 47

Appendix E
Classes Taught at Iliff School of Theology

The list of classes taught is contained in the Iliff Archives, box 44, file folder 8.

As Instructor:

1939 Christian Theology I
1939 Christian Theology II
1947-48 God in Contemporary Thought

As Associate Professor:

1950 God in Contemporary Thought
1950 Man, Sin and Salvation
1951 Man, Sin and Salvation

As Professor:

1952 God in Contemporary Thought
1952 Man, Sin and Salvation
1952 The History of Christian Thought
1952 Salvation
1952 Immortality
1952 Theology and the Devotional Life
1952 Christology
1952 Recent Religious
1952 European Theological Thought
1952 Problems on Theology
1952 The Problem of God
1952 Personal Counseling
1952 The Minister and Social Work Agency (with Prof. Stotts)
1953 God in Contemporary Thought
1953 Man, Sin and Salvation
1953 The History of Christian Thought
1953 Salvation
1953 Immortality
1953 Theology and the Devotional Life
1953 Christology
1953 Recent Religious Movements
1953 European Theological Thought
1953 Problems on Theology
1953 The Problem of God
1953 Personal Counseling
1953 Introduction to Pastoral Care and Personal Counseling
1953 Planning a Preaching Program
1954 God in Contemporary Thought
1954 Man, Sin and Salvation
1954 The History of Christian Thought
1954 Salvation
1954 Immortality
1954 Theology and the Devotional Life
1954 Christology
1954 Recent Religious Movements
1954 European Theological Thought
1954 Problems on Theology
1954 The Problem of God
1954 Personal Counseling

1954 Introduction to Pastoral Care and Personal Counseling
1954 Planning a Preaching Program
1955 God in Contemporary Thought
1955 Man, Sin and Salvation
1955 The History of Christian Thought
1955 Salvation
1955 Immortality
1955 Theology and the Devotional Life
1955 Christology
1955 Recent Religious Movements
1955 European Theological Thought
1955 Problems on Theology
1955 The Problem of God
1955 Personal Counseling
1955 Introduction to Pastoral Care and Personal Counseling
1955 Planning a Preaching Program
1955 Theology in the Methodist Church
1955 The Theology of Tillich
1956 God in Contemporary Thought
1956 Man, Sin and Salvation
1956 The History of Christian Thought
1956 Salvation
1956 Immortality
1956 Theology and the Devotional Life
1956 Christology
1956 Recent Religious Movements
1956 European Theological Thought
1956 Problems on Theology
1956 The Problem of God
1956 Personal Counseling
1956 Planning a Preaching Program
1956 Theology in the Methodist Church
1956 The Theology of Tillich
1956 Theological Issues Today
1957 God in Contemporary Thought
1957 Man, Sin and Salvation
1957 The History of Christian Thought
1957 Salvation
1957 Immortality
1957 Theology and the Devotional Life
1957 Christology
1957 Recent Religious Movements
1957 European Theological Thought
1957 Problems on Theology
1957 The Problem of God
1957 Personal Counseling
1957 Planning a Preaching Program
1957 Theology in the Methodist Church
1957 The Theology of Tillich
1957 Theological Issues Today
1958 God in Contemporary Thought
1958 Man, Sin and Salvation
1958 The History of Christian Thought
1958 Salvation
1958 Immortality
1958 Theology and the Devotional Life
1958 Christology
1958 Recent Religious Movements
1958 European Theological Thought
1958 Problems on Theology
1958 The Problem of God

APPENDIX E: CLASSES TAUGHT AT ILIFF SCHOOL OF THEOLOGY

1958	Personal Counseling
1958	Planning a Preaching Program
1958	Theology in the Methodist Church
1958	The Theology of Tillich
1958	Theological Issues Today
1958	Nature and Function of the Church
1958	Credo
1959	Man, Sin and Salvation
1959	The History of Christian Thought
1959	Salvation
1959	Immortality
1959	Theology and the Devotional Life
1959	Christology
1959	Recent Religious Movements
1959	European Theological Thought
1959	Problems on Theology
1959	The Problem of God
1959	Personal Counseling
1959	Planning a Preaching Program
1959	Theology in the Methodist Church
1959	The Theology of Tillich
1959	Theological Issues Today
1959	Credo
1959	Introduction to Christian Theology
1960	Man, Sin and Salvation
1960	The History of Christian Thought
1960	Salvation
1960	Immortality
1960	Theology and the Devotional Life
1960	Christology
1960	Recent Religious Movements
1960	European Theological Thought
1960	Problems on Theology
1960	The Problem of God
1960	Personal Counseling
1960	Planning a Preaching Program
1960	Theology in the Methodist Church
1960	The Theology of Tillich
1960	Theological Issues Today
1960	Credo
1960	Introduction to Christian Theology
1960	Nature and Function of the Church
1960	Christian Theology: An Integrative Course
1960	The Theology and the Work of the Minister (with Mr. Stewart)
1961	Man, Sin and Salvation
1961	The History of Christian Thought
1961	Salvation
1961	Immortality
1961	Theology and the Devotional Life
1961	Christology
1961	Recent Religious Movements
1961	European Theological Thought
1961	Problems on Theology
1961	The Problem of God
1961	Personal Counseling
1961	Planning a Preaching Program
1961	Theology in the Methodist Church
1961	The Theology of Tillich
1961	Theological Issues Today
1961	Credo
1961	Introduction to Christian Theology

1961 Nature and Function of the Church
1961 Christian Theology: An Integrative Course
1961 The Theology and the Work of the Minister
1962-63 Man, Sin and Salvation
1962-63 The History of Christian Thought
1962-63 Salvation
1962-63 Immortality
196263 Theology and the Devotional Life
196263 Christology
196263 Recent Religious Movements
196263 European Theological Thought
196263 Problems on Theology
1962-63 The Problem of God
1962-63 Personal Counseling
1962-63 Planning a Preaching Program
1962-63 Theology in the Methodist Church
1962-63 The Theology of Tillich
1962-63 Theological Issues Today
1962-63 Credo
1962-63 Introduction to Christian Theology
1962-63 Nature and Function of the Church
1962-63 Christian Theology: An Integrative Course
1962-63 The Theology and the Work of the Minister
1962-63 The Theology of the Reformed Churches
1964-65 Man, Sin and Salvation
1964-65 The History of Christian Thought
1964-65 Salvation
1964-65 Immortality
1964-65 Theology and the Devotional Life
1964-65 Christology
1964-65 Recent Religious Movements
1964-65 European Theological Thought
1964-65 Problems on Theology
1964-65 The Problem of God
1964-65 Personal Counseling
1964-65 Planning a Preaching Program
1964-65 Theology in the Methodist Church
1964-65 The Theology of Tillich
1964-65 Theological Issues Today
1964-65 Credo
1964-65 Introduction to Christian Theology
1964-65 Nature and Function of the Church
1964-65 Christian Theology: An Integrative Course
1964-65 The Theology and the Work of the Minister
1964-65 The Theology of the Reformed Churches
1964-65 Theology and Psychiatry in Dialogue (with Mr. Gavin)
1966-67 Man, Sin and Salvation
1966-67 The History of Christian Thought
1966-67 Salvation
1966-67 Immortality
1966-67 Theology and the Devotional Life
1966-67 Christology
1966-67 Recent Religious Movements
1966-67 European Theological Thought
1966-67 Problems on Theology
1966-67 The Problem of God
1966-67 Personal Counseling
1966-67 Theology in the Methodist Church
1966-67 The Theology of Tillich

APPENDIX E: CLASSES TAUGHT AT ILIFF SCHOOL OF THEOLOGY

1966-67 Theological Issues Today
1966-67 Credo
1966-67 Introduction to Christian Theology
1966-67 Nature and Function of the Church
1966-67 Christian Theology: An Integrative Course
1966-67 The Theology and the Work of the Minister
1966-67 The Theology of the Reformed Churches
1966-67 Theology and Psychiatry in Dialogue
1968-69 Man, Sin and Salvation
1968-69 Salvation
1968-69 Theology and the Devotional Life
1968-69 Christology
1968-69 European Theological Thought
1968-69 Problems on Theology
1968-69 The Problem of God
1968-69 Personal Counseling
1968-69 Theology in the Methodist Church
1968-69 The Theology of Tillich
1968-69 Theological Issues Today
1968-69 Credo
1968-69 Introduction to Christian Theology
1968-69 Nature and Function of the Church
1968-69 Christian Theology: An Integrative Course
1968-69 The Theology and the Work of the Minister
1968-69 The Theology of the Reformed Churches
1968-69 Theology and Psychiatry in Dialogue
1968-69 Death in Theological Perspective
1969-70 Theology and the Devotional Life
1969-70 Christology
1969-70 European Theological Thought
1969-70 Problems on Theology
1969-70 The Problem of God
1969-70 Personal Counseling
1969-70 Theology in the Methodist Church
1969-70 Theological Issues Today
1969-70 Credo
1969-70 Introduction to Christian Theology
1969-70 Nature and Function of the Church
1969-70 Christian Theology: An Integrative Course
1969-70 The Theology and the Work of the Minister
1969-70 Theology and Psychiatry in Dialogue
1969-70 Death in Theological Perspective
1969-70 Lay-Clergy Theological Dialogue
1970-71 Theology and the Devotional Life
1970-71 Christology
1970-71 European Theological Thought
1970-71 Problems on Theology
1970-71 The Problem of God
1970-71 Personal Counseling
1970-71 Theology in the Methodist Church
1970-71 Theological Issues Today
1970-71 Credo
1970-71 Introduction to Christian Theology
1970-71 Christian Theology: An Integrative Course
1970-71 The Theology and the Work of the Minister
1970-71 Theology and Psychiatry in Dialogue
1970-71 Death in Theological Perspective

1970-71	Lay-Clergy Theological Dialogue
1970-71	History of the Ecumenical Movement (with Mr. Van Sickle)
1970-71	The Philosophy of Whitehead
1970-71	The Theology of Ministry
1970-71	Man, Sin and Salvation
1971	The Theology of Ministry (Summer)
1971-72	Theology and the Devotional Life
1971-72	Christology
1971-72	European Theological Thought
1971-72	Problems on Theology
1971-72	The Problem of God
1971-72	Personal Counseling
1971-72	Theology in the Methodist Church
1971-72	Theological Issues Today
1971-72	Credo
1971-72	Introduction to Christian Theology
1971-72	Christian Theology: An Integrative Course
1971-72	The Theology and the Work of the Minister
1971-72	Theology and Psychiatry in Dialogue
1971-72	Death in Theological Perspective
1971-72	Lay-Clergy Theological Dialogue
1971-72	History of the Ecumenical Movement (with Mr. Van Sickle)
1971-72	The Philosophy of Whitehead
1971-72	The Theology of Ministry
1971-72	Man, Sin and Salvation
1972-73	Theology and the Devotional Life
1972-73	Christology
1972-73	European Theological Thought
1972-73	Problems on Theology
1972-73	The Problem of God
1972-73	Personal Counseling
1972-73	Theology in the Methodist Church
1972-73	Theological Issues Today
1972-73	Credo
1972-73	Introduction to Christian Theology
1972-73	Christian Theology: An Integrative Course
1972-73	The Theology and the Work of the Minister
1972-73	Theology and Psychiatry in Dialogue
1972-73	Death in Theological Perspective
1972-73	Lay-Clergy Theological Dialogue
1972-73	History of the Ecumenical Movement
1972-73	The Philosophy of Whitehead
1972-73	The Theology of Ministry
1972-73	Man, Sin and Salvation
1973	Theological Issues Today: Hope (Summer)
1973	Theology of Ministry (Summer)
1973-74	Theology and the Devotional Life
1973-74	Christology
1973-74	European Theological Thought
1973-74	Problems on Theology
1973-74	The Problem of God
1973-74	Personal Counseling
1973-74	Theology in the Methodist Church
1973-74	Theological Issues Today
1973-74	Credo
1973-74	Introduction to Christian Theology

APPENDIX E: CLASSES TAUGHT AT ILIFF SCHOOL OF THEOLOGY

1973-74 Christian Theology: An Integrative Course
1973-74 The Theology and the Work of the Minister
1973-74 Theology and Psychiatry in Dialogue
1973-74 Death in Theological Perspective
1973-74 Lay-Clergy Theological Dialogue
1973-74 History of the Ecumenical Movement
1973-74 The Philosophy of Whitehead
1973-74 The Theology of Ministry
1973-74 Man, Sin and Salvation
1973-74 Empirical Theologies from Schleiermacher to the Present
1973-74 Doctoral Preaching (with Mr. Pennington)
1974 Theological Issues Today (Summer) Iliff-at-Aspen
1974-75 Theology and the Devotional Life
1974-75 Christology
1974-75 European Theological Thought
1974-75 Problems on Theology
1974-75 The Problem of God
1974-75 Personal Counseling
1974-75 Theology in the Methodist Church
1974-75 Theological Issues Today
1974-75 Credo
1974-75 Introduction to Christian Theology
1974-75 Christian Theology: An Integrative Course
1974-75 The Theology and the Work of the Minister
1974-75 Theology and Psychiatry in Dialogue
1974-75 Death in Theological Perspective
1974-75 Lay-Clergy Theological Dialogue
1974-75 History of the Ecumenical Movement
1974-75 The Philosophy of Whitehead
1974-75 The Theology of Ministry
1974-75 Man, Sin and Salvation
1974-75 Empirical Theologies from Schleiermacher to the Present
1974-75 Doctoral Preaching
1975 Theologies of Ministry (Summer)
1975 Clergy-Physician Dialogue (Summer) Iliff-at-Aspen
1975-76 Theology and the Devotional Life
1975-76 Christology
1975-76 European Theological Thought
1975-76 Problems on Theology
1975-76 The Problem of God
1975-76 Personal Counseling
1975-76 Theology in the Methodist Church
1975-76 Theological Issues Today
1975-76 Credo
1975-76 Introduction to Christian Theology
1975-76 The Theology and the Work of the Minister
1975-76 Theology and Psychiatry in Dialogue
1975-76 Death in Theological Perspective
1975-76 Lay-Clergy Theological Dialogue
1975-76 History of the Ecumenical Movement
1975-76 The Philosophy of Whitehead
1975-76 The Theology of Ministry
1975-76 Man, Sin and Salvation

1975-76	Empirical Theologies from Schleiermacher to the Present
1975-76	Doctoral Preaching
1976	Modern Cosmologies and Religious Faith (Summer) Iliff-at-Aspen
1976	Theology of the Body (Summer) Iliff-at-Aspen
1976-77	Theology and the Devotional Life
1976-77	Christology
1976-77	European Theological Thought
1976-77	Problems on Theology
1976-77	The Problem of God
1976-77	Personal Counseling
1976-77	Theology in the Methodist Church
1976-77	Theological Issues Today
1976-77	Credo
1976-77	Introduction to Christian Theology
1976-77	The Theology and the Work of the Minister
1976-77	Theology and Psychiatry in Dialogue
1976-77	Death in Theological Perspective
1976-77	Lay-Clergy Theological Dialogue
1976-77	History of the Ecumenical Movement
1976-77	The Philosophy of Whitehead
1976-77	The Theology of Ministry
1976-77	Empirical Theologies from Schleiermacher to the Present
1976-77	Doctoral Preaching
1976-77	The Person, Sin and Salvation
1976-77	Theological Uses of Process Philosophy
1976-77	Modern Cosmologies and Religious Faith
1976-77	Theology of the Body
1977-78	Theology and the Devotional Life
1977-78	Christology
1977-78	Problems on Theology
1977-78	The Problem of God
1977-78	Personal Counseling
1977-78	Theology in the Methodist Church
1977-78	Theological Issues Today
1977-78	Credo
1977-78	Introduction to Christian Theology
1977-78	The Theology and the Work of the Minister
1977-78	Theology and Psychiatry in Dialogue
1977-78	Death in Theological Perspective
1977-78	Lay-Clergy Theological Dialogue
1977-78	History of the Ecumenical Movement
1977-78	The Philosophy of Whitehead
1977-78	The Theology of Ministry
1977-78	Empirical Theologies from Schleiermacher to the Present
1977-78	Doctoral Preaching
1977-78	The Person, Sin and Salvation
1977-78	Theological Uses of Process Philosophy
1977-78	Modern Cosmologies and Religious Faith
1977-78	Theology of the Body
1978	Aging and the Life Cycle (Summer) Iliff-at-Aspen
1978-79	Theology and the Devotional Life
1978-79	Christology
1978-79	Problems on Theology

APPENDIX E: CLASSES TAUGHT AT ILIFF SCHOOL OF THEOLOGY

1978-79	The Problem of God
1978-79	Personal Counseling
1978-79	Theology in the Methodist Church
1978-79	Theological Issues Today
1978-79	Credo
1978-79	Introduction to Christian Theology
1978-79	The Theology and the Work of the Minister
1978-79	Theology and Psychiatry in Dialogue
1978-79	Death in Theological Perspective
1978-79	Lay-Clergy Theological Dialogue
1978-79	History of the Ecumenical Movement
1978-79	The Philosophy of Whitehead
1978-79	The Theology of Ministry
1978-79	Empirical Theologies from Schleiermacher to the Present
1978-79	Doctoral Preaching
1978-79	The Person, Sin and Salvation
1978-79	Theological Uses of Process Philosophy
1978-79	Modern Cosmologies and Religious Faith
1978-79	Theology of the Body
1979	Religious Faith and Mental Health (Summer) Iliff-at-Aspen
1979-80	Theology and the Devotional Life
1979-80	Christology
1979-80	The Problem of God
1979-80	Personal Counseling
1979-80	Theology in the Methodist Church
1979-80	Theological Issues Today
1979-80	Credo
1979-80	Introduction to Christian Theology
1979-80	The Theology and the Work of the Minister
1979-80	Theology and Psychiatry in Dialogue
1979-80	Death in Theological Perspective
1979-80	Lay-Clergy Theological Dialogue
1979-80	History of the Ecumenical Movement
1979-80	The Philosophy of Whitehead
1979-80	The Theology of Ministry
1979-80	Empirical Theologies from Schleiermacher to the Present
1979-80	Doctoral Preaching
1979-80	The Person, Sin and Salvation
1979-80	Theological Uses of Process Philosophy
1979-80	Modern Cosmologies and Religious Faith
1979-80	Theology of the Body
1979-80	Aging, Dying and Death in Theological Perspective
1979-80	Death in Theological Perspective
1980	Religious Faith and the Search for Meaning (Summer) Iliff-at-Aspen
1980-81	Theology and the Devotional Life
1980-81	Christology
1980-81	The Problem of God
1980-81	Personal Counseling
1980-81	Theology in the Methodist Church
1980-81	Credo
1980-81	Introduction to Christian Theology
1980-81	The Theology and the Work of the Minister

1980-81	Theology and Psychiatry in Dialogue
1980-81	Death in Theological Perspective
1980-81	Lay-Clergy Theological Dialogue
1980-81	History of the Ecumenical Movement
1980-81	The Philosophy of Whitehead
1980-81	The Theology of Ministry
1980-81	Empirical Theologies from Schleiermacher to the Present
1980-81	Doctoral Preaching
1980-81	The Person, Sin and Salvation
1980-81	Modern Cosmologies and Religious Faith
1980-81	Theology of the Body
1980-81	Aging, Dying and Death in Theological Perspective
1980-81	Death in Theological Perspective
1980-81	The Theology of Harvey Potthoff
1981	Loneliness in the Aging Process: Preventing, Coping, Surmounting (Summer)
1981	Process Theology and the Issues of Life (Summer) Iliff-at-Aspen
1984	Explorations in Religious Naturalism (Summer)
1984	The Search for a Contemporary Spirituality (Summer) Iliff-at-Breckenridge
1985	Theology of Ministry (Summer)
1985	A Theology of Wholeness (Summer) Iliff-at-Breckenridge
1986	Emerging Images of God (Summer) Iliff-at-Aspen
1988	A Dialogue on Science and Religion (Summer) Iliff-at-Aspen
1989	Aging, Diminishment, and Death in Religious Perspective (Summer) Iliff-at-Aspen
1990	Theology of Ministry (Summer)
1990	Humor and Struggle: Ingredients of Faith (Summer)

As Professor Emeritus:

1991	Aging, Diminishment, and Death in Religious Perspective (Summer)
1991	A Modern Theology of Earth (Summer) Iliff-at-Aspen
1992	Spirituality Old and New (Summer) Iliff-at-Aspen
1993	Process Theology and Life's Meaning (Summer) Iliff-at- Aspen

Appendix F
Articles about Harvey H. Potthoff

"Reverend Potthoff Appointed to Iliff Faculty." *Protestant Herald* (May 1952). [Iliff Archives, box 32, file folder 2.]

"More Church Education is Advocated." *Rocky Mountain News* (June 28, 1962). [Iliff Archives, box 4, file folder 16.]

"'God Is Dead': Focus on Vital Issues" by Wes French. *Rocky Mountain News* (March 3, 1966). [Iliff Archives, box 4, file folder 16.]

"Professor Potthoff and the Celebration of Life" by William H. Bernhardt. *The Iliff Review* 26, no. 3 (Fall 1969). [Iliff Archives, box 4, file folder 16.]

"Hope Theme of Easter Service Here." *Colorado Springs Sun* 7, no. 110 (April 19, 1977). [Iliff Archives, box 32, file folder 2.]

"Loneliness Part of Human Condition" by Virginia Culver. *Denver Post* (April 8, 1977):5BB. [Iliff Archives, box 4, file folder 16.]

"Harvey Potthoff to Address 44 Degree Candidates at Iliff." *Rocky Mountain United Methodist Reporter* 1 (May 20, 1977). [Iliff Archives, box 4, file folder 16.]

"Harvey Potthoff to Address Lay/Clergy Retreat on the Christmas Story." *Rocky Mountain News* (January 27, 1978). [Iliff Archives, box 4, file folder 16.]

"Archeology Grows More Scientific" by Peter J. Scarlett. *Salt Lake Tribune* (February 14, 1978): 15, 17. [Iliff Archives, box 4, file folder 16.]

"Trustees Establish Potthoff Chair." *Iliff Reporter* 32, no. 4 (December 1980). [Iliff Archives, box32, file folder 2.]

"Iliff Week Promises Variety, Milestones - Reception to Honor Dr. Potthoff" by Gary Arnold. *Rocky Mountain United Methodist Reporter* (January 16, 1981). [Iliff Archives, box 4, file folder 16.]

"Dr. Potthoff Recently Honored" by Gary Arnold *Rocky Mountain United Methodist Reporter* (February 27, 1981). [Iliff Archives, box 4, file folder 16.]

"Iliff Names Potthoff, Wood Interim Chief Executives." *Iliff Reporter* 33, no. 1 (March 1981). [Iliff Archives, box 32, file folder 2.]

"Dr. Harvey H. Potthoff Honored at Iliff Week." *Iliff Reporter* 33; no. 1 (March 1981). [Iliff Archives, box 32, file folder 2.]

."Potthoff Heads Symposium" by Met Shafer. *The Nebraska Wesleyan* 21, no. 3: (September 24, 1982): 1. [Iliff Archives, box 4, file folder 16.]

"Harvey H. Potthoff Chair Fully Funded." *Iliff Reporter* 36, no. 1 (Spring 1983). [Iliff Archives, box32, file folder 2.]

"Potthoff Chair Fully Funded." *Rocky Mountain United Methodist Reporter* (May 28, 1983). [Iliff Archives, box 32, file folder 2.]

"Methodists See Real 'Endowed Chair'" by Wes French. *Rocky Mountain News* (June 11, 1983). [Iliff Archives, box 4, file folder 16.]

"Dr. Harvey Potthoff to Return" by Sandra Rooney. *The Nebraska Wesleyan University Alumnews* (March 1984): 4-5. [Iliff Archives, box 4, file folder 16.]

"Dr. Potthoff to Return to Nebraska Wesleyan" by Sandra Rooney. *The Nebraska Messenger* (March 1984):1. [Iliff Archives, box 4, file folder 16.]

."Famed Theologian Named to Religion Chair at Mesa" by Dave Fiskell. *The Daily Sentinel*, Grand Junction, CO (April 28, 1984): 5. [Iliff Archives, box 4, file folder 16.]

"Professor Says Living an Art" by Steve McMillan. *The Daily Sentinel*, Grand Junction, CO (November 16, 1984): 4B. [Iliff Archives, box 4, file folder 16.]

"Theologian Aims at Head and Heart" by Terry Mattingly. *Rocky Mountain News* (January 8, 1986):118. [Iliff Archives, box 4, file folder 16.]

"Theologian Potthoff: Let Us All Love Alike" by Betty Stevens. *Lincoln Star-Journal* (January 22, 1986). [Iliff Archives, box 4, file folder 16.]

"Potthoff Encourages Youth to Enrich Personal Journey, Professor Focus" by Lori Hand. *The Wesleyan - The Official Voice of Nebraska Wesleyan* (September 14, 1986). [Iliff Archives, box 4, file folder 16.]

"Celebrating Life: Harvey Potthoff Finds Fulfillment in People and Experiences." *Celebrating Excellence, Nebraska Wesleyan University* [1987 Annual Report] Vol. 87, no. 2 (September 1987): 17-19. [Iliff Archives, box 4, file folder 16.]

"Harvey Potthoff Receives Honorary Degree [From Nebraska Wesleyan University]" *The Iliff Reporter* (1988). Iliff Archives, box 4, file folder 16.

"Harvey Potthoff Receives Honorary Degree From Nebraska Wesleyan University." *Nebraska Messenger* (October 1988). [Iliff Archives, box 4, file folder 16.]

"He's Getting the Hang of Living" by Don Walton. *Lincoln Star-Journal* (May 19, 1989):7. [Iliff Archives, box 4, file folder 16.]

"Harvey H. Potthoff [his life and scholarship]" by David E. Conner. *An Intellectual History of The Iliff School of Theology: A Centennial Tribute*, 1892 – 1992 (1992): 259 – 278. [Iliff Archives, box 6, file folder 7.]

"Commencement Speaker: Harvey H. Potthoff, Mattingly Distinguished Visiting Professor of Religion" *Commencement Booklet, Nebraska Wesleyan University* (May 16, 1992). [Iliff Archives, box 6, file folder 7.]

"A Most Unforgettable Character: by Timothy L. Bryan and Pamela Dillman. *FaithLink Participant Pages* – (July 27, 1997): 3-4 [Iliff Archives, box 4, file folder 16.]

Appendix G
Roles in Church and Community

Dates	Position	Organization	Location
1934-35	Associate Pastor	Christ Methodist Church	Denver, CO
1936	Ordained Minister	Methodist Episcopal Church	Denver, CO
1936-52	Minister	Christ Methodist Church	Denver, CO
1937-52	Faculty Part -time	Iliff School of Theology	Denver, CO
1942-64	Chairman	Board of Ministerial Training	Denver, CO
1944-64	Chairman	Rocky Mountain Conference Student Aid Committee	
1944-64	Member	United Methodist Student Foundation Board of Directors - University of Denver	Denver, CO
1948-80	Delegate	Western Jurisdictional Conference	
1950	Chairman	Denver County Unit of the White House Conference on Children and Youth	Denver, CO
1950-74	Director of Honor	Morningside College Board of Directors	Sioux City, IA
1952	Delegate	General Conference of the Methodist and United Methodist Church	
1952-58	Editor	*The Iliff Review*	Denver, CO
1952-70	Chairman	Western Jurisdictional Committee on Episcopacy	
1952-81	Professor of of Christian Theology	Iliff School of Theology	Denver, CO
1955-61	Chairman	Board of Trustees, Rocky Mountain Methodist Homes, Inc. (Now Frasier Meadows Retirement Community)	Denver, CO
1955-68	Member	Board of Trustees, Rocky Mountain Mountain Methodist Homes, Inc. (Now Frasier Meadows Retirement Community)	Denver, CO

Dates	Position	Organization	Location
1956	Chairman	Subcommittee on Program of the Western Jurisdictional Conference	
1956	Delegate	General Conference of the Methodist and United Methodist Church	
1958-72	Member	Curriculum Committee of the Methodist and United Methodist Churches	
1960-72	Member	Board of Education of the Methodist and United Methodist Church	
1960	Chairman	Subcommittee on Entertainment and Programs of the Western Jurisdictional Conference	
1960	Delegate	General Conference of the Methodist and United Methodist Church	
1963-65	President	Methodist Conference on Christian Education	
1964	Delegate	General Conference of the Methodist and United Methodist Church	
1964	Dean	Colorado Delegation of Western Jurisdictional Conference	
1966	Delegate	World Methodist Conference	London, UK
1966	Delegate	World Methodist Conference	Denver, CO
1966-72	Chairman	Denver Regional Missionary Personnel Committee	Denver, CO
1968	Delegate	General Conference of the Methodist and United Methodist Church	
1968	Delegate	World Council of Churches, Fourth Assembly	Uppsala, Sweden
1968-72	Member	General Conference Theological Study Commission on Doctrine and Doctrinal Standards	
1970	Member	General Conference Education Legislative Committee	
1971	Delegate	World Methodist Conference	Denver, CO
1971-74	Chairman	Morningside College Board of Directors Long-Range Planning Committee	Sioux City, IA
1972	Member	Commission on Education	
1972	Delegate	General Conference of the Methodist and United Methodist Churches	

APPENDIX G: ROLES IN CHURCH AND COMMUNITY

Dates	Position	Organization	Location
1972	Chairman	General Conference Legislative Committee	
1972	Chairman	General Conference Fraternal Delegate Committee	
1973	Establishing Member	Iliff-at-Aspen	Aspen, CO
1976	Delegate	General Conference of the Methodist and United Methodist Church	
1976-80	Chairman	Inter-jurisdictional Committee on Episcopacy	
1980	Delegate	General Conference of the Methodist and United Methodist Church	
1981	Chief Academic Officer ad Interim	Iliff School of Theology	Denver, CO
1981-92	Mattingly Distinguished Visiting Professor of Religion	Nebraska Wesleyan University	Lincoln, NE
1994-95	Chairman	University Park United Methodist Church Interim Ministerial Team	Denver, CO
	Member	Board of the Diaconal Ministry	
	Member	Board of Directors United Methodist Student Foundation, University of Denver	Denver, CO
	Chairman	Adult Section of Curriculum Committee of the Methodist and UMC	
	Member	Colorado Family and Children's Service Board of Directors	
	President	Denver Council of Churches, Social Services Department	Denver, CO
	President	Rocky Mountain Conference Board of Directors	
	Member	American Association of University Professors	
	Member	American Academy of Religion	
	Member	Colorado Authors' League	

Appendix H
Honors and Awards

Dates	Position	Organization	Location	Box, Folder
1941	Doctorate	Iliff School of Theology. Doctoral Diploma	Denver, CO	32, 1
1961	Literary Honorary Doctorate	Morningside College	Sioux City, IA	
1965	HHP Honored by HHP Scholarship endowed by Carl Potthoff (HHP's brother)	Iliff School of Theology	Denver, CO	
1969	Alumnus of the Year	Iliff School of Theology.	Denver, CO	37
1975	Plaque of Appreciation	Pacific Air Forces Command Chaplain		32, 3
1975	Member of the Order of Morningside	Morningside College	Sioux City, IA	39
1980	Vote to Establish Harvey H. Potthoff Endowed Chair	Iliff Board of Trustees (documented in *The Iliff Review*)	Denver, CO	
1981	Following in In Tribute to ... Award	Iliff Faculty	Denver, CO	37
1981	Professor Emeritus of Christian Theology	Iliff School of Theology	Denver, CO	37
1981	Retirement Award Recipient	Rocky Mountain Annual Conference	Denver, CO	37
1981	Contribution Award Recipient	Iliff School of Theology Board of Trustees	Denver, CO	39
1982	Membership Invitation	Phi Kappa Phi. Nebraska Wesleyan University	Lincoln, NE	32, 3
1982-83	Dedicated Issue	Student Directory. Nebraska Wesleyan University	Lincoln, NE	36, 1
1983	Harvey H. Potthoff Chair of Christian Theology Fully Endowed	Iliff School of Theology	Denver, CO	32, 2

APPENDIX H: HONORS AND AWARDS

Dates	Position	Organization	Location	Box, Folder
1985	Golden Anniversary Alumnus of the Year	Iliff School of Theology	Denver, CO	37
1985	Invited to be a Member Sigma Tau Delta National English Honorary	Nebraska Wesleyan University	Lincoln, NE	32, 3
1986	Award Recipient for 50 Years of Service	United Methodist Church		
1986	Award for Distinguished Alumnus	Iliff School of Theology	Denver, CO	37
1987	Dedicated to Harvey H. Potthoff *The Flintlock, A Magazine of Creative Expression*	Student Senate. Nebraska Wesleyan University	Lincoln, NE	32, 3
1987-88	Centennial Award for Exemplary Commitment	Board of Governors Nebraska Wesleyan University	Lincoln, NE	38
1988	Honorary Doctor of Humane Letters	Nebraska Wesleyan University	Lincoln, NE	32, 3
1990	Tree Planted in Honor of Harvey Potthoff	Alice Abel Arboretum. Nebraska Wesleyan University	Lincoln, NE	32, 2
1992	A Concert Dedicated to Harvey H. Potthoff on the Occasion of his Retirement	The Nebraska Wesleyan Choir and the Lincoln Civic Choir	Lincoln, NE	32, 2
1992	Second Century Award	Nebraska Wesleyan University	Lincoln, NE	
1992	Commencement Speaker	Nebraska Wesleyan University	Lincoln, NE	36, 1
1994	Certificate of Appreciation	University Park UMC	Denver, CO	39

Dates	Position	Organization	Location	Box, Folder
1995	Francis Asbury Award in Ministry	General Board of Higher Education Iliff School of Theology	Denver, CO	
1998	Dedication of Harvey H. Potthoff Seminar Room		Denver, CO	32, 3
2001	HHP Scholarship Endowment increased by gift from HHP, making it the HHP Presidential Scholarship	Iliff School of Theology	Denver, CO	

Index